SEVEN SEAS ENTERTAINMENT PRESENTS

Wonderland Vol. 3

6/21

story and art by YUGO ISHIKAWA

TRANSLATION
Molly Rabbitt

ADAPTATION
Marykate Jasper

LETTERING AND RETOUCH
James Gaubatz

ORIGINAL COVER DESIGN
Mikiyo Kobayashi＋Bay Bridge Studio

COVER DESIGN
KC Fabellon

PROOFREADER
Kurestin Armada
B. Lana Guggenheim

EDITOR
Jenn Grunigen

PRODUCTION MANAGER
Lissa Pattillo

EDITOR-IN-CHIEF
Adam Arnold

PUBLISHER
Jason DeAngelis

WONDERLAND VOL. 3 by Yugo ISHIKAWA
© 2015 Yugo ISHIKAWA
All rights reserved.
Original Japanese edition published by SHOGAKUKAN.
English translation rights in the United States of America, Canada, and the
United Kingdom arranged with SHOGAKUKAN through Tuttle-Mori Agency, Inc.

Seven Seas press and purchase enquiries can be sent to Marketing Manager
Lianne Sentar at press@gomanga.com. Information regarding the distribution
and purchase of digital editions is available from Digital Manager CK Russell
at digital@gomanga.com.

Seven Seas and the Seven Seas logo are trademarks of
Seven Seas Entertainment. All rights reserved.

ISBN: 978-1-642751-27-7

Printed in Canada

First Printing: August 2019

10 9 8 7 6 5 4 3 2 1

FOLLOW US ONLINE: *www.sevenseasentertainment.com*

READING DIRECTIO

This book reads from *right to left*, Japan
If this is your first time reading manga,
reading from the top right panel on each page and
take it from there. If you get lost, just follow the
numbered diagram here. It may seem backwards at
first, but you'll get the hang of it! Have fun!!

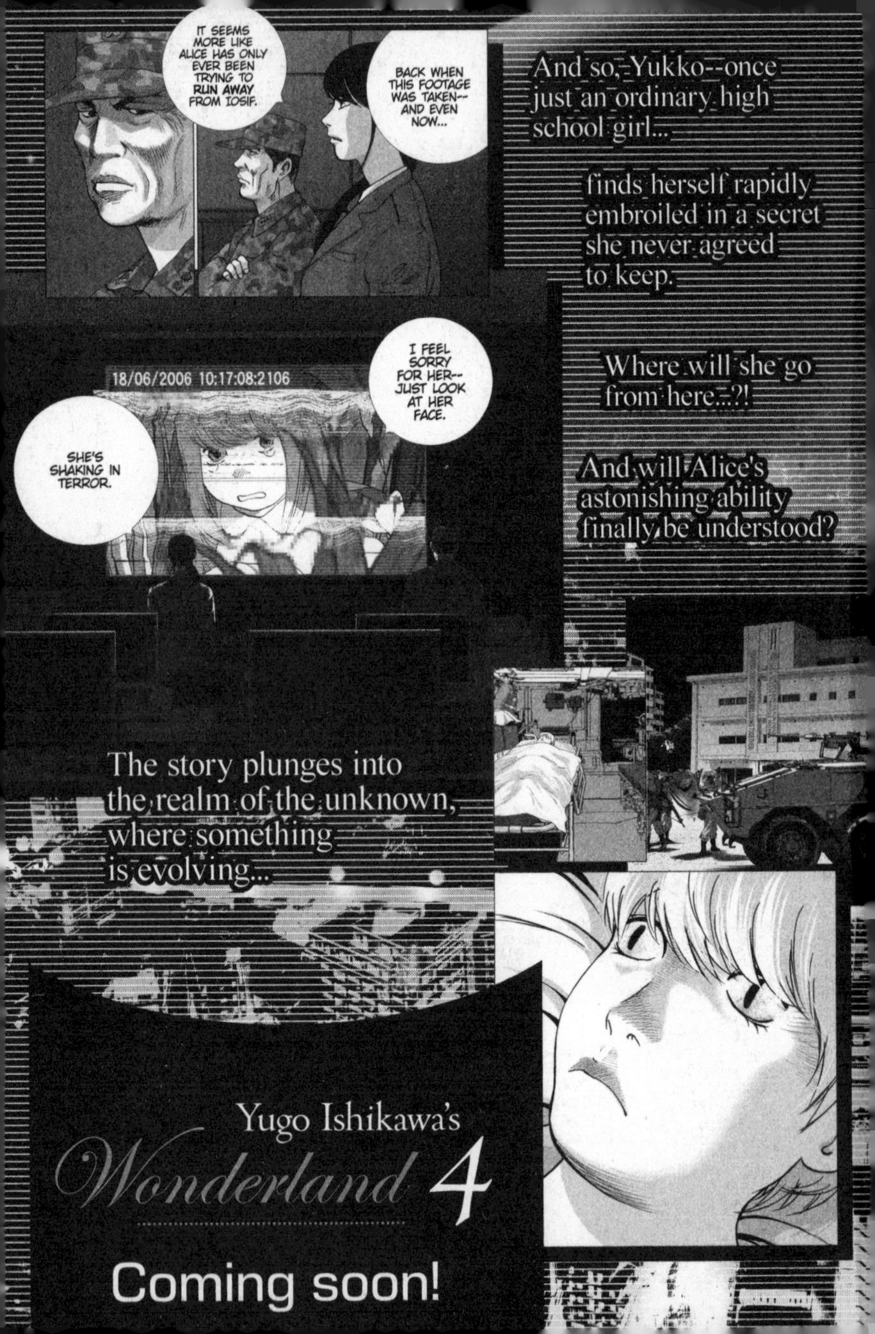
And so, Yukko--once just an ordinary high school girl...
finds herself rapidly embroiled in a secret she never agreed to keep.
BACK WHEN THIS FOOTAGE WAS TAKEN-- AND EVEN NOW...
IT SEEMS MORE LIKE ALICE HAS ONLY EVER BEEN TRYING TO RUN AWAY FROM IOSIF.
Where will she go from here...?!
And will Alice's astonishing ability finally be understood?
18/06/2006 10:17:08:2106
I FEEL SORRY FOR HER-- JUST LOOK AT HER FACE.
SHE'S SHAKING IN TERROR.
The story plunges into the realm of the unknown, where something is evolving...
Yugo Ishikawa's
Wonderland 4
Coming soon!

Wonderland

STORY & ART BY
Yugo Ishikawa

3

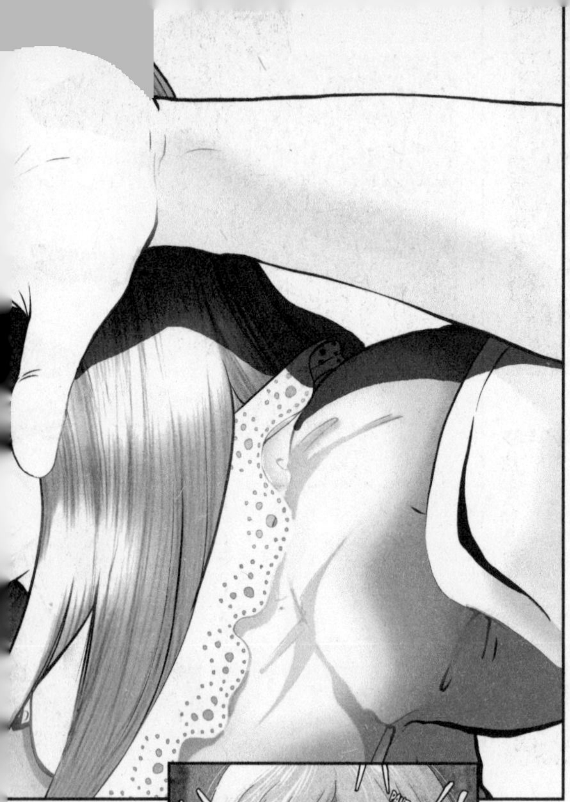

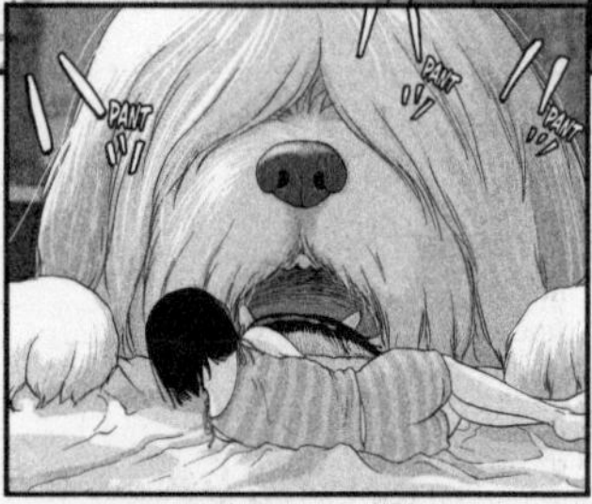
PANT
PANT
PANT

Could the mysterious girl Alice be the key to this strange situation?!

Story

High school student Yukko lives a quiet, normal life with her parents, cat, and dog--until she wakes up one morning and discovers that she and her parents have been shrunk. Her mother and father are cruelly (and accidentally) murdered by their cat. When she ventures into the outside world for help, she finds that all her neighbors have been shrunk, too--and they're being chased by feral cats and crows.

To address this extraordinary situation, the Self-Defense Force (SDF) has been called in. However, their mission isn't merely search and rescue; they're also here to find and capture the strange girl, Alice, who's on the run with Yukko!

To track them down, the SDF brings in their secret weapon: a boy named Iosif, who also has superpowers.

Everything is about to be revealed and brought to light...

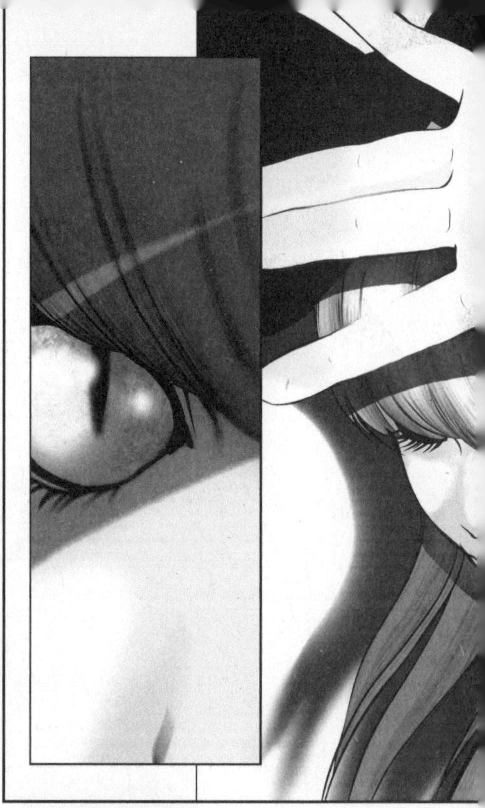

Characters

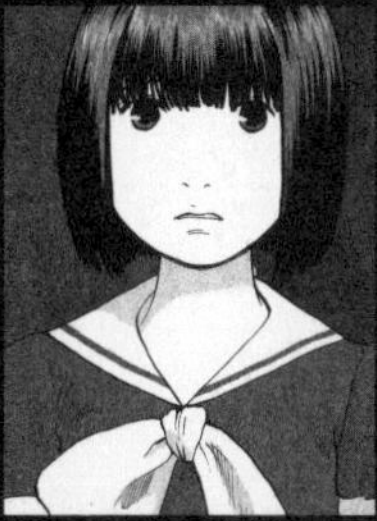

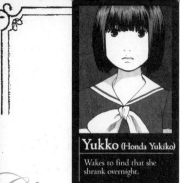

Yukko (Honda Yukiko)

Wakes to find that she shrank overnight.

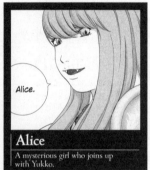

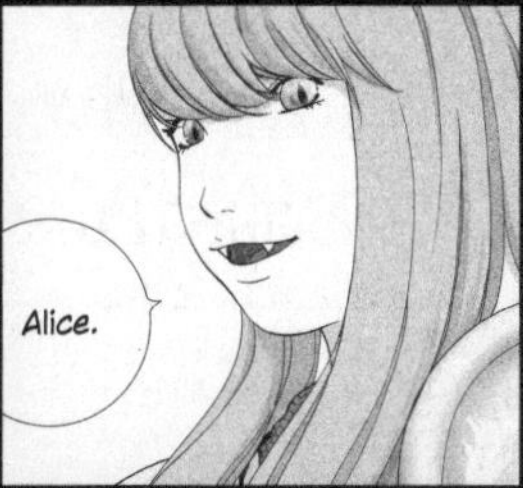
Alice.

Alice

A mysterious girl who joins up with Yukko.

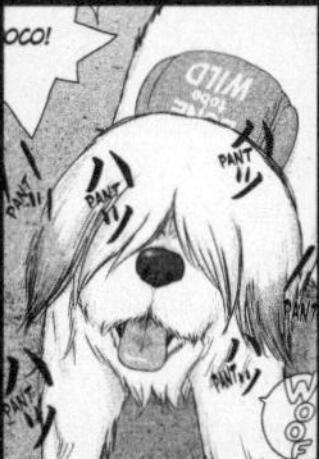
PANT
PANT
WOOF

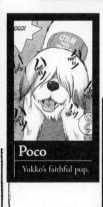

Poco

Yukko's faithful pup.

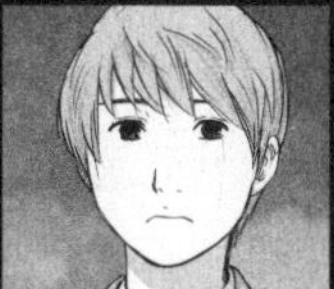

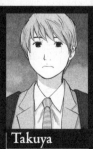

Takuya

Yukko's boyfriend.

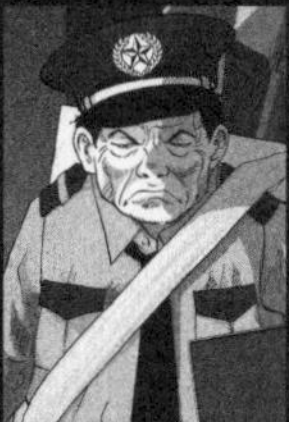

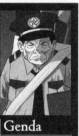

Genda

A mall security guard who's been helping Yukko and Alice.

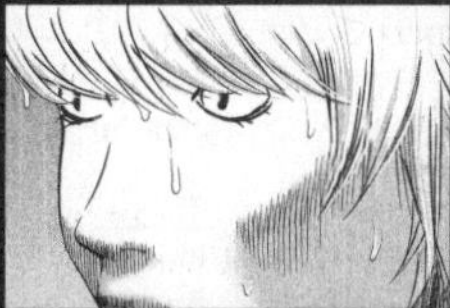

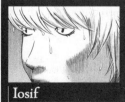

Iosif

A mysterious boy with superpowers.

Contents

Chapter 19: Contact

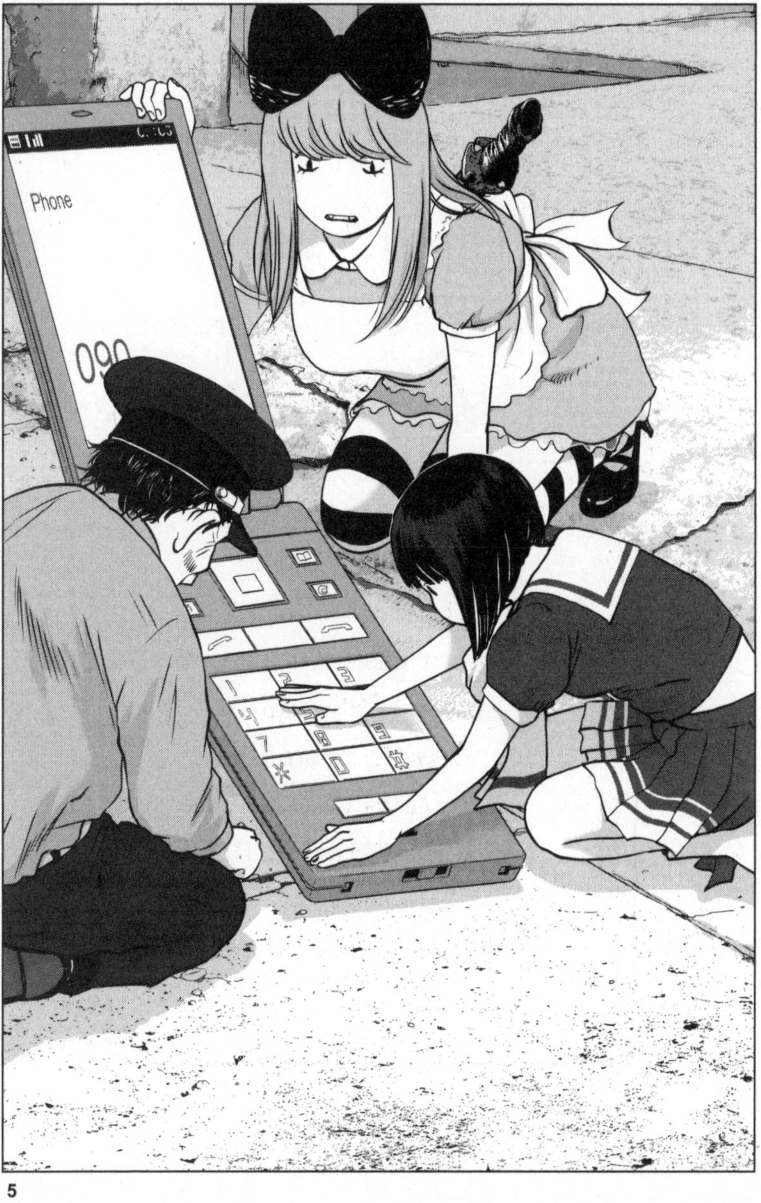
Phone
090

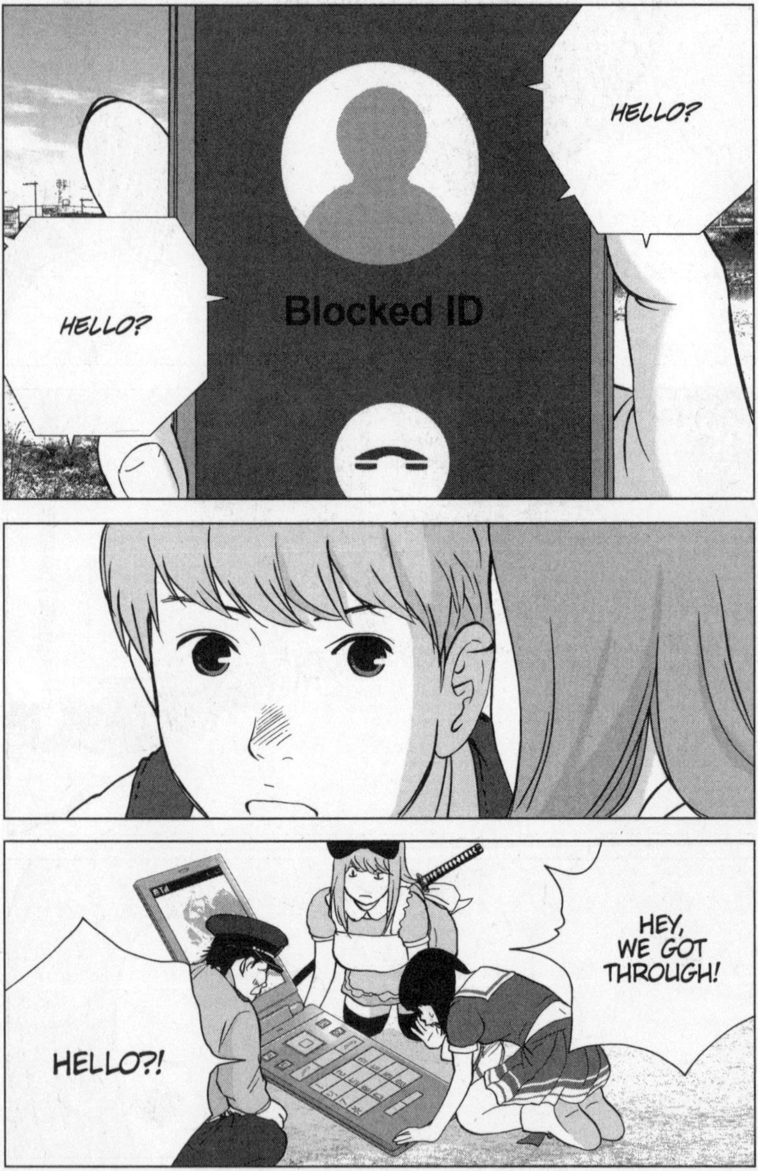
HELLO?
Blocked ID
HELLO?
HEY, WE GOT THROUGH!
HELLO?!

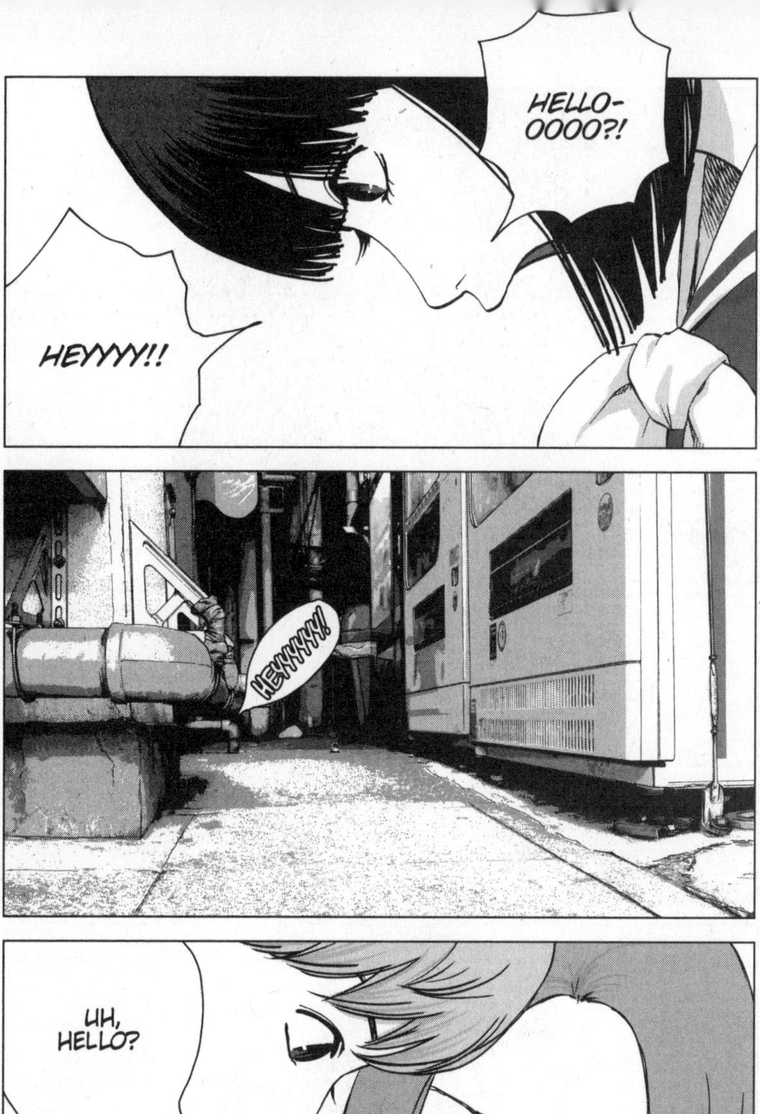
HELLO-OOOO?!
HEYYYY!!
HEYYYYYY!
UH, HELLO?

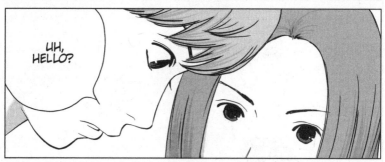

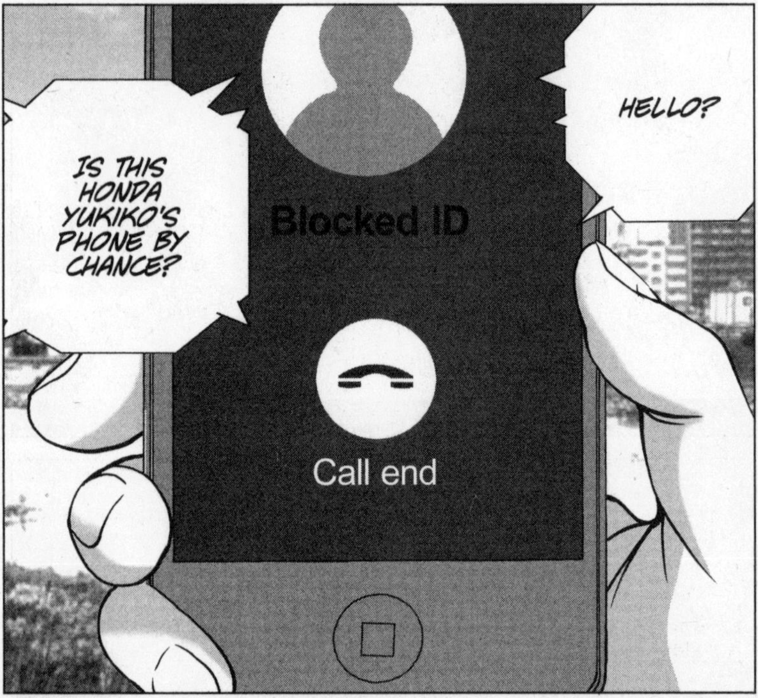
HELLO?
Blocked ID
IS THIS HONDA YUKIKO'S PHONE BY CHANCE?
Call end

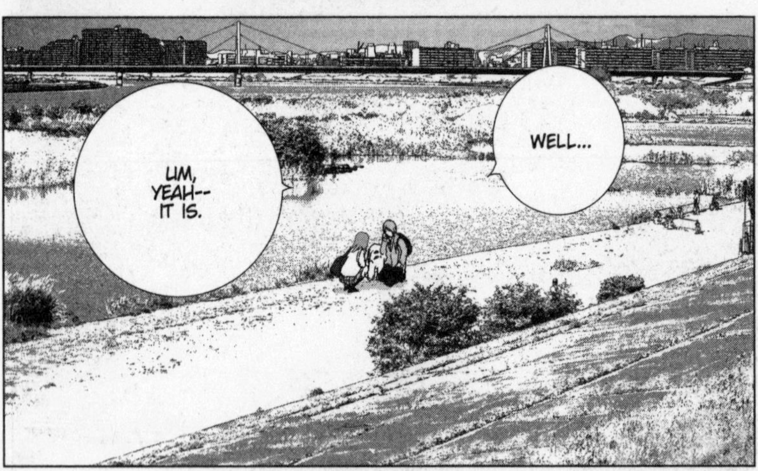
WELL...
UM, YEAH-- IT IS.

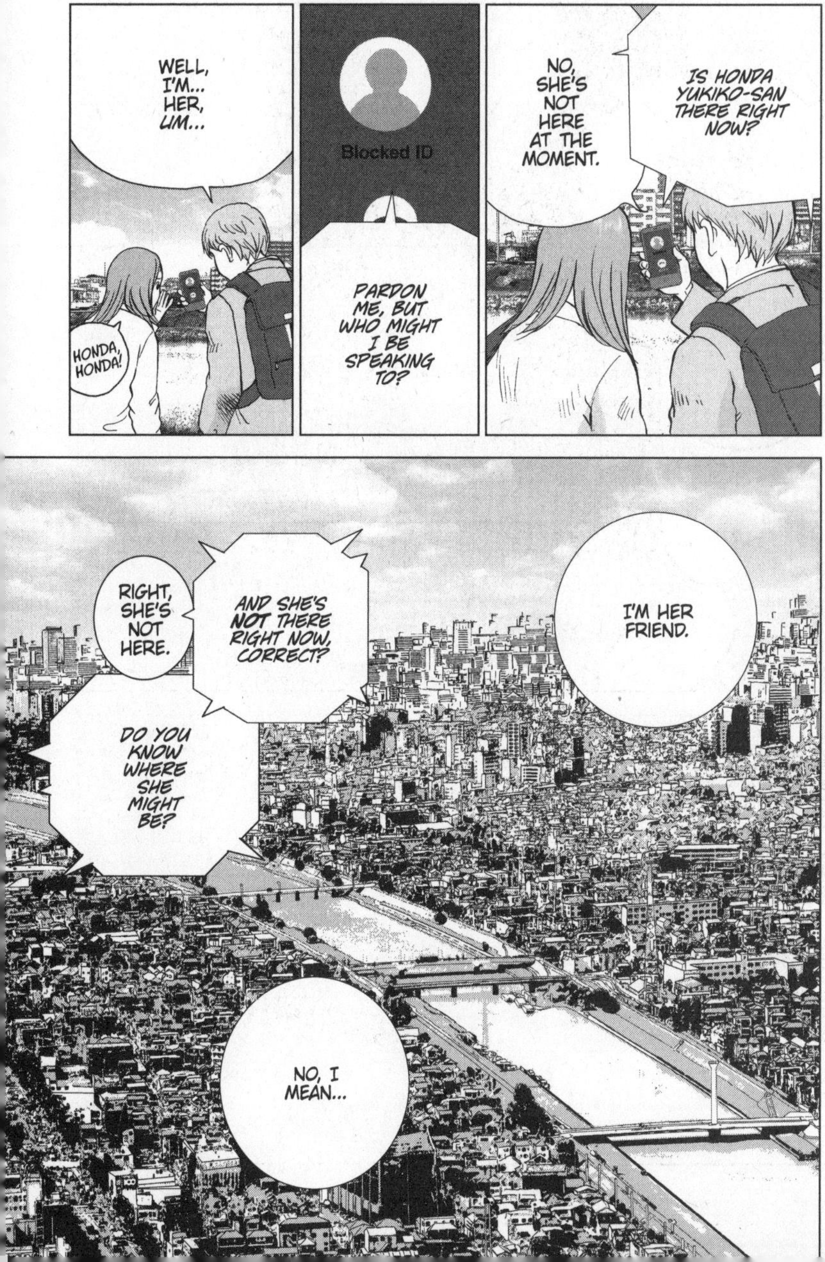
IS HONDA YUKIKO-SAN THERE RIGHT NOW?
NO, SHE'S NOT HERE AT THE MOMENT.
Blocked ID
PARDON ME, BUT WHO MIGHT I BE SPEAKING TO?
WELL, I'M... HER, UM...
HONDA, HONDA!
I'M HER FRIEND.
AND SHE'S **NOT** THERE RIGHT NOW, CORRECT?
RIGHT, SHE'S NOT HERE.
DO YOU KNOW WHERE SHE MIGHT BE?
NO, I MEAN...

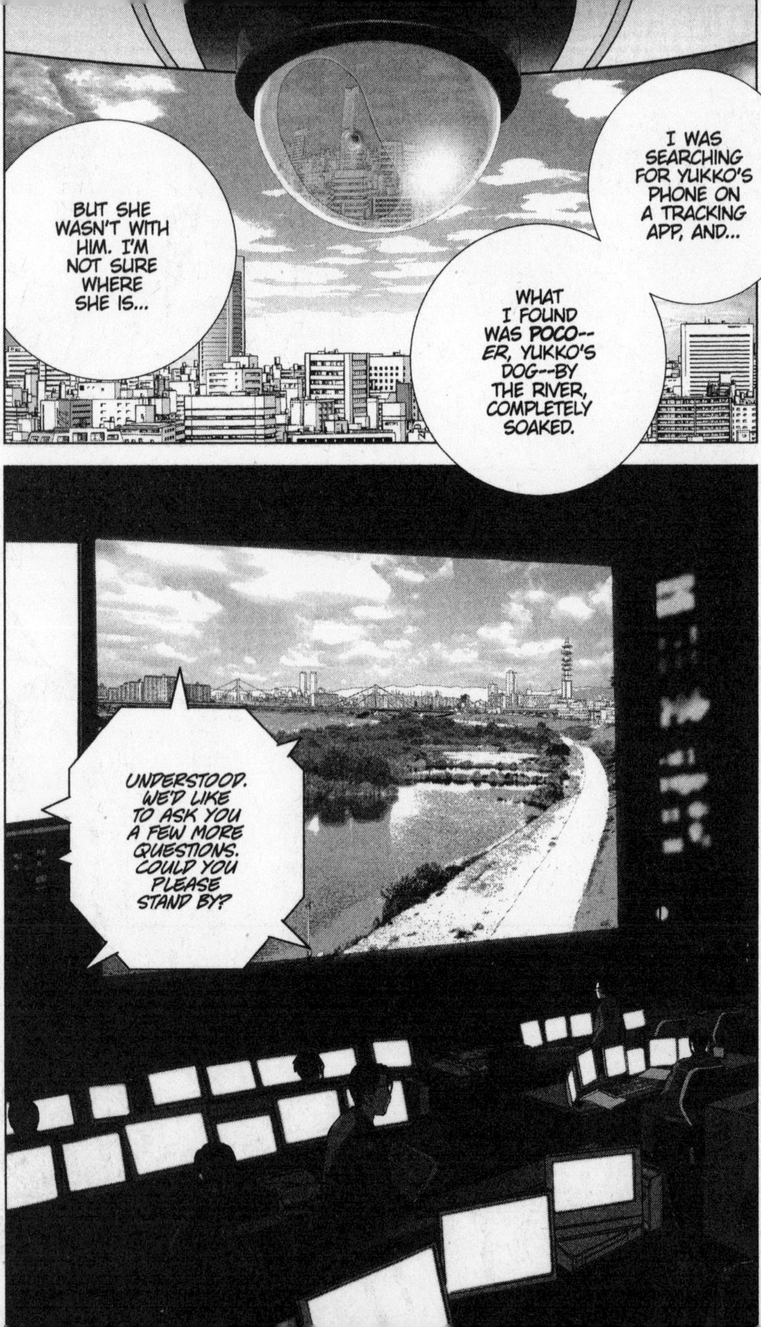
I WAS SEARCHING FOR YUKKO'S PHONE ON A TRACKING APP, AND...
WHAT I FOUND WAS POCO-- ER, YUKKO'S DOG--BY THE RIVER, COMPLETELY SOAKED.
BUT SHE WASN'T WITH HIM. I'M NOT SURE WHERE SHE IS...
UNDERSTOOD. WE'D LIKE TO ASK YOU A FEW MORE QUESTIONS. COULD YOU PLEASE STAND BY?

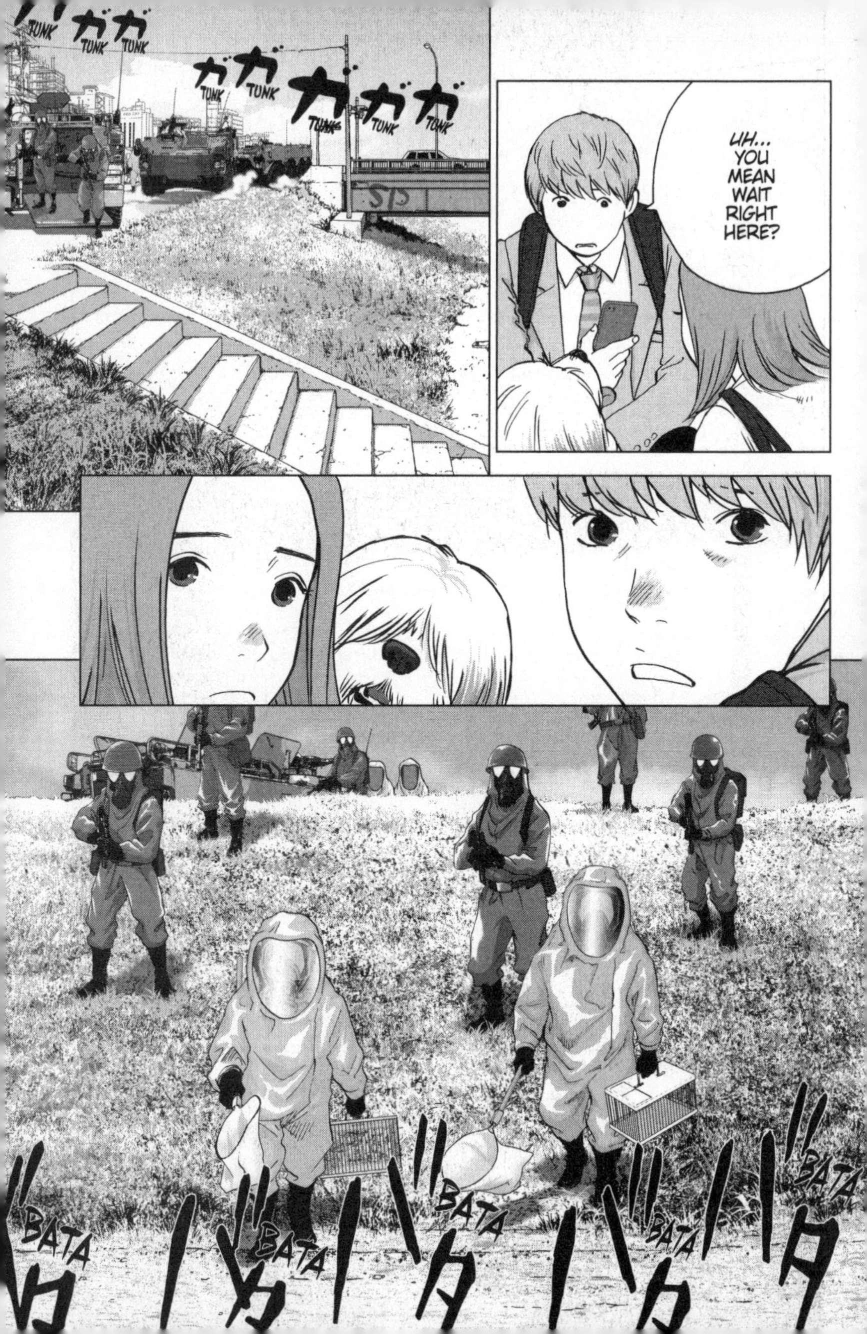
UH... YOU MEAN WAIT RIGHT HERE?
TUNK
TUNK
TUNK
TUNK
TUNK
TUNK
TUNK
TUNK
BATA
BATA
BATA
BATA
BATA

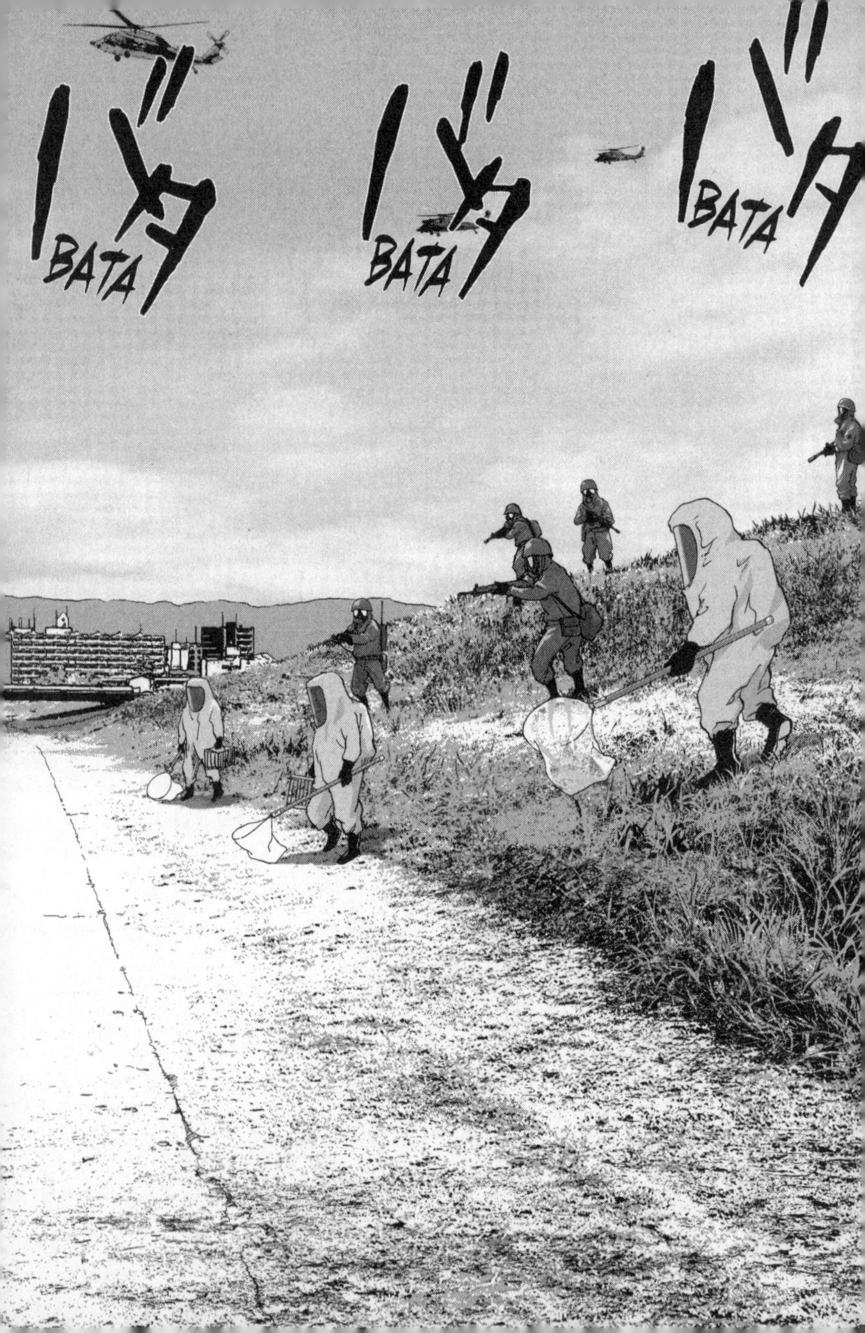

バタ
BATA
バタ
BATA
バタ
BATA

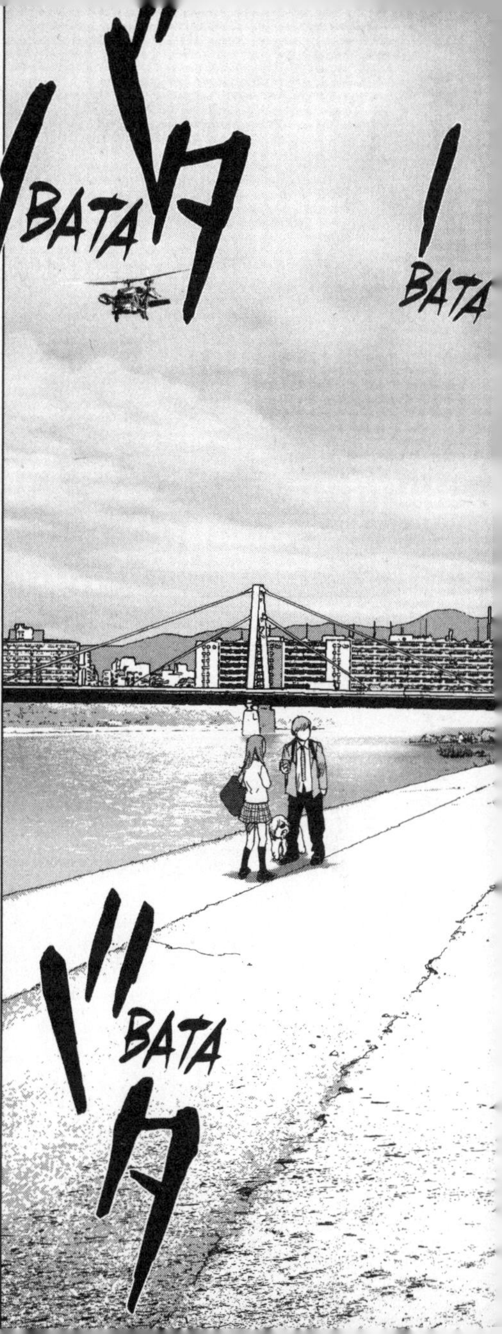
BATA
BATA
BATA
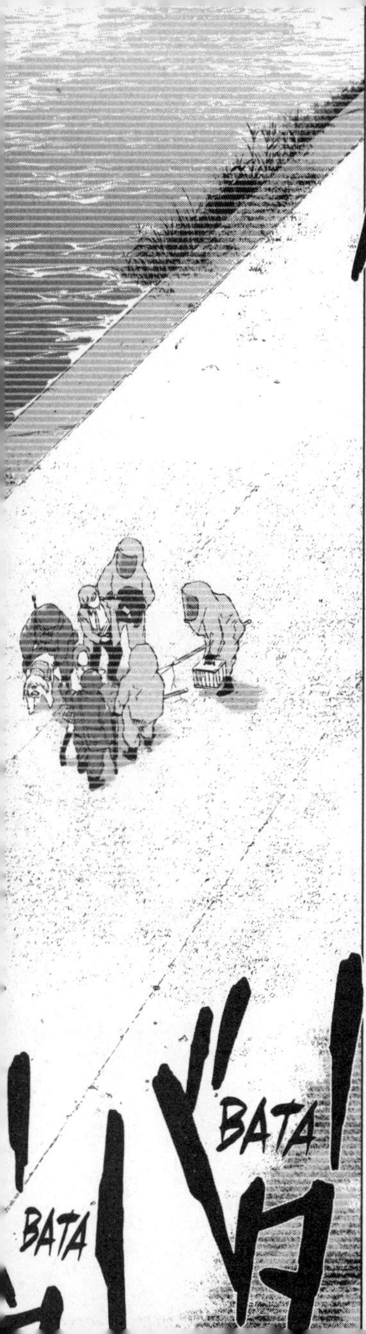
BATA
BATA

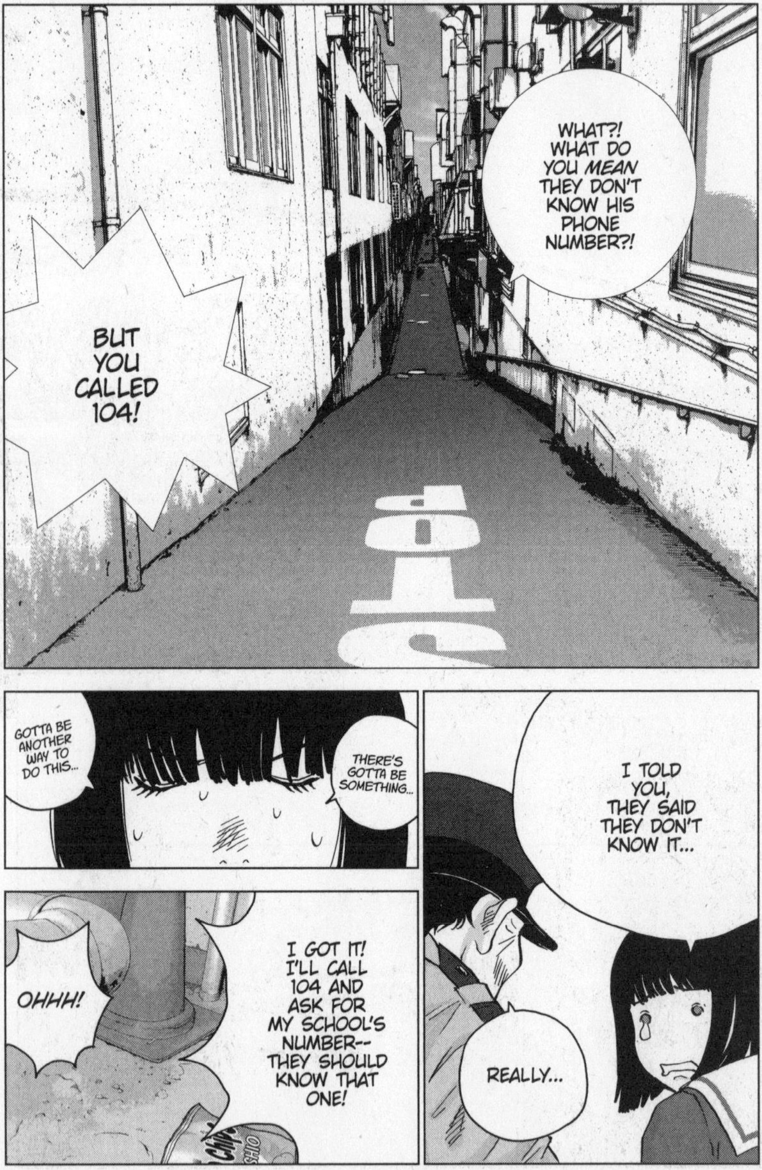
WHAT?! WHAT DO YOU *MEAN* THEY DON'T KNOW HIS PHONE NUMBER?!
BUT YOU CALLED 104!
I TOLD YOU, THEY SAID THEY DON'T KNOW IT...
REALLY...
THERE'S GOTTA BE SOMETHING...
GOTTA BE ANOTHER WAY TO DO THIS...
I GOT IT! I'LL CALL 104 AND ASK FOR MY SCHOOL'S NUMBER-- THEY SHOULD KNOW THAT ONE!
OHHH!

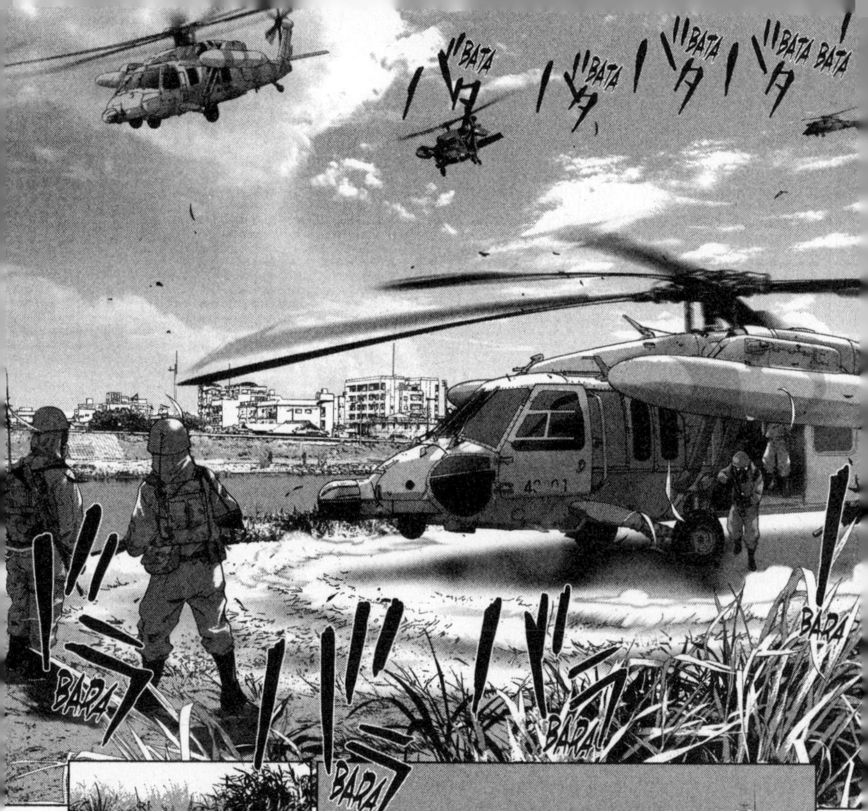
バタバタバタバタ!
BATA BATA BATA BATA BATA
バラバラバラバラ!
BARA BARA BARA BARA

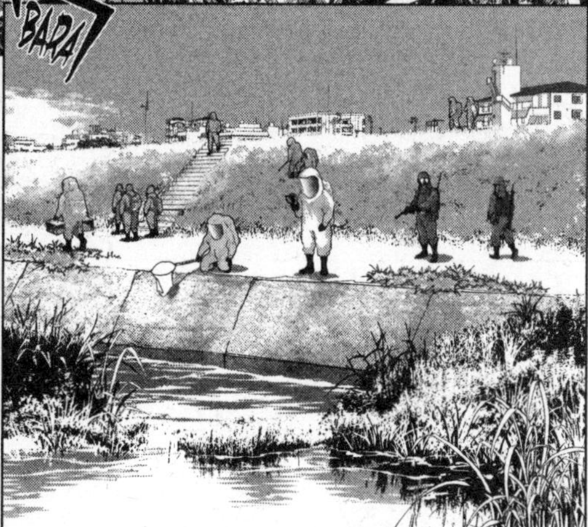

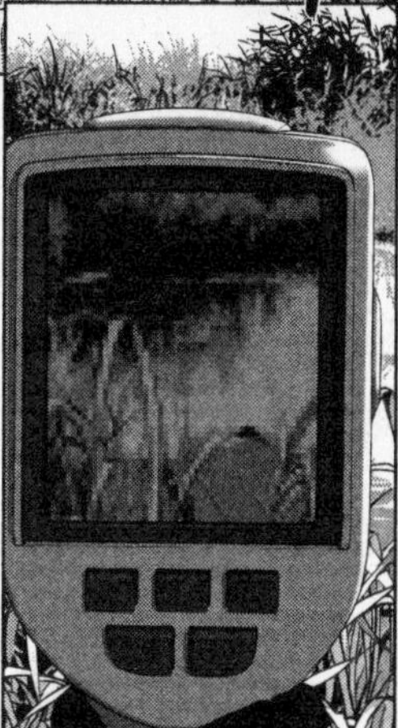

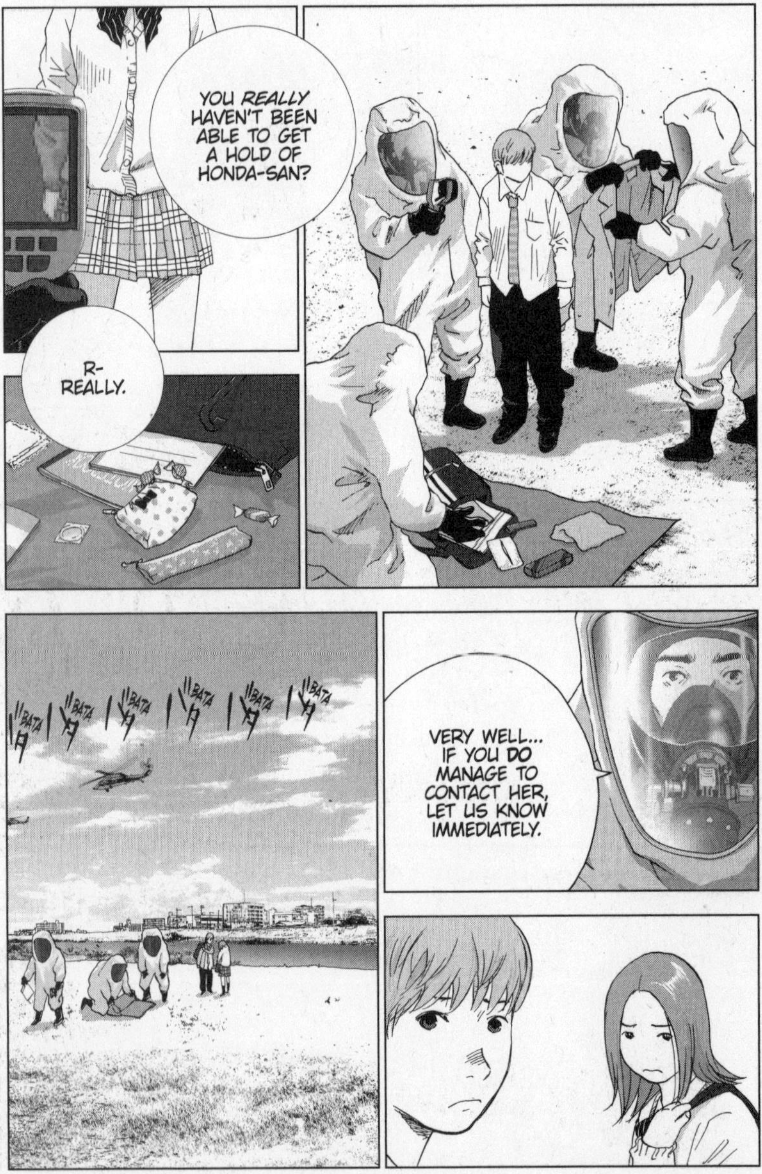
YOU REALLY HAVEN'T BEEN ABLE TO GET A HOLD OF HONDA-SAN?
R- REALLY.
VERY WELL... IF YOU DO MANAGE TO CONTACT HER, LET US KNOW IMMEDIATELY.
BATA BATA BATA BATA BATA BATA

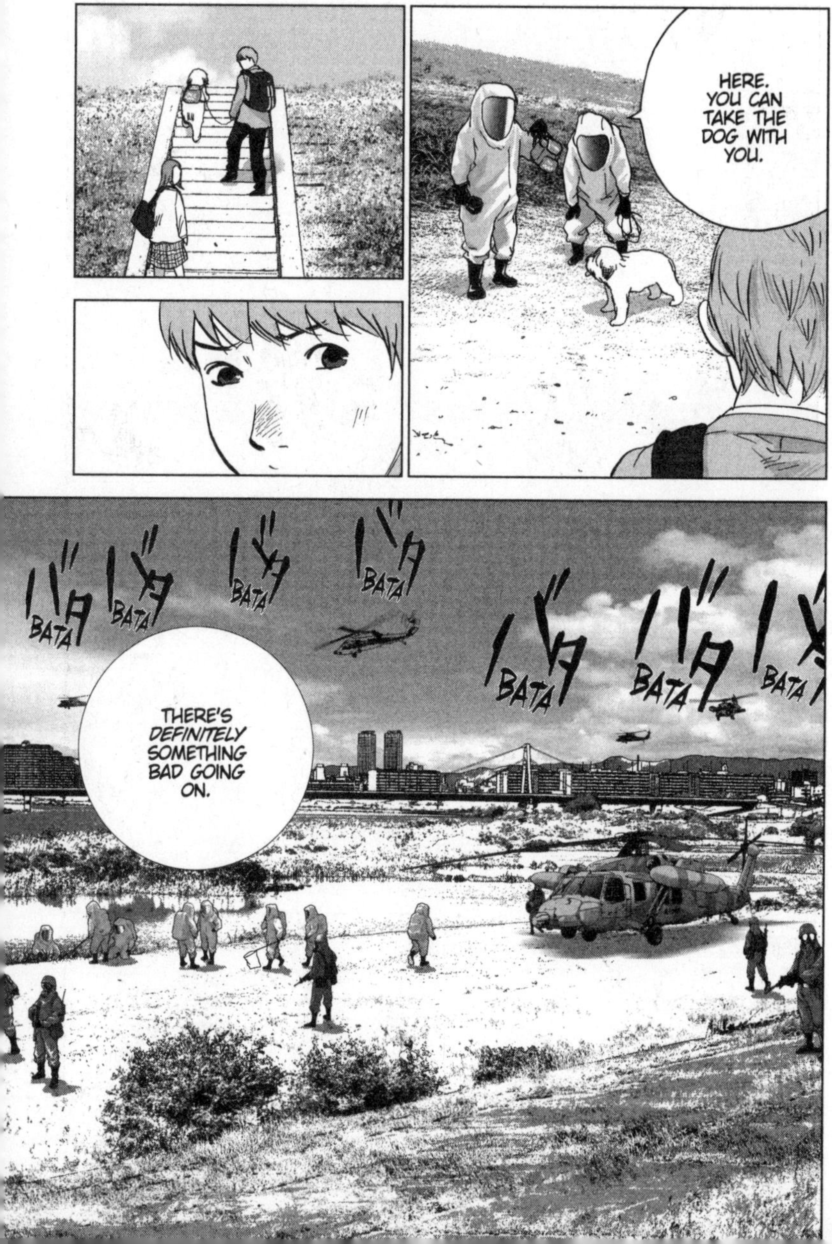
HERE. YOU CAN TAKE THE DOG WITH YOU.
バタ BATA
バタ BATA
バタ BATA
バタ BATA
バタ BATA
バタ BATA
バタ BATA
THERE'S DEFINITELY SOMETHING BAD GOING ON.

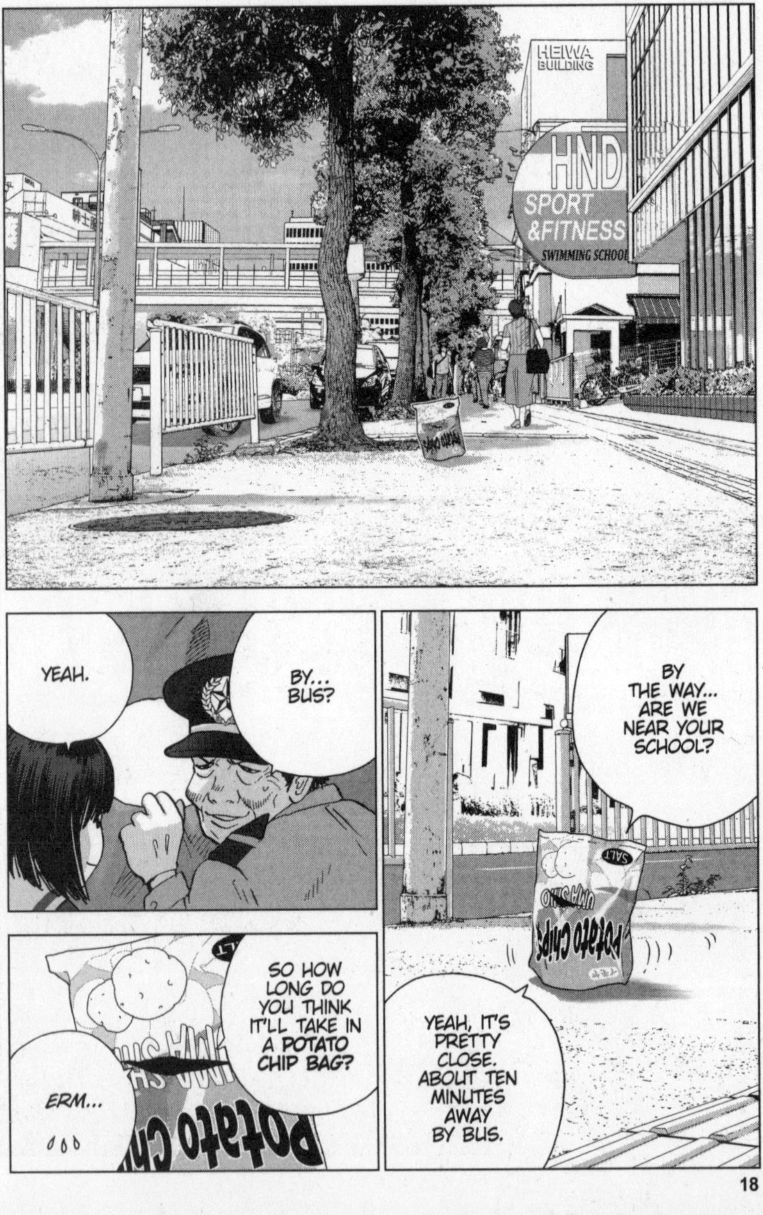
HEIWA BUILDING
HND SPORT &FITNESS SWIMMING SCHOOL
BY THE WAY... ARE WE NEAR YOUR SCHOOL?
YEAH, IT'S PRETTY CLOSE. ABOUT TEN MINUTES AWAY BY BUS.
BY... BUS?
YEAH.
SO HOW LONG DO YOU THINK IT'LL TAKE IN A POTATO CHIP BAG?
ERM...

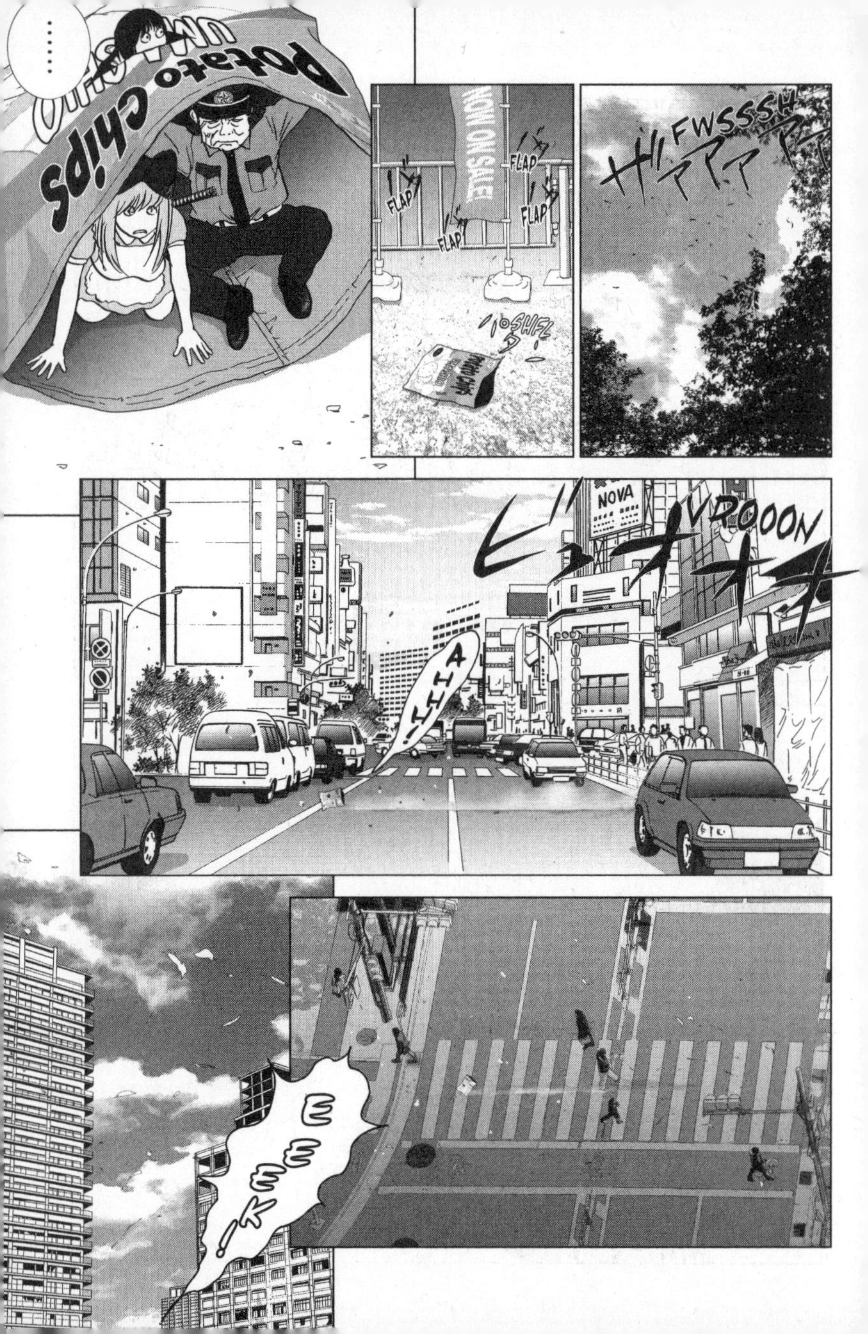
FWSSSH
NOW ON SALE!
FLAP
FLAP
FLAP
FLAP
SHFL
......
Potato Chips
NOVA
VROOON
AHHH!
EEEEK!

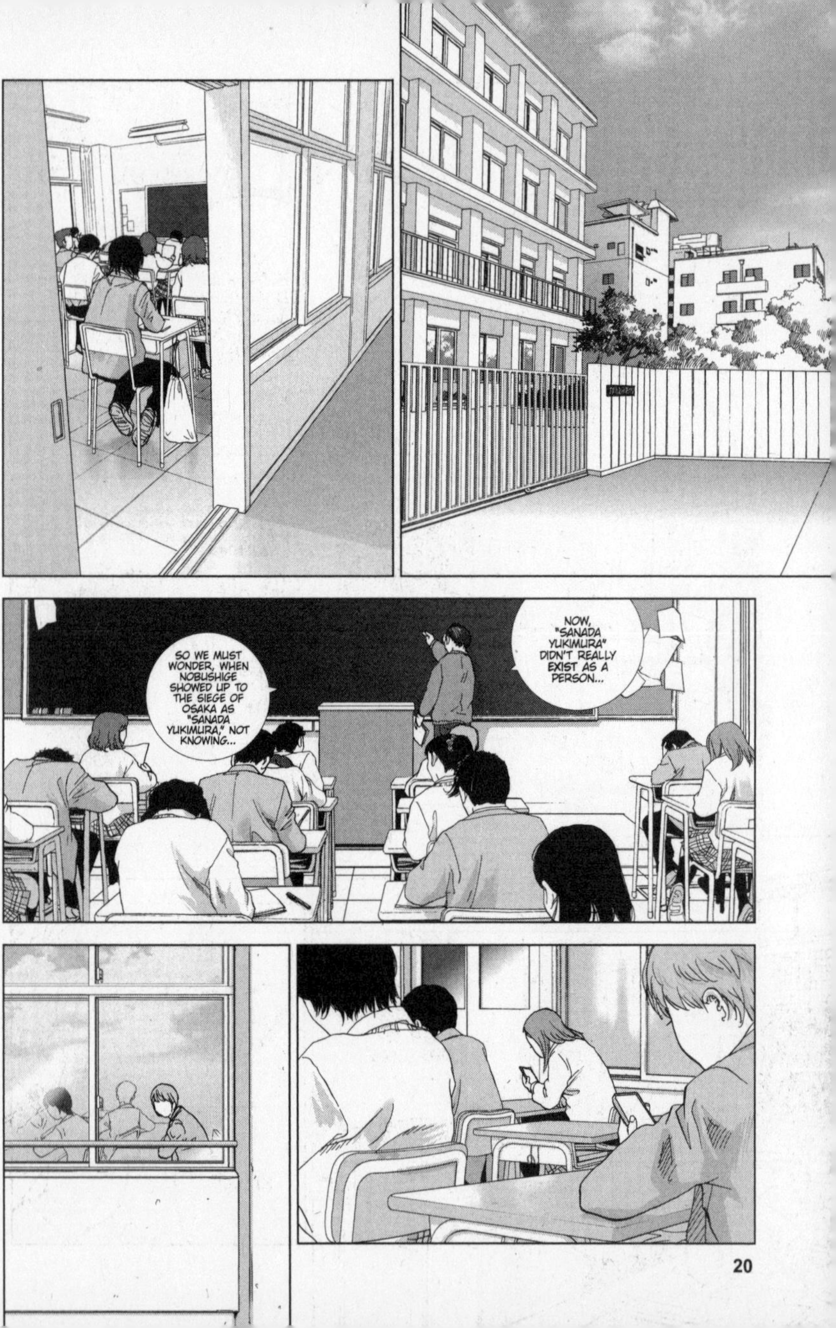
NOW, "SANADA YUKIMURA" DIDN'T REALLY EXIST AS A PERSON...
SO WE MUST WONDER, WHEN NOBUSHIGE SHOWED UP TO THE SIEGE OF OSAKA AS "SANADA YUKIMURA," NOT KNOWING...

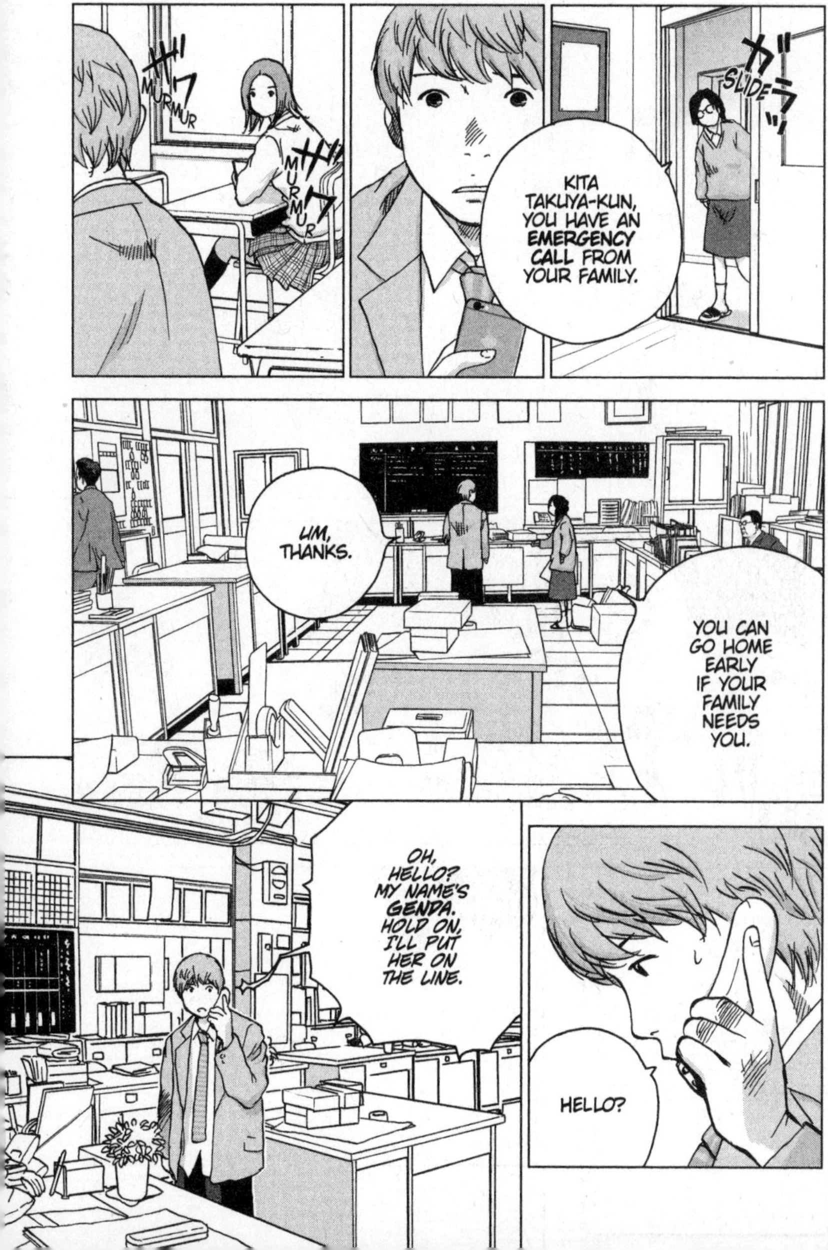
SLIDE
KITA TAKUYA-KUN, YOU HAVE AN EMERGENCY CALL FROM YOUR FAMILY.
MURMUR
MURMUR
YOU CAN GO HOME EARLY IF YOUR FAMILY NEEDS YOU.
UM, THANKS.
HELLO?
OH, HELLO? MY NAME'S GENDA. HOLD ON, I'LL PUT HER ON THE LINE.

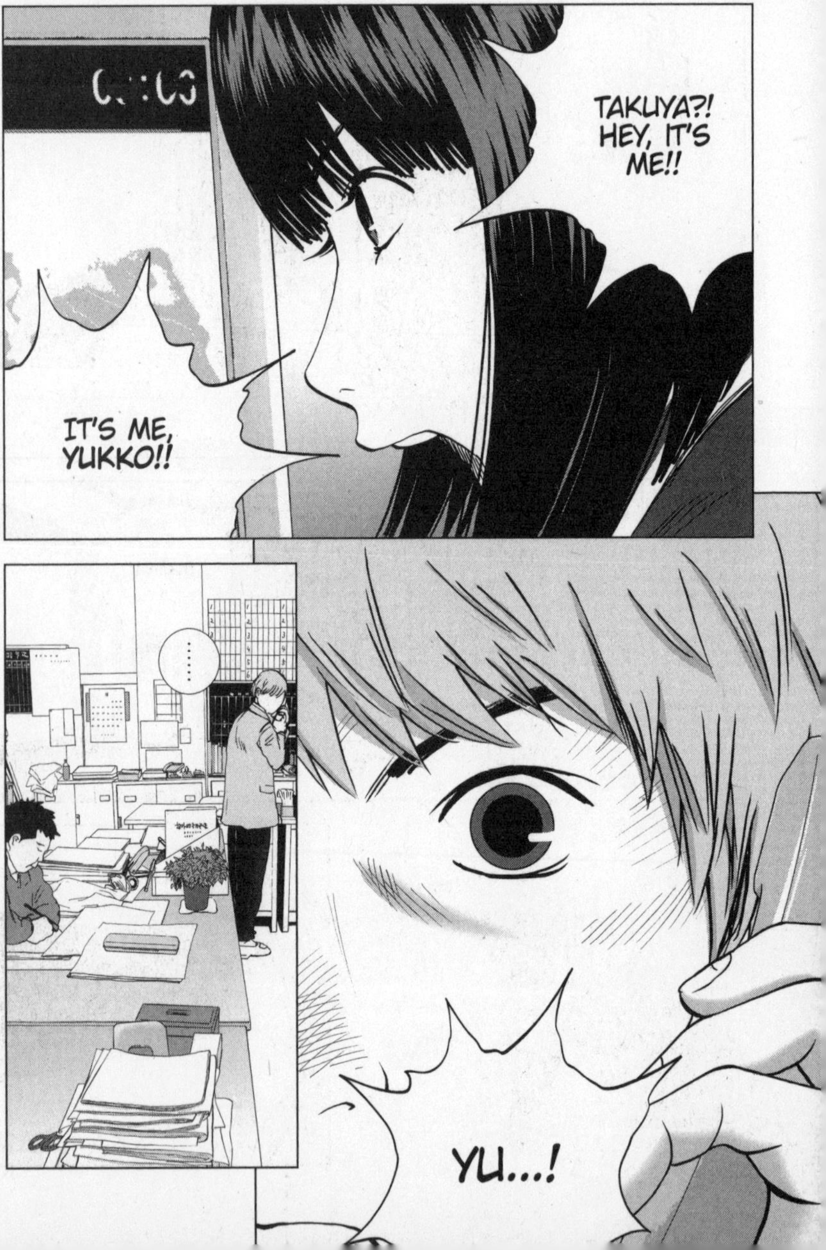
TAKUYA?! HEY, IT'S ME!!
IT'S ME, YUKKO!!
YU...!
......

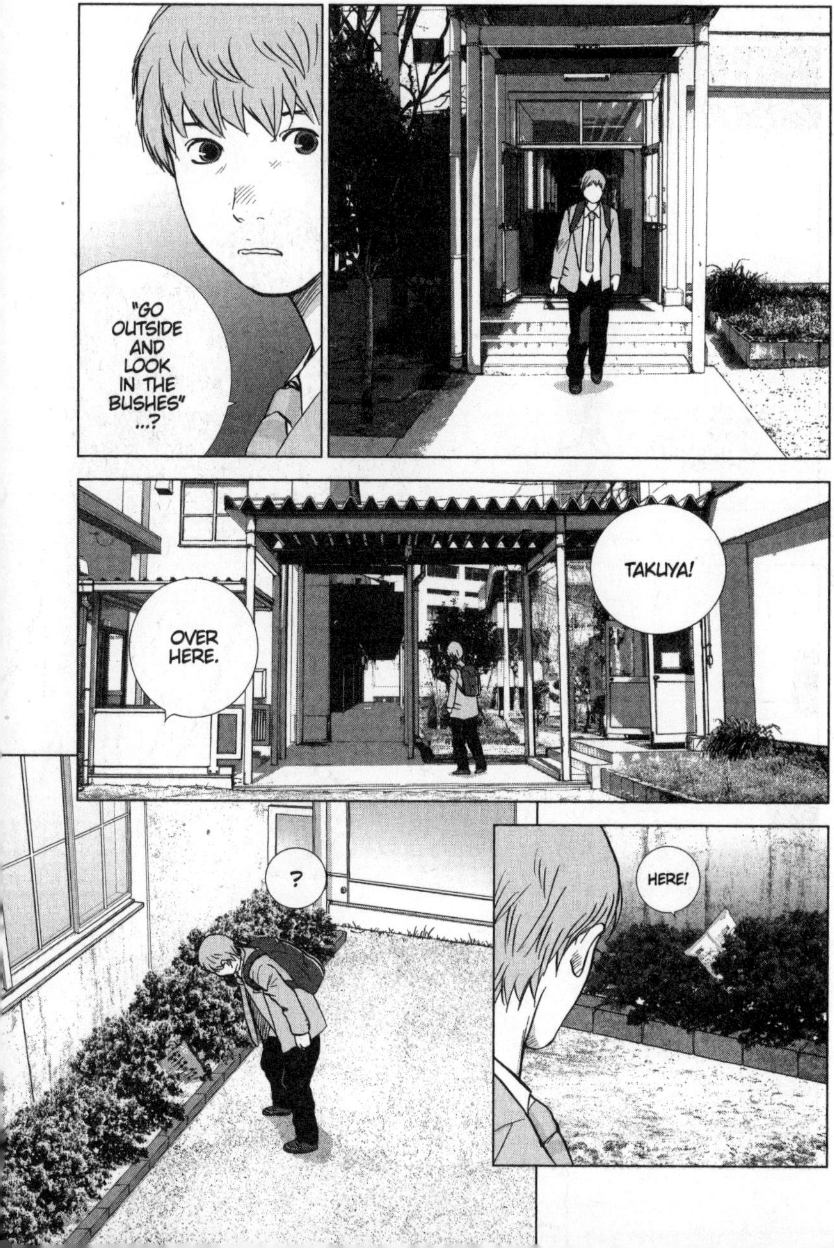
"GO OUTSIDE AND LOOK IN THE BUSHES" ...?
TAKUYA!
OVER HERE.
HERE!
?

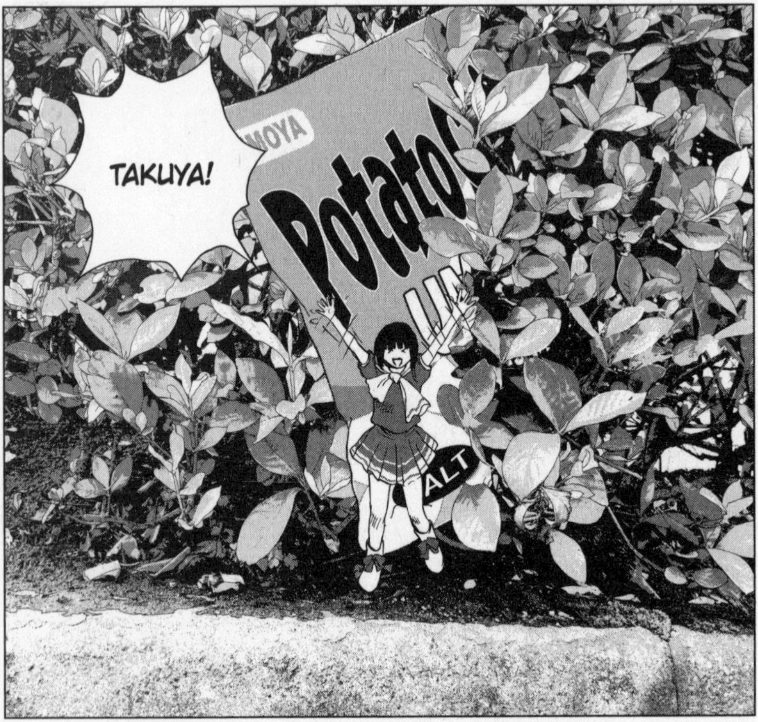
TAKUYA!

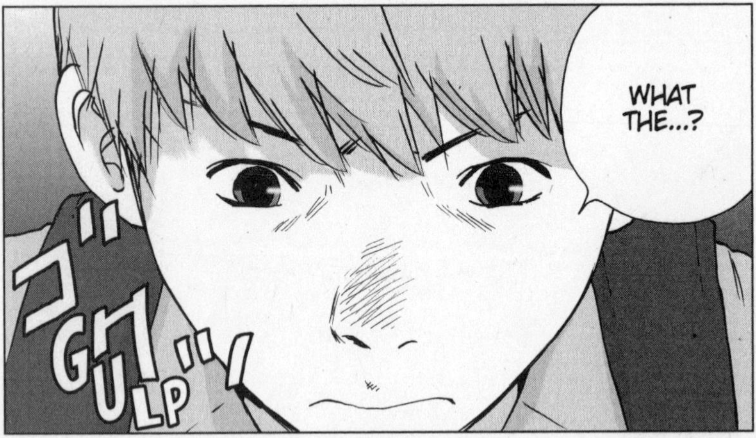
WHAT THE...?
GULP

Chapter 20: Reunion

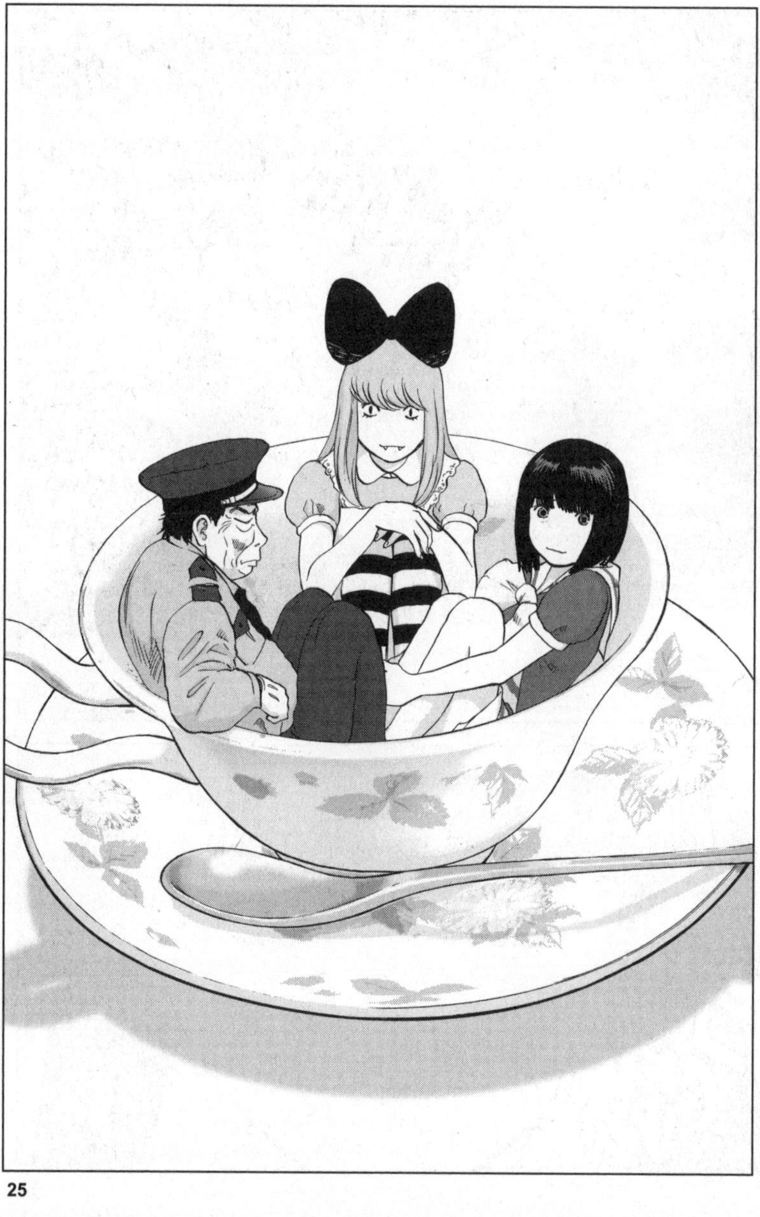

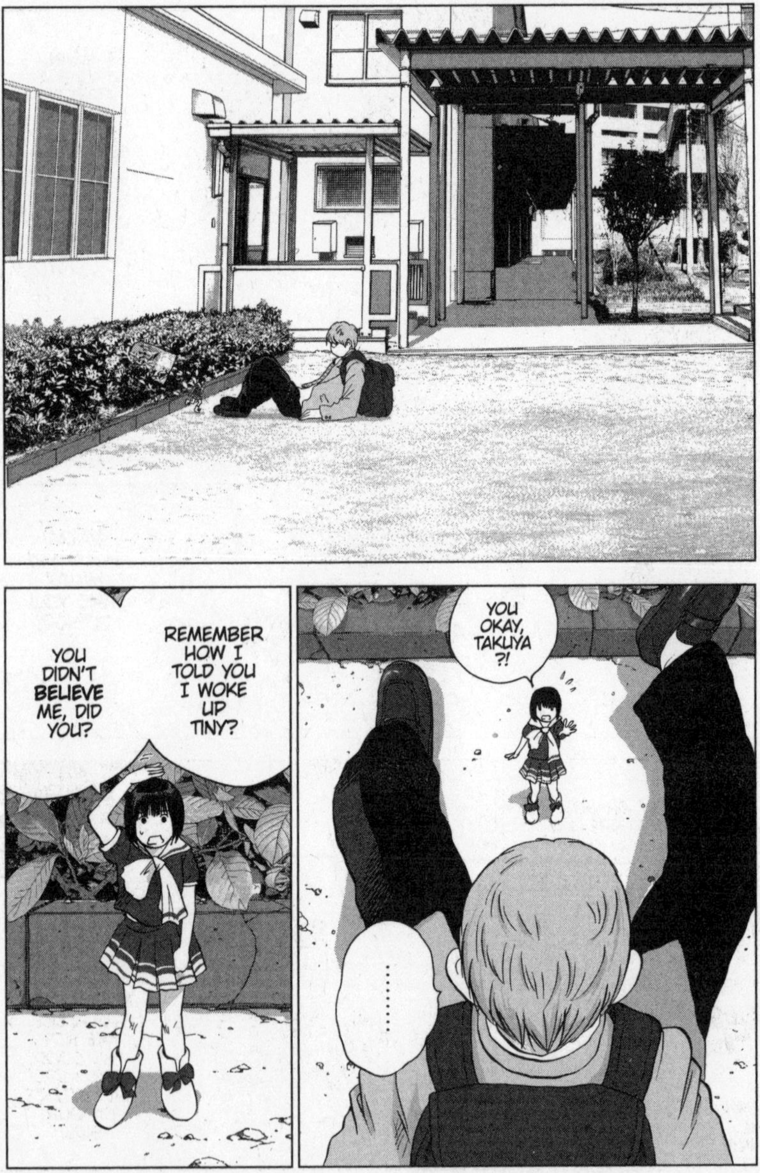
YOU OKAY, TAKUYA ?!
......
REMEMBER HOW I TOLD YOU I WOKE UP TINY?
YOU DIDN'T BELIEVE ME, DID YOU?

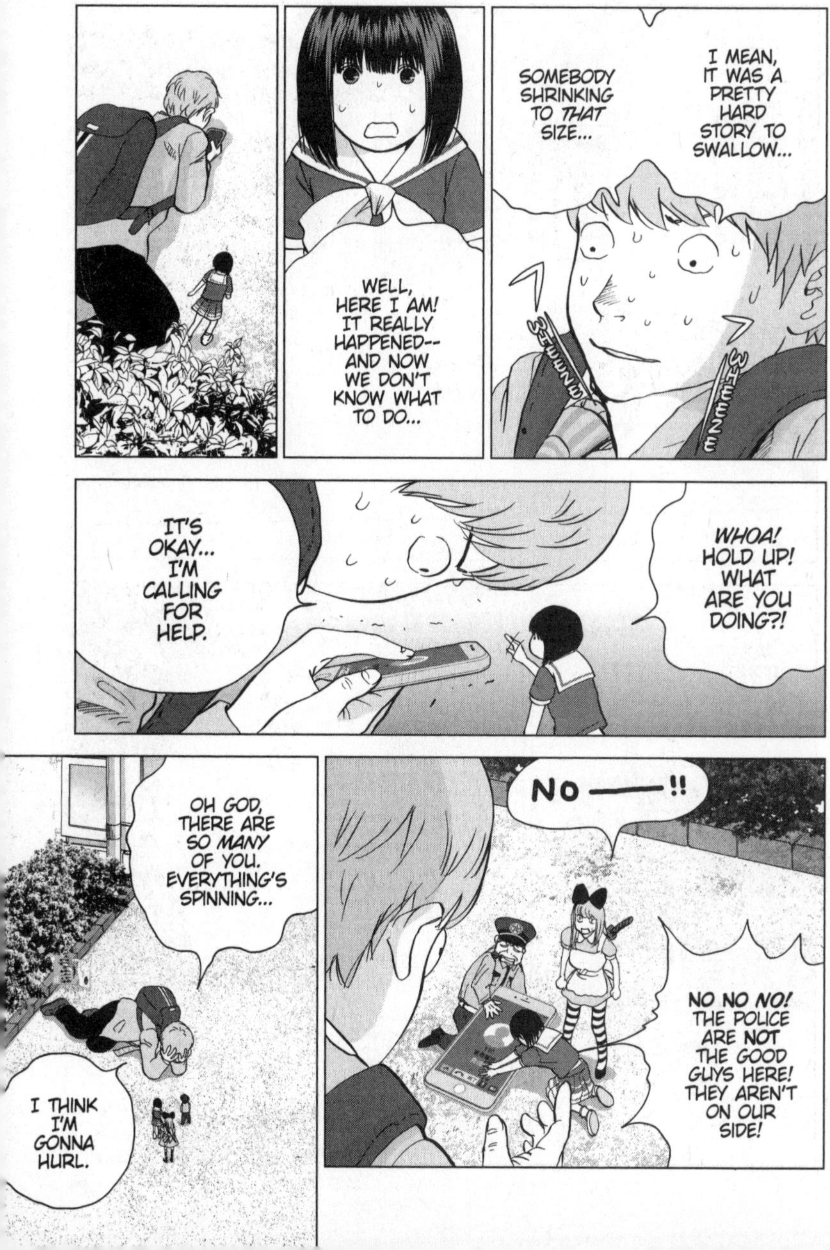
I MEAN, IT WAS A PRETTY HARD STORY TO SWALLOW...
SOMEBODY SHRINKING TO *THAT* SIZE...
WELL, HERE I AM! IT REALLY HAPPENED-- AND NOW WE DON'T KNOW WHAT TO DO...
WHOA! HOLD UP! WHAT ARE YOU DOING?!
IT'S OKAY... I'M CALLING FOR HELP.
NO——!!
NO NO *NO!* THE POLICE ARE **NOT** THE GOOD GUYS HERE! THEY AREN'T ON OUR SIDE!
OH GOD, THERE ARE SO *MANY* OF YOU. EVERYTHING'S SPINNING...
I THINK I'M GONNA HURL.

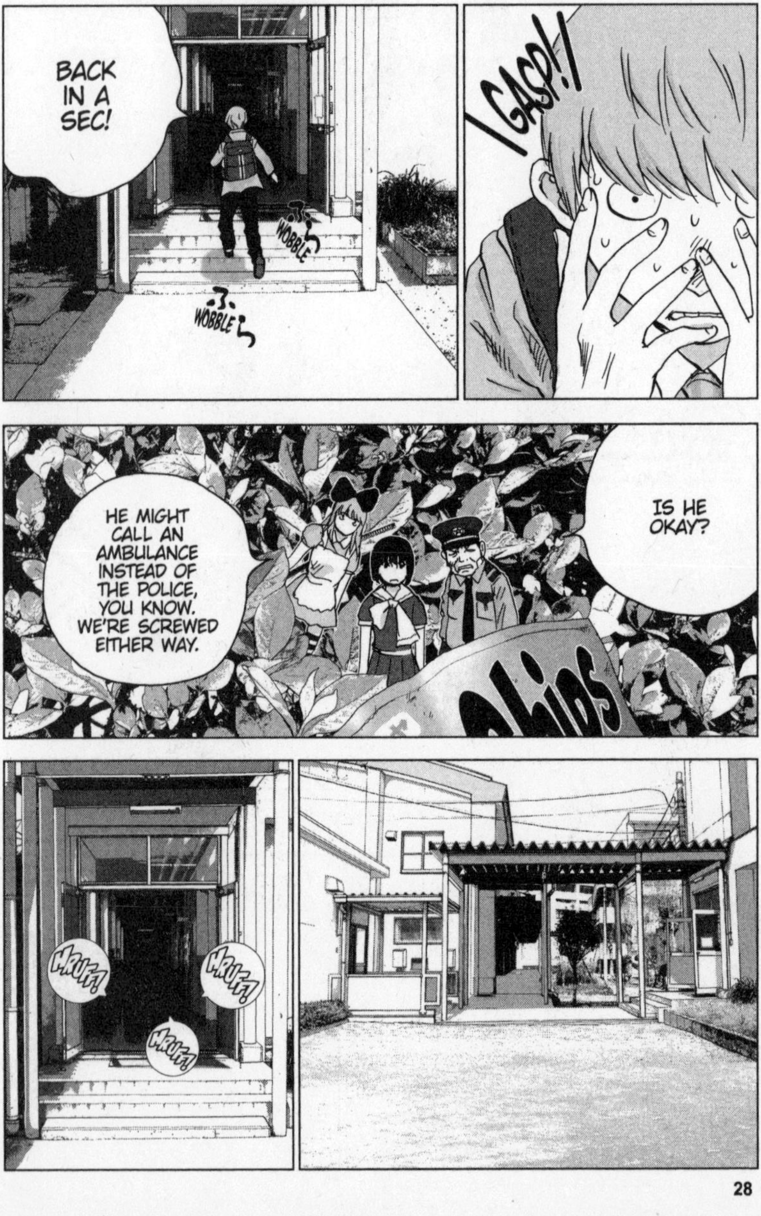
GASP!!
BACK IN A SEC!
WOBBLE
WOBBLE
IS HE OKAY?
HE MIGHT CALL AN AMBULANCE INSTEAD OF THE POLICE, YOU KNOW. WE'RE SCREWED EITHER WAY.
HRUFF!
HRUFF!
HRUFF!

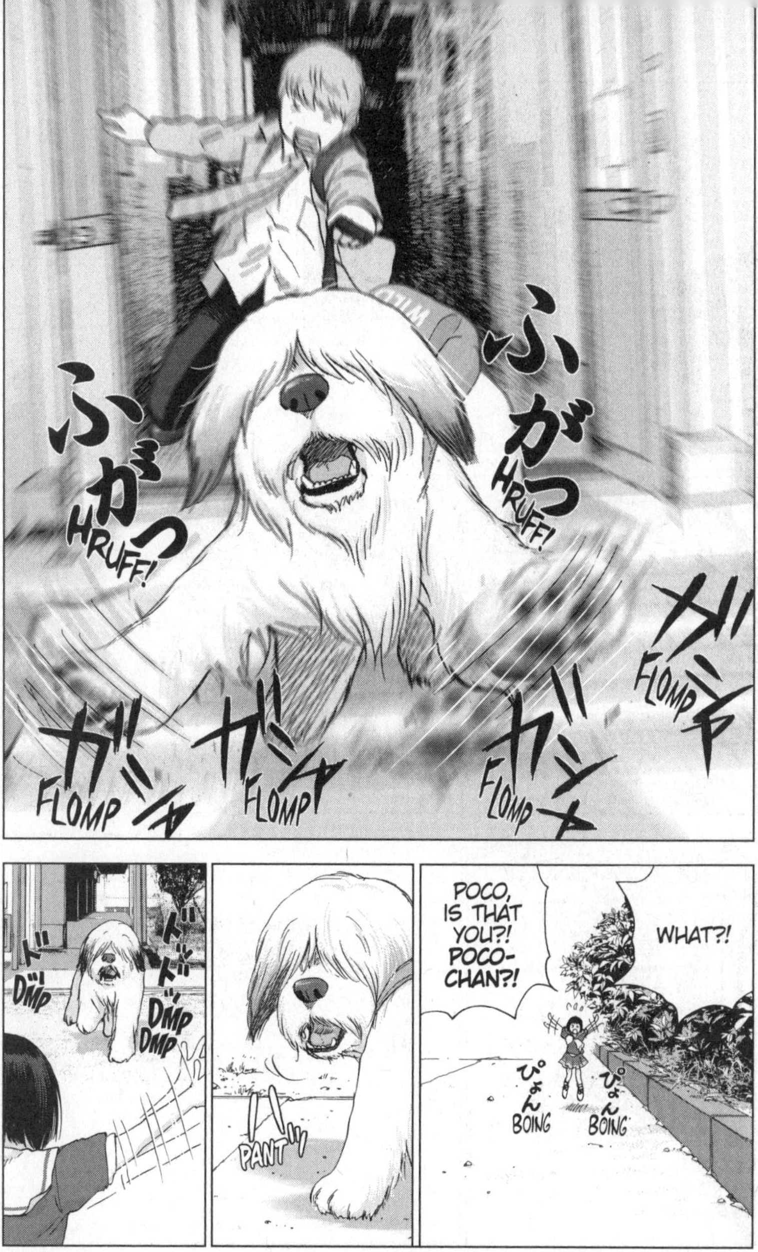
ふがっ
HRUFF!
ふがっ
HRUFF!
ガシャ
FLOMP
ガシャ
FLOMP
ガシャ
FLOMP
ガシャ
FLOMP
WHAT?!
POCO, IS THAT YOU?! POCO-CHAN?!
ぴょん
BOING
ぴょん
BOING
PANT
ドドド
DMP
DMP
DMP

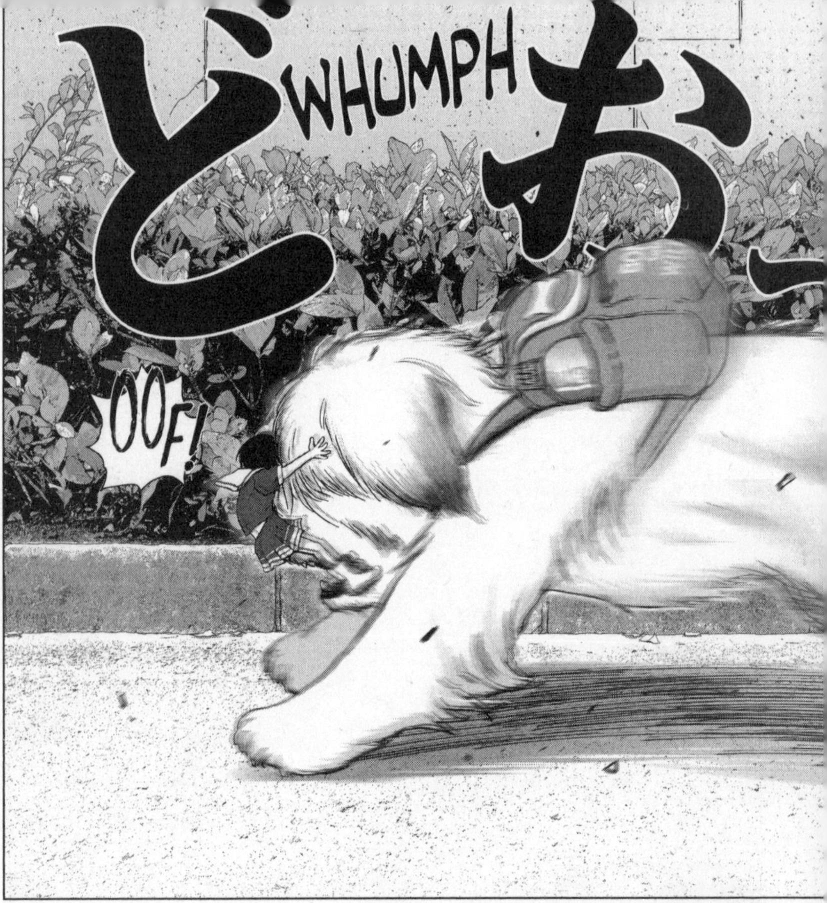
WHUMPH
OOF!
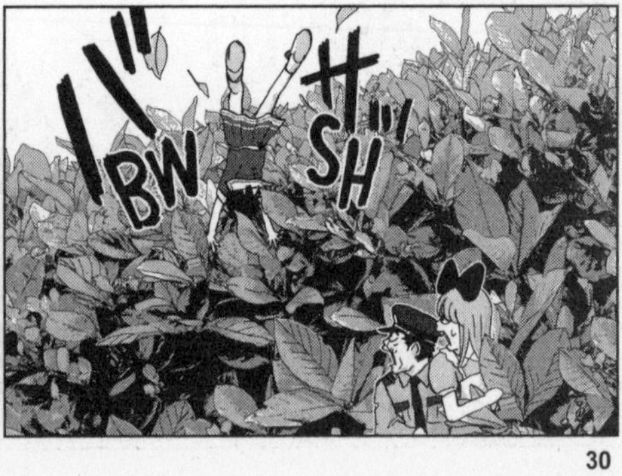
BW
SH
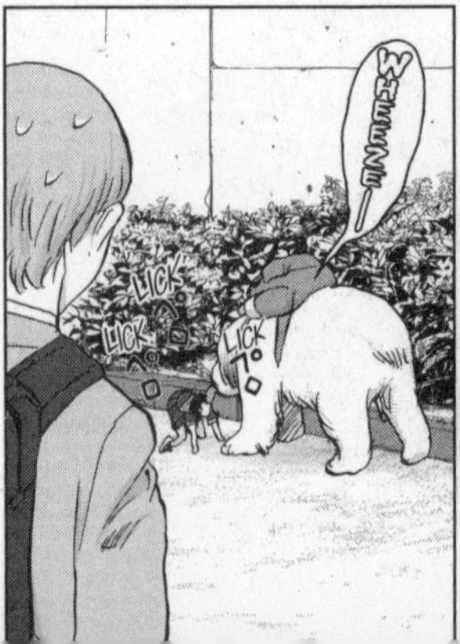
LICK
LICK
LICK

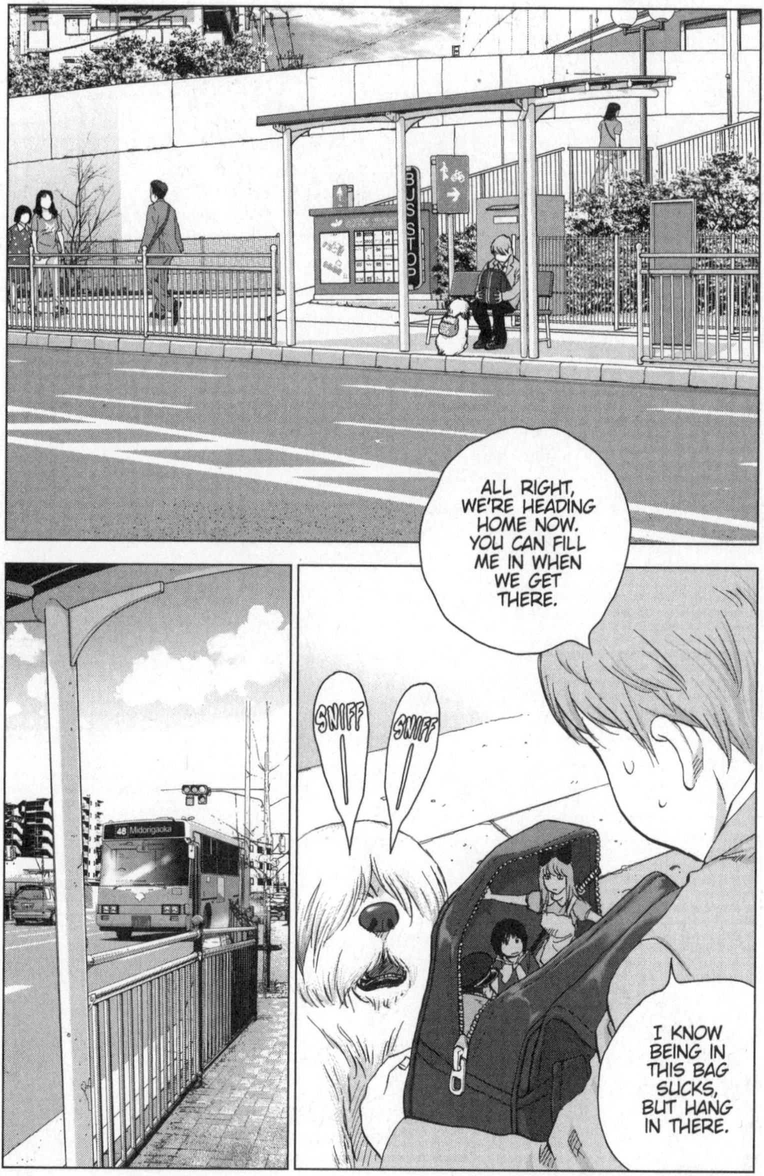
BUS STOP
ALL RIGHT, WE'RE HEADING HOME NOW. YOU CAN FILL ME IN WHEN WE GET THERE.
SNIFF
SNIFF
I KNOW BEING IN THIS BAG SUCKS, BUT HANG IN THERE.
48 Midorigaoka

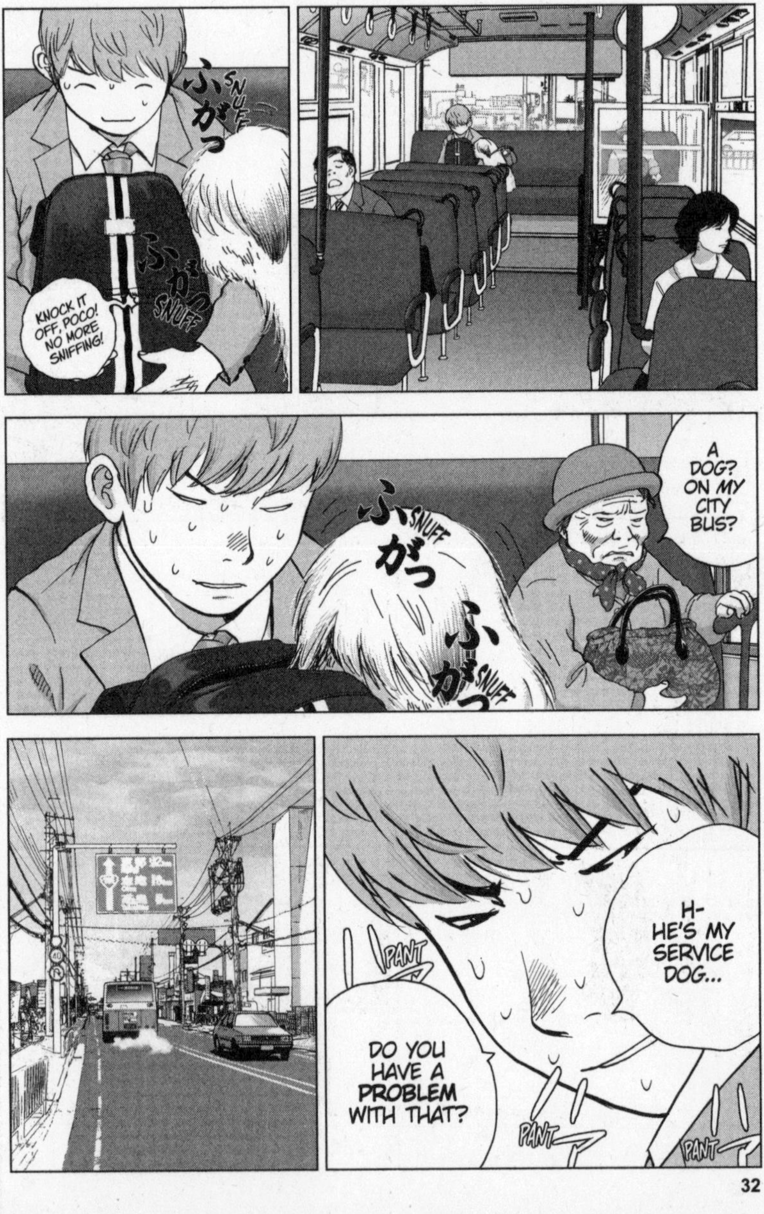
ふがっ SNUFF
ふがっ SNUFF
KNOCK IT OFF, POCO! NO MORE SNIFFING!
A DOG? ON MY CITY BUS?
ふがっ SNUFF
ふがっ SNUFF
H- HE'S MY SERVICE DOG...
PANT
DO YOU HAVE A PROBLEM WITH THAT?
PANT
PANT

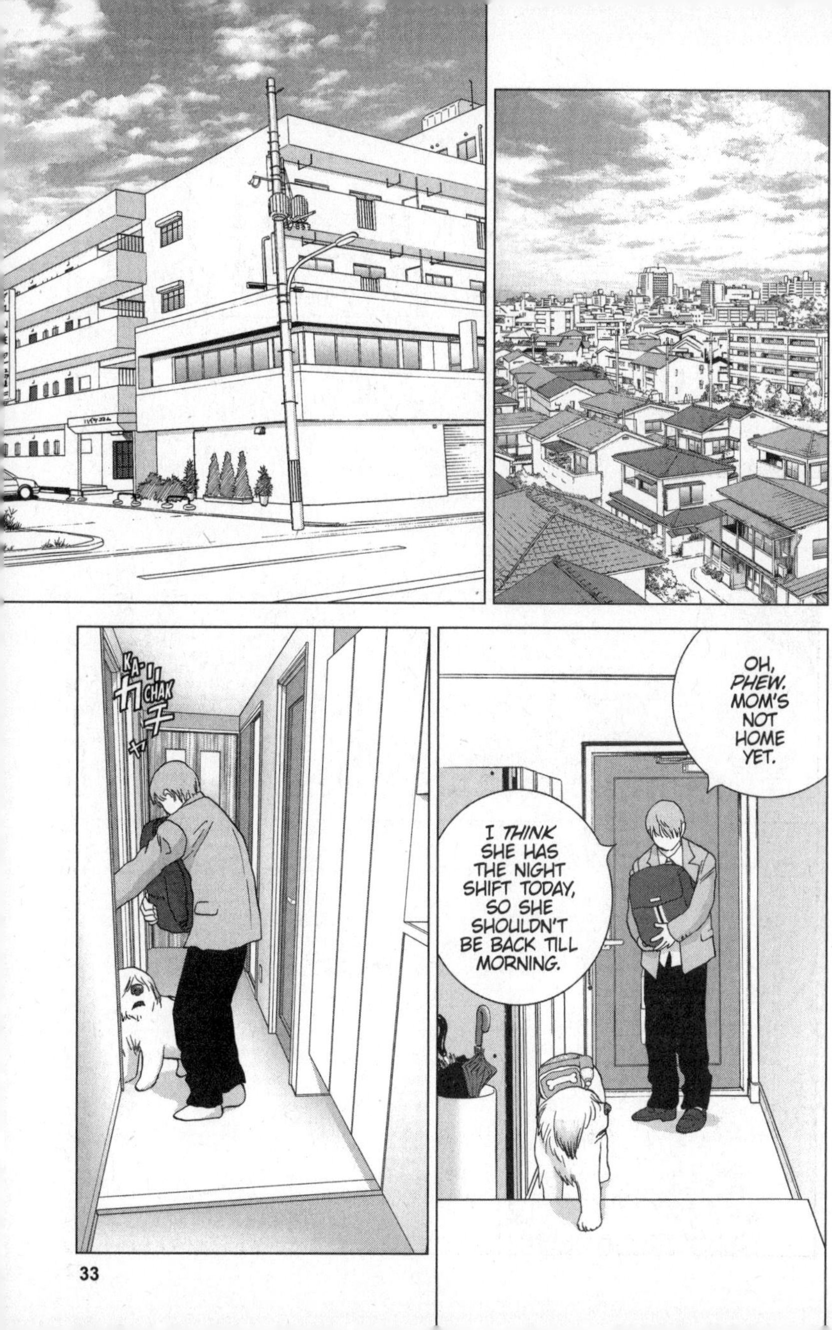
OH, *PHEW*. MOM'S NOT HOME YET.
I *THINK* SHE HAS THE NIGHT SHIFT TODAY, SO SHE SHOULDN'T BE BACK TILL MORNING.
KA-CHAK

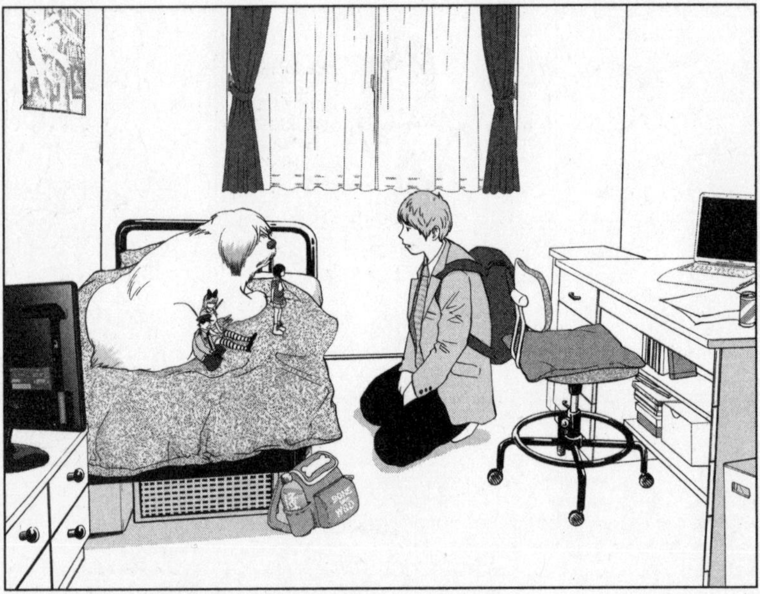

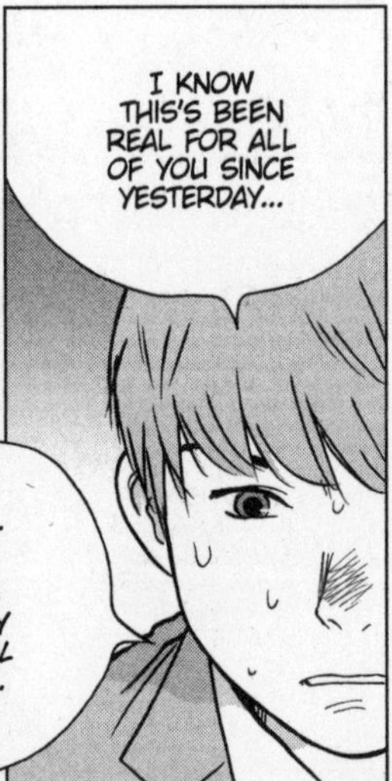
I KNOW THIS'S BEEN REAL FOR ALL OF YOU SINCE YESTERDAY...

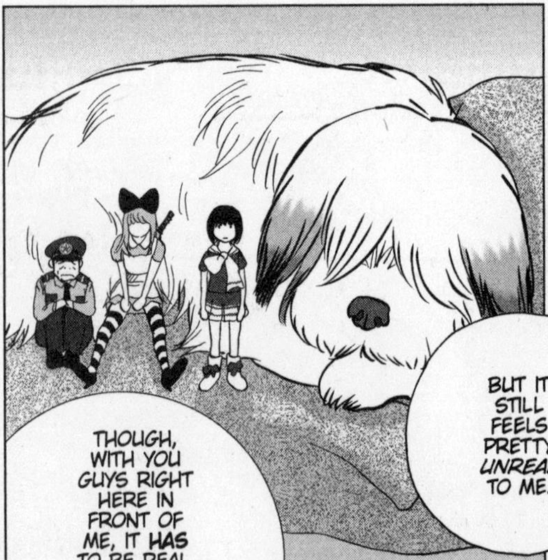
BUT IT STILL FEELS PRETTY *UNREAL* TO ME.
THOUGH, WITH YOU GUYS RIGHT HERE IN FRONT OF ME, IT **HAS** TO BE REAL, RIGHT?

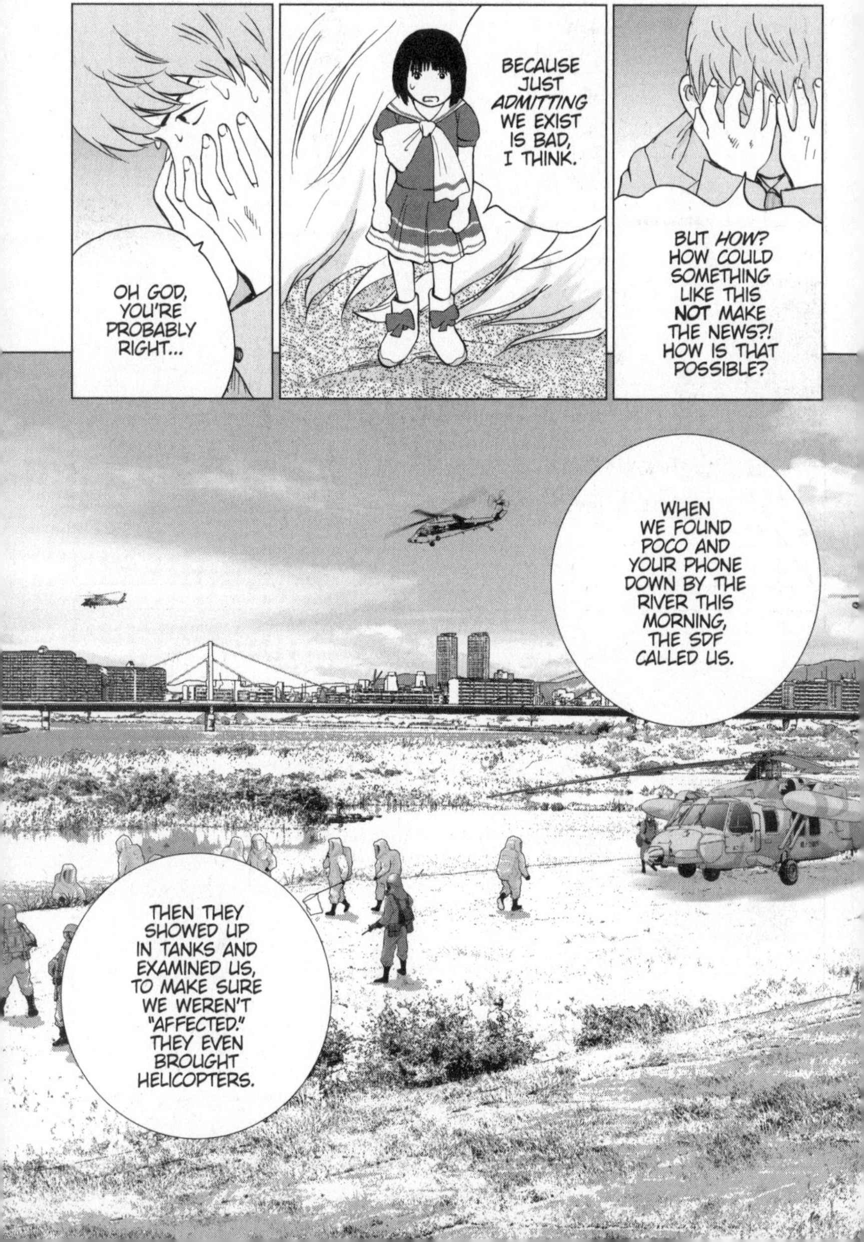
BUT *HOW?* HOW COULD SOMETHING LIKE THIS **NOT** MAKE THE NEWS?! HOW IS THAT POSSIBLE?
BECAUSE JUST *ADMITTING* WE EXIST IS BAD, I THINK.
OH GOD, YOU'RE PROBABLY RIGHT...
WHEN WE FOUND POCO AND YOUR PHONE DOWN BY THE RIVER THIS MORNING, THE SDF CALLED US.
THEN THEY SHOWED UP IN TANKS AND EXAMINED US, TO MAKE SURE WE WEREN'T "AFFECTED." THEY EVEN BROUGHT HELICOPTERS.

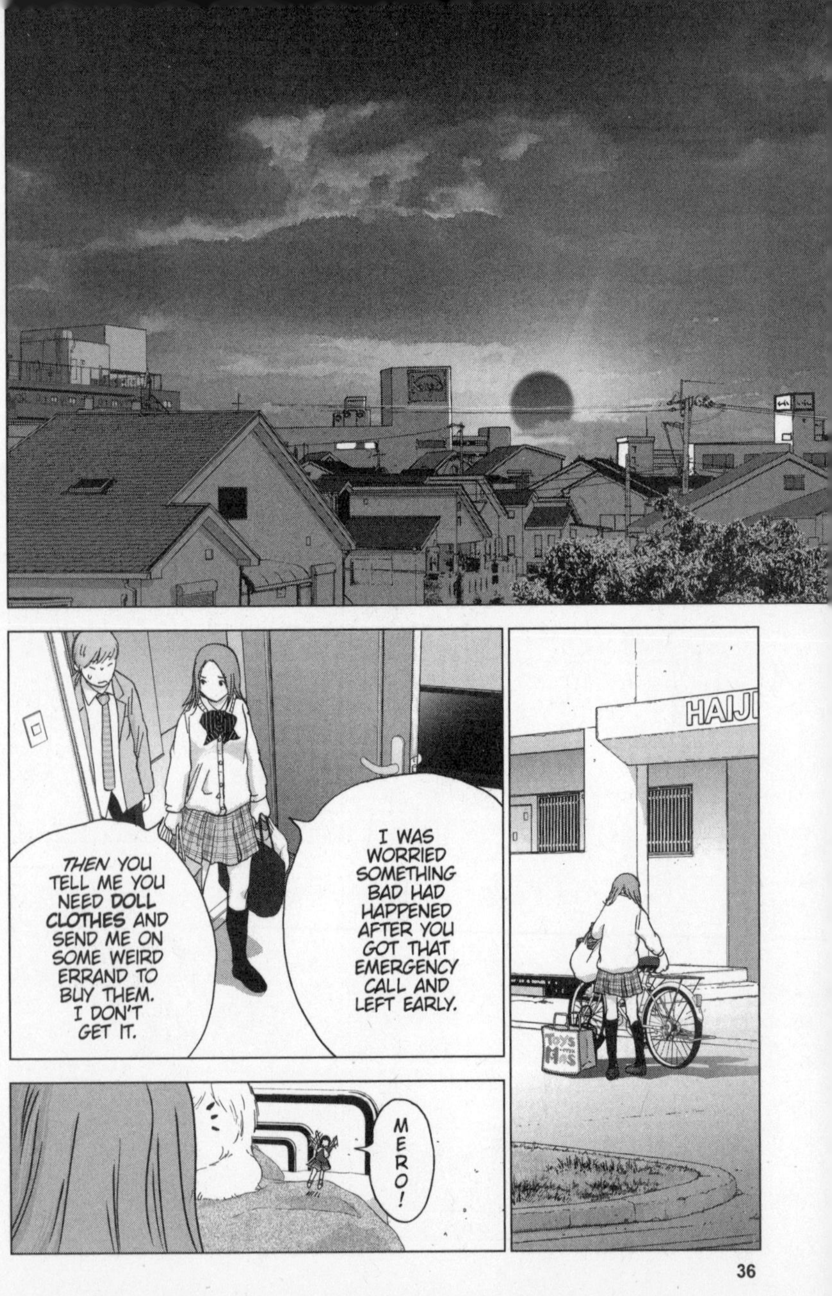
I WAS WORRIED SOMETHING BAD HAD HAPPENED AFTER YOU GOT THAT EMERGENCY CALL AND LEFT EARLY.
THEN YOU TELL ME YOU NEED **DOLL CLOTHES** AND SEND ME ON SOME WEIRD ERRAND TO BUY THEM. I DON'T GET IT.
MERO!

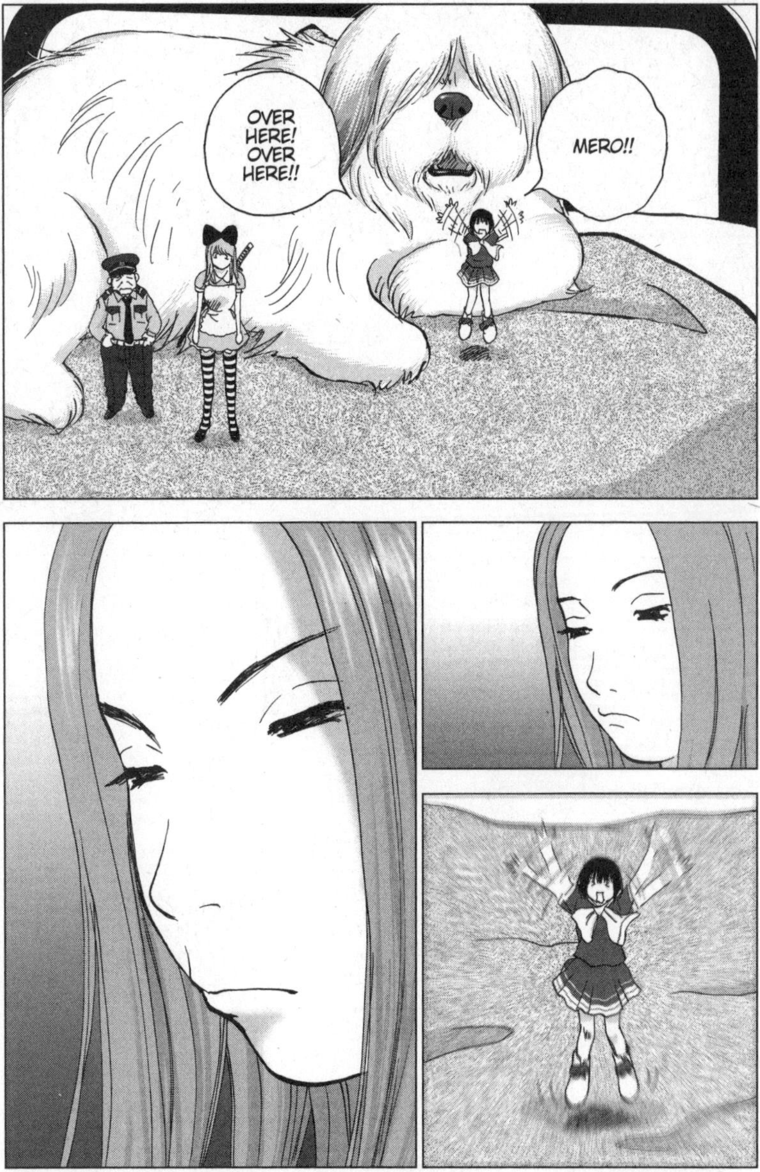
MERO!!
OVER HERE! OVER HERE!!

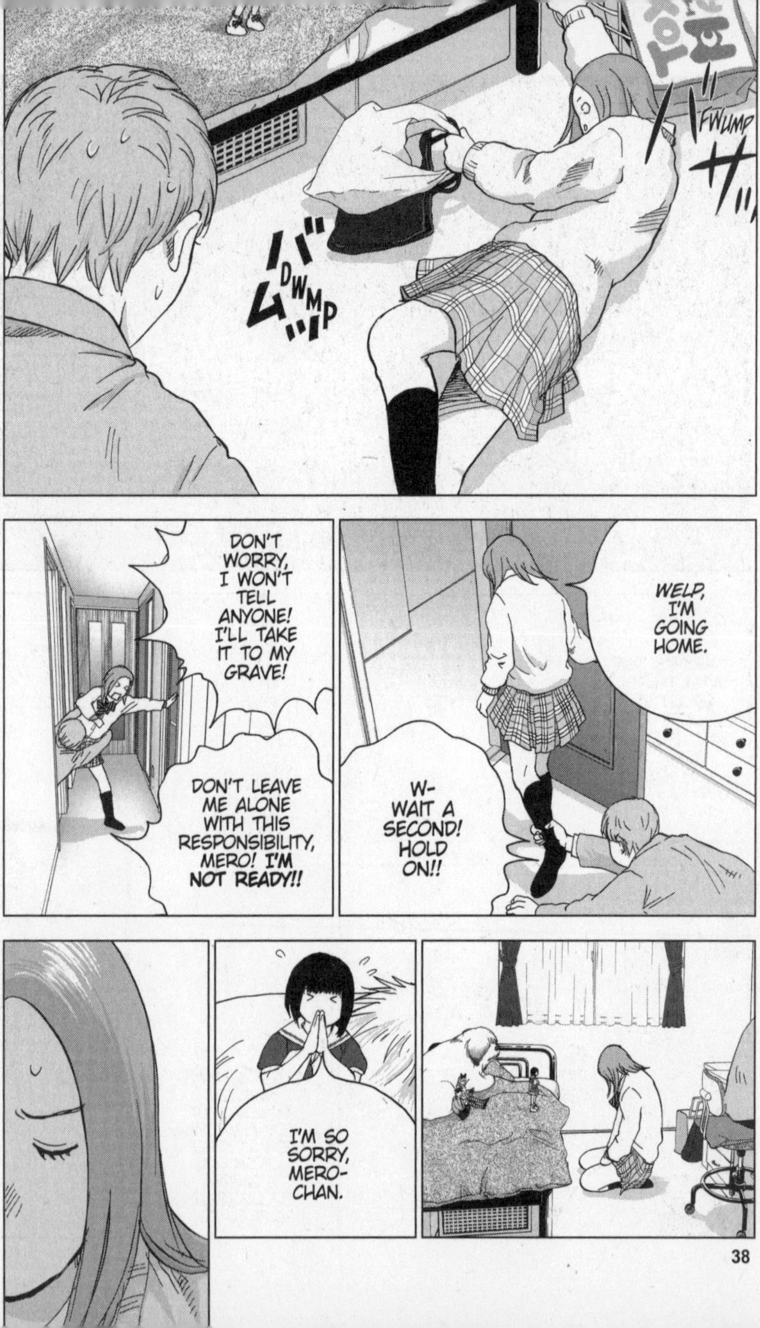
FWUMP
DWMP
WELP, I'M GOING HOME.
W- WAIT A SECOND! HOLD ON!!
DON'T WORRY, I WON'T TELL ANYONE! I'LL TAKE IT TO MY GRAVE!
DON'T LEAVE ME ALONE WITH THIS RESPONSIBILITY, MERO! I'M NOT READY!!
I'M SO SORRY, MERO-CHAN.

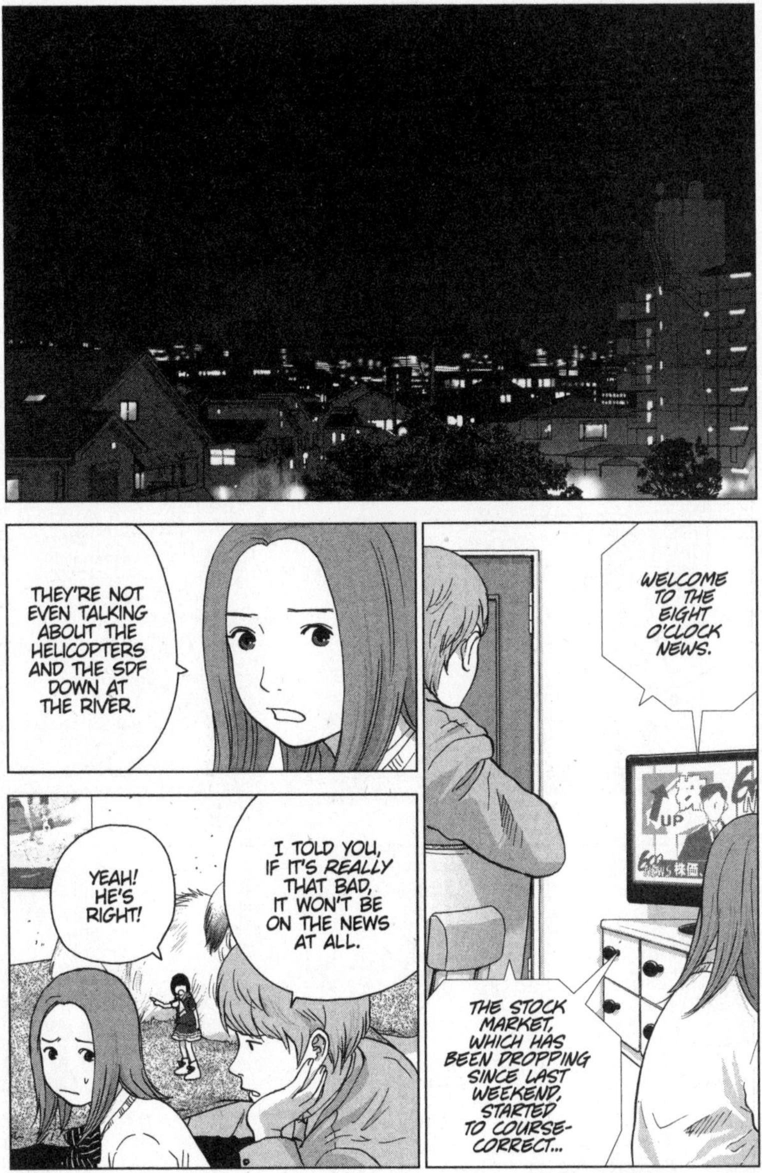
WELCOME TO THE EIGHT O'CLOCK NEWS.
THE STOCK MARKET, WHICH HAS BEEN DROPPING SINCE LAST WEEKEND, STARTED TO COURSE-CORRECT...
THEY'RE NOT EVEN TALKING ABOUT THE HELICOPTERS AND THE SDF DOWN AT THE RIVER.
I TOLD YOU, IF IT'S *REALLY* THAT BAD, IT WON'T BE ON THE NEWS AT ALL.
YEAH! HE'S RIGHT!

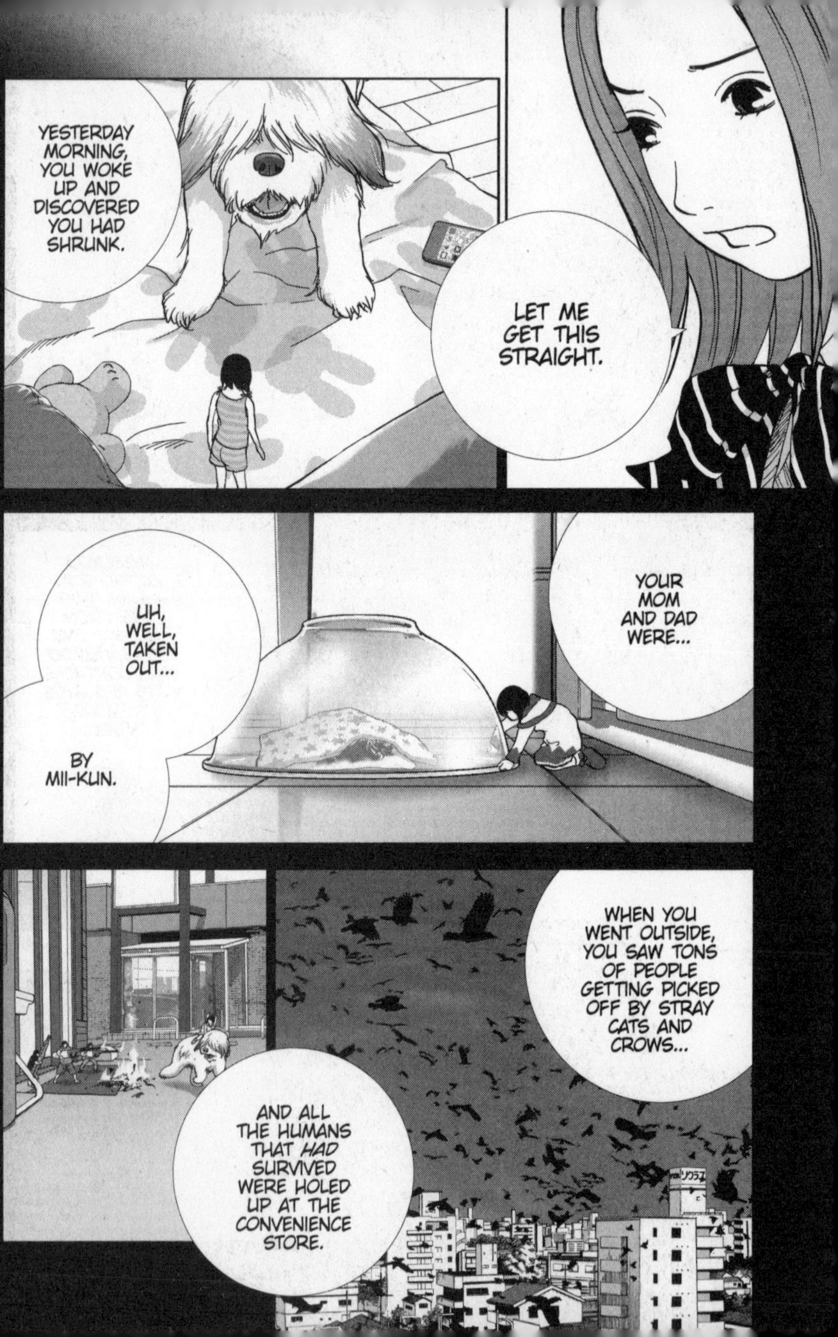
LET ME GET THIS STRAIGHT.
YESTERDAY MORNING, YOU WOKE UP AND DISCOVERED YOU HAD SHRUNK.
YOUR MOM AND DAD WERE...
UH, WELL, TAKEN OUT...
BY MII-KUN.
WHEN YOU WENT OUTSIDE, YOU SAW TONS OF PEOPLE GETTING PICKED OFF BY STRAY CATS AND CROWS...
AND ALL THE HUMANS THAT *HAD* SURVIVED WERE HOLED UP AT THE CONVENIENCE STORE.

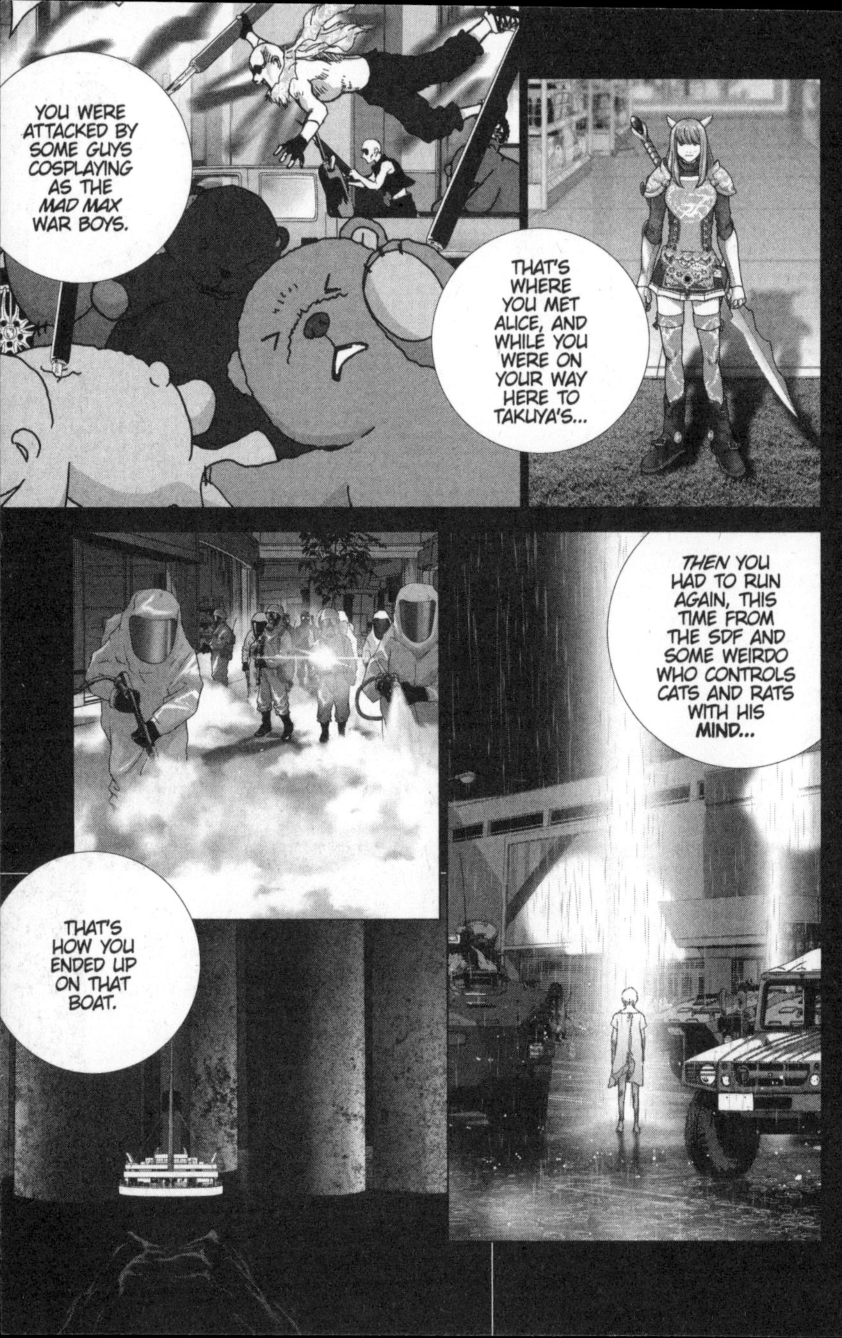
YOU WERE ATTACKED BY SOME GUYS COSPLAYING AS THE *MAD MAX* WAR BOYS.
THAT'S WHERE YOU MET ALICE, AND WHILE YOU WERE ON YOUR WAY HERE TO TAKUYA'S...
THEN YOU HAD TO RUN AGAIN, THIS TIME FROM THE SDF AND SOME WEIRDO WHO CONTROLS CATS AND RATS WITH HIS MIND...
THAT'S HOW YOU ENDED UP ON THAT BOAT.

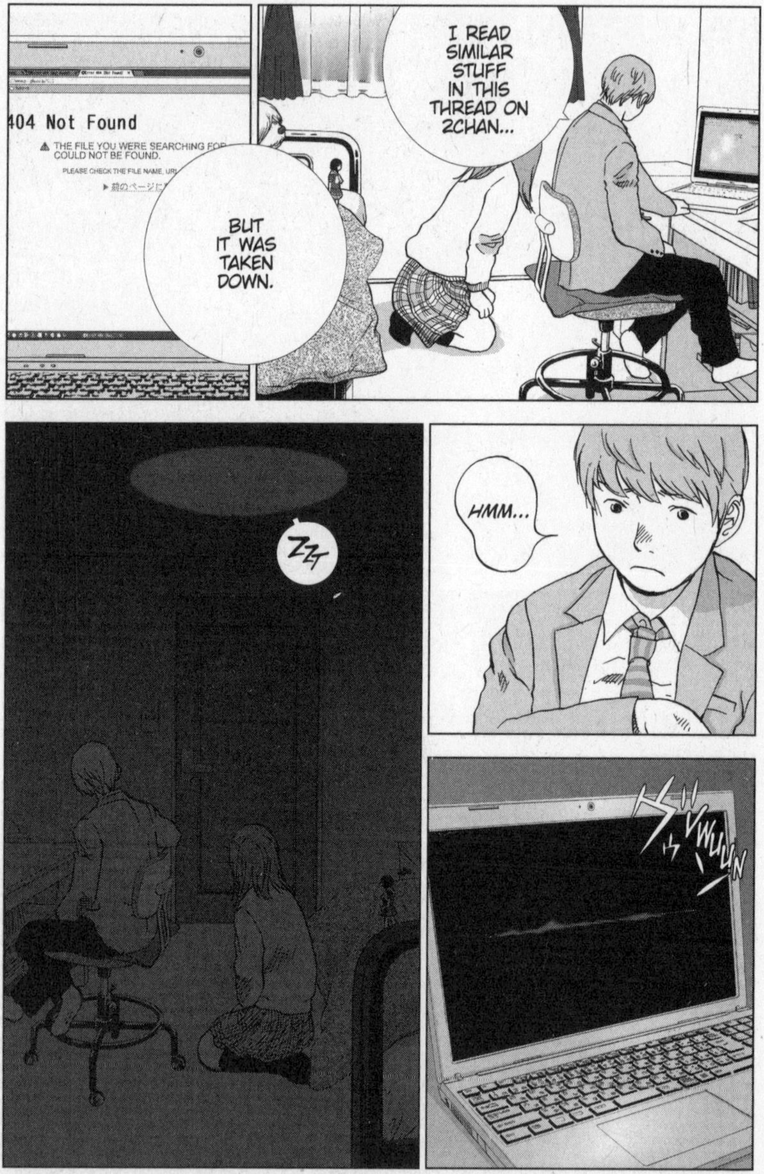
I READ SIMILAR STUFF IN THIS THREAD ON 2CHAN...
BUT IT WAS TAKEN DOWN.
404 Not Found
THE FILE YOU WERE SEARCHING FOR COULD NOT BE FOUND.
PLEASE CHECK THE FILE NAME, URL
HMM...
VWUUN
ZZZ

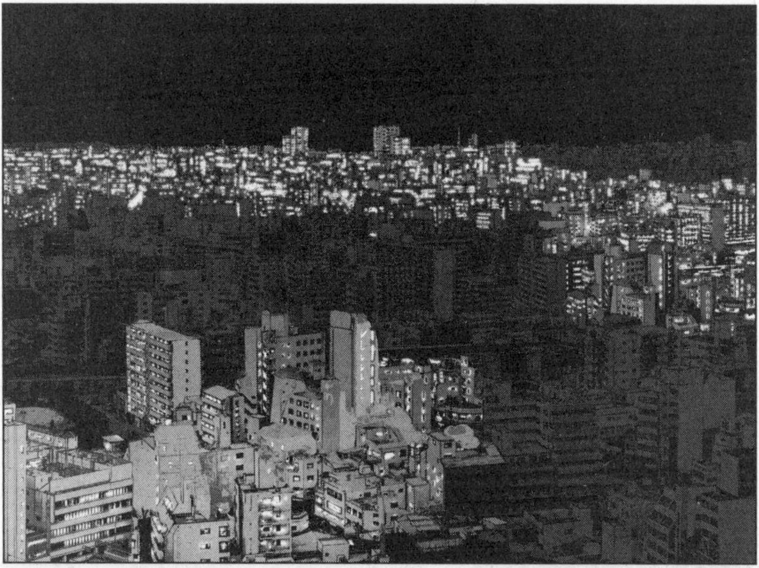

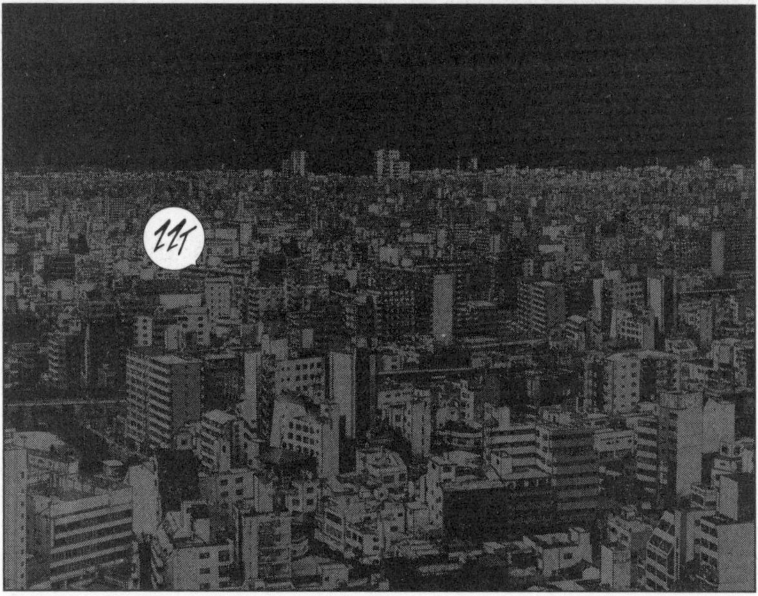
ZZT

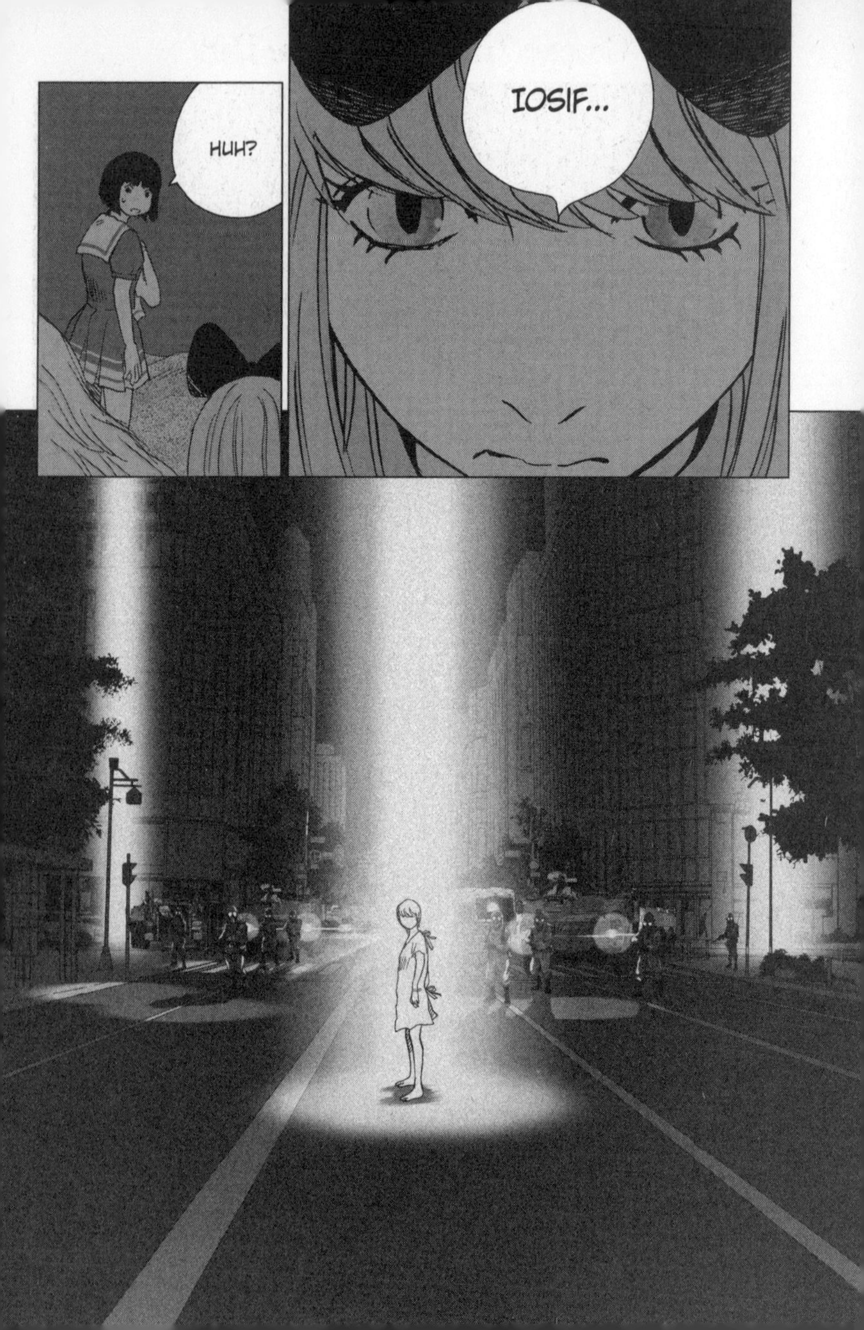
IOSIF...
HUH?

Chapter 21: Hunters in the Dark

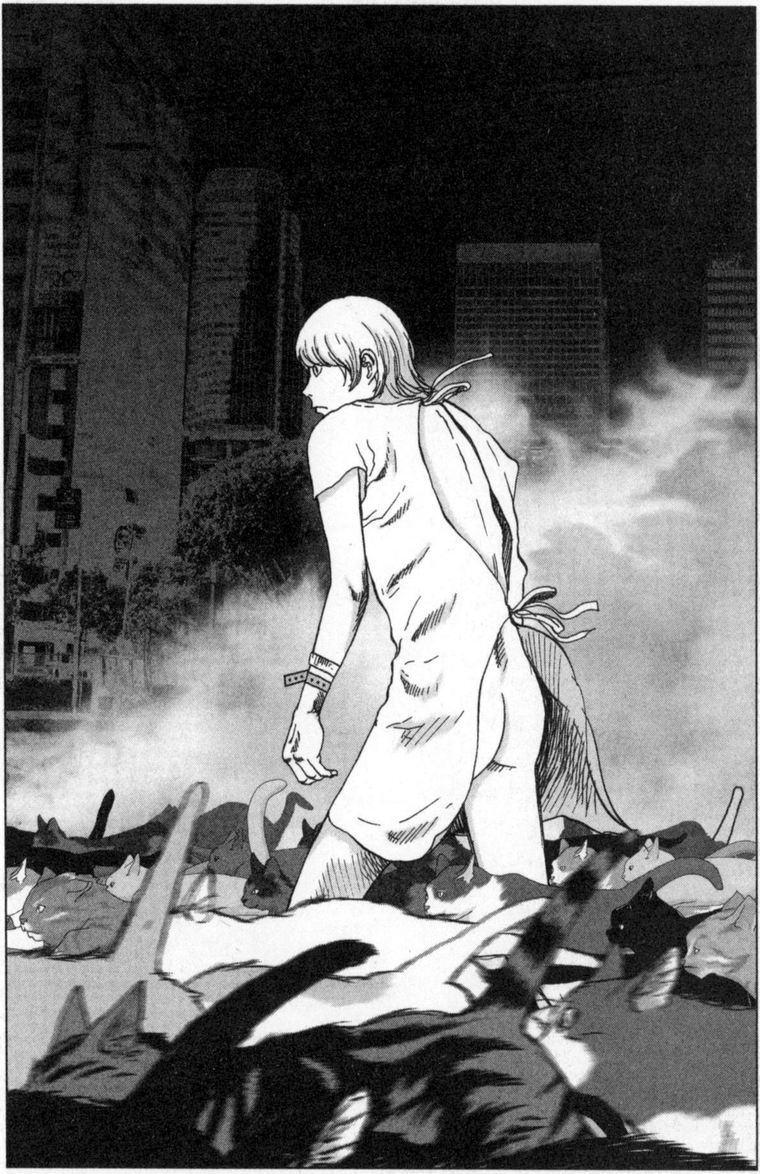

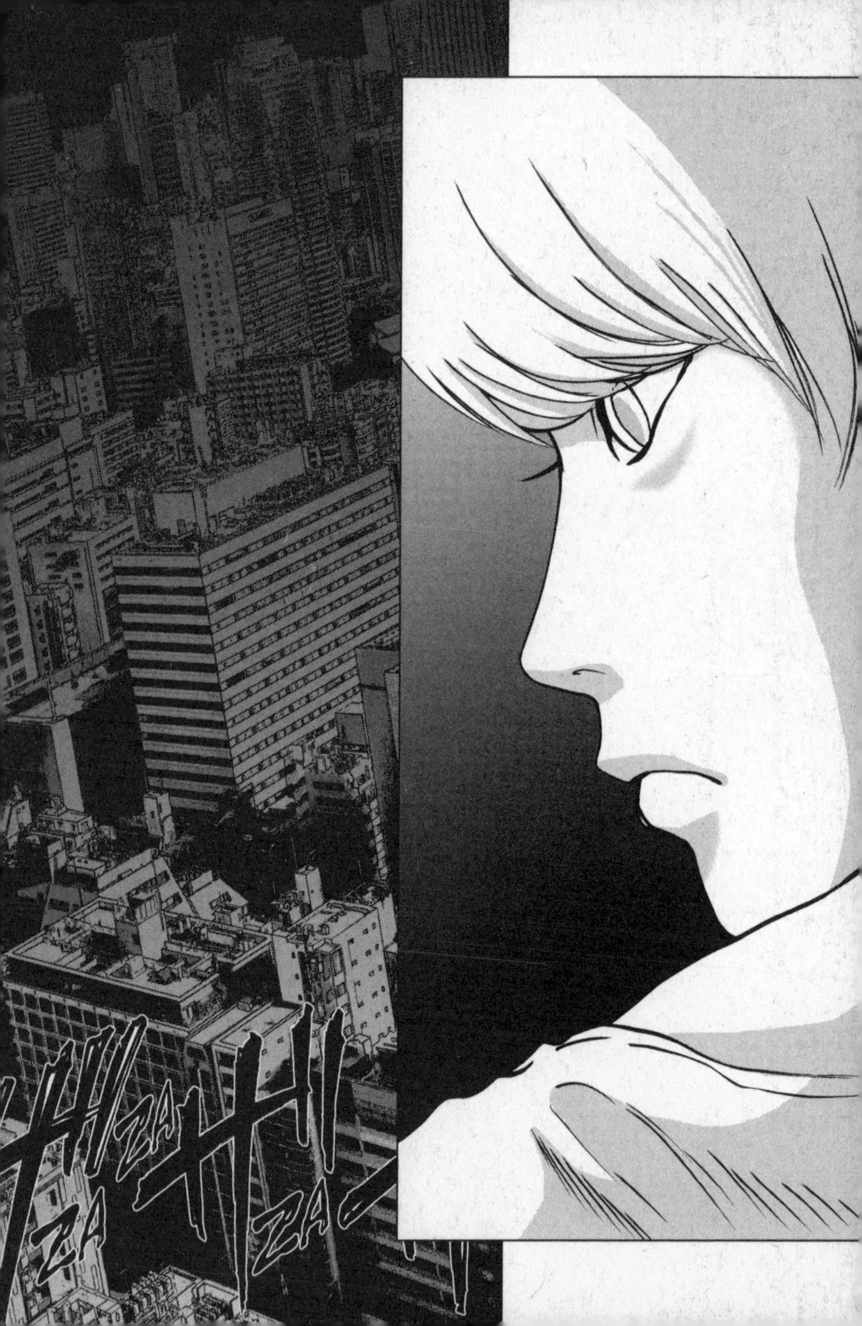
ZA
ZA
ZA

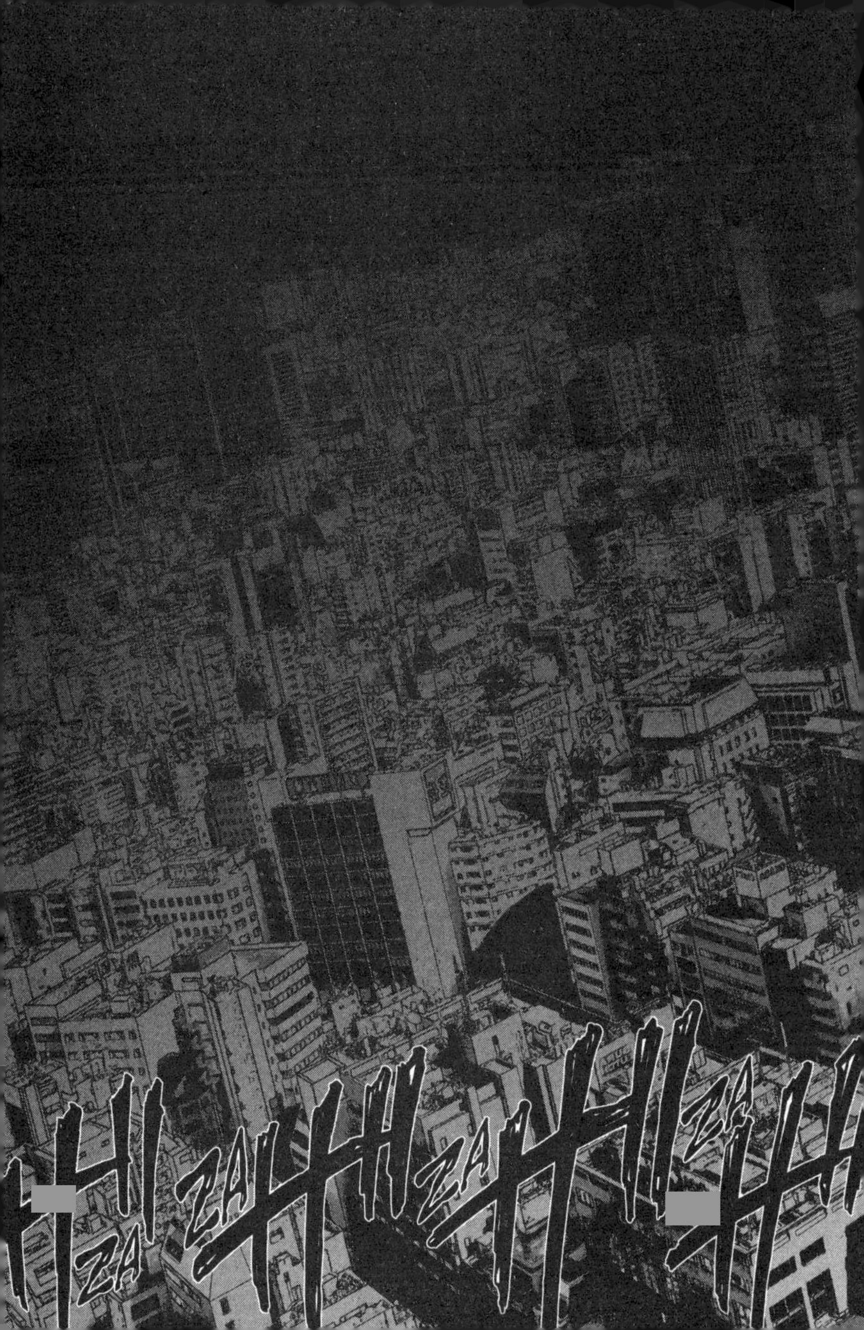
ZA
ZA
ZA
ZA

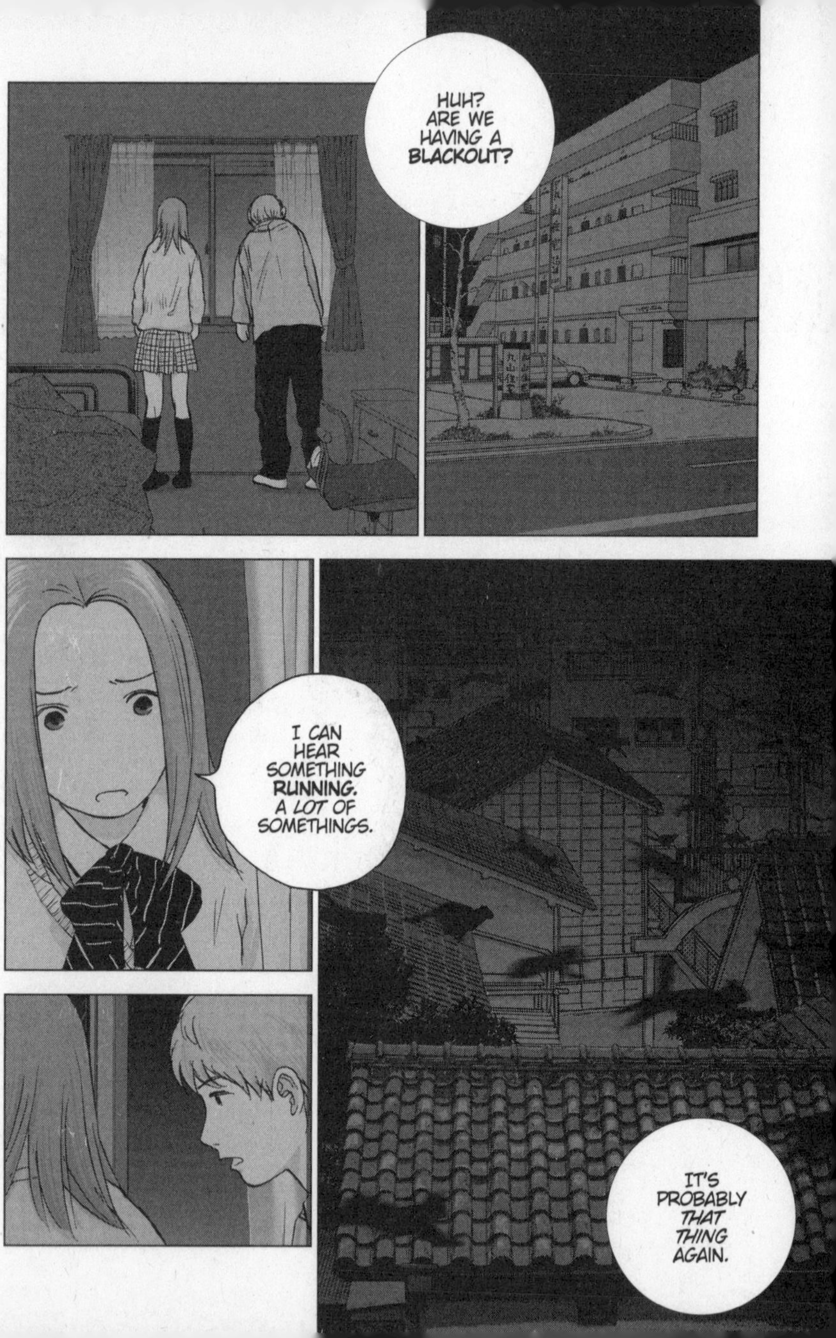
HUH? ARE WE HAVING A BLACKOUT?
I CAN HEAR SOMETHING **RUNNING.** A *LOT* OF SOMETHINGS.
IT'S PROBABLY *THAT THING* AGAIN.

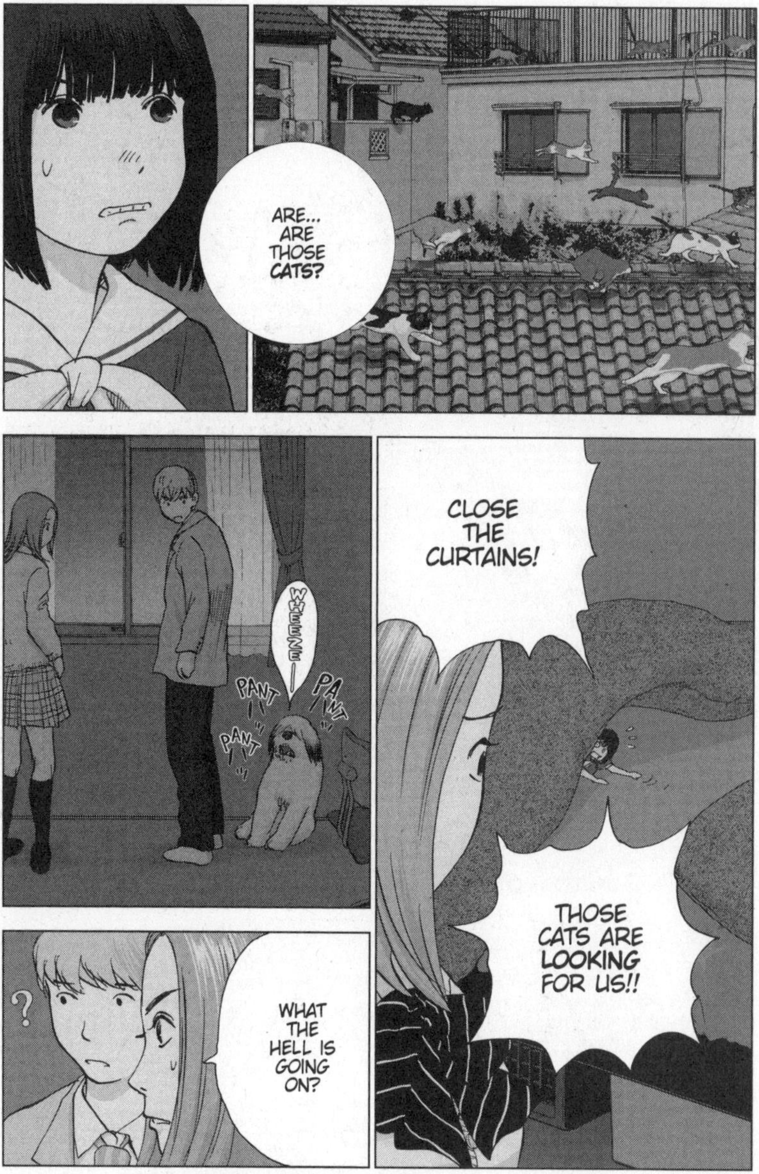
ARE... ARE THOSE CATS?
CLOSE THE CURTAINS!
THOSE CATS ARE LOOKING FOR US!!
WHEEZE
PANT
PANT
PANT
?
WHAT THE HELL IS GOING ON?

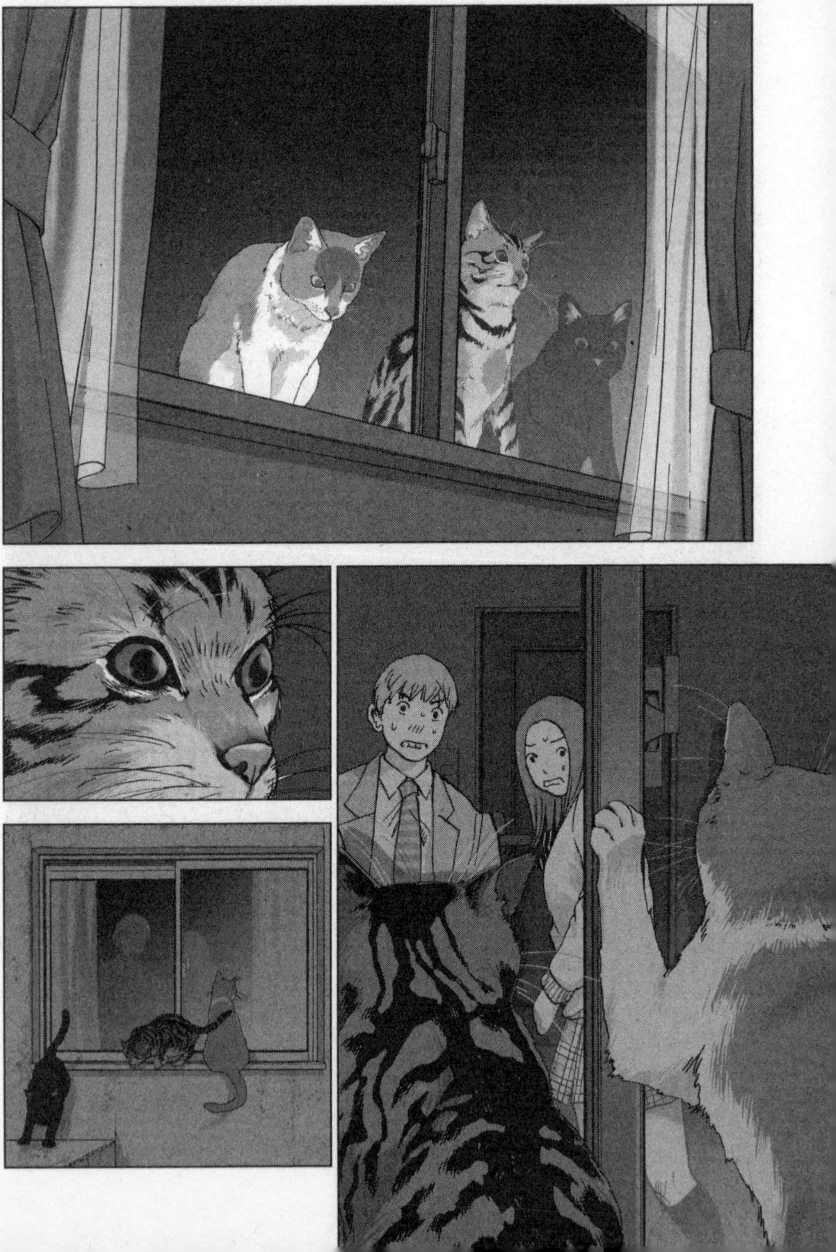

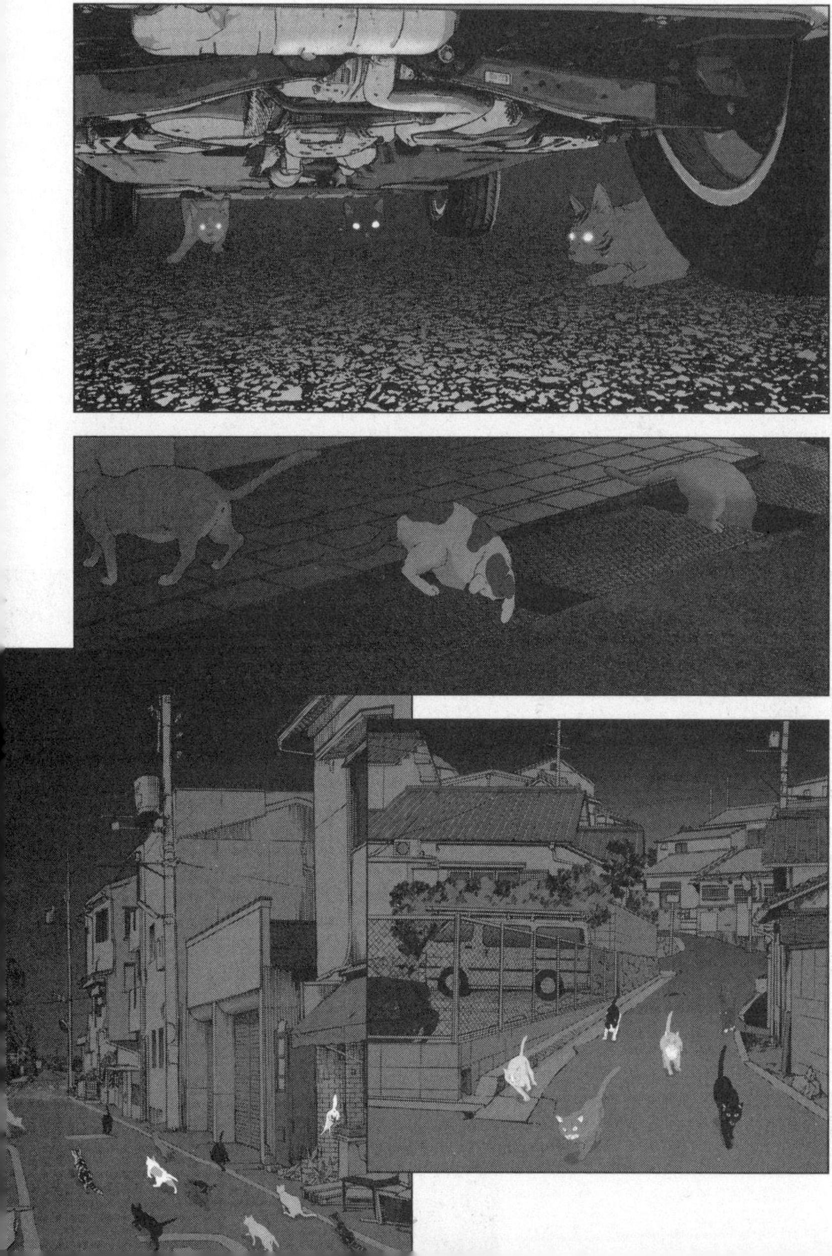

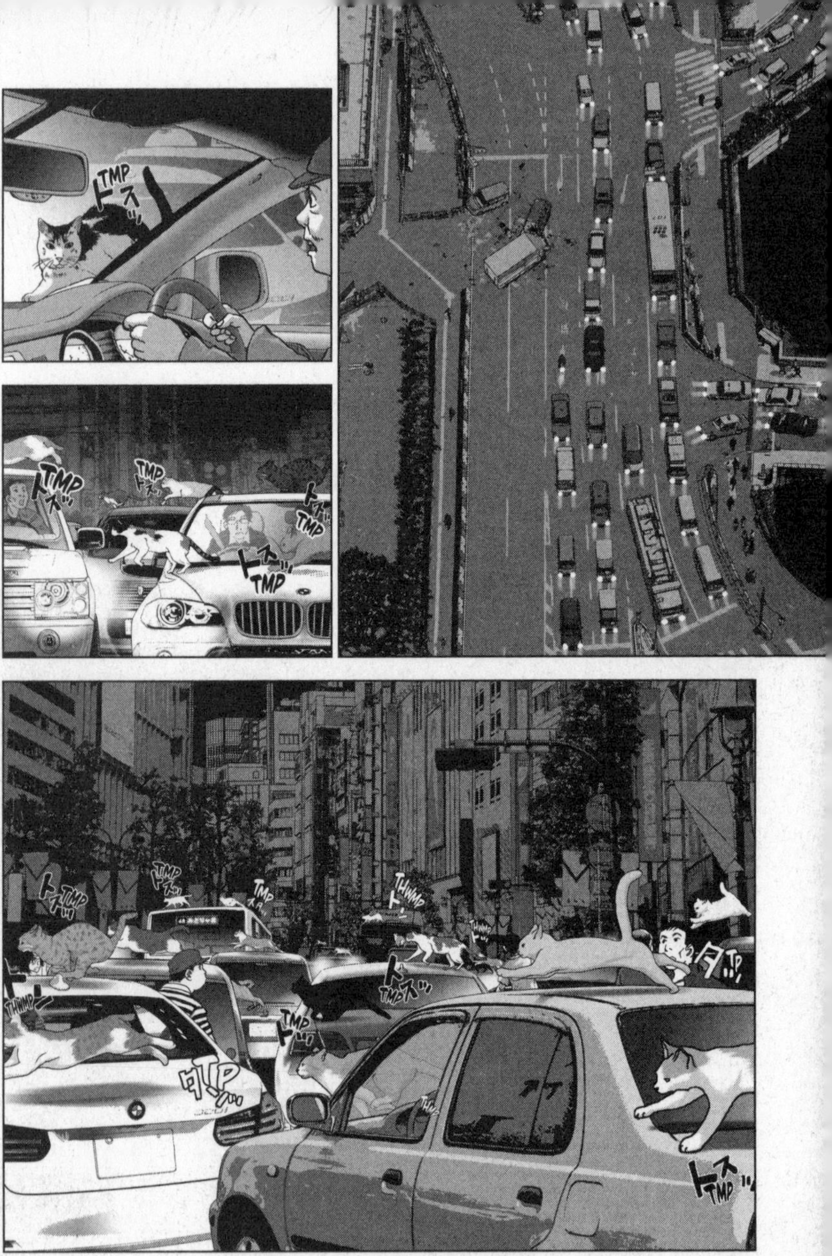
TMP
TMP
TMP
TMP
TMP
TP
TMP
THWMP
THWMP
TMP
TMP
TMP
TMP
THWMP
TMP
TP

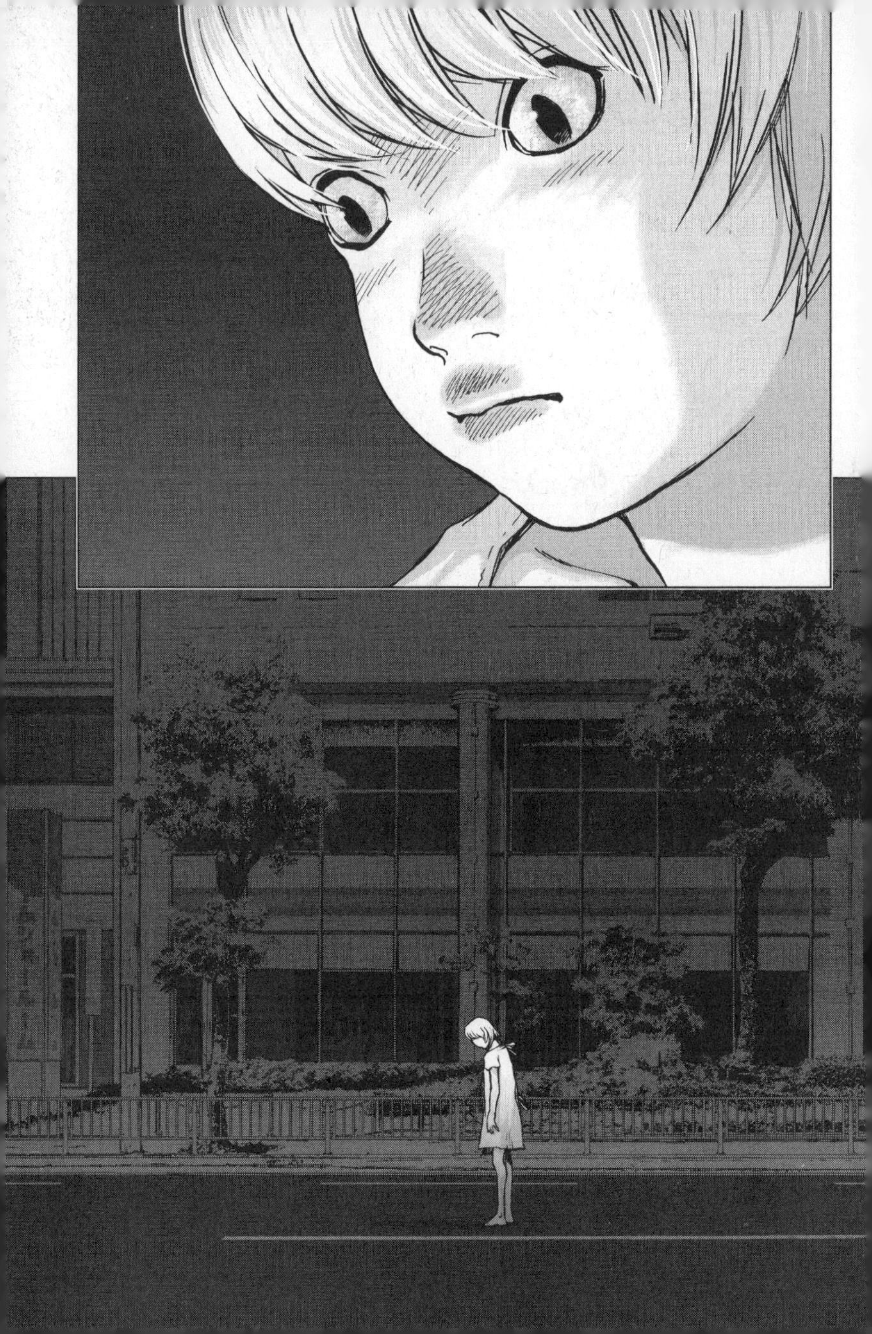

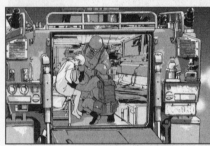

BLOCK ONE, SEARCH COMPLETE.

TARGET ACQUIIRED.

MOVE OUT.

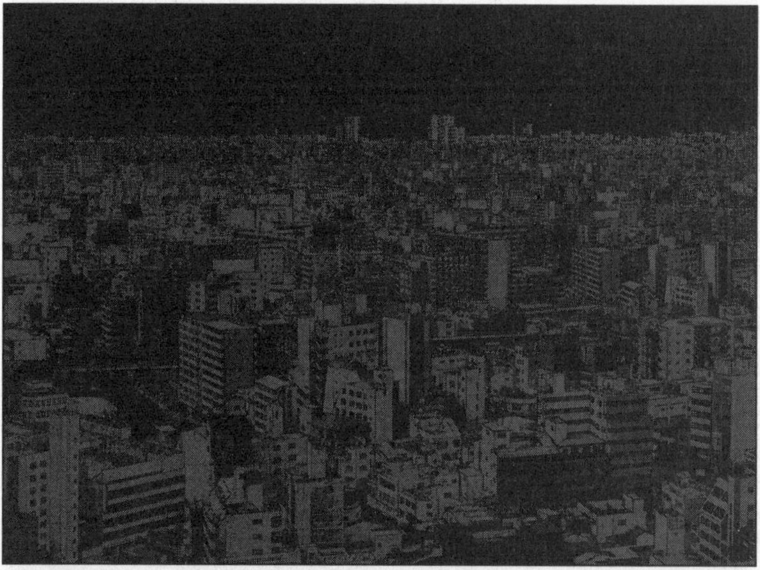
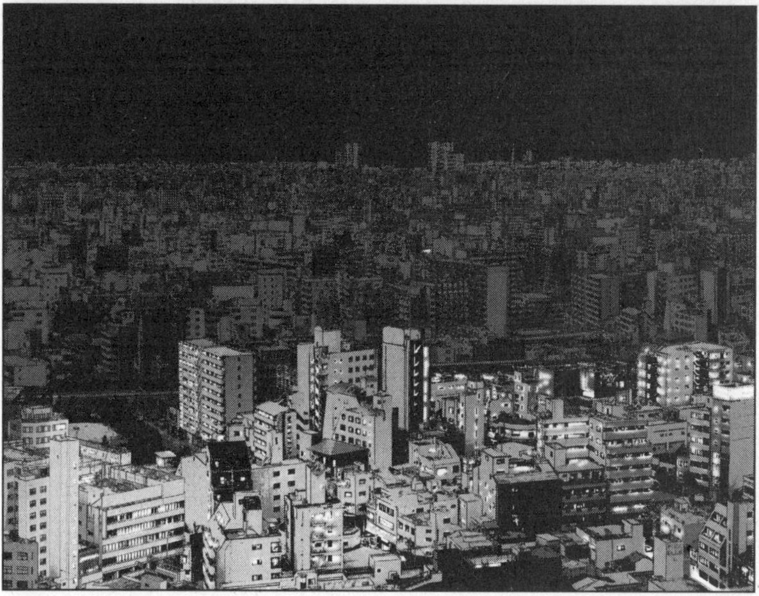

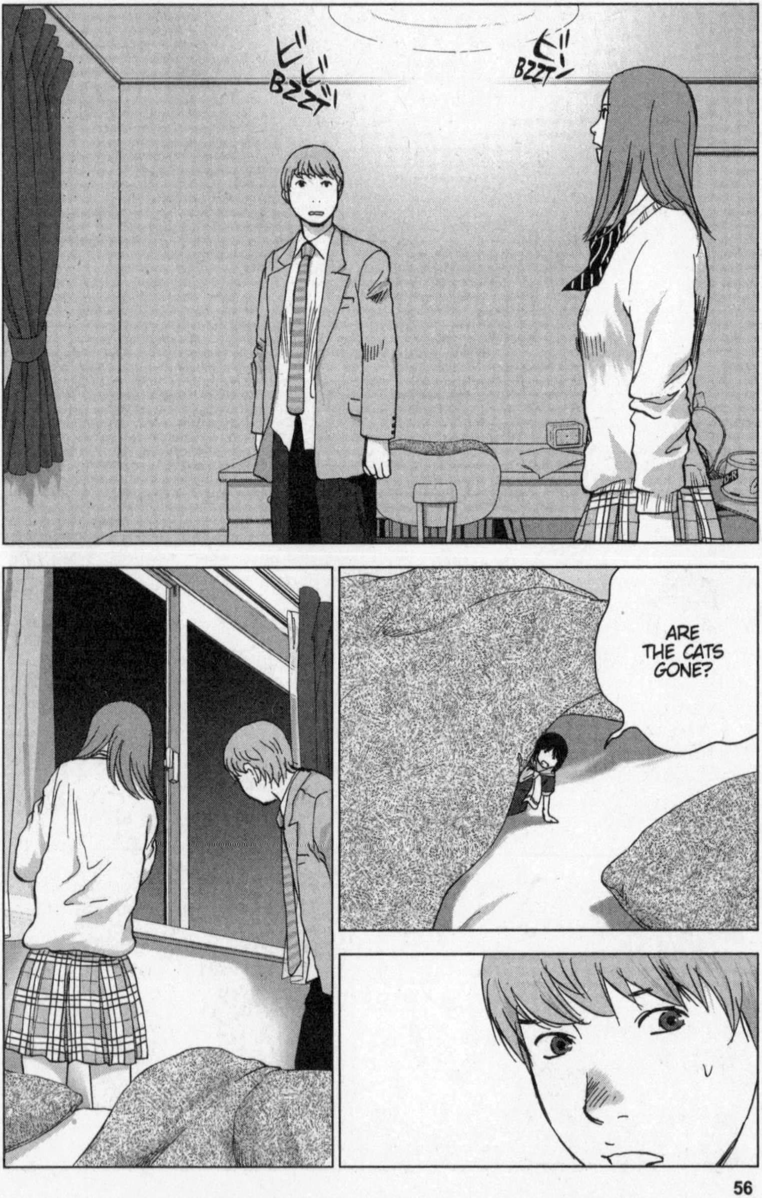
ビ
BZZT
ビビ
BZZZT
ARE THE CATS GONE?

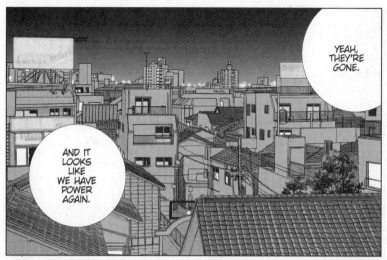

YEAH, THEY'RE GONE.
AND IT LOOKS LIKE WE HAVE POWER AGAIN.
WHAT *WAS* THAT JUST NOW? IT WAS SO **CREEPY**.
I CAN'T REALLY EXPLAIN IT, BUT THERE'S A BOY NAMED IOSIF WHO CAN CONTROL CATS AND MICE-- AND HE'S USING THEM TO **LOOK** FOR US.
WHAT THE HELL? WHAT DO YOU MEAN, HE *USES* THEM?
THAT'S RIGHT! HE ALSO USES BABIES.
HE USES **BABIES**, TOO.

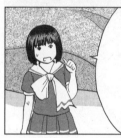

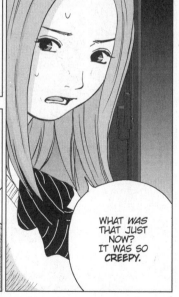

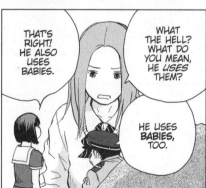

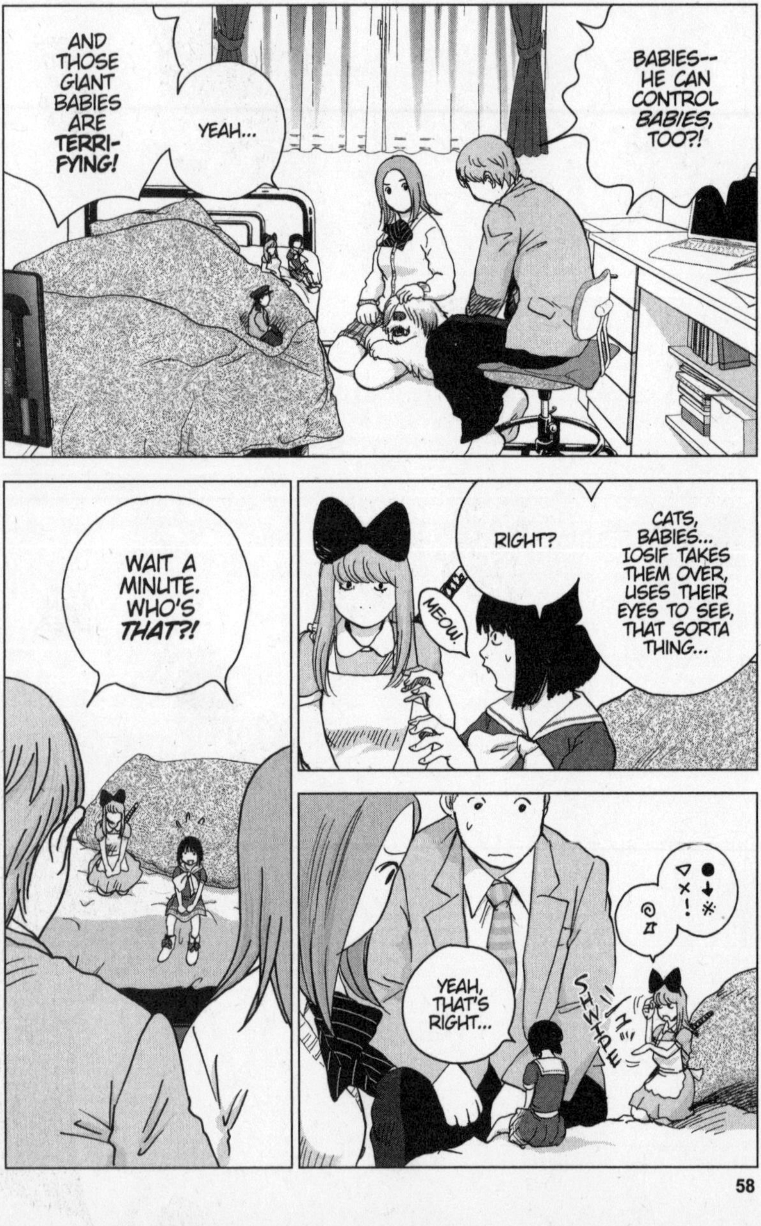
AND THOSE GIANT BABIES ARE TERRIFYING!
YEAH...
BABIES-- HE CAN CONTROL BABIES, TOO?!
CATS, BABIES... IOSIF TAKES THEM OVER, USES THEIR EYES TO SEE, THAT SORTA THING...
RIGHT?
MEOW.
SHWIPE
YEAH, THAT'S RIGHT...
WAIT A MINUTE. WHO'S THAT?!

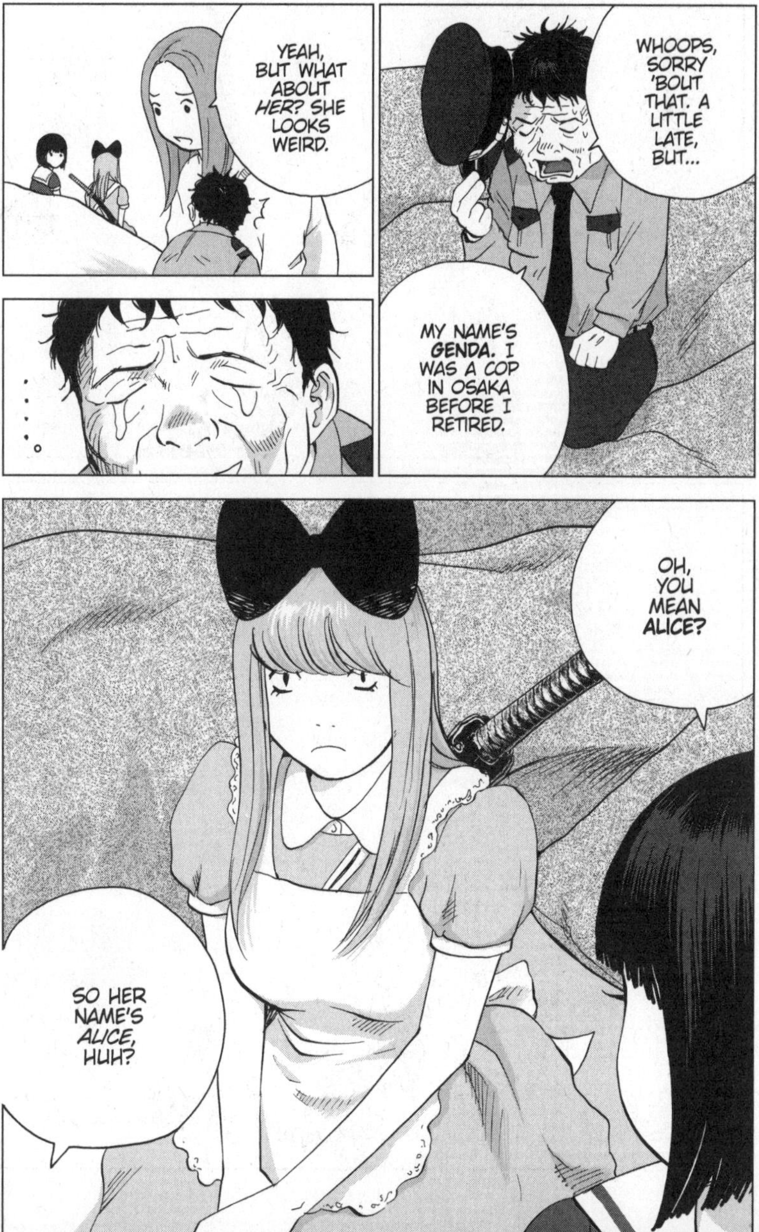
WHOOPS, SORRY 'BOUT THAT. A LITTLE LATE, BUT...
MY NAME'S GENDA. I WAS A COP IN OSAKA BEFORE I RETIRED.
YEAH, BUT WHAT ABOUT HER? SHE LOOKS WEIRD.
.....
OH, YOU MEAN ALICE?
SO HER NAME'S ALICE, HUH?

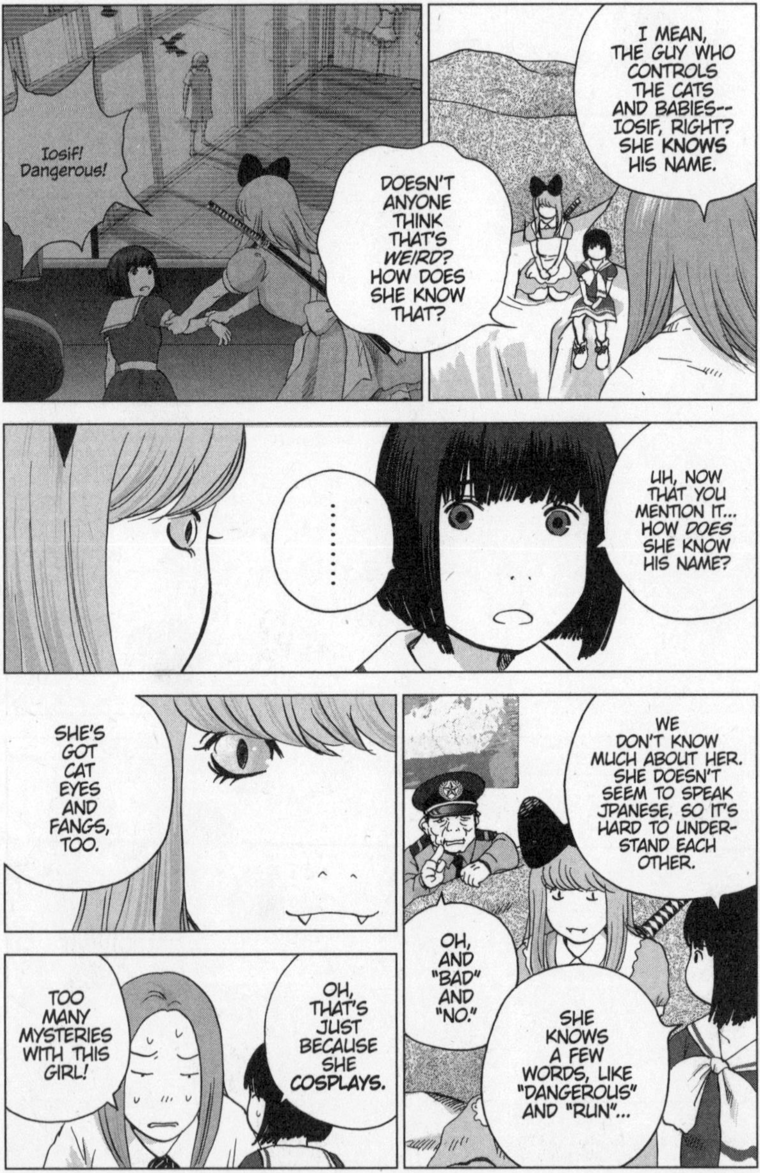
I MEAN, THE GUY WHO CONTROLS THE CATS AND BABIES-- IOSIF, RIGHT? SHE KNOWS HIS NAME.
DOESN'T ANYONE THINK THAT'S *WEIRD*? HOW DOES SHE KNOW THAT?
Iosif! Dangerous!
UH, NOW THAT YOU MENTION IT... HOW *DOES* SHE KNOW HIS NAME?
....
WE DON'T KNOW MUCH ABOUT HER. SHE DOESN'T SEEM TO SPEAK JPANESE, SO IT'S HARD TO UNDERSTAND EACH OTHER.
SHE KNOWS A FEW WORDS, LIKE "DANGEROUS" AND "RUN"...
OH, AND "BAD" AND "NO."
SHE'S GOT CAT EYES AND FANGS, TOO.
OH, THAT'S JUST BECAUSE SHE COSPLAYS.
TOO MANY MYSTERIES WITH THIS GIRL!

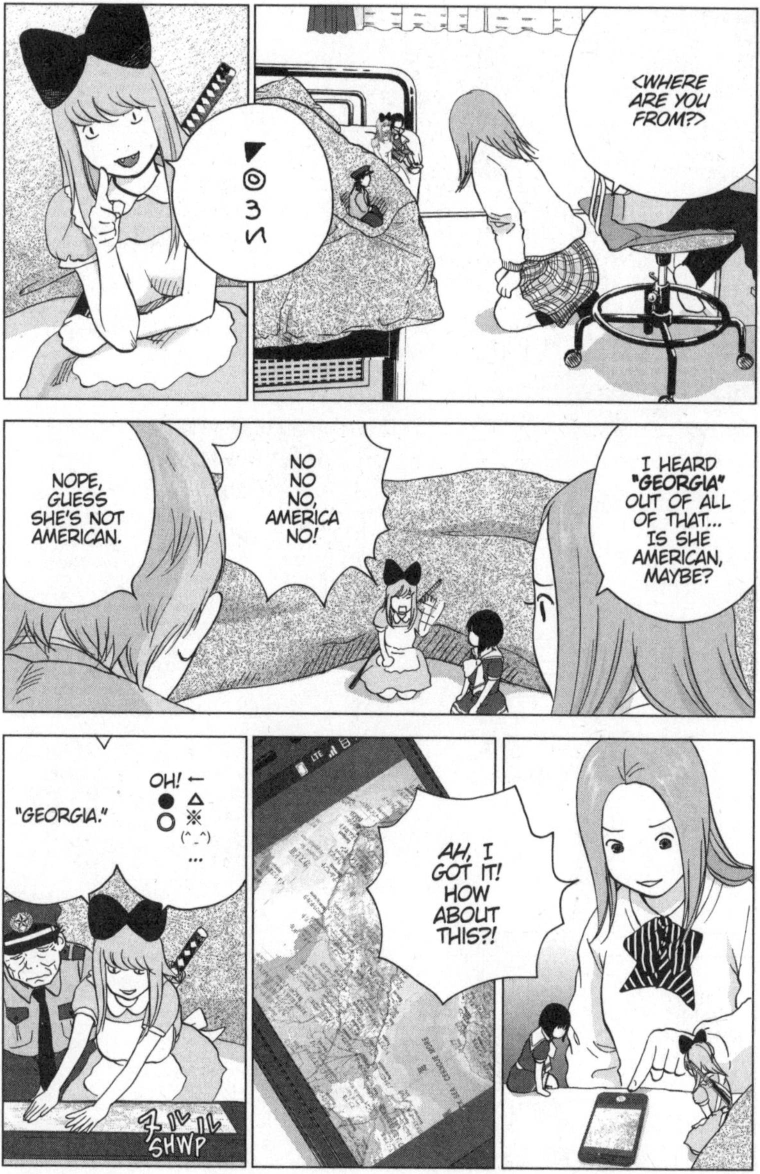
<WHERE ARE YOU FROM?>
I HEARD "GEORGIA" OUT OF ALL OF THAT... IS SHE AMERICAN, MAYBE?
NO NO NO, AMERICA NO!
NOPE, GUESS SHE'S NOT AMERICAN.
AH, I GOT IT! HOW ABOUT THIS?!
OH! ← ● △ ○ ※ (^_^) ...
"GEORGIA."
SHWP

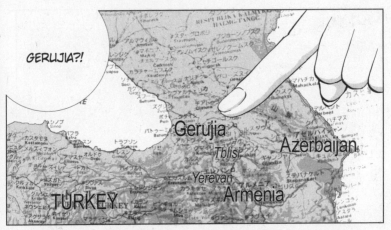

GERUJIA?!
Gerujia
Tblisi
Azerbaijan
Yerevan
Armenia
TURKEY
AH, OKAY. IT USED TO BE CALLED "GERUJIA" UNTIL A FEW YEARS AGO. NOW IT'S CALLED GEORGIA.
SO ALICE CAME TO JAPAN TO COSPLAY OR SOMETHING, THEN SHRUNK AND GOT STUCK HERE?
STUCK IN A FOREIGN COUNTRY, SO FAR AWAY FROM HOME...
AND THEN SHE GETS INVOLVED IN *THIS* MESS. I FEEL SORRY FOR HER.
SNIFF
SNIFF
WHAT LANGUAGE DO THEY SPEAK THERE? RUSSIAN, MAYBE?
WHY DON'T WE TRY USING A TRANSLATION APP ON YOUR PHONE?

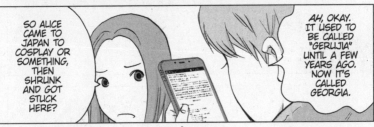

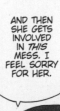

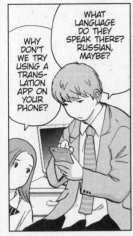

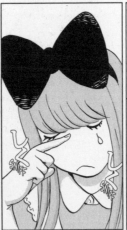

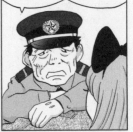

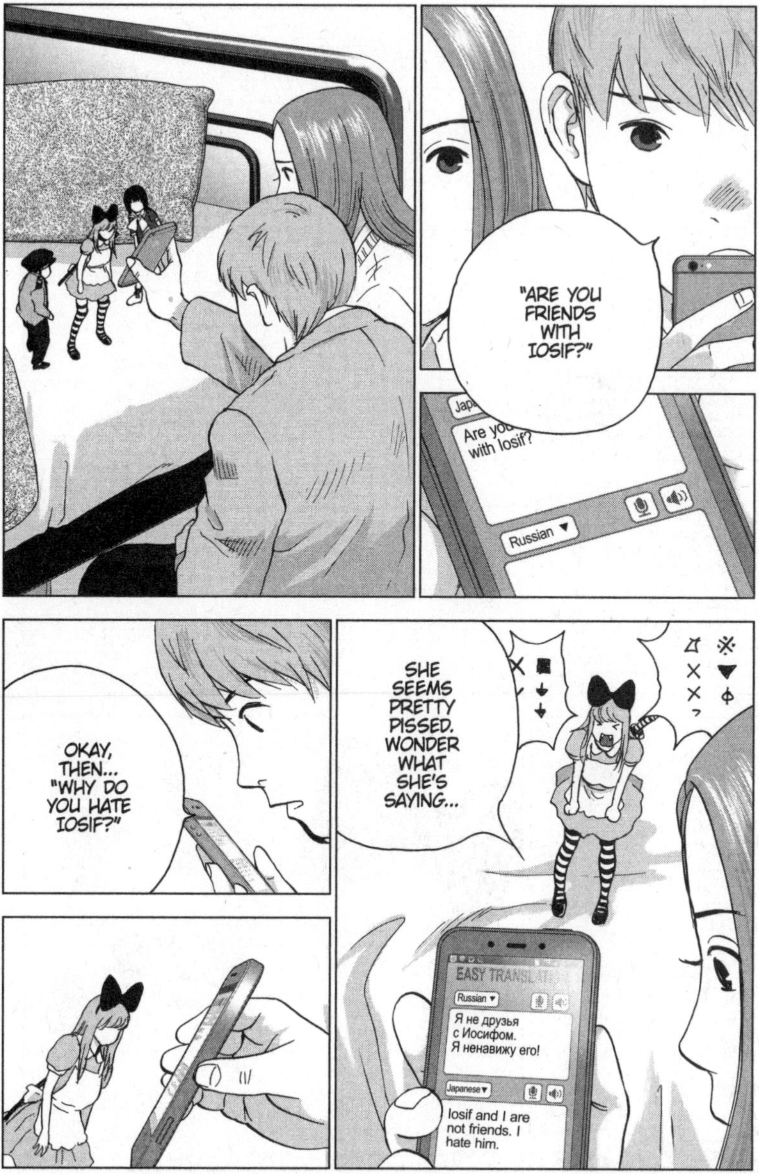
"ARE YOU FRIENDS WITH IOSIF?"
Are you
with Iosif?
Russian
SHE SEEMS PRETTY PISSED. WONDER WHAT SHE'S SAYING...
Russian
Я не друзья с Иосифом. Я ненавижу его!
Japanese
Iosif and I are not friends. I hate him.
OKAY, THEN... "WHY DO YOU HATE IOSIF?"

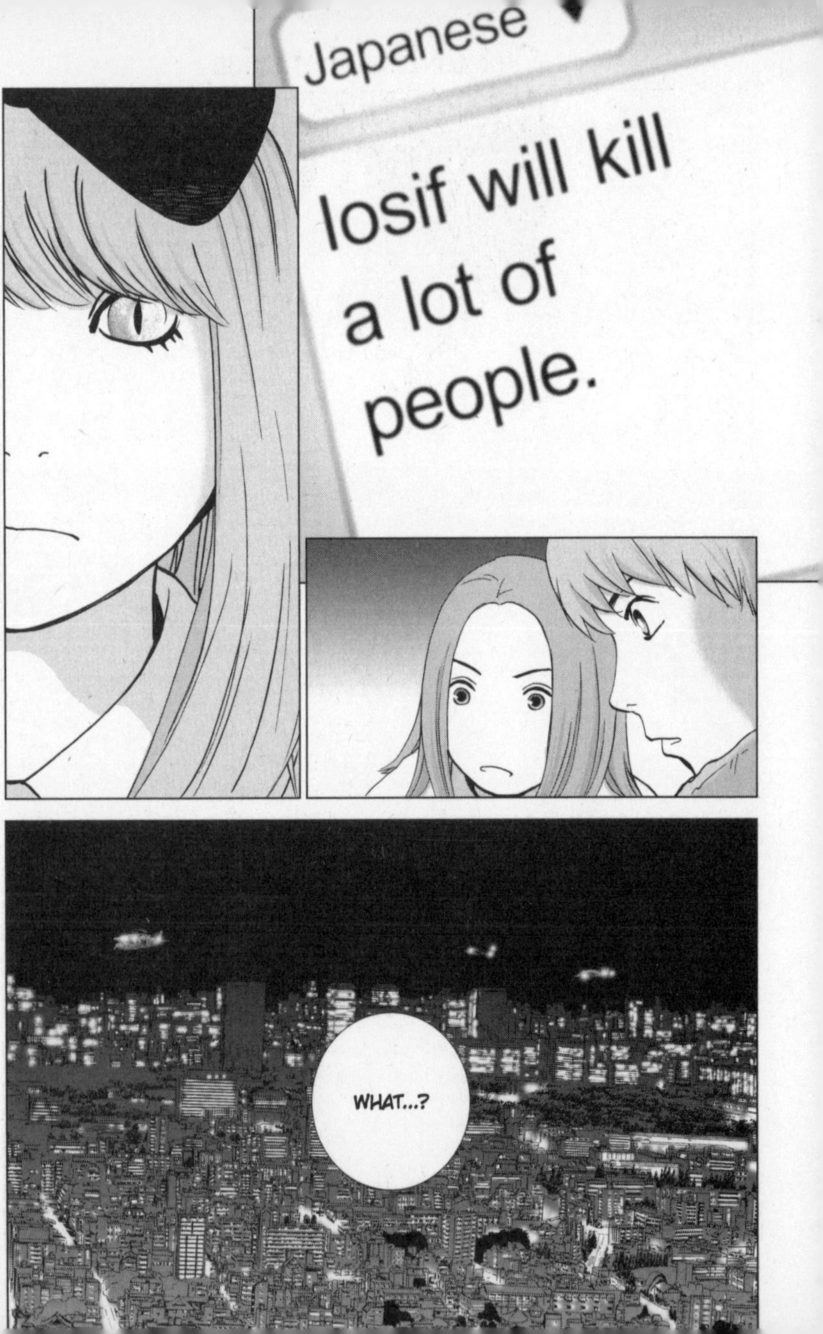
Japanese
Iosif will kill a lot of people.
WHAT...?

Chapter 22: Information

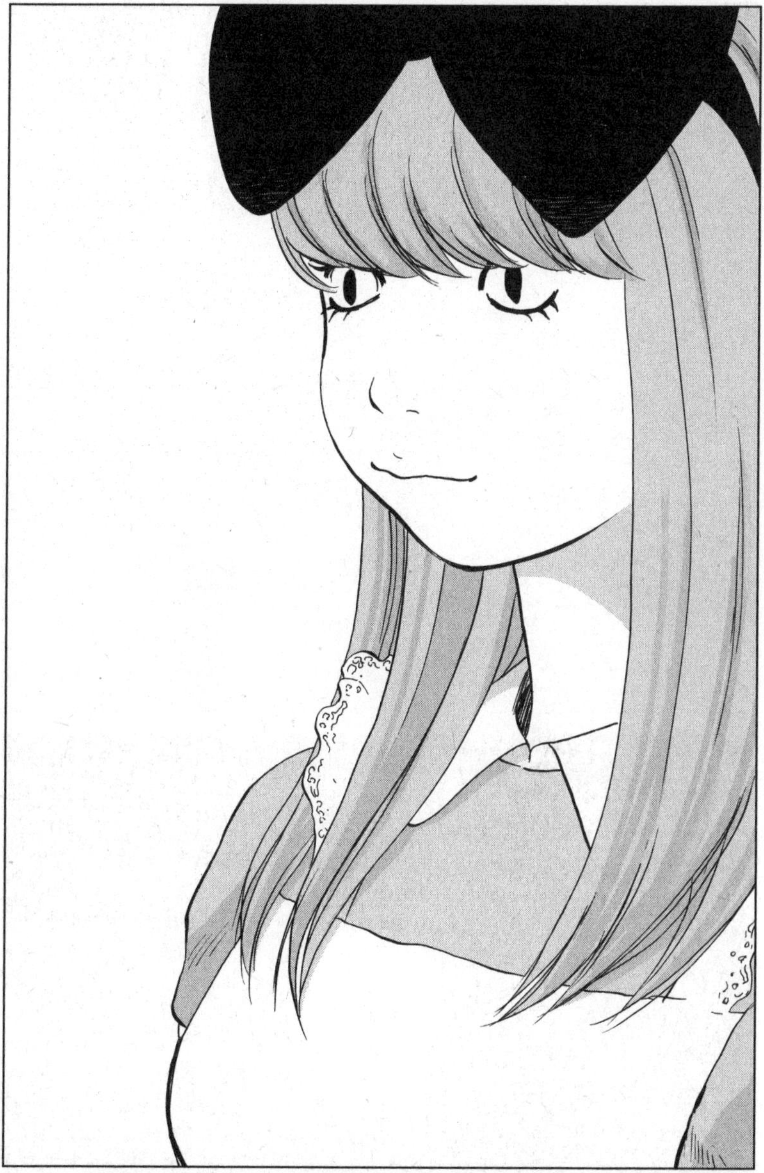

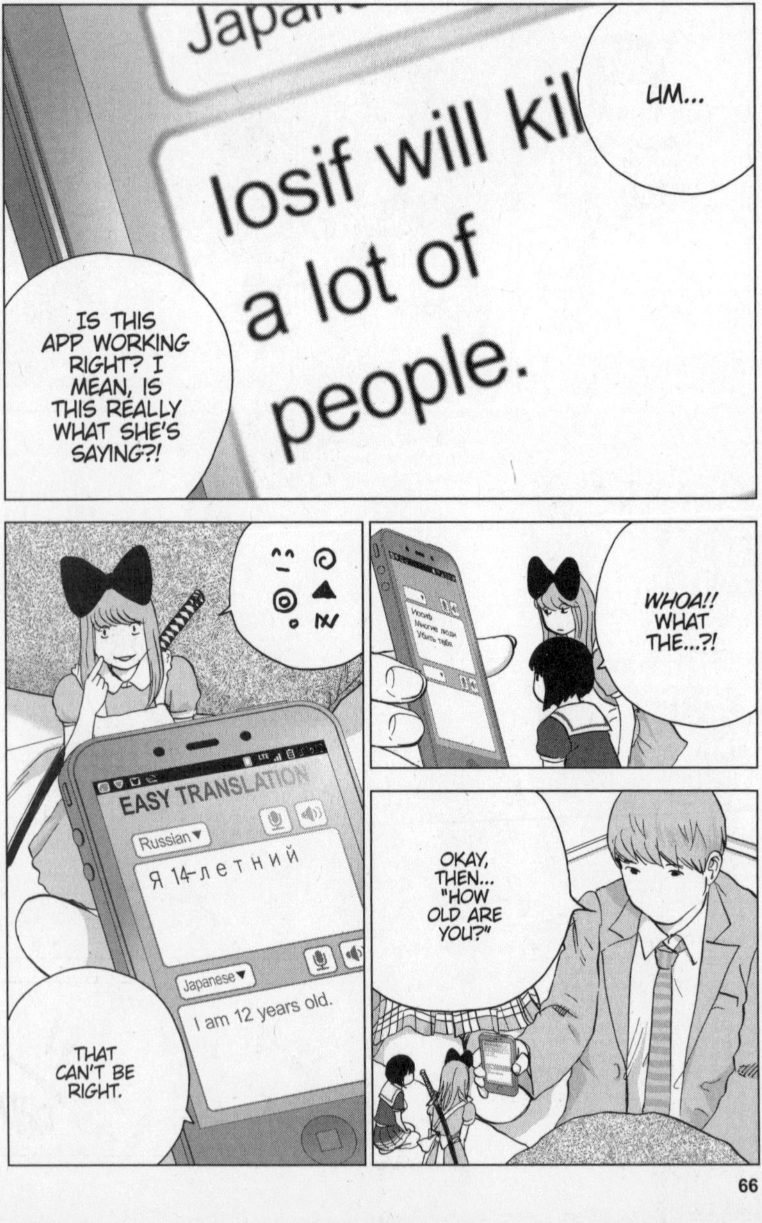
UM...
Iosif will kil
a lot of
people.
IS THIS APP WORKING RIGHT? I MEAN, IS THIS REALLY WHAT SHE'S SAYING?!
WHOA!! WHAT THE...?!
OKAY, THEN... "HOW OLD ARE YOU?"
EASY TRANSLATION
Russian
Я 14-летний
Japanese
I am 12 years old.
THAT CAN'T BE RIGHT.

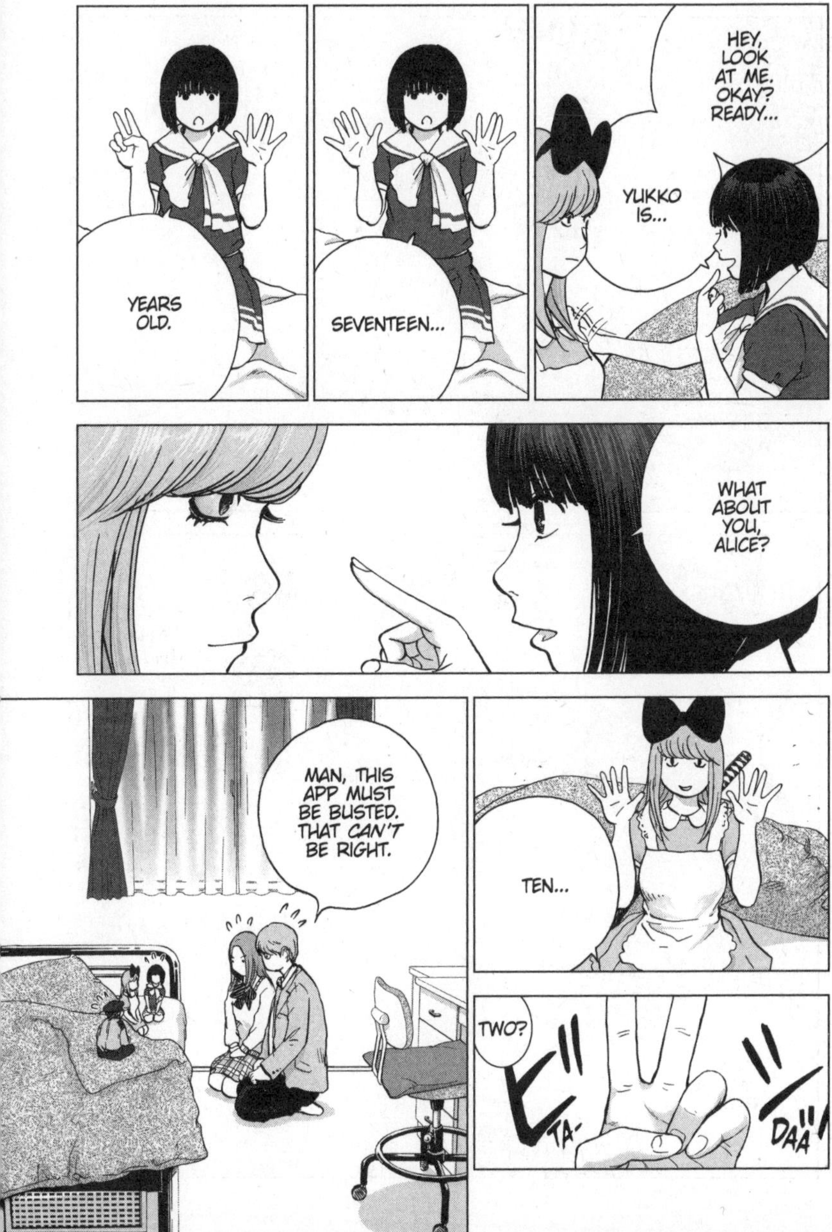
HEY, LOOK AT ME. OKAY? READY...
YUKKO IS...
SEVENTEEN...
YEARS OLD.
WHAT ABOUT YOU, ALICE?
TEN...
TWO?
TA-
DAA
MAN, THIS APP MUST BE BUSTED. THAT *CAN'T* BE RIGHT.

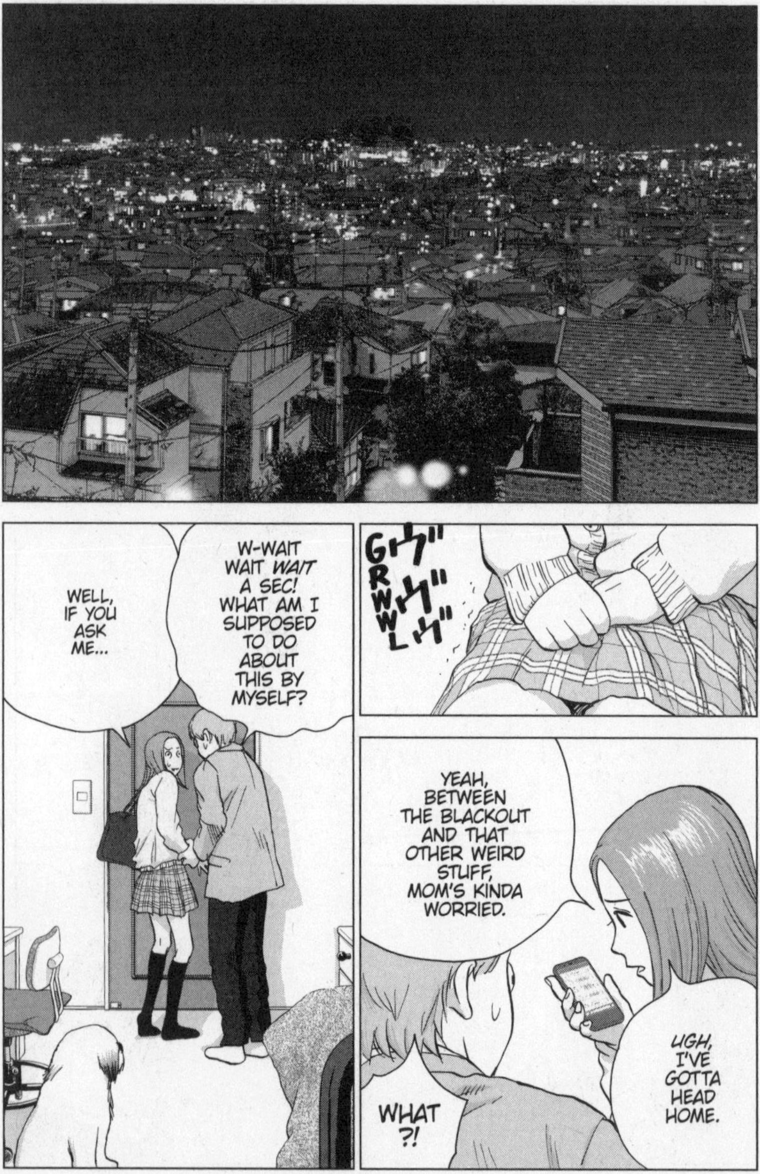
GRWWL
YEAH, BETWEEN THE BLACKOUT AND THAT OTHER WEIRD STUFF, MOM'S KINDA WORRIED.
UGH, I'VE GOTTA HEAD HOME.
WHAT?!
W-WAIT WAIT WAIT A SEC! WHAT AM I SUPPOSED TO DO ABOUT THIS BY MYSELF?
WELL, IF YOU ASK ME...

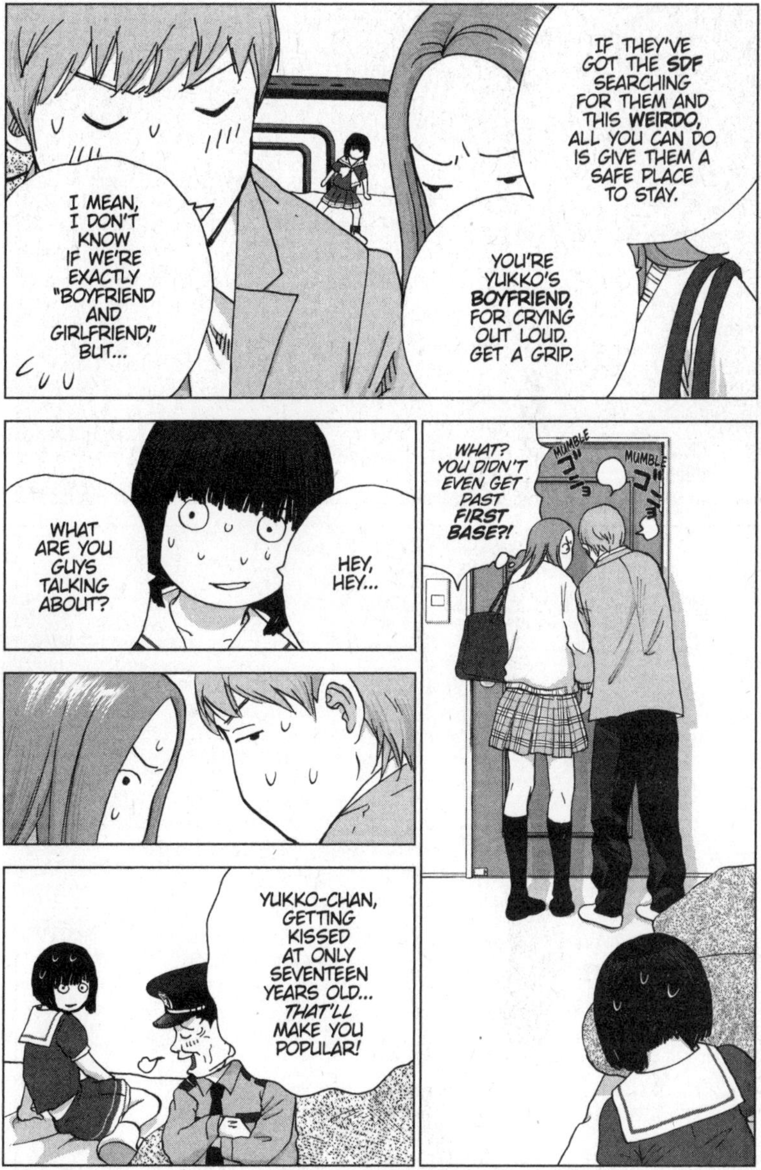
IF THEY'VE GOT THE SDF SEARCHING FOR THEM AND THIS WEIRDO, ALL YOU CAN DO IS GIVE THEM A SAFE PLACE TO STAY.
YOU'RE YUKKO'S BOYFRIEND, FOR CRYING OUT LOUD. GET A GRIP.
I MEAN, I DON'T KNOW IF WE'RE EXACTLY "BOYFRIEND AND GIRLFRIEND," BUT...
MUMBLE
MUMBLE
WHAT? YOU DIDN'T EVEN GET PAST FIRST BASE?!
HEY, HEY...
WHAT ARE YOU GUYS TALKING ABOUT?
YUKKO-CHAN, GETTING KISSED AT ONLY SEVENTEEN YEARS OLD... THAT'LL MAKE YOU POPULAR!

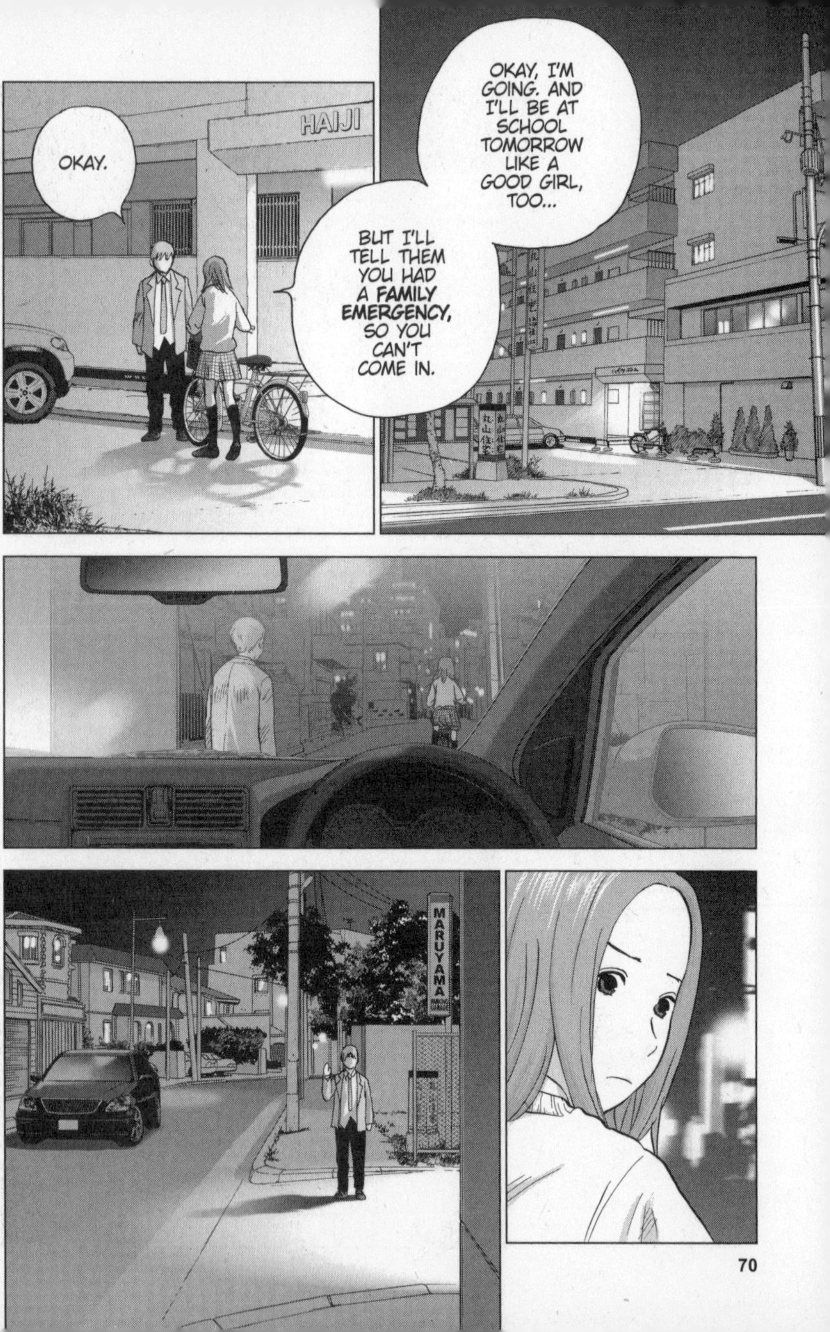
OKAY, I'M GOING. AND I'LL BE AT SCHOOL TOMORROW LIKE A GOOD GIRL, TOO...
BUT I'LL TELL THEM YOU HAD A **FAMILY EMERGENCY,** SO YOU CAN'T COME IN.
HAIJI
OKAY.
MARUYAMA

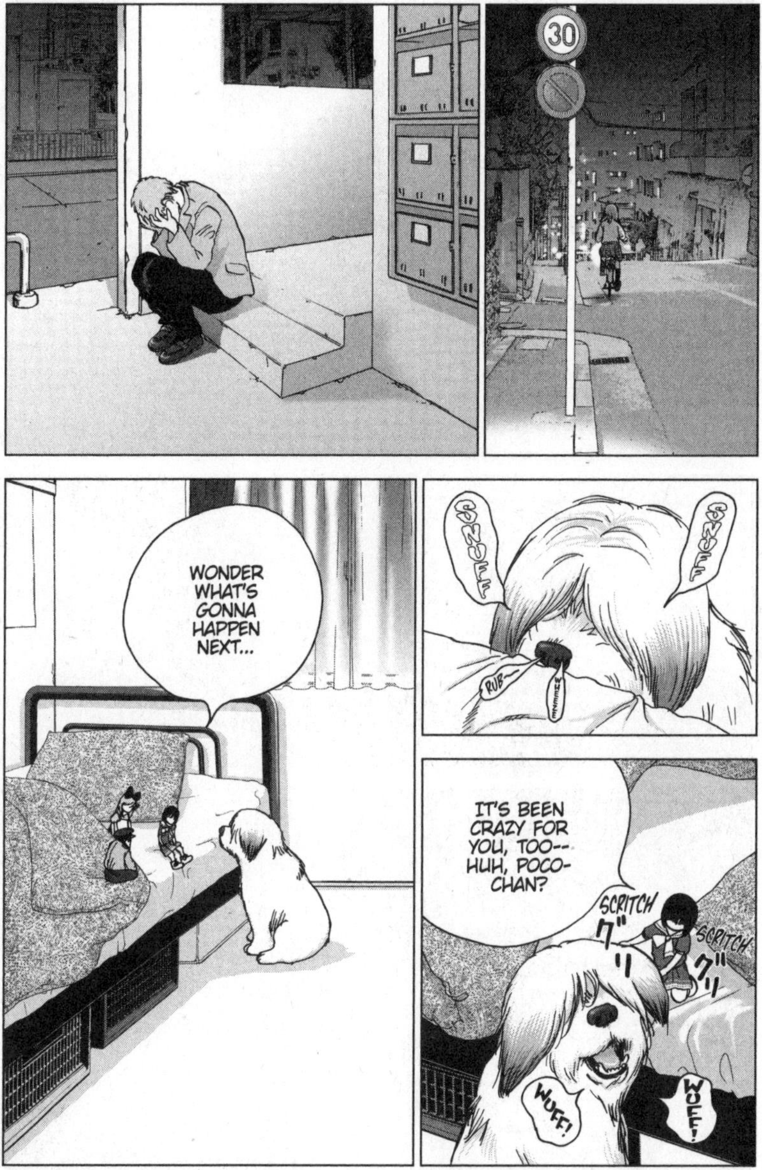
SNUFF
SNUFF
RUB
IT'S BEEN CRAZY FOR YOU, TOO-- HUH, POCO-CHAN?
SCRITCH
SCRITCH
WUFF!
WUFF!
WONDER WHAT'S GONNA HAPPEN NEXT...

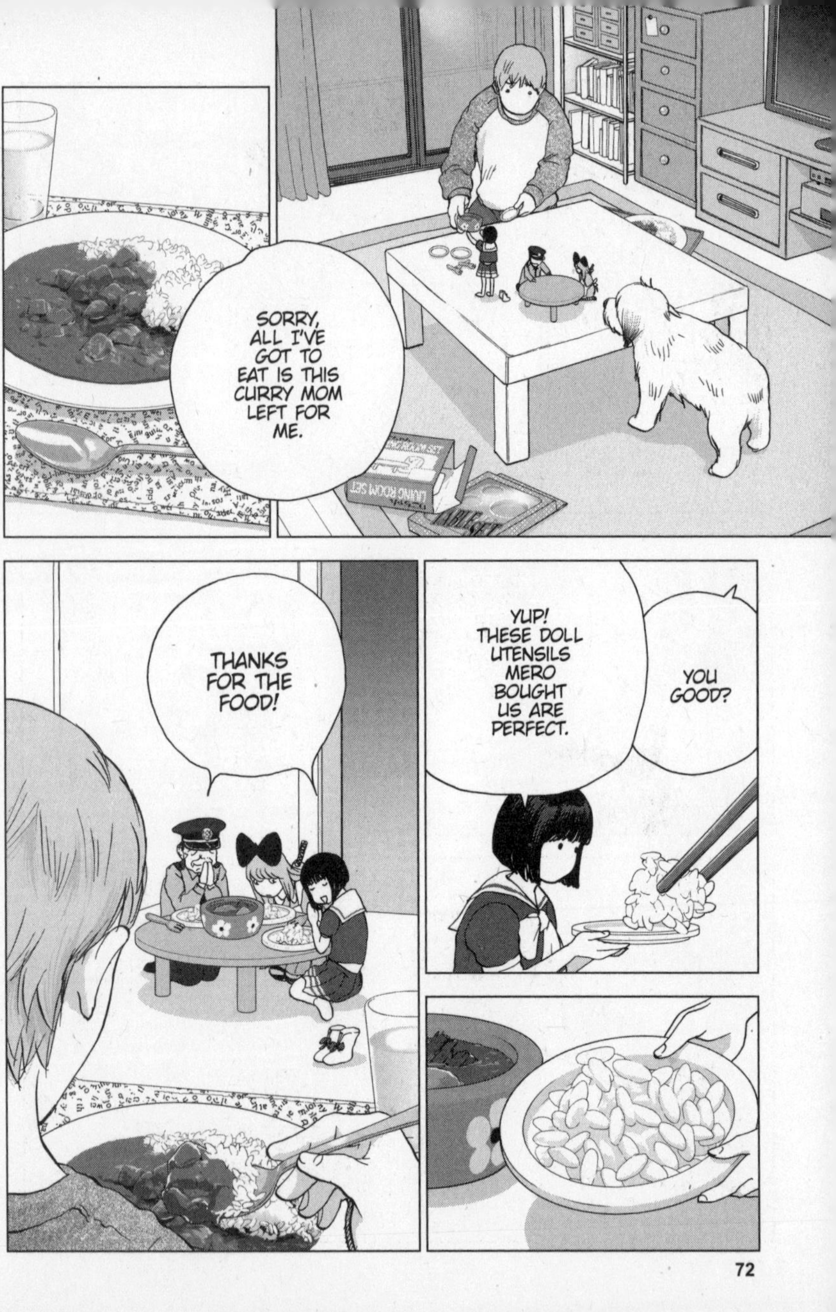
SORRY, ALL I'VE GOT TO EAT IS THIS CURRY MOM LEFT FOR ME.
LIVING ROOM SET
YOU GOOD?
YUP! THESE DOLL UTENSILS MERO BOUGHT US ARE PERFECT.
THANKS FOR THE FOOD!

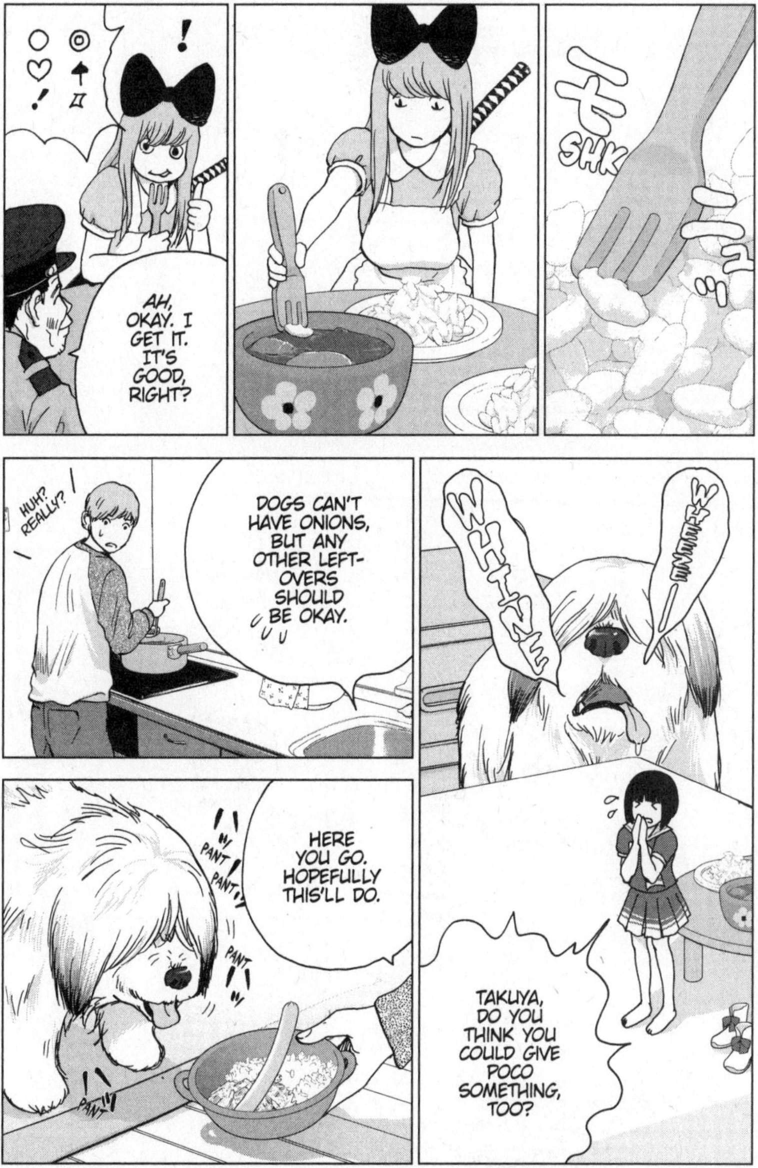
SHK
!
AH, OKAY. I GET IT. IT'S GOOD, RIGHT?
WHINE
TAKUYA, DO YOU THINK YOU COULD GIVE POCO SOMETHING, TOO?
HUH? REALLY?
DOGS CAN'T HAVE ONIONS, BUT ANY OTHER LEFT-OVERS SHOULD BE OKAY.
PANT PANT
HERE YOU GO. HOPEFULLY THIS'LL DO.
PANT
PANT

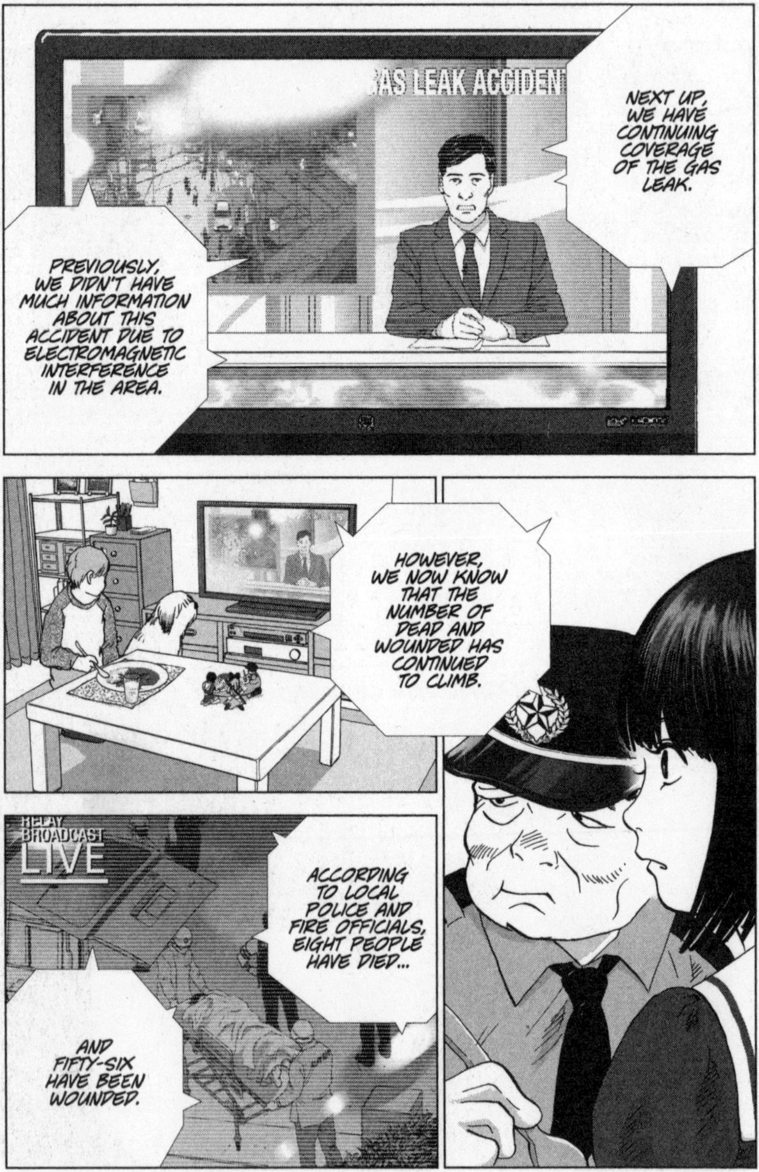

NEXT UP, WE HAVE CONTINUING COVERAGE OF THE GAS LEAK.
AS LEAK ACCIDEN
PREVIOUSLY, WE DIDN'T HAVE MUCH INFORMATION ABOUT THIS ACCIDENT DUE TO ELECTROMAGNETIC INTERFERENCE IN THE AREA.
HOWEVER, WE NOW KNOW THAT THE NUMBER OF DEAD AND WOUNDED HAS CONTINUED TO CLIMB.
RELAY BROADCAST
LIVE
ACCORDING TO LOCAL POLICE AND FIRE OFFICIALS, EIGHT PEOPLE HAVE DIED...
AND FIFTY-SIX HAVE BEEN WOUNDED.

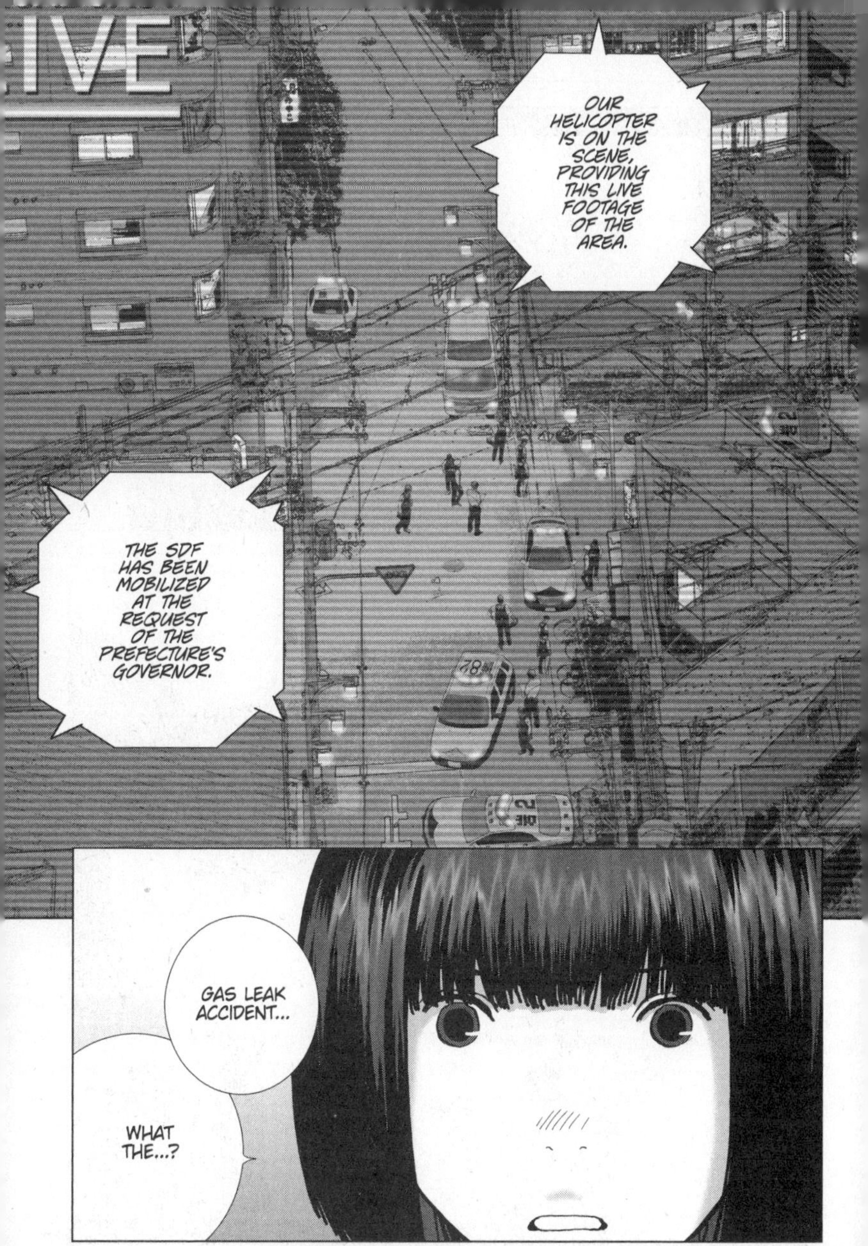
LIVE
OUR HELICOPTER IS ON THE SCENE, PROVIDING THIS LIVE FOOTAGE OF THE AREA.
THE SDF HAS BEEN MOBILIZED AT THE REQUEST OF THE PREFECTURE'S GOVERNOR.
GAS LEAK ACCIDENT...
WHAT THE...?

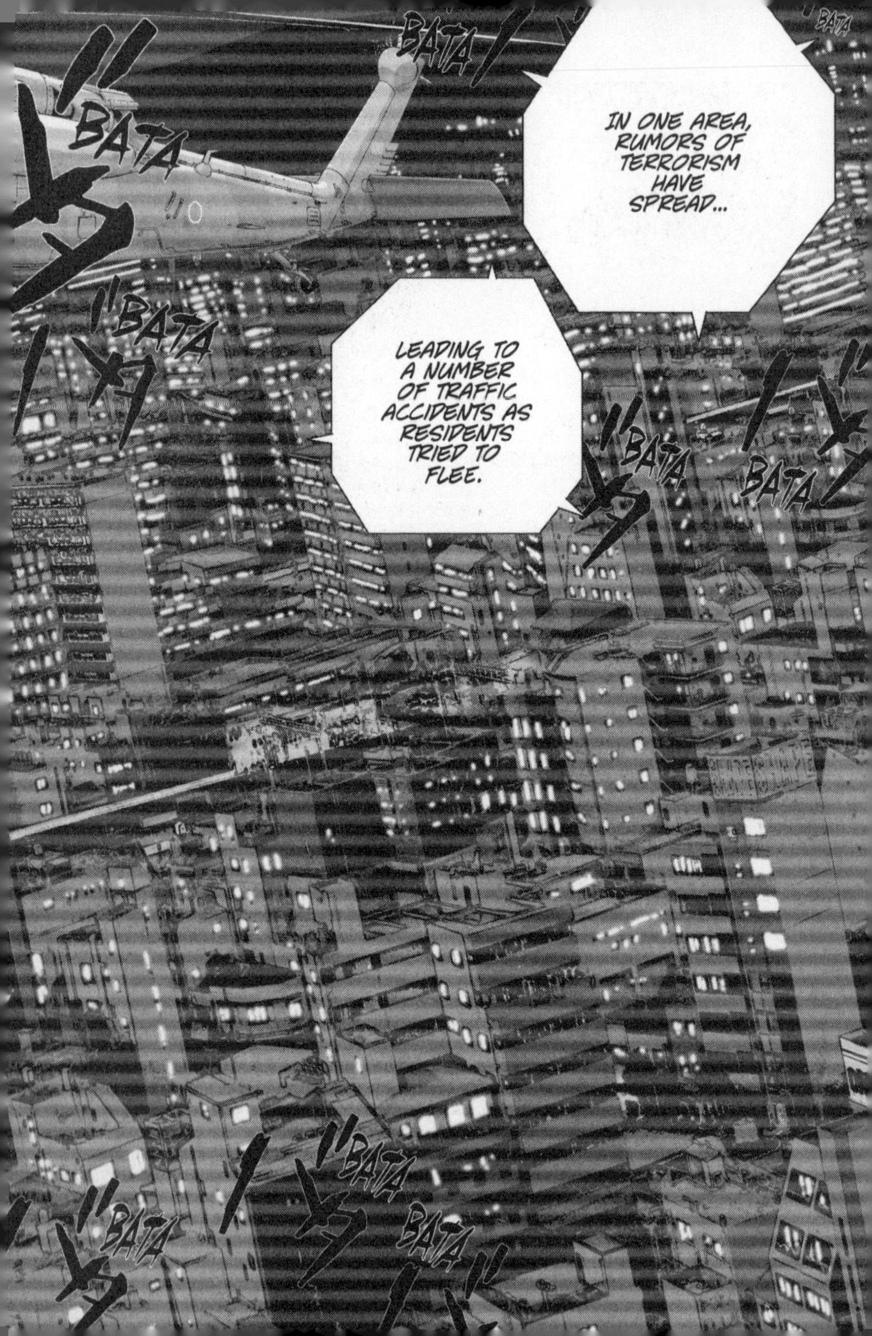
BATA
BATA
IN ONE AREA, RUMORS OF TERRORISM HAVE SPREAD...
BATA
BATA
LEADING TO A NUMBER OF TRAFFIC ACCIDENTS AS RESIDENTS TRIED TO FLEE.
BATA
BATA
BATA
BATA
BATA

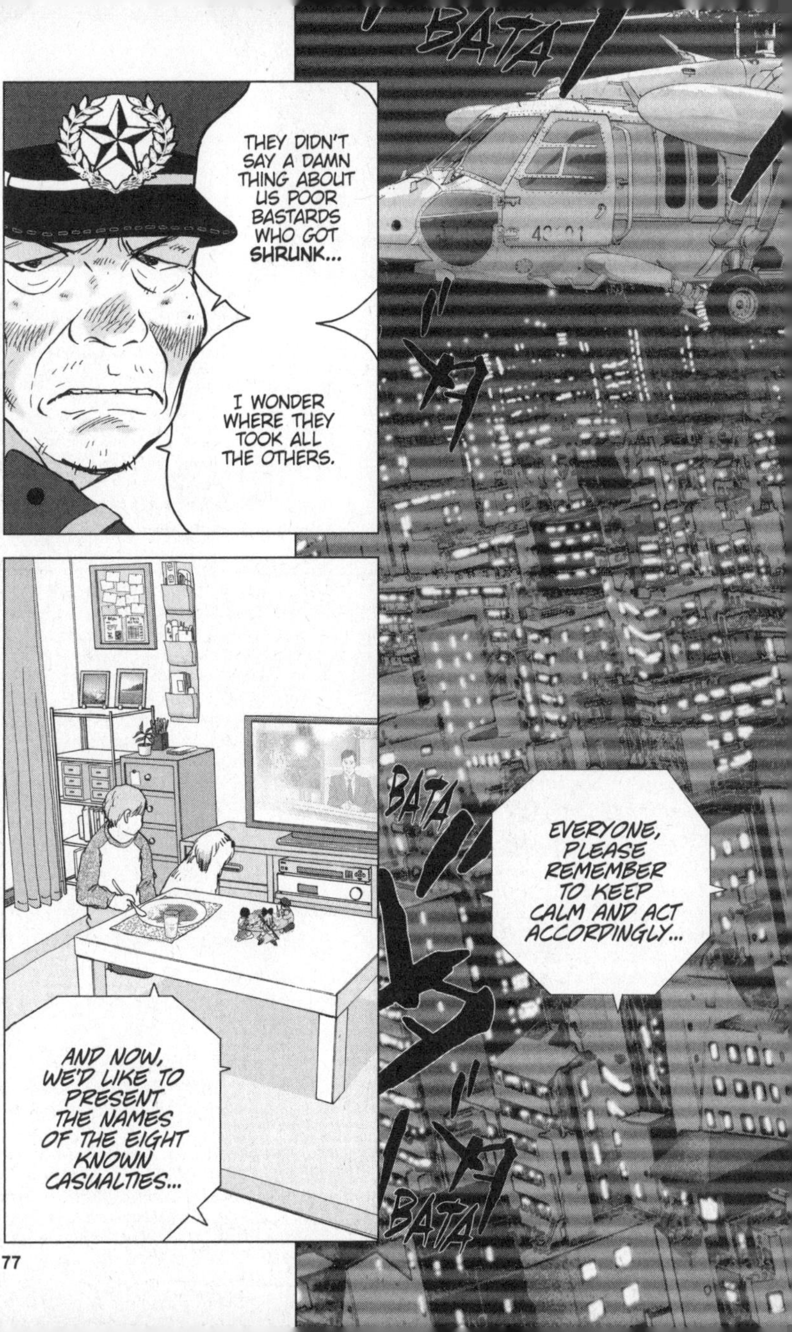
BATA
BATA
EVERYONE, PLEASE REMEMBER TO KEEP CALM AND ACT ACCORDINGLY...
BATA
THEY DIDN'T SAY A DAMN THING ABOUT US POOR BASTARDS WHO GOT **SHRUNK**...
I WONDER WHERE THEY TOOK ALL THE OTHERS.
AND NOW, WE'D LIKE TO PRESENT THE NAMES OF THE EIGHT KNOWN CASUALTIES...

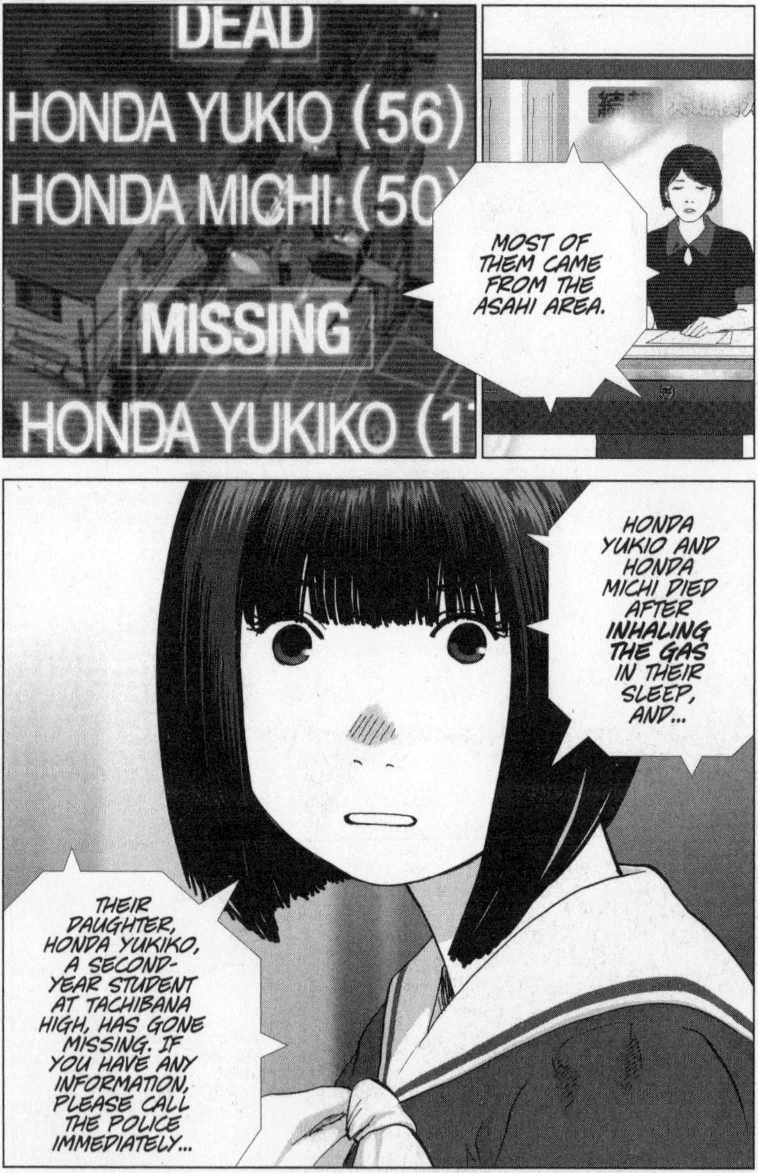
MOST OF THEM CAME FROM THE ASAHI AREA.
DEAD
HONDA YUKIO (56)
HONDA MICHI (50
MISSING
HONDA YUKIKO (1
HONDA YUKIO AND HONDA MICHI DIED AFTER INHALING THE GAS IN THEIR SLEEP, AND...
THEIR DAUGHTER, HONDA YUKIKO, A SECOND-YEAR STUDENT AT TACHIBANA HIGH, HAS GONE MISSING. IF YOU HAVE ANY INFORMATION, PLEASE CALL THE POLICE IMMEDIATELY...

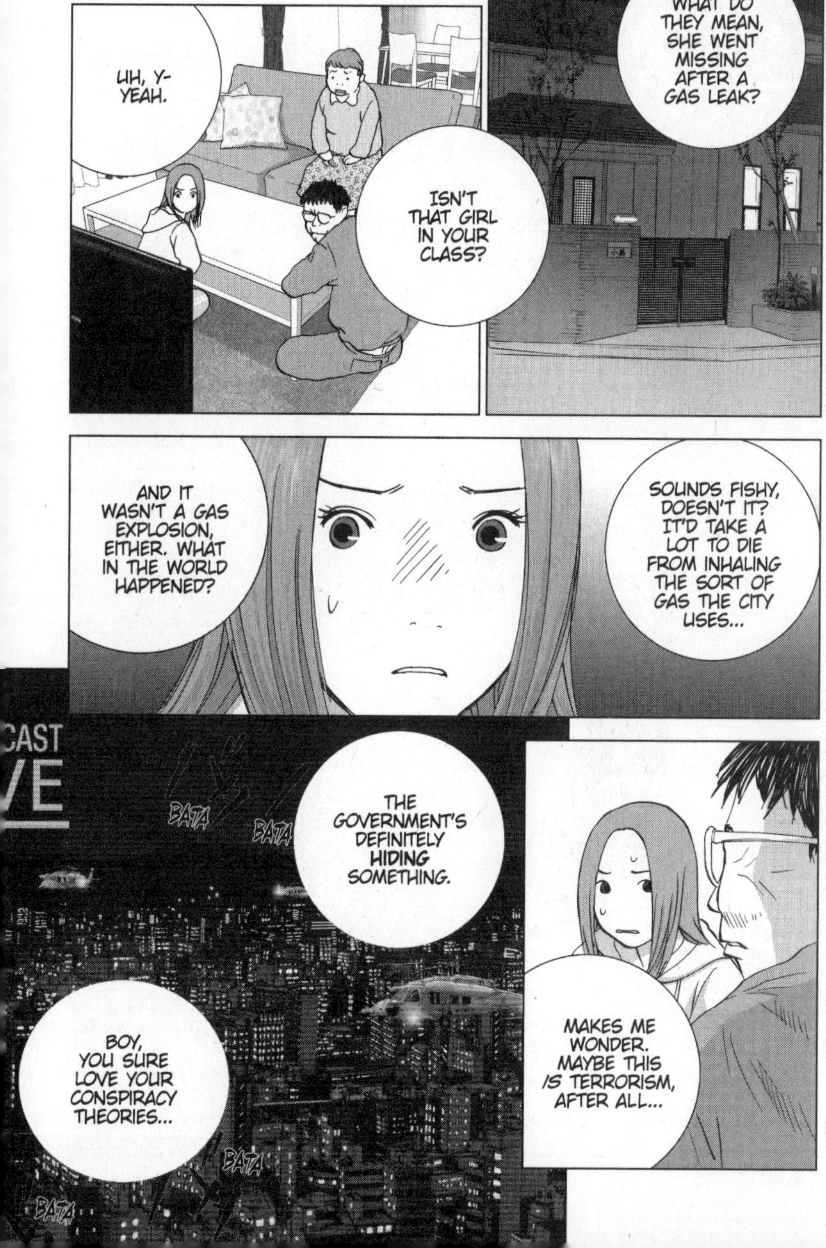
WHAT DO THEY MEAN, SHE WENT MISSING AFTER A GAS LEAK?
ISN'T THAT GIRL IN YOUR CLASS?
UH, Y-YEAH.
SOUNDS FISHY, DOESN'T IT? IT'D TAKE A LOT TO DIE FROM INHALING THE SORT OF GAS THE CITY USES...
AND IT WASN'T A GAS EXPLOSION, EITHER. WHAT IN THE WORLD HAPPENED?
MAKES ME WONDER. MAYBE THIS *IS* TERRORISM, AFTER ALL...
CAST
BATA
BATA
THE GOVERNMENT'S DEFINITELY **HIDING** SOMETHING.
BOY, YOU SURE LOVE YOUR CONSPIRACY THEORIES...
BATA
BATA

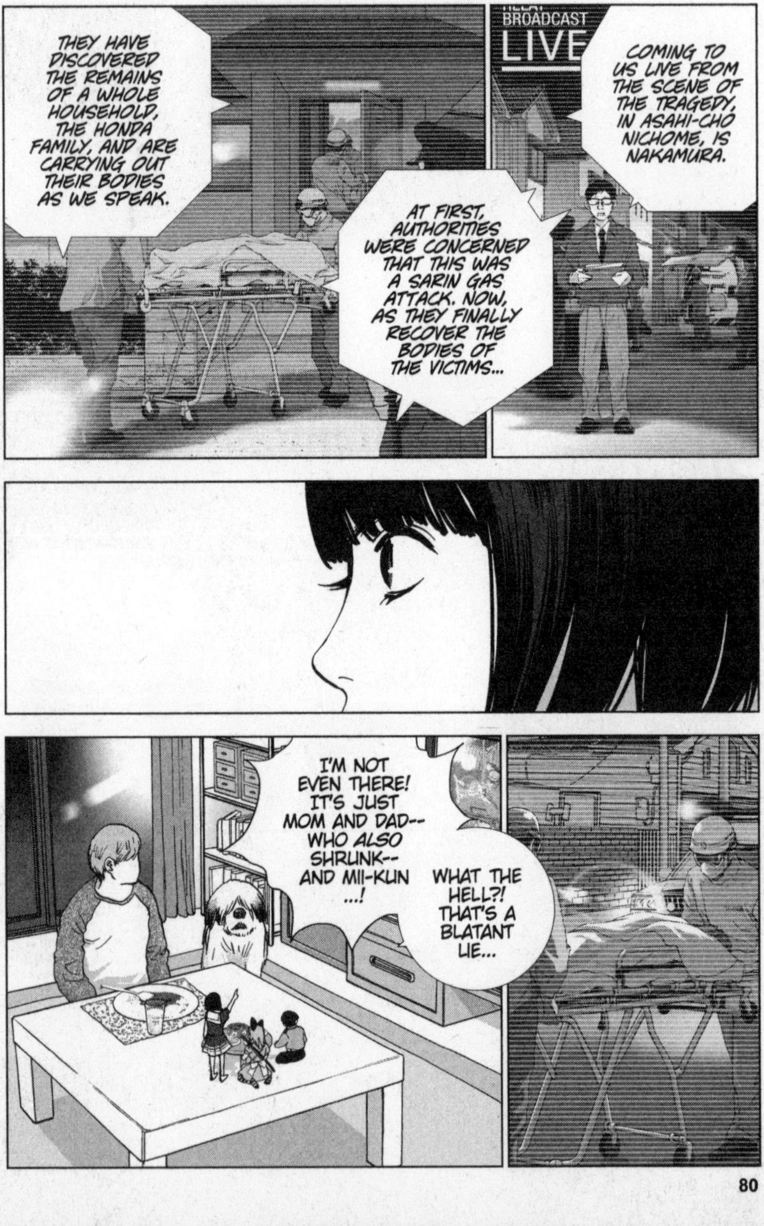
BROADCAST
LIVE
COMING TO US LIVE FROM THE SCENE OF THE TRAGEDY, IN ASAHI-CHO NICHOME, IS NAKAMURA.
THEY HAVE DISCOVERED THE REMAINS OF A WHOLE HOUSEHOLD, THE HONDA FAMILY, AND ARE CARRYING OUT THEIR BODIES AS WE SPEAK.
AT FIRST, AUTHORITIES WERE CONCERNED THAT THIS WAS A SARIN GAS ATTACK. NOW, AS THEY FINALLY RECOVER THE BODIES OF THE VICTIMS...
WHAT THE HELL?! THAT'S A BLATANT LIE...
I'M NOT EVEN THERE! IT'S JUST MOM AND DAD-- WHO ALSO SHRUNK-- AND MII-KUN ...!

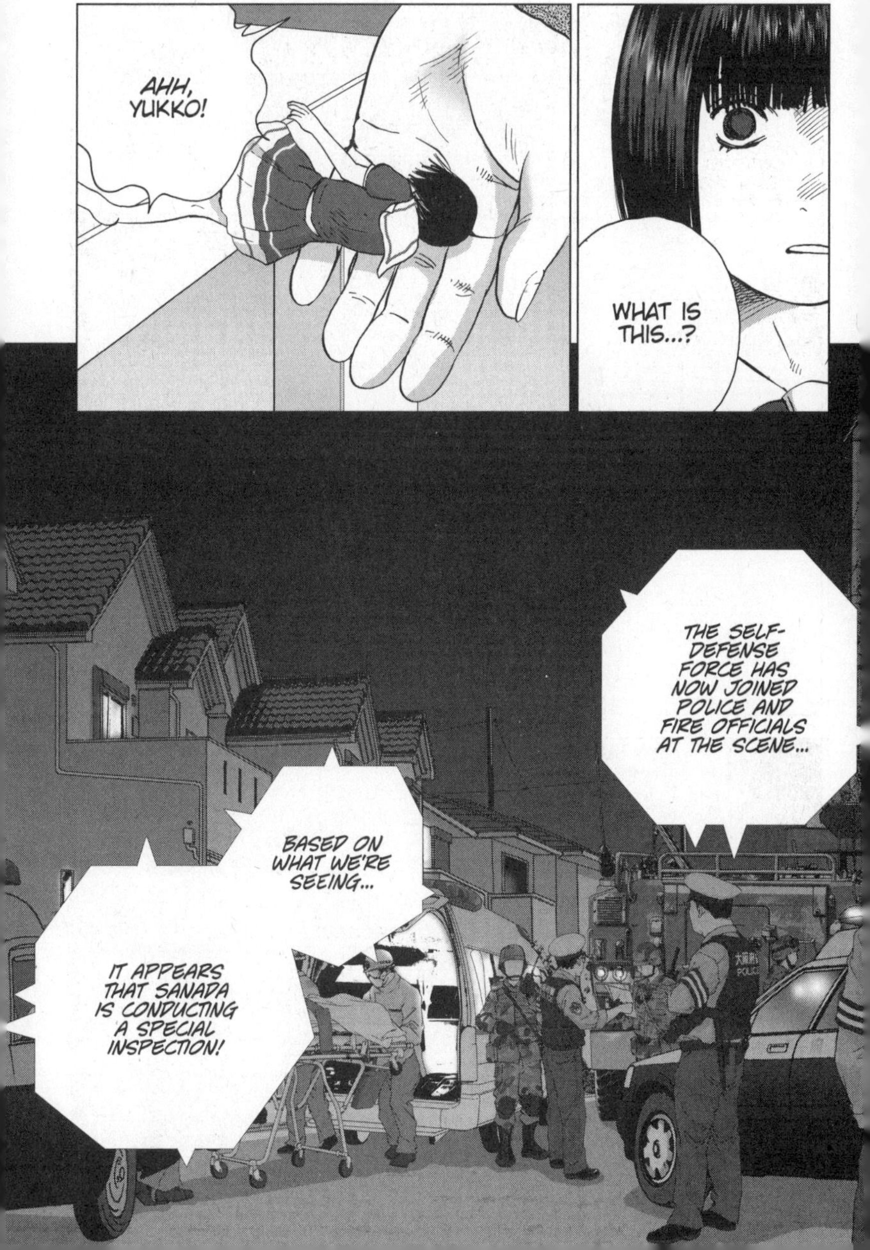
WHAT IS THIS...?
AHH, YUKKO!
THE SELF-DEFENSE FORCE HAS NOW JOINED POLICE AND FIRE OFFICIALS AT THE SCENE...
BASED ON WHAT WE'RE SEEING...
IT APPEARS THAT SANADA IS CONDUCTING A SPECIAL INSPECTION!

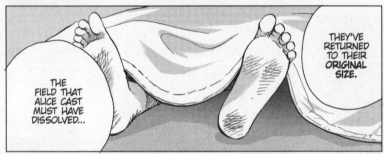

THEY'VE RETURNED TO THEIR ORIGINAL SIZE.

THE FIELD THAT ALICE CAST MUST HAVE DISSOLVED...

AND WITH IT, THE SHRINKING EFFECT.

BUT WHERE IS ALICE NOW?

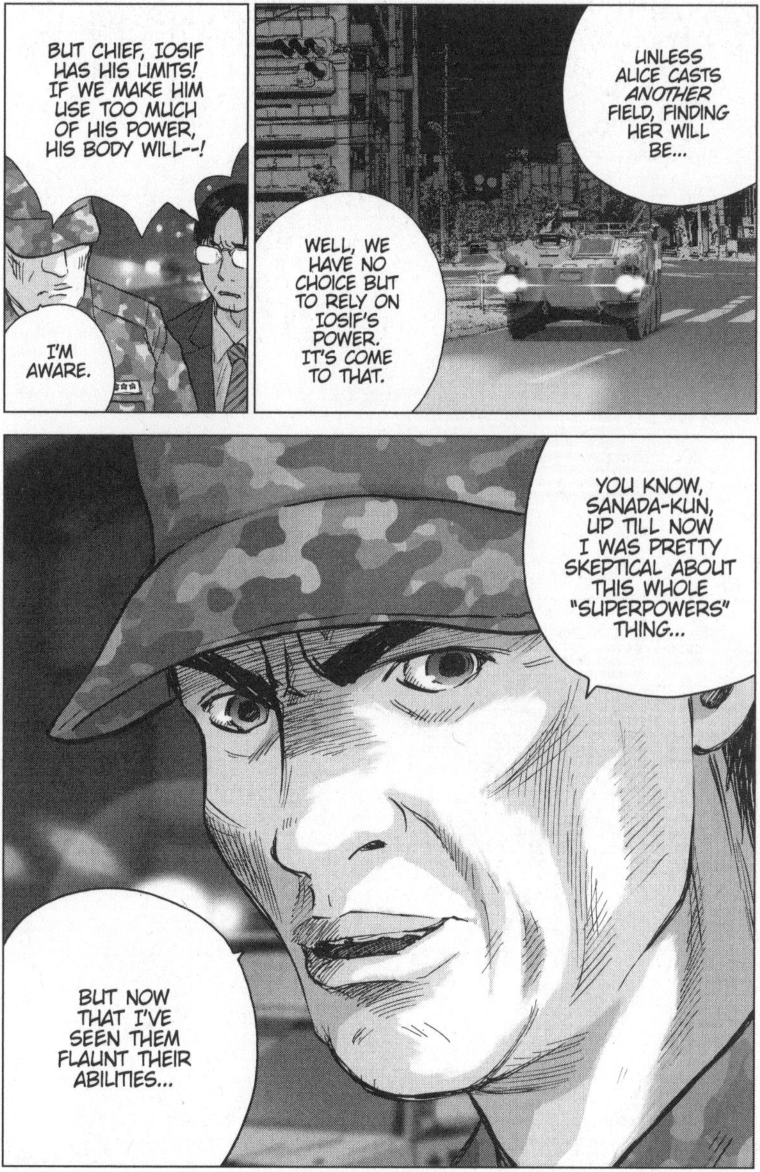
UNLESS ALICE CASTS *ANOTHER* FIELD, FINDING HER WILL BE...
WELL, WE HAVE NO CHOICE BUT TO RELY ON IOSIF'S POWER. IT'S COME TO THAT.
BUT CHIEF, IOSIF HAS HIS LIMITS! IF WE MAKE HIM USE TOO MUCH OF HIS POWER, HIS BODY WILL--!
I'M AWARE.
YOU KNOW, SANADA-KUN, UP TILL NOW I WAS PRETTY SKEPTICAL ABOUT THIS WHOLE "SUPERPOWERS" THING...
BUT NOW THAT I'VE SEEN THEM FLAUNT THEIR ABILITIES...

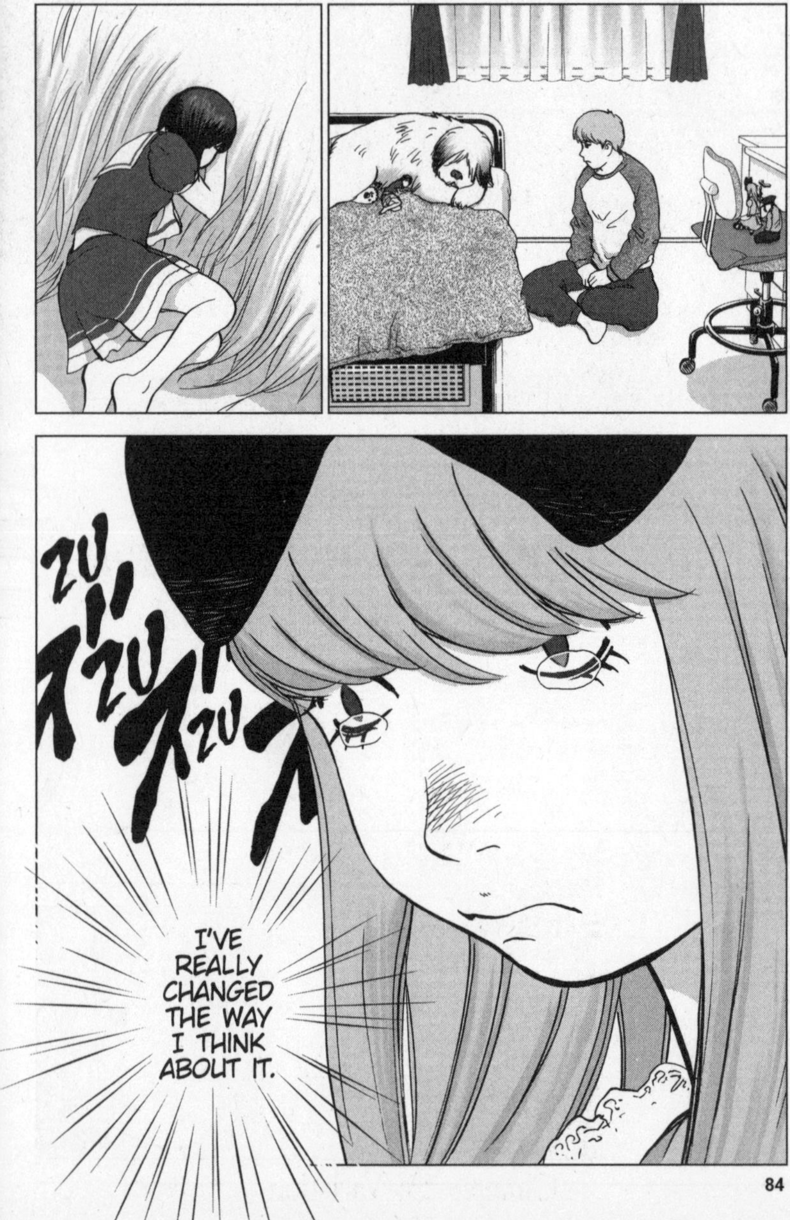
ZU ZU ZU
I'VE REALLY CHANGED THE WAY I THINK ABOUT IT.

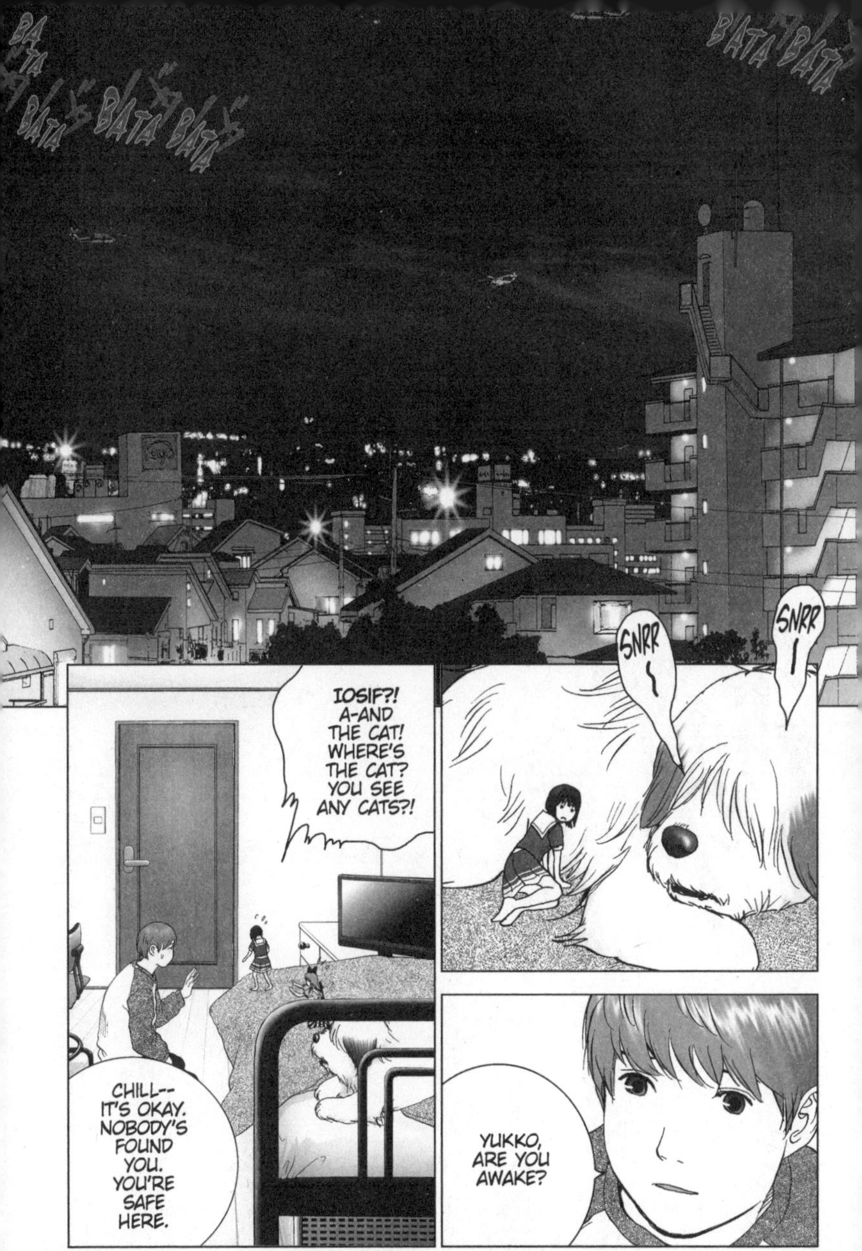
BATA BATA BATA
BATA BATA BATA BATA
SNRR
SNRR
YUKKO, ARE YOU AWAKE?
IOSIF?! A-AND THE CAT! WHERE'S THE CAT? YOU SEE ANY CATS?!
CHILL-- IT'S OKAY. NOBODY'S FOUND YOU. YOU'RE SAFE HERE.

Chapter 23: Variation

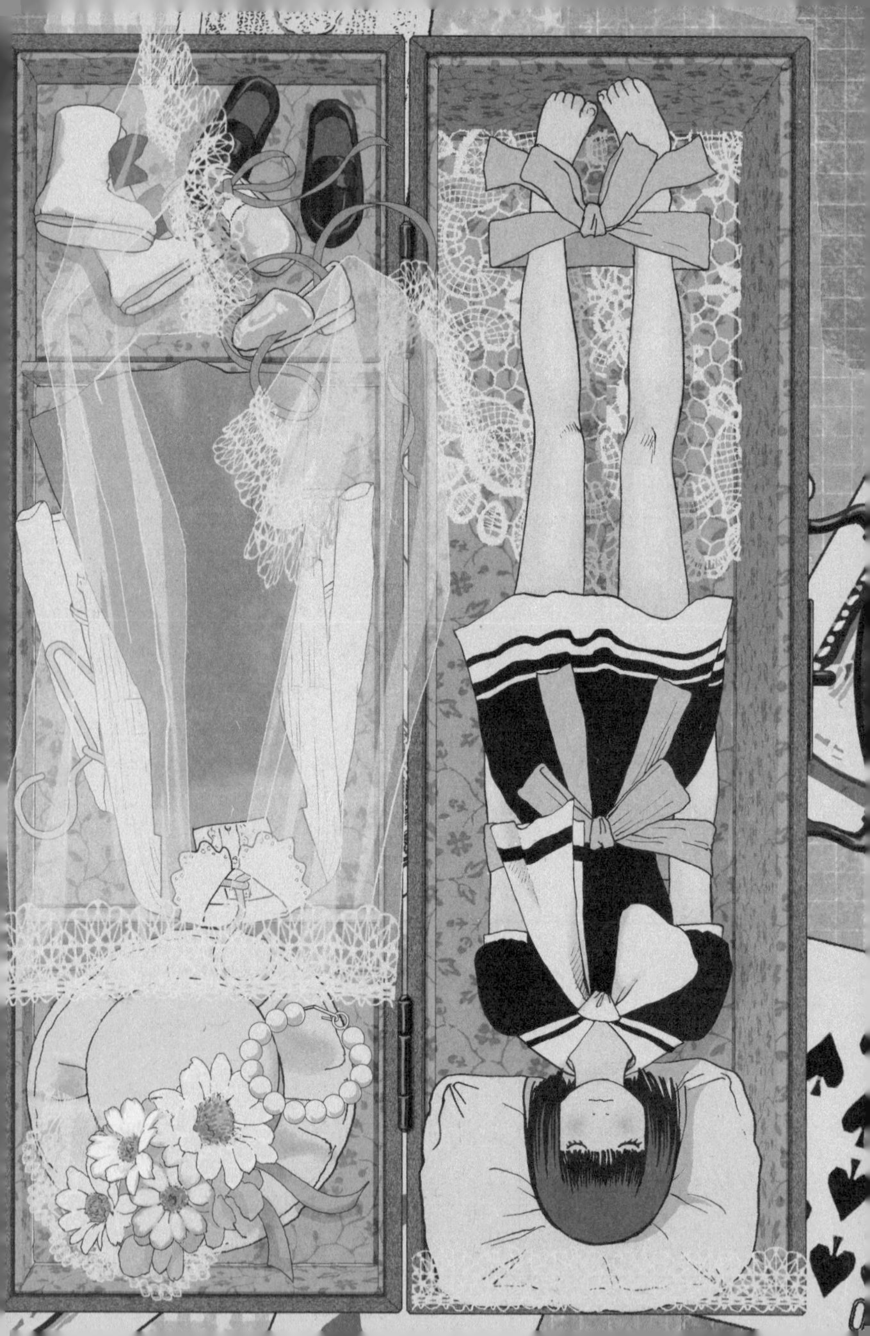

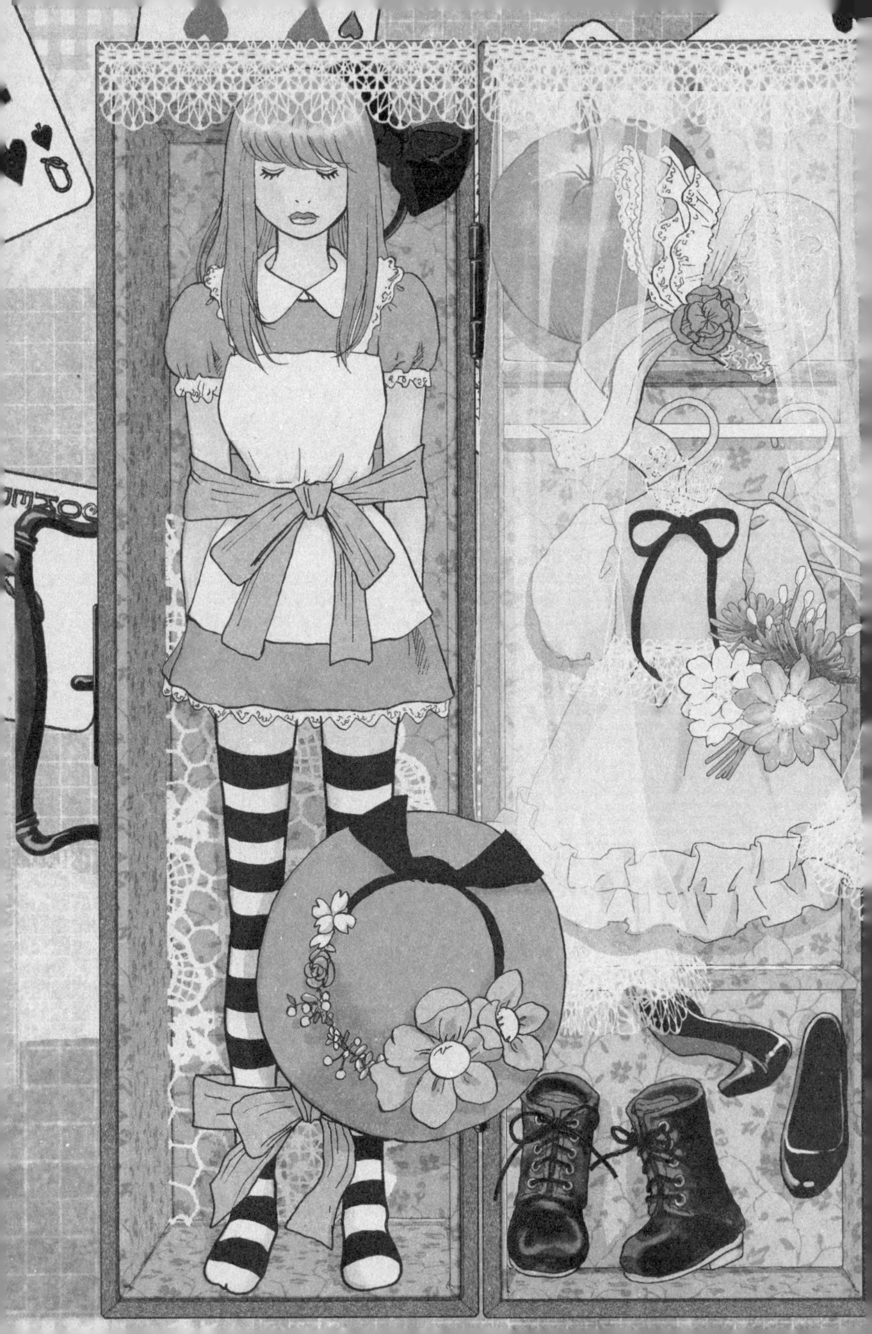

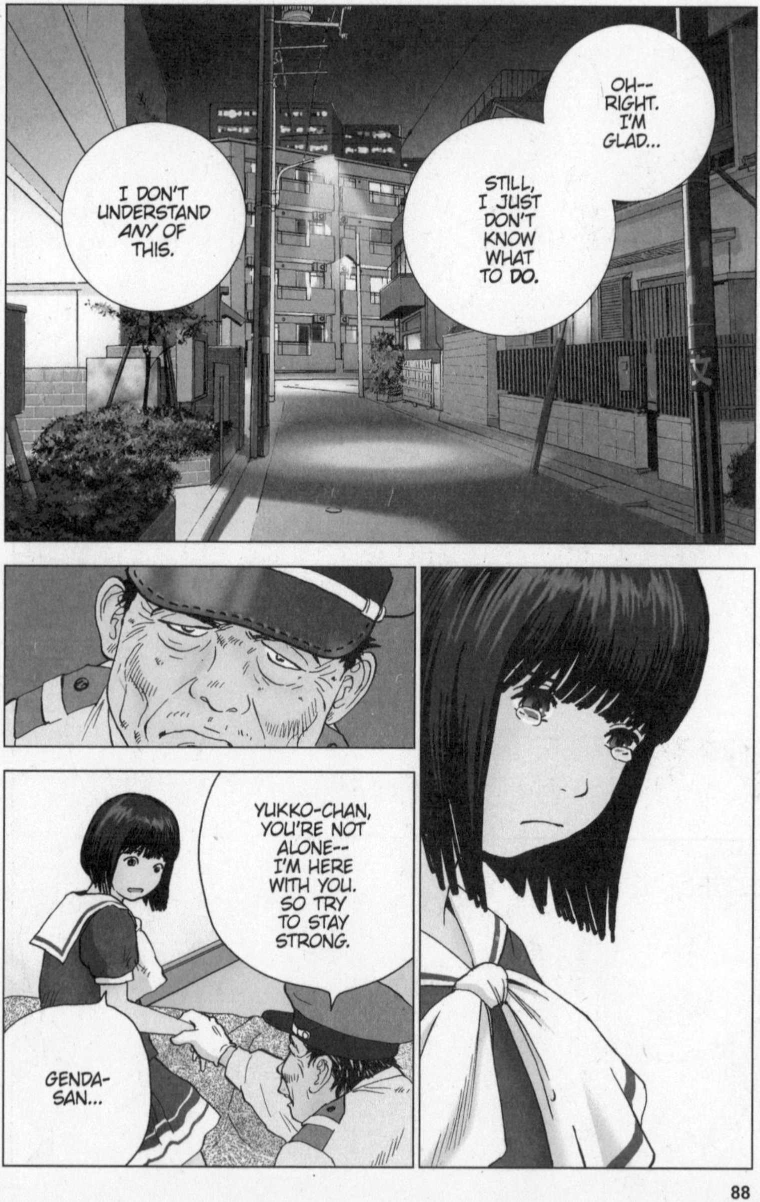
OH-- RIGHT. I'M GLAD...
STILL, I JUST DON'T KNOW WHAT TO DO.
I DON'T UNDERSTAND ANY OF THIS.
YUKKO-CHAN, YOU'RE NOT ALONE-- I'M HERE WITH YOU. SO TRY TO STAY STRONG.
GENDA-SAN...

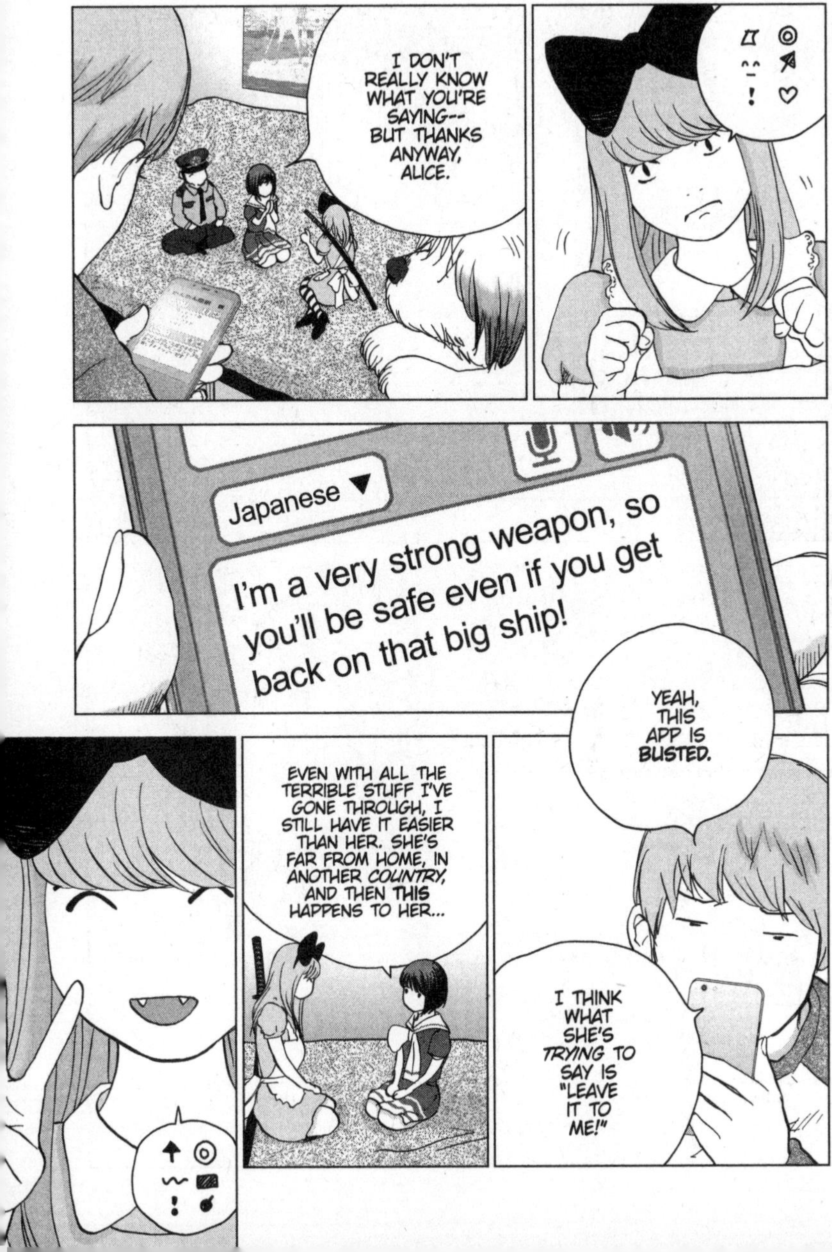
I DON'T REALLY KNOW WHAT YOU'RE SAYING-- BUT THANKS ANYWAY, ALICE.
Japanese
I'm a very strong weapon, so you'll be safe even if you get back on that big ship!
YEAH, THIS APP IS BUSTED.
I THINK WHAT SHE'S *TRYING* TO SAY IS "LEAVE IT TO ME!"
EVEN WITH ALL THE TERRIBLE STUFF I'VE GONE THROUGH, I STILL HAVE IT EASIER THAN HER. SHE'S FAR FROM HOME, IN ANOTHER *COUNTRY,* AND THEN THIS HAPPENS TO HER...

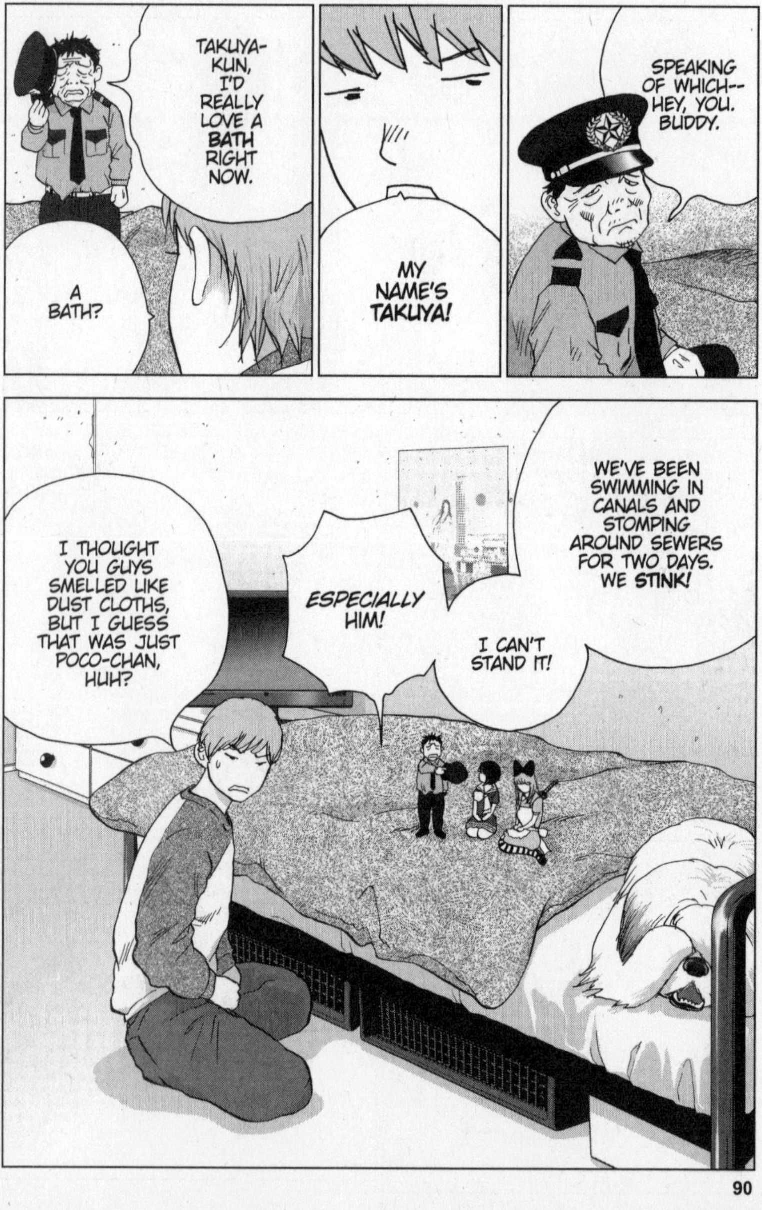
SPEAKING OF WHICH-- HEY, YOU. BUDDY.
MY NAME'S TAKUYA!
TAKUYA-KUN, I'D REALLY LOVE A BATH RIGHT NOW.
A BATH?
WE'VE BEEN SWIMMING IN CANALS AND STOMPING AROUND SEWERS FOR TWO DAYS. WE STINK!
I CAN'T STAND IT!
ESPECIALLY HIM!
I THOUGHT YOU GUYS SMELLED LIKE DUST CLOTHS, BUT I GUESS THAT WAS JUST POCO-CHAN, HUH?

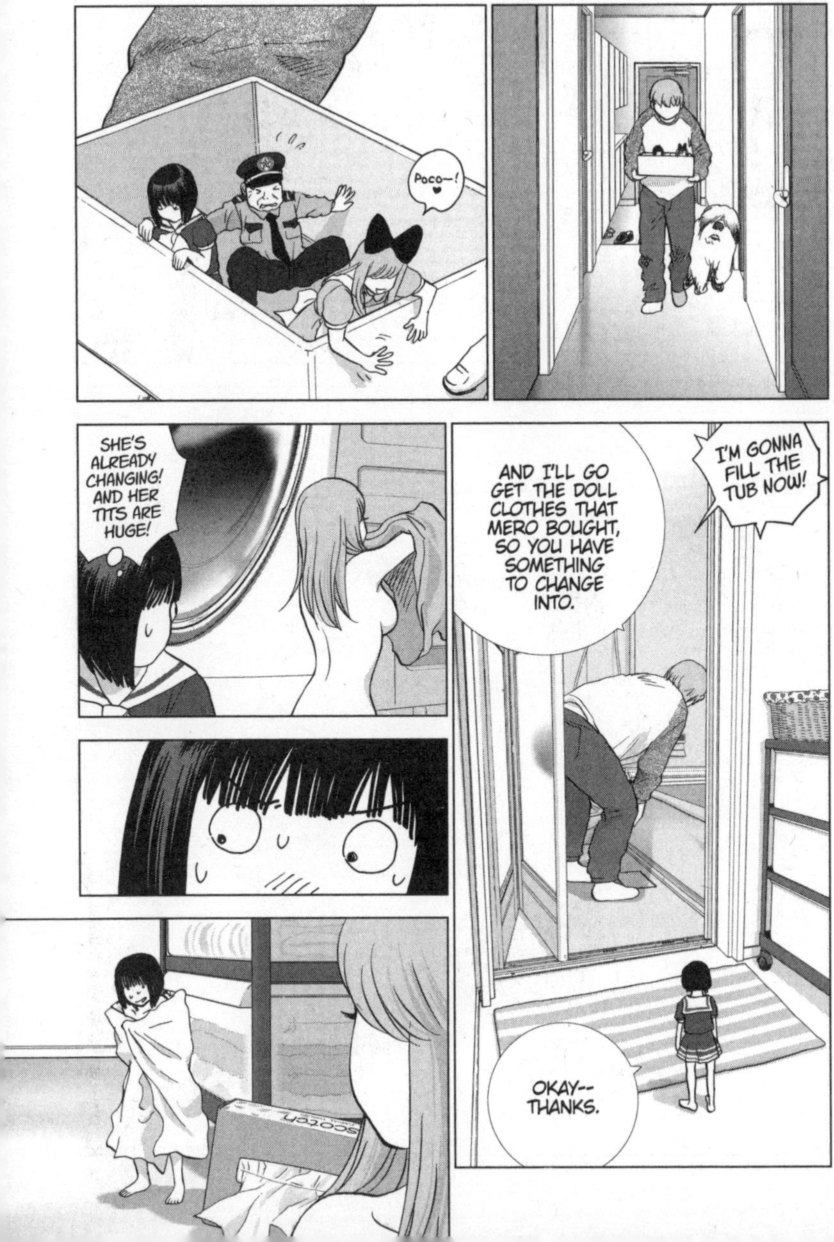
Poco~!
I'M GONNA FILL THE TUB NOW!
AND I'LL GO GET THE DOLL CLOTHES THAT MERO BOUGHT, SO YOU HAVE SOMETHING TO CHANGE INTO.
OKAY-- THANKS.
SHE'S ALREADY CHANGING! AND HER TITS ARE HUGE!
scotch

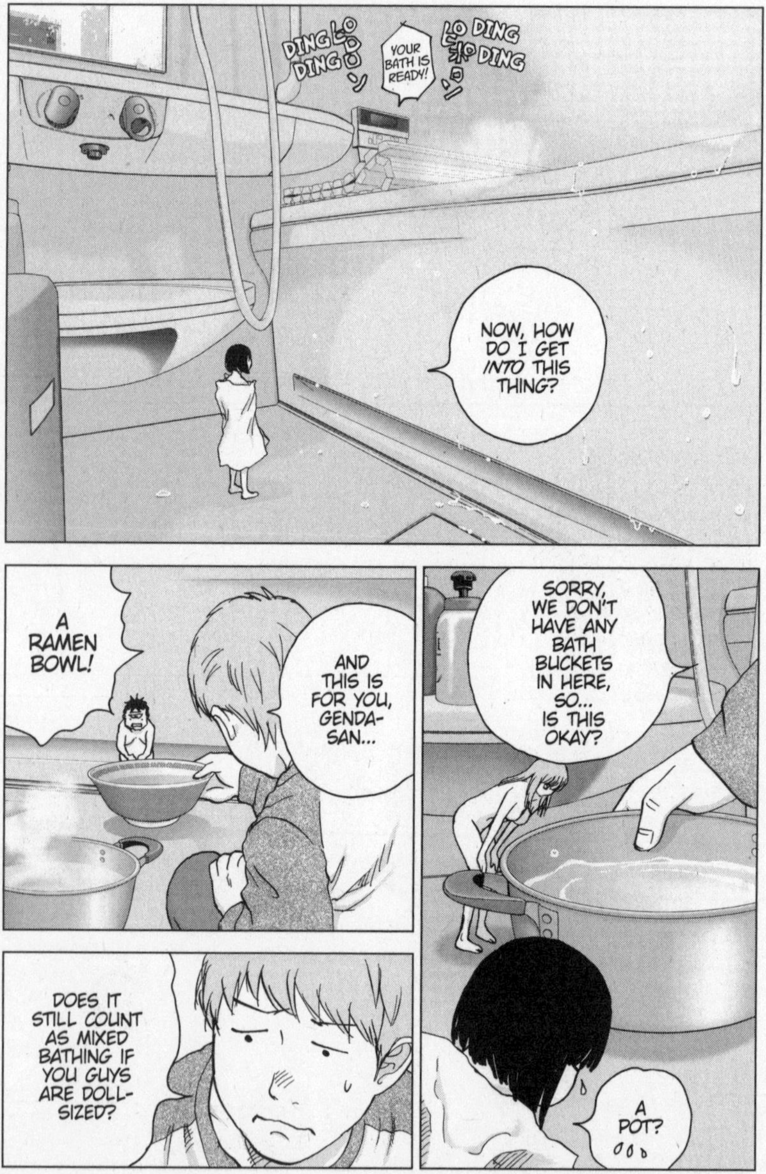
LO DING DING
YOUR BATH IS READY!
DING LO DING
NOW, HOW DO I GET *INTO* THIS THING?
SORRY, WE DON'T HAVE ANY BATH BUCKETS IN HERE, SO... IS THIS OKAY?
A POT?
AND THIS IS FOR YOU, GENDA-SAN...
A RAMEN BOWL!
DOES IT STILL COUNT AS MIXED BATHING IF YOU GUYS ARE DOLL-SIZED?

ARE YOU OKAY?

SNIFFLE

SAY WHAT YOU WANT, THIS IS ABSOLUTELY HEAVENLY.

AND BECAUSE WE'RE TINY, OUR WATER BILL WILL BE, TOO. ♥

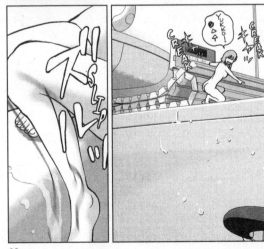

YUUKO!

HEY, ALICE-- WHAT ARE YOU DOING? THAT'S DANGEROUS!

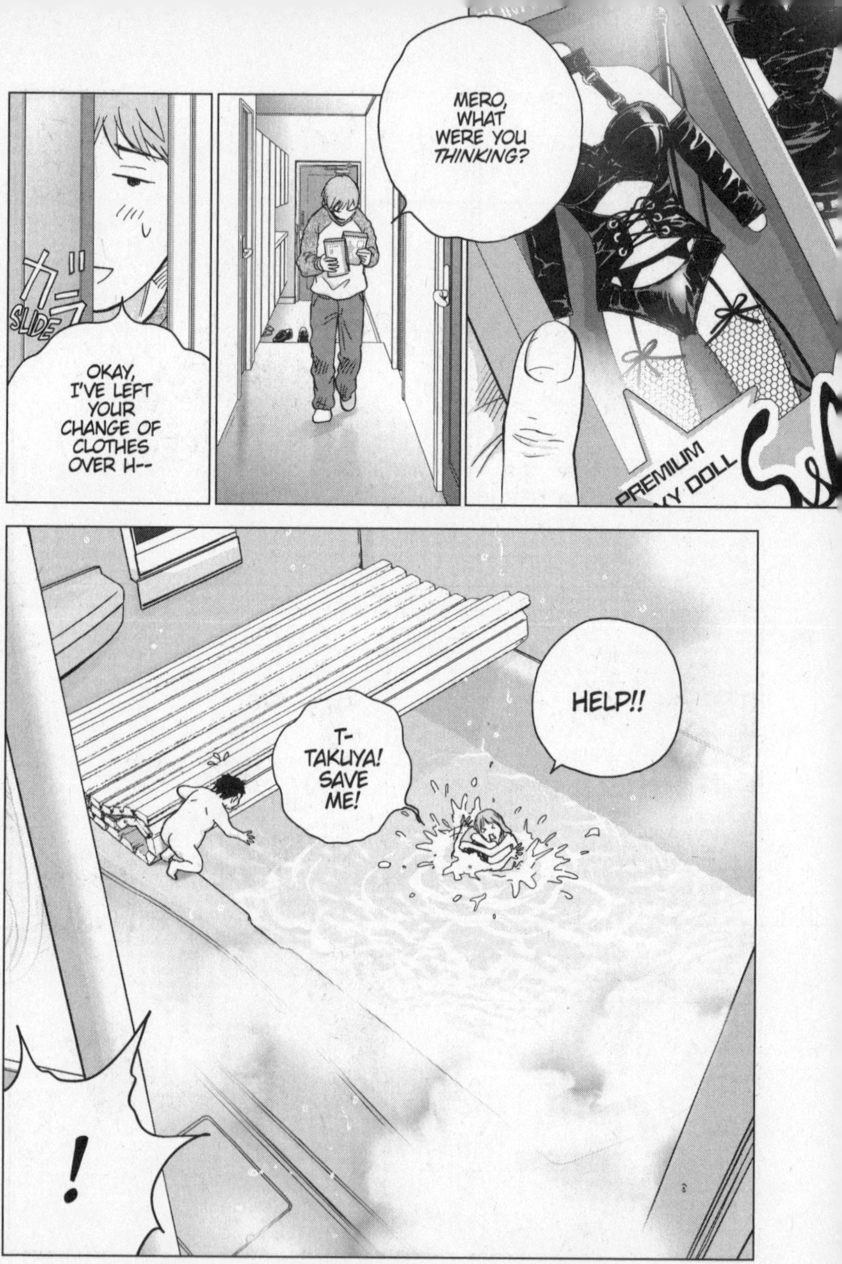
MERO, WHAT WERE YOU THINKING?
PREMIUM
XY DOLL
カラ
SLIDE
OKAY, I'VE LEFT YOUR CHANGE OF CLOTHES OVER H--
HELP!!
T-TAKUYA! SAVE ME!
!

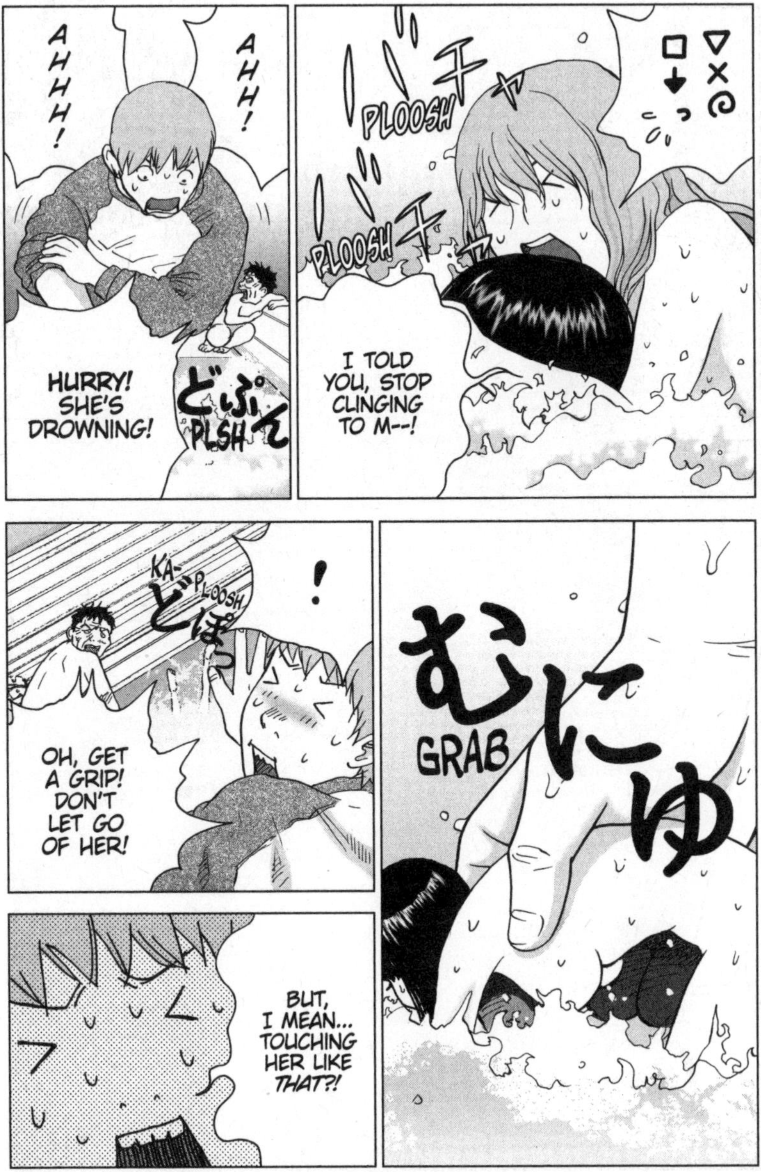

PLOOSH
PLOOSH
I TOLD YOU, STOP CLINGING TO M--!
AHHH!
AHH!
HURRY! SHE'S DROWNING!
PLSH
GRAB
KA-PLOOSH
!
OH, GET A GRIP! DON'T LET GO OF HER!
BUT, I MEAN... TOUCHING HER LIKE *THAT*?!

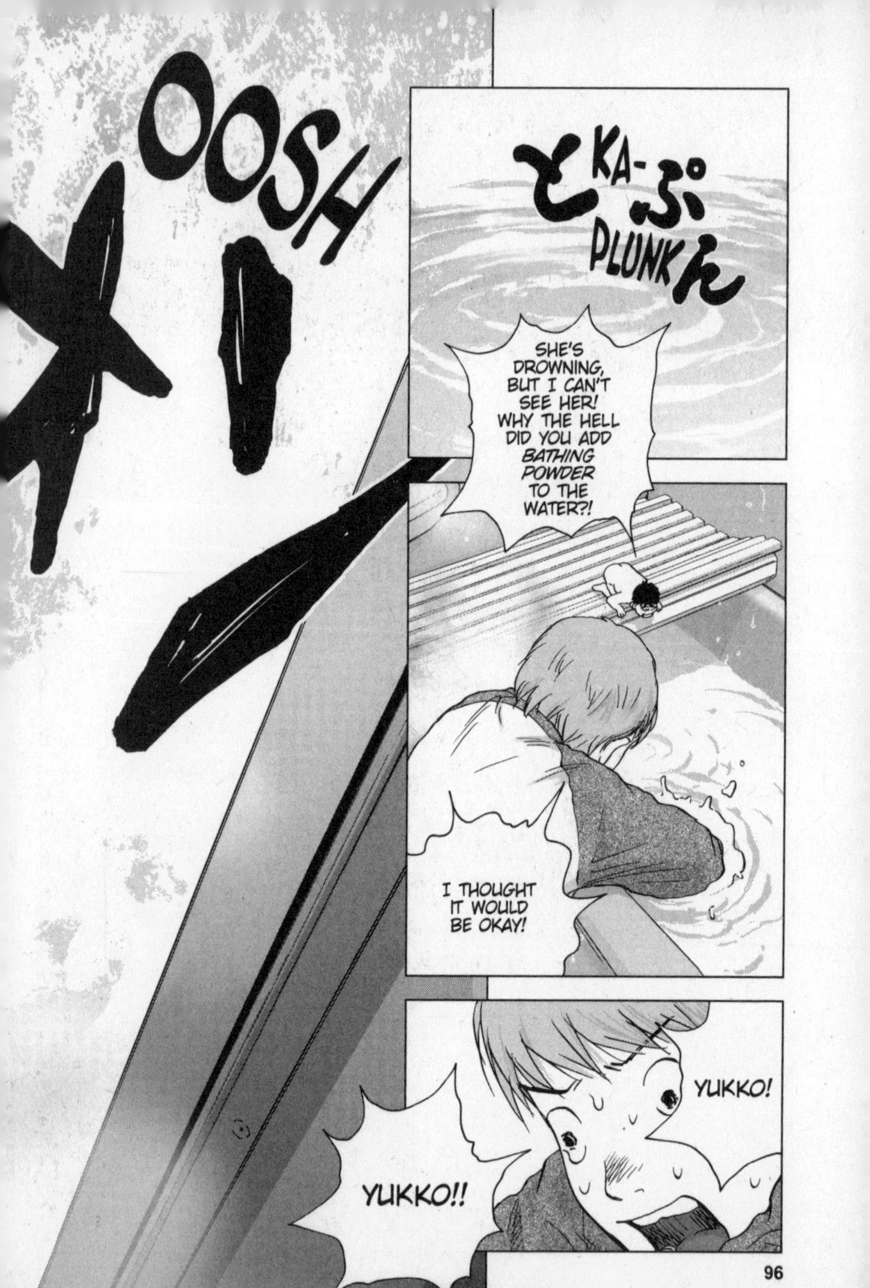
とKA-ぷPLUNKん
SHE'S DROWNING, BUT I CAN'T SEE HER! WHY THE HELL DID YOU ADD *BATHING POWDER* TO THE WATER?!
I THOUGHT IT WOULD BE OKAY!
YUKKO!
YUKKO!!
OOSH

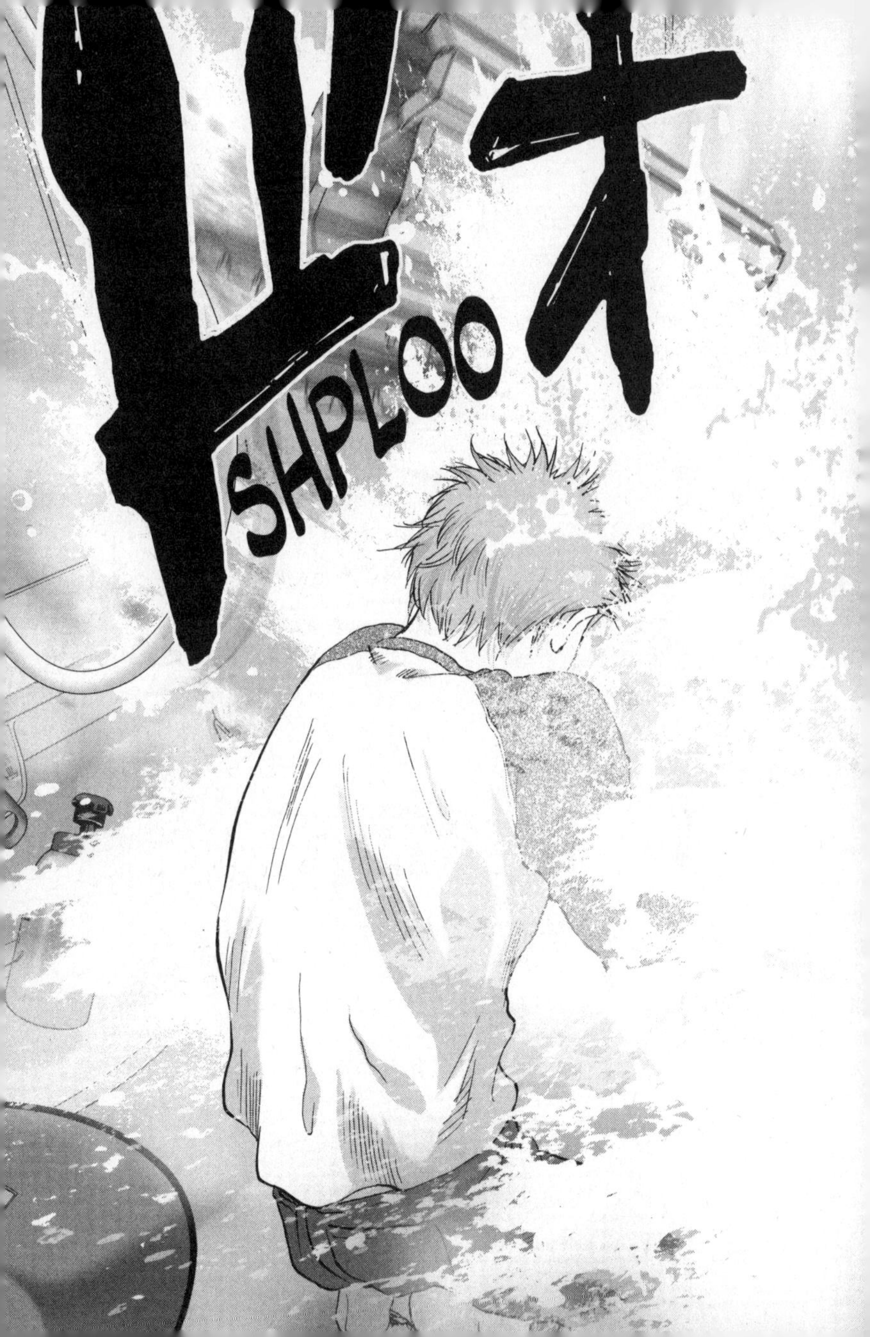
SHPLOO

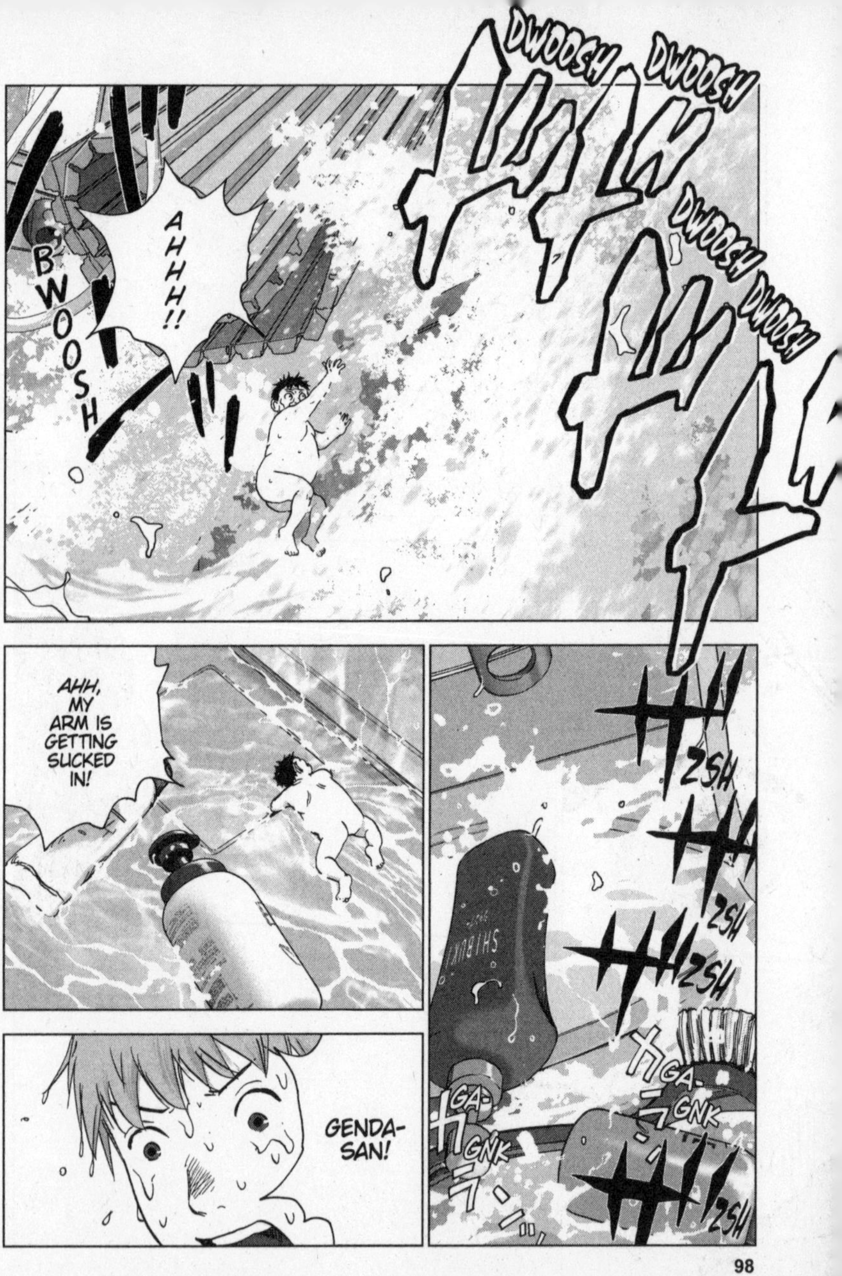
DWOOSH
DWOOSH
DWOOSH
DWOOSH
AHHH!!
BWOOSH
ZSH
ZSH
ZSH
SHIBUKI
GA-GNK
GA-GNK
ZSH
AHH, MY ARM IS GETTING SUCKED IN!
GENDA-SAN!

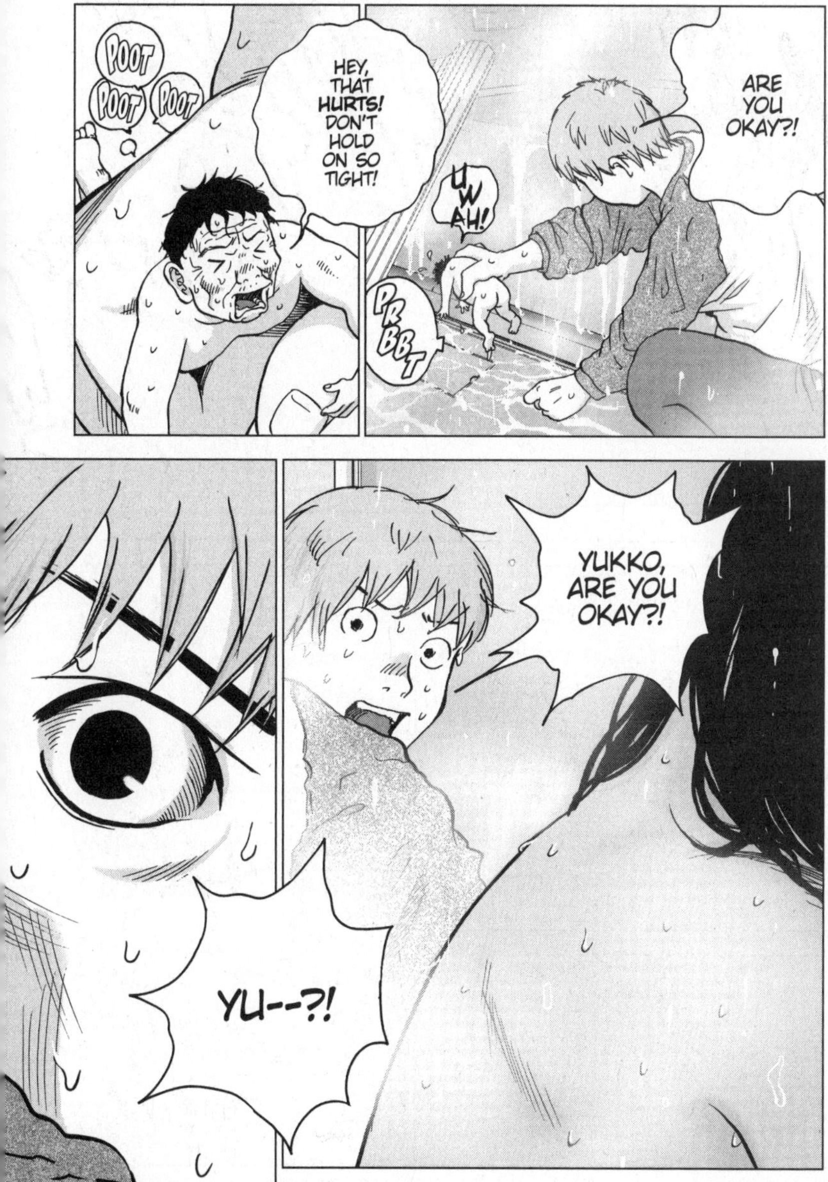
ARE YOU OKAY?!
UWAH!
PRBBT
HEY, THAT HURTS! DON'T HOLD ON SO TIGHT!
POOT
POOT
POOT
YUKKO, ARE YOU OKAY?!
YU--?!

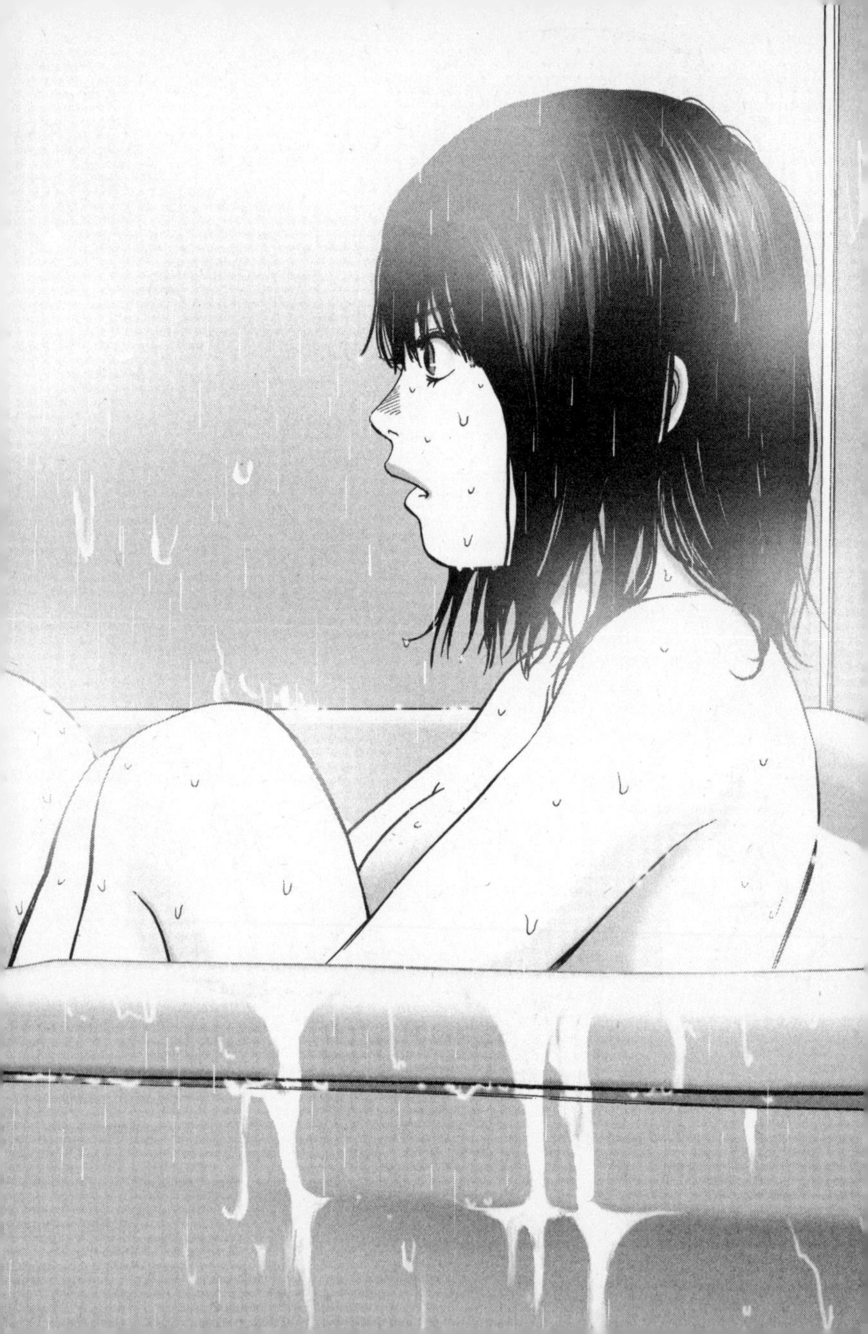

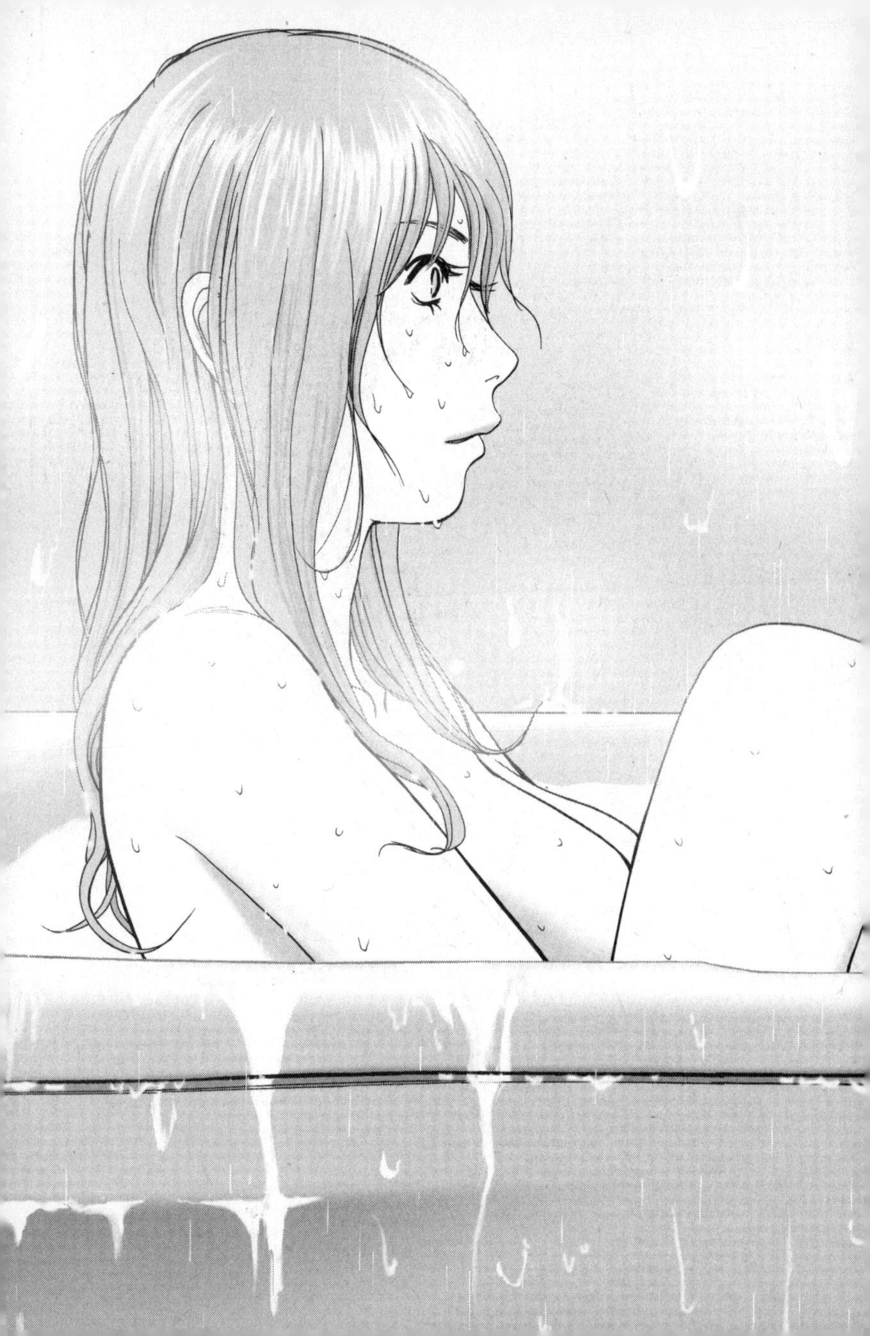

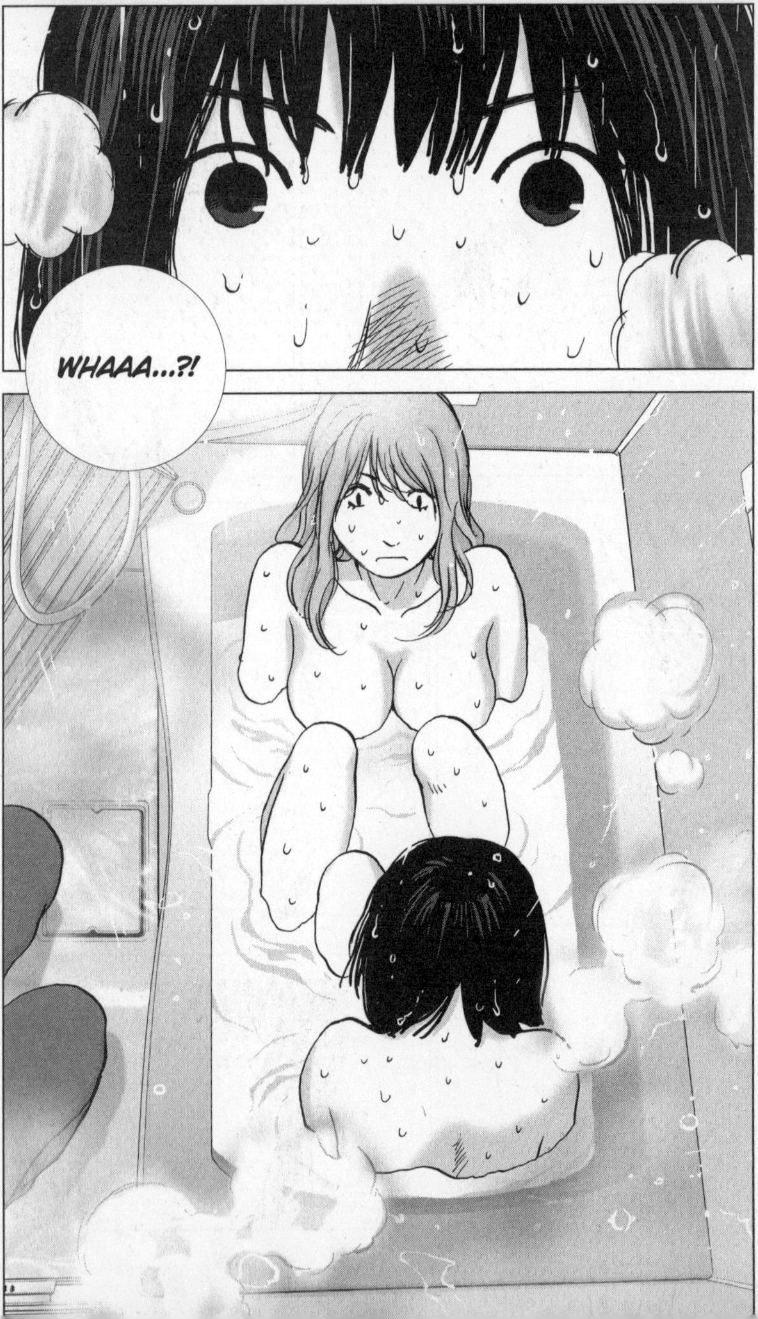
WHAAA...?!

ピトン
PLIP
ポチュン
PLISH
PLAP
ペタ
ペタ
PLAP
ペタ
PLAP
KA-
PLOOSH

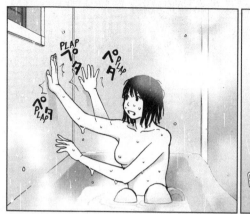

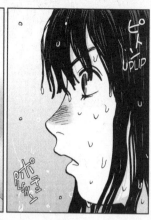

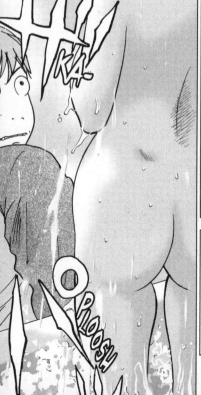

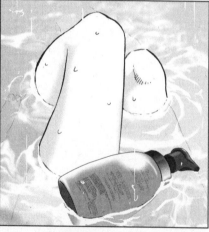

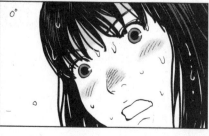

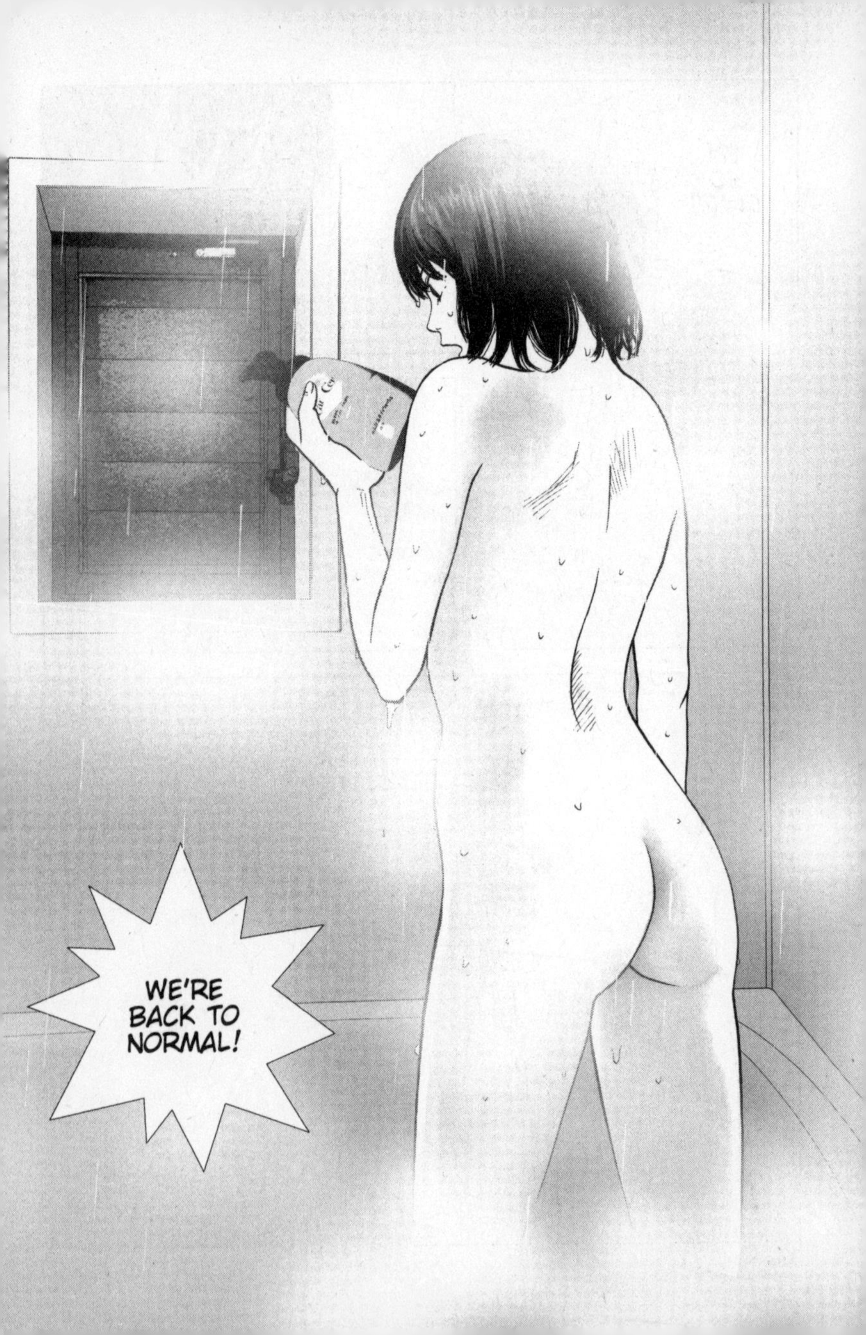
WE'RE BACK TO NORMAL!

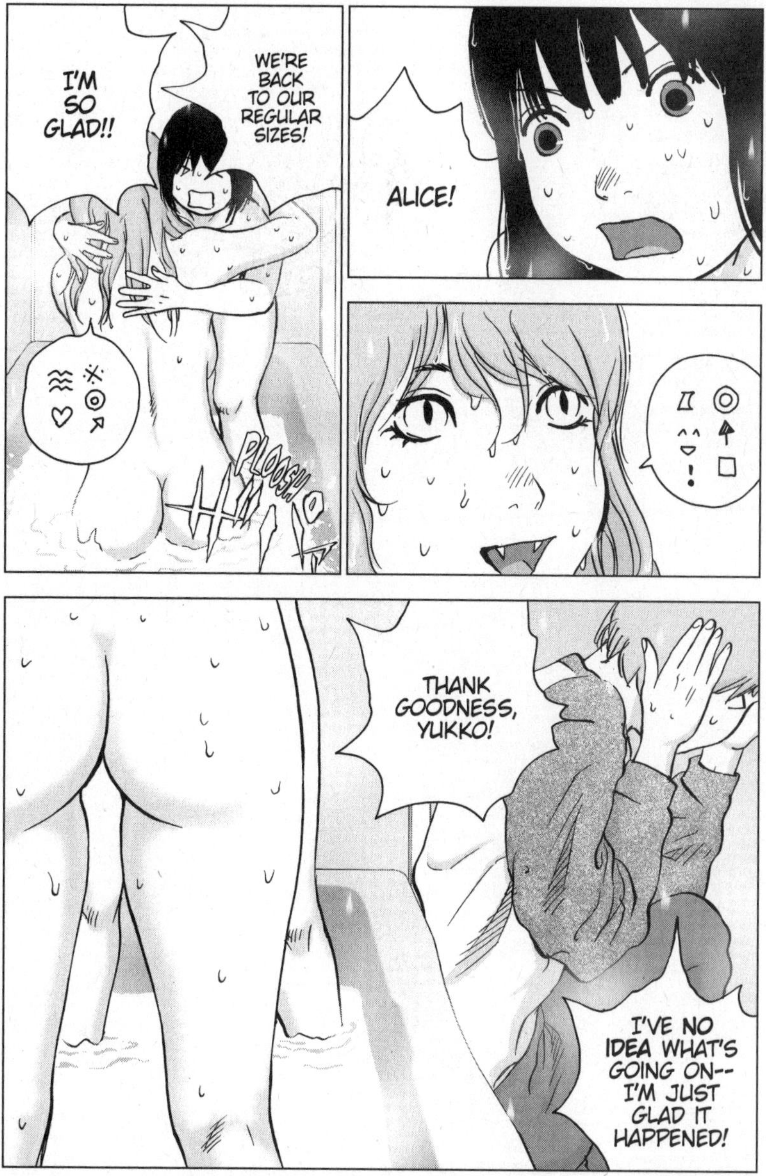
ALICE!
WE'RE BACK TO OUR REGULAR SIZES!
I'M SO GLAD!!
PLOOSH
THANK GOODNESS, YUKKO!
I'VE NO IDEA WHAT'S GOING ON-- I'M JUST GLAD IT HAPPENED!

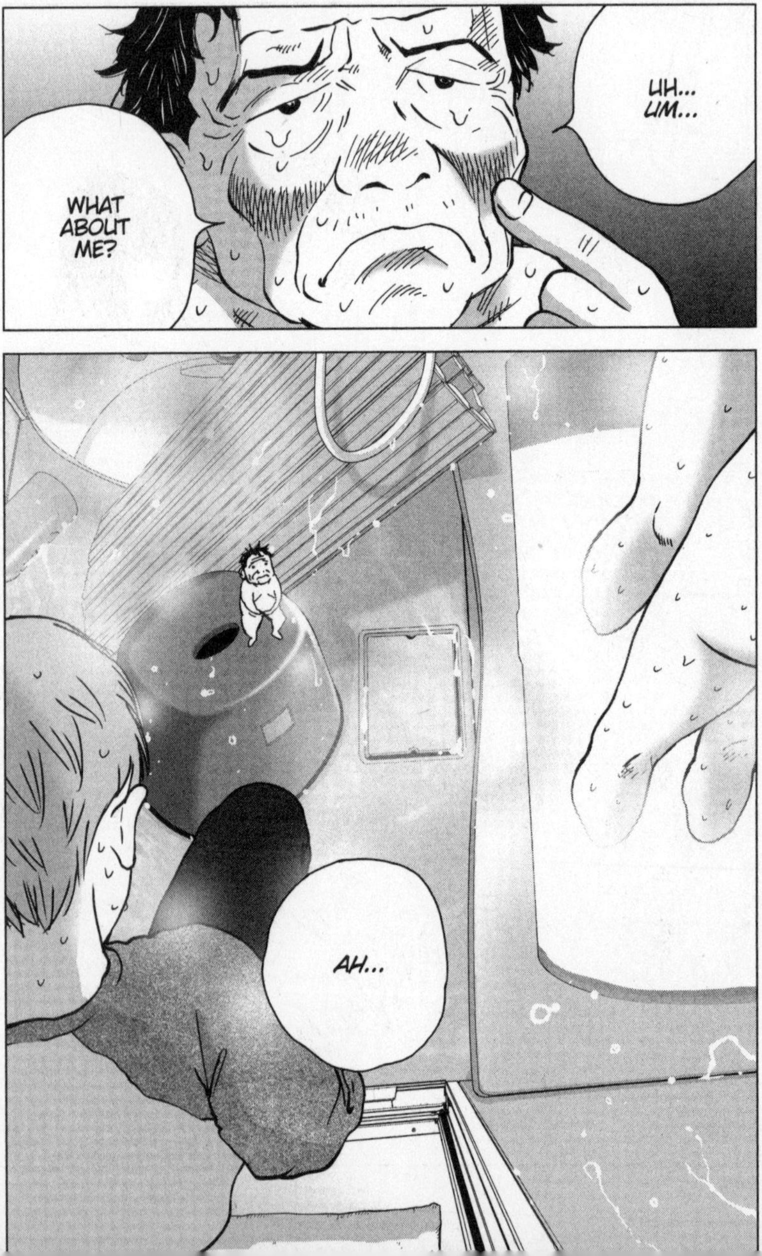
UH... UM...
WHAT ABOUT ME?
AH...

Chapter 24: The Gifted Ones

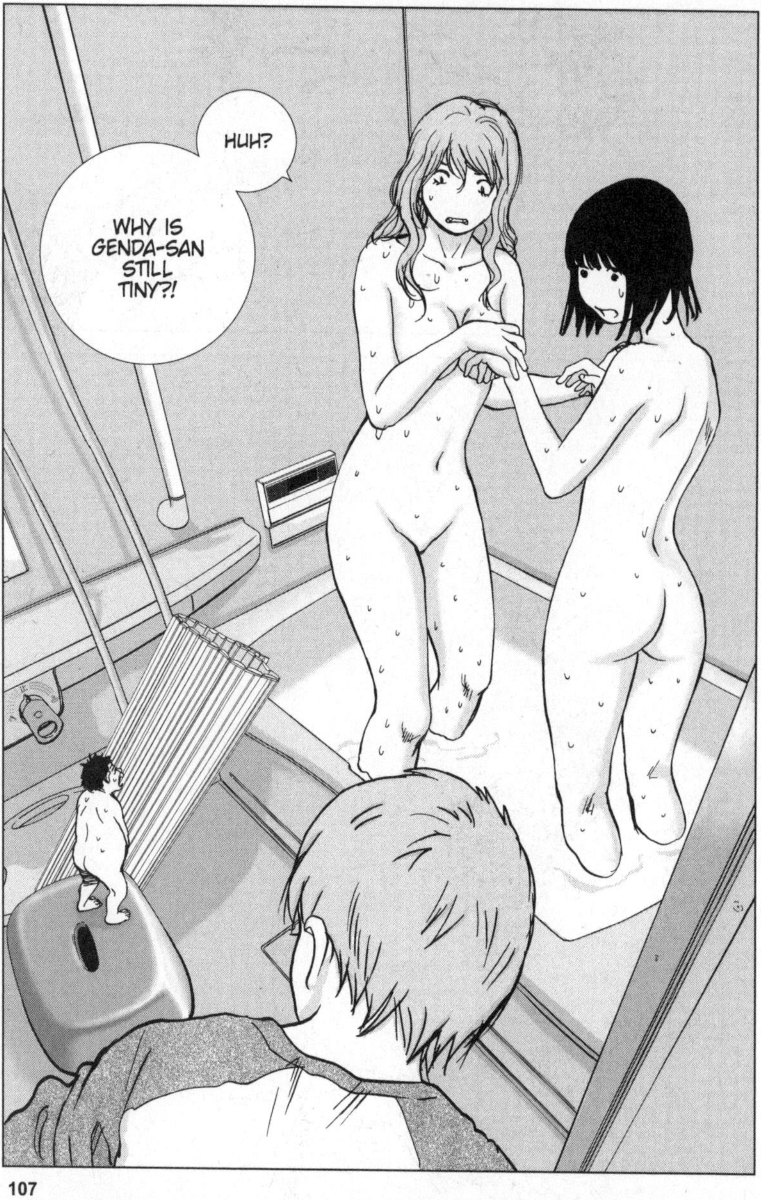
HUH?
WHY IS GENDA-SAN STILL TINY?!

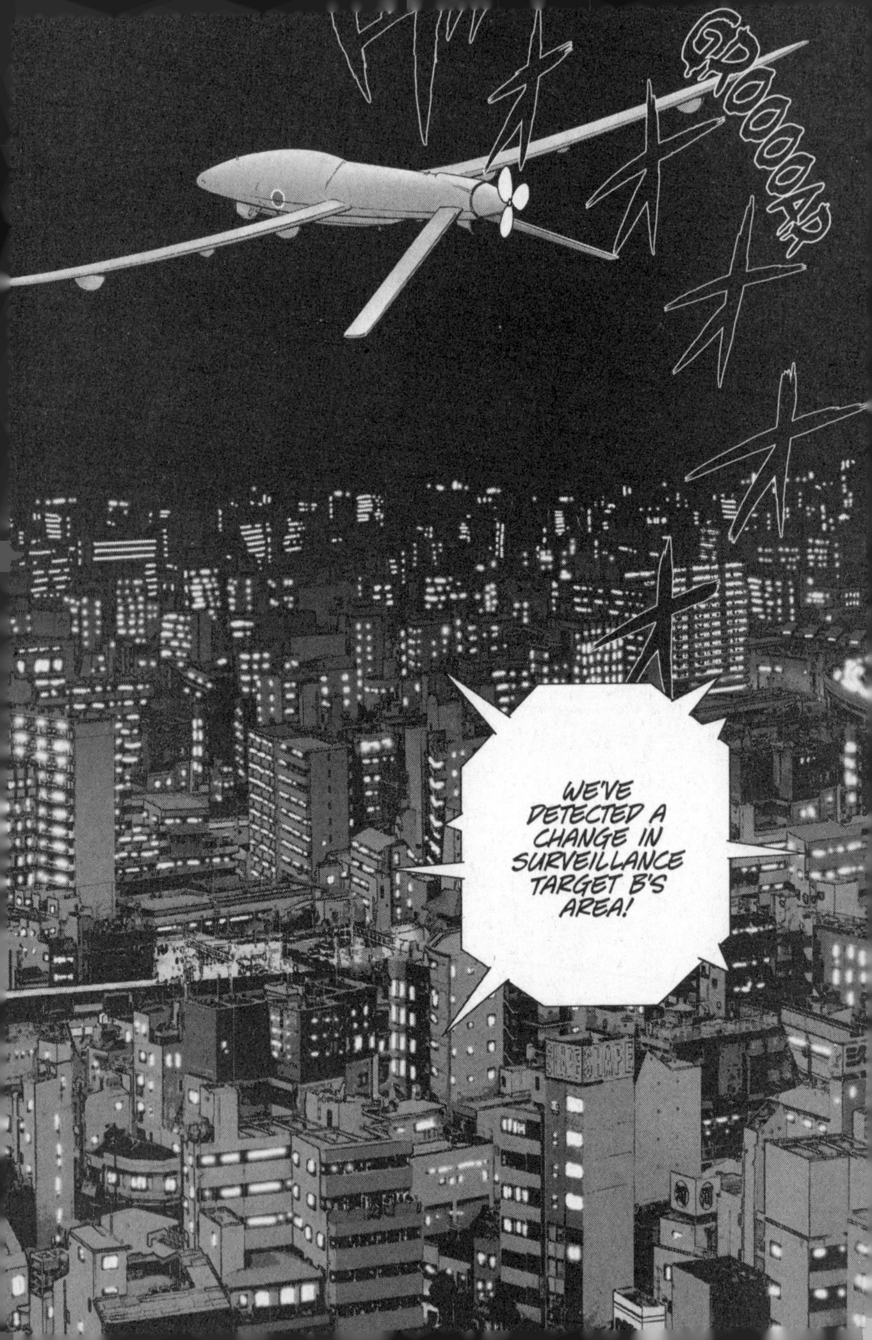
GROOOOAR
WE'VE DETECTED A CHANGE IN SURVEILLANCE TARGET B'S AREA!

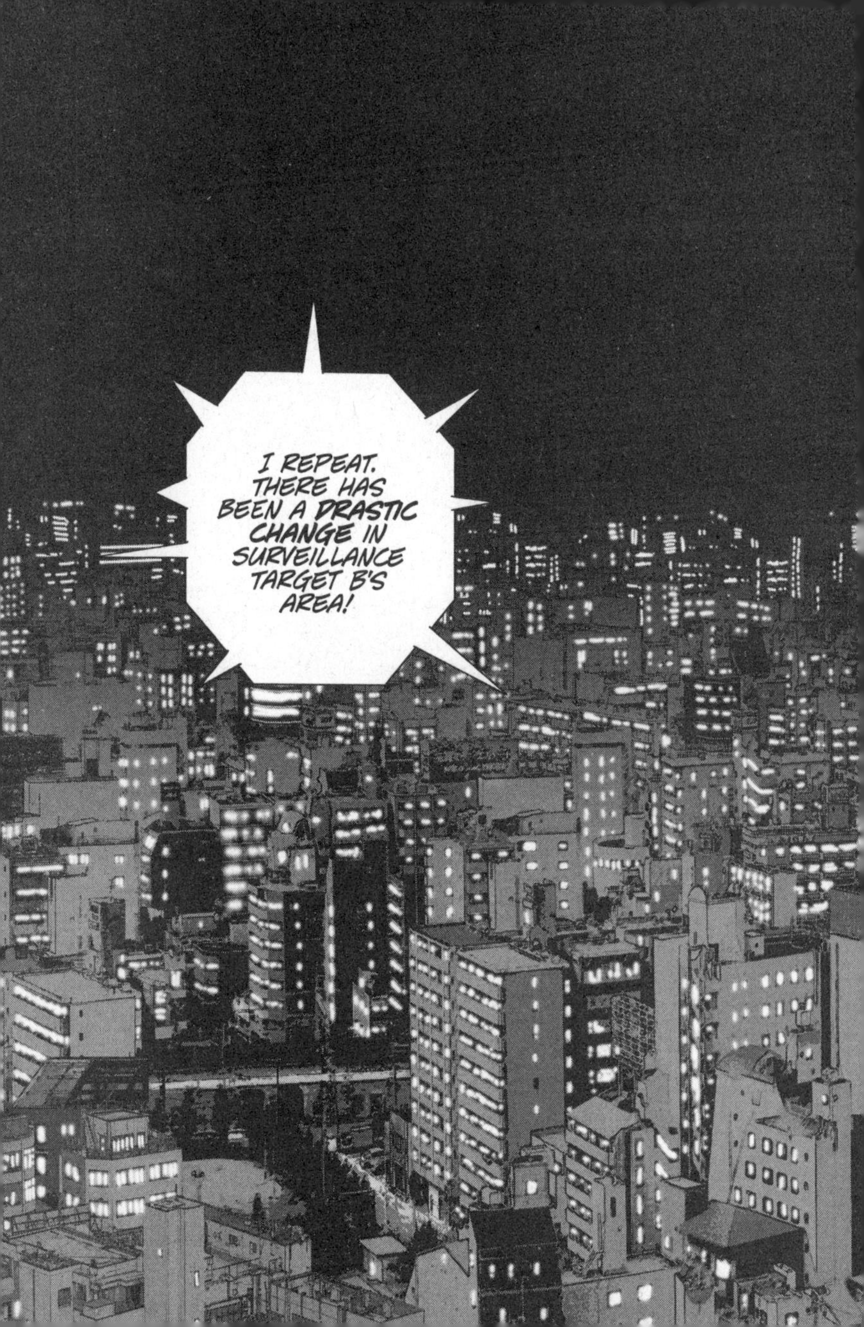
I REPEAT. THERE HAS BEEN A DRASTIC CHANGE IN SURVEILLANCE TARGET B'S AREA!

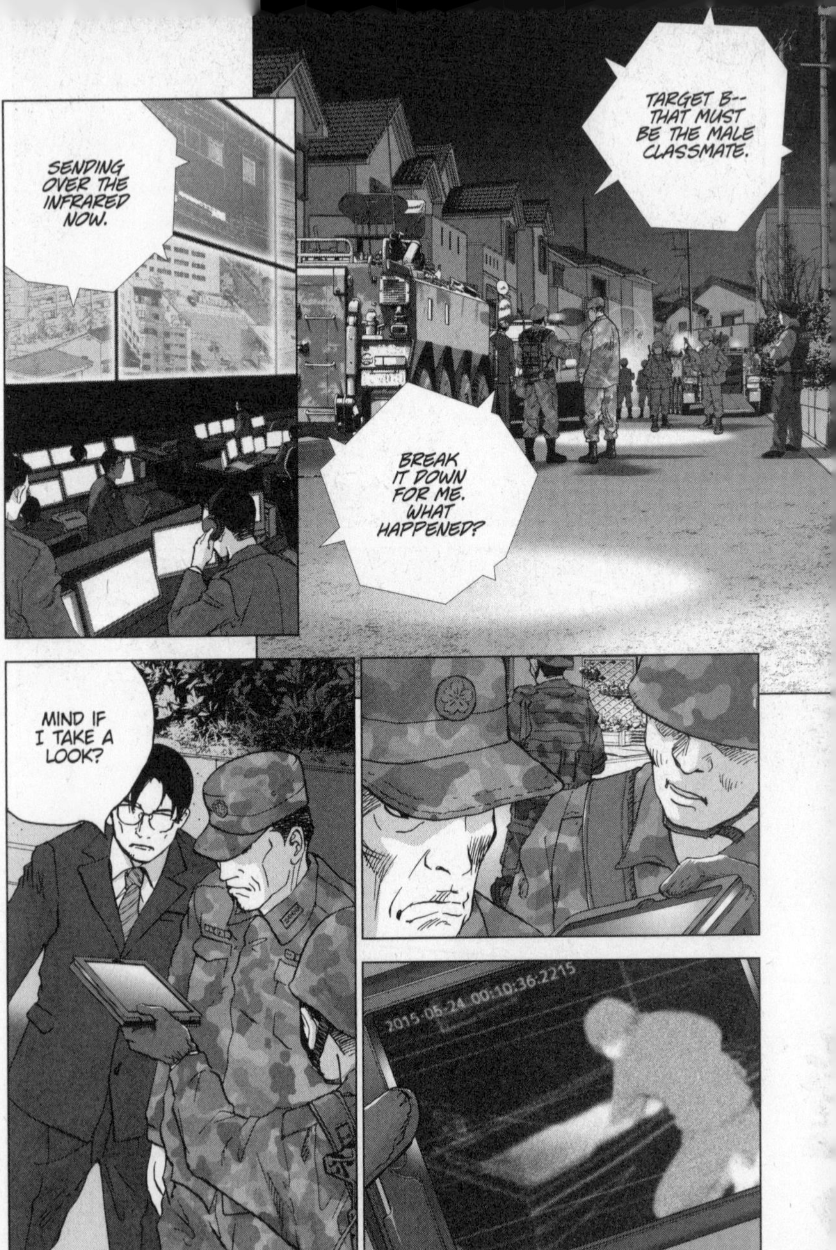
TARGET B-- THAT MUST BE THE MALE CLASSMATE.
BREAK IT DOWN FOR ME. WHAT HAPPENED?
SENDING OVER THE INFRARED NOW.
2015-06-24 00:10:36:2215
MIND IF I TAKE A LOOK?

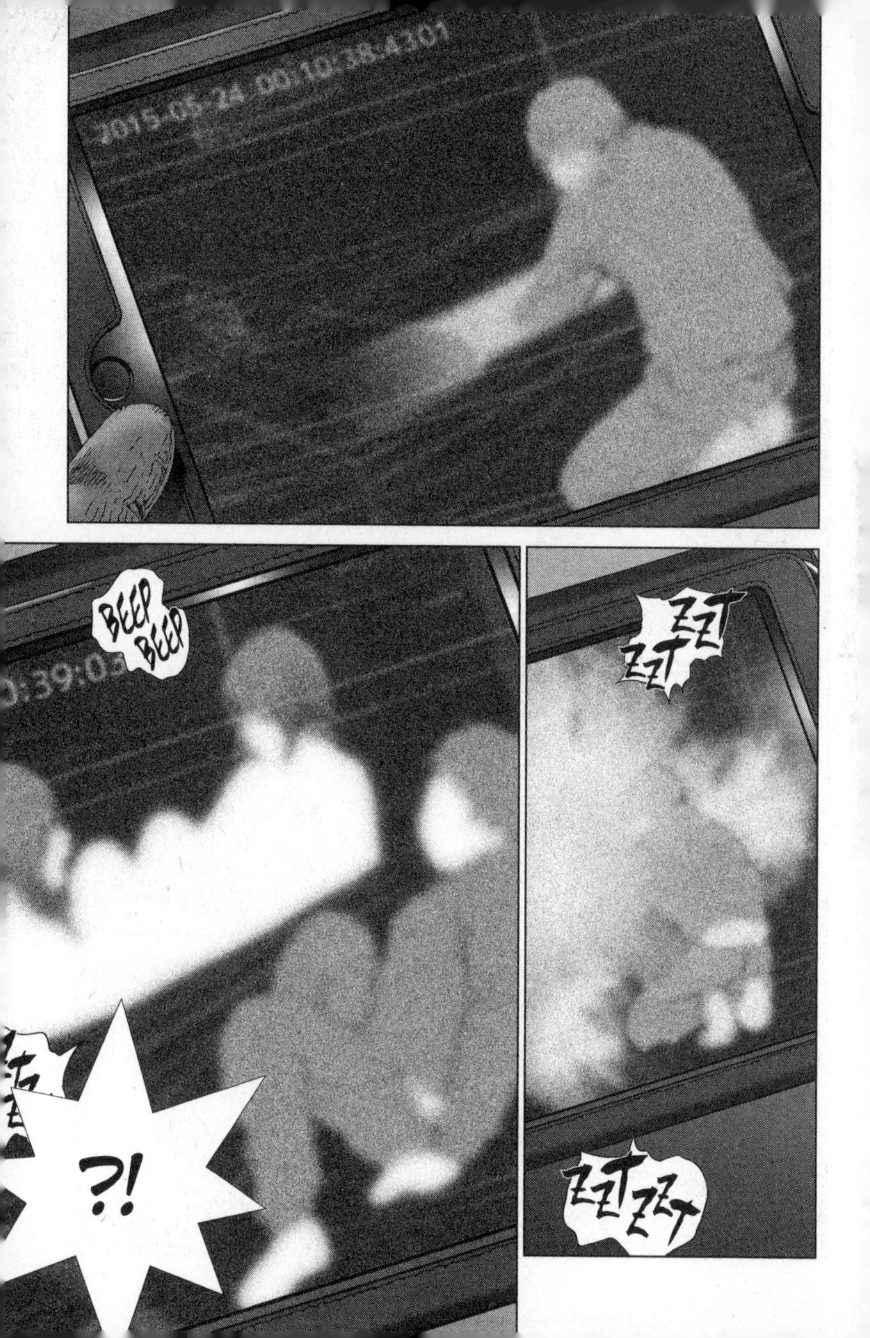
2015-05-24 00:10:38.4301
ZZT ZZT
ZZT ZZT
BEEP BEEP
0:39:03
?!

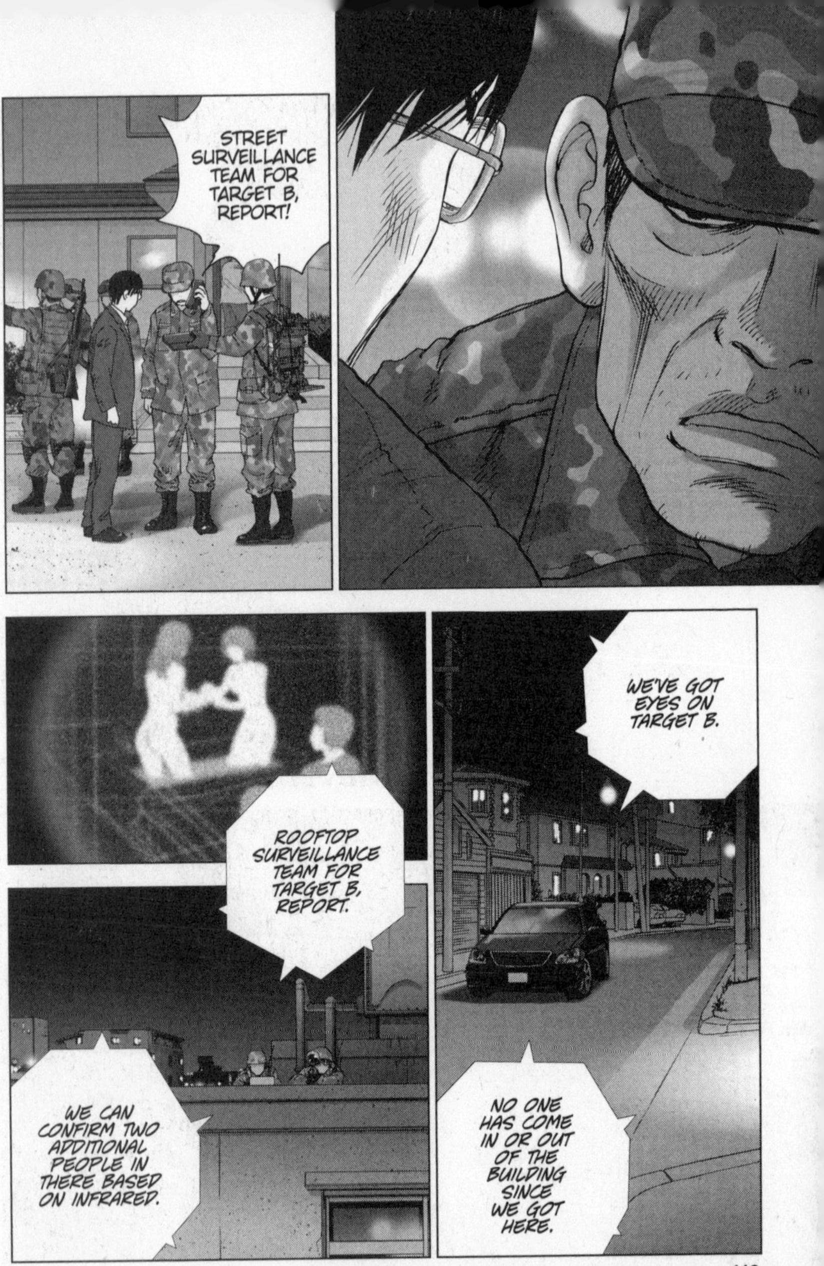
STREET SURVEILLANCE TEAM FOR TARGET B, REPORT!
WE'VE GOT EYES ON TARGET B.
NO ONE HAS COME IN OR OUT OF THE BUILDING SINCE WE GOT HERE.
ROOFTOP SURVEILLANCE TEAM FOR TARGET B, REPORT.
WE CAN CONFIRM TWO ADDITIONAL PEOPLE IN THERE BASED ON INFRARED.

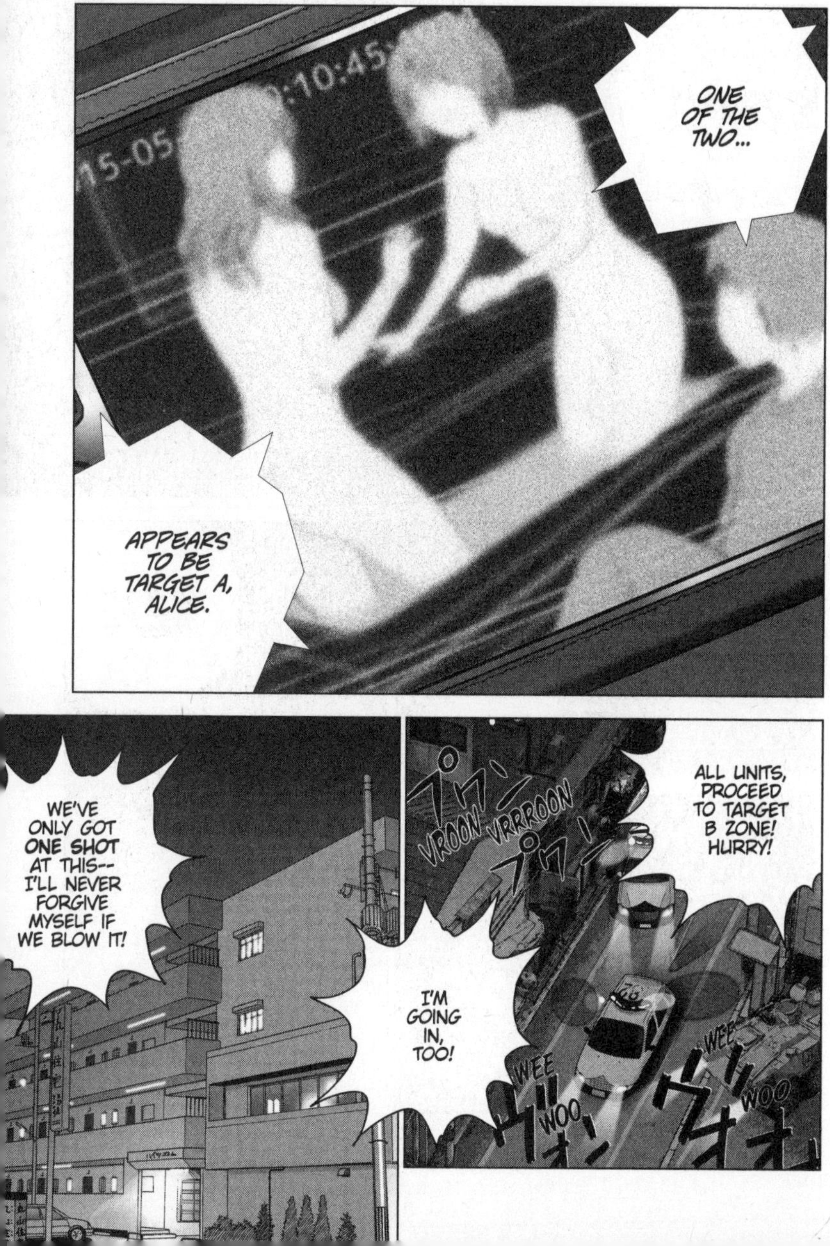
ONE OF THE TWO...
APPEARS TO BE TARGET A, ALICE.
ALL UNITS, PROCEED TO TARGET B ZONE! HURRY!
VROOON
VRRROON
WEE WOO
WEE WOO
WE'VE ONLY GOT ONE SHOT AT THIS-- I'LL NEVER FORGIVE MYSELF IF WE BLOW IT!
I'M GOING IN, TOO!

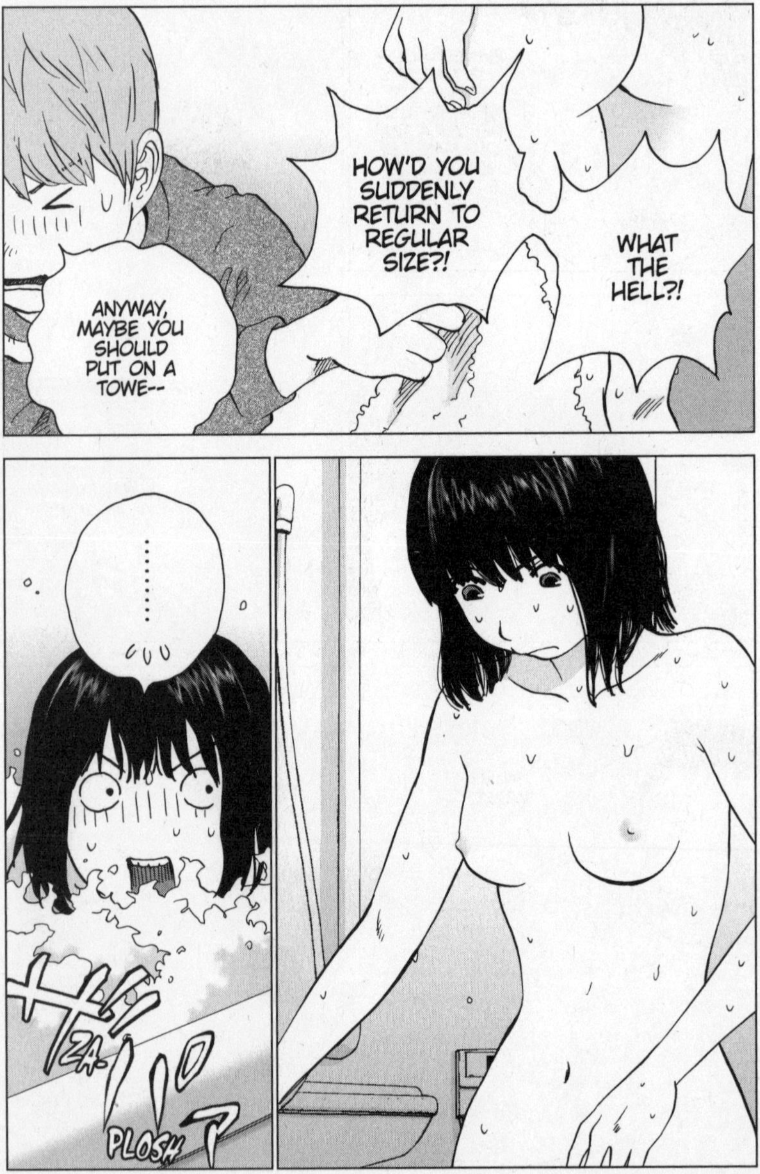
WHAT THE HELL?!
HOW'D YOU SUDDENLY RETURN TO REGULAR SIZE?!
ANYWAY, MAYBE YOU SHOULD PUT ON A TOWE--
......
ZA-
PLOSH

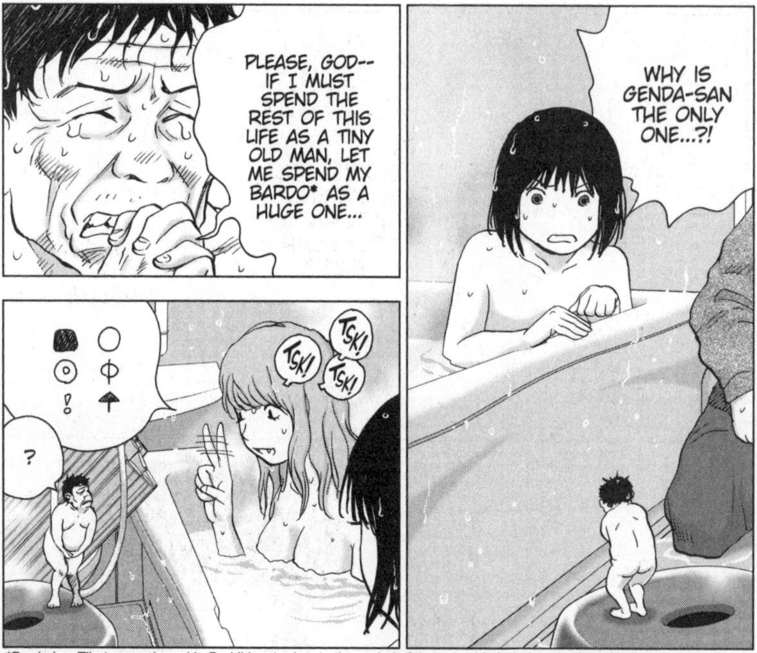
WHY IS GENDA-SAN THE ONLY ONE...?!
PLEASE, GOD-- IF I MUST SPEND THE REST OF THIS LIFE AS A TINY OLD MAN, LET ME SPEND MY BARDO* AS A HUGE ONE...
TSK! TSK! TSK!
?
!

*Bardo is a Tibetan word used in Buddhism to denote the period of time spent in between death and rebirth.

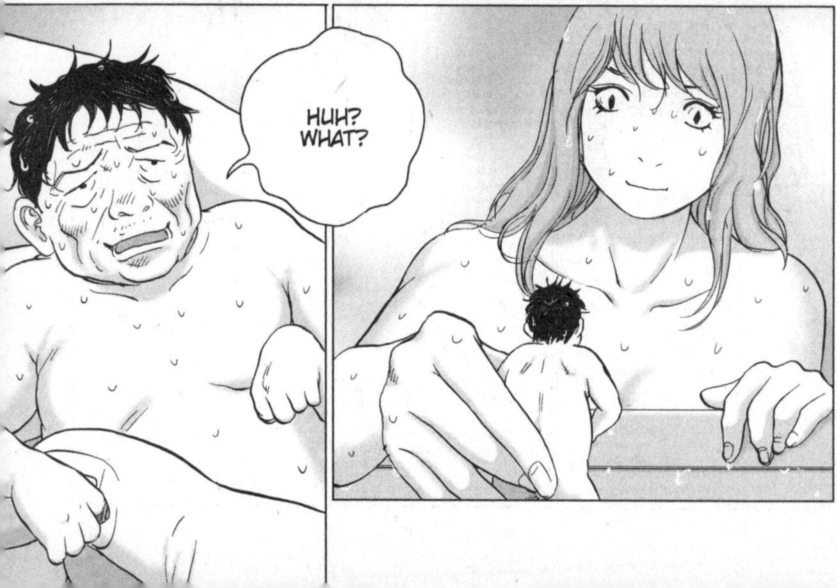
HUH? WHAT?

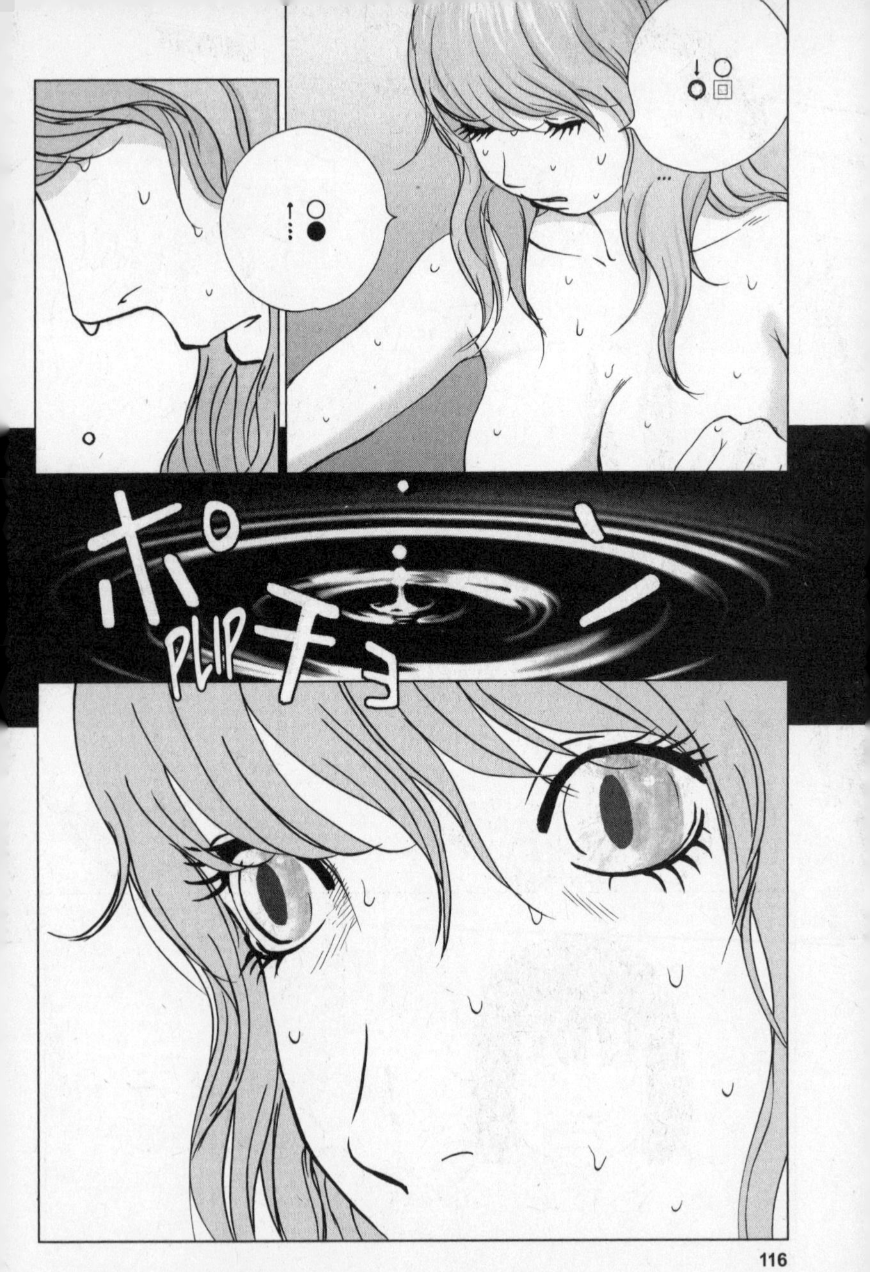
ポチョーン
PLIP

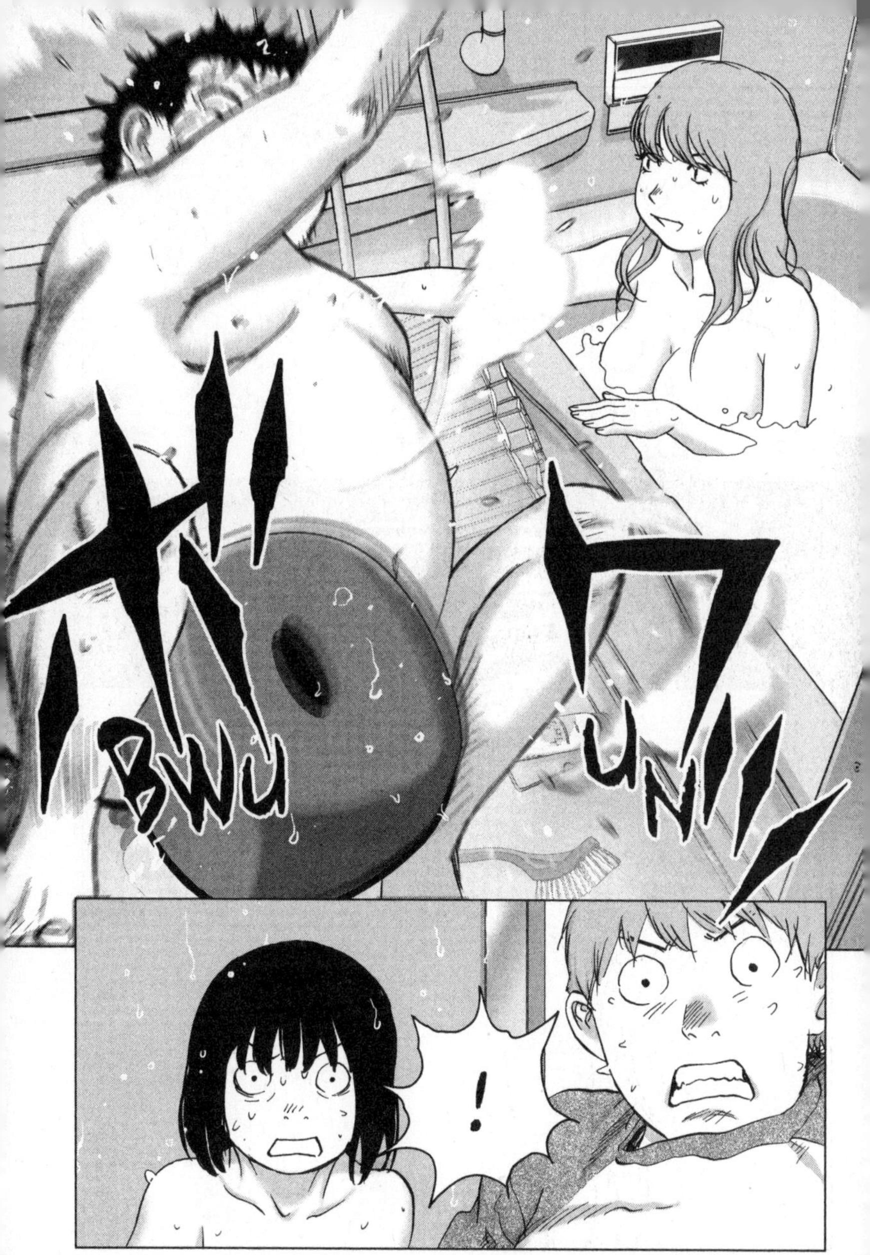
BWU
UN!!
!

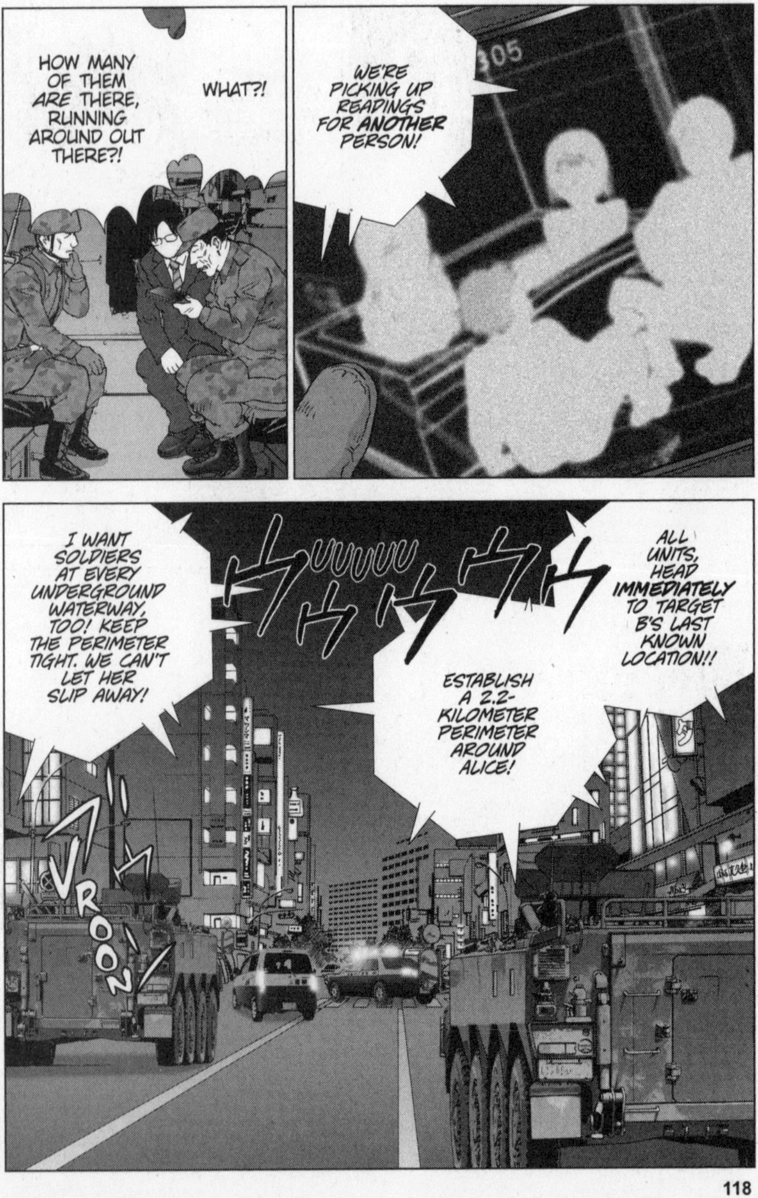
WE'RE PICKING UP READINGS FOR ANOTHER PERSON!
WHAT?!
HOW MANY OF THEM ARE THERE, RUNNING AROUND OUT THERE?!
ALL UNITS, HEAD IMMEDIATELY TO TARGET B'S LAST KNOWN LOCATION!!
UUUUUU
ESTABLISH A 2.2-KILOMETER PERIMETER AROUND ALICE!
I WANT SOLDIERS AT EVERY UNDERGROUND WATERWAY, TOO! KEEP THE PERIMETER TIGHT. WE CAN'T LET HER SLIP AWAY!
VROON!

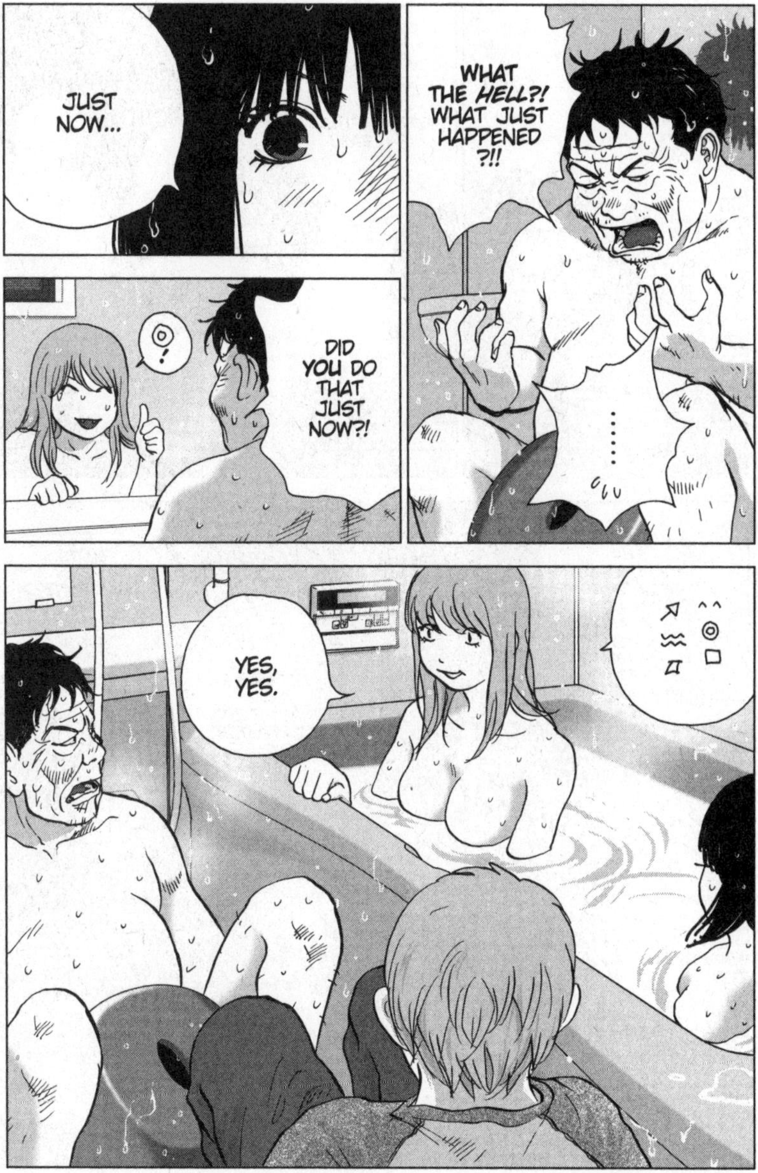
WHAT THE *HELL*?! WHAT JUST HAPPENED ?!!
......
JUST NOW...
DID YOU DO THAT JUST NOW?!
YES, YES.

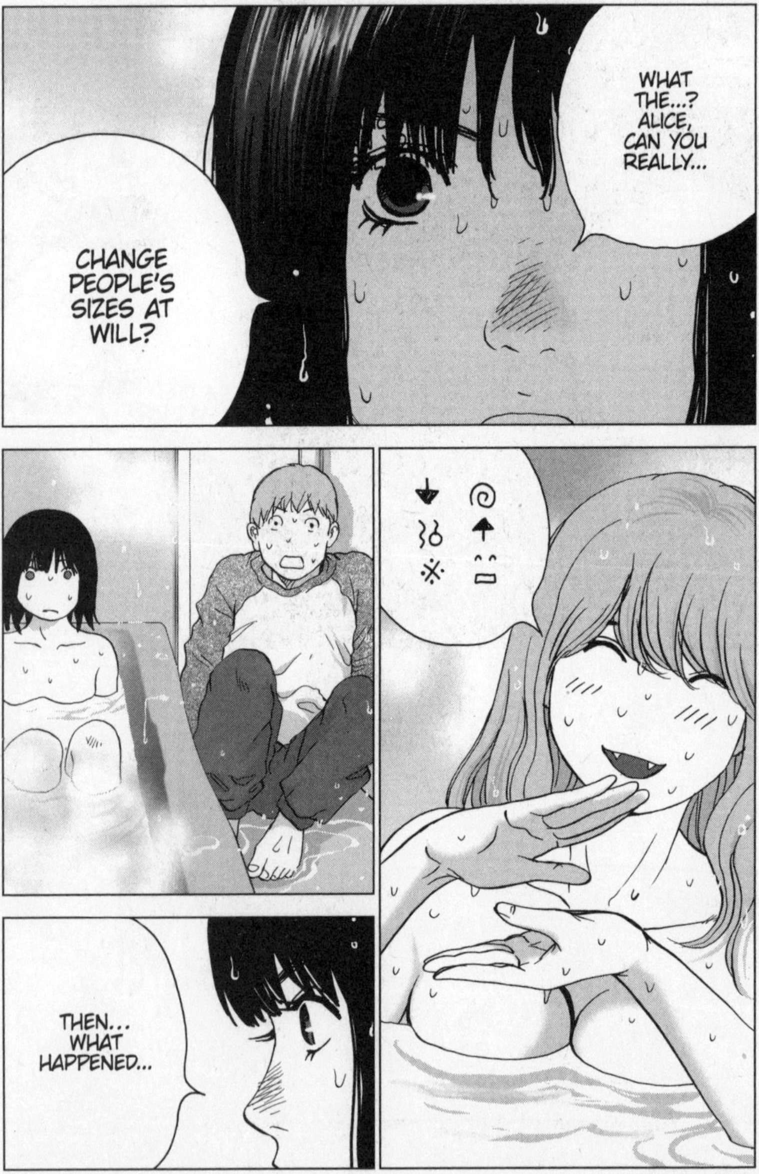
WHAT THE...? ALICE, CAN YOU REALLY...
CHANGE PEOPLE'S SIZES AT WILL?
THEN... WHAT HAPPENED...

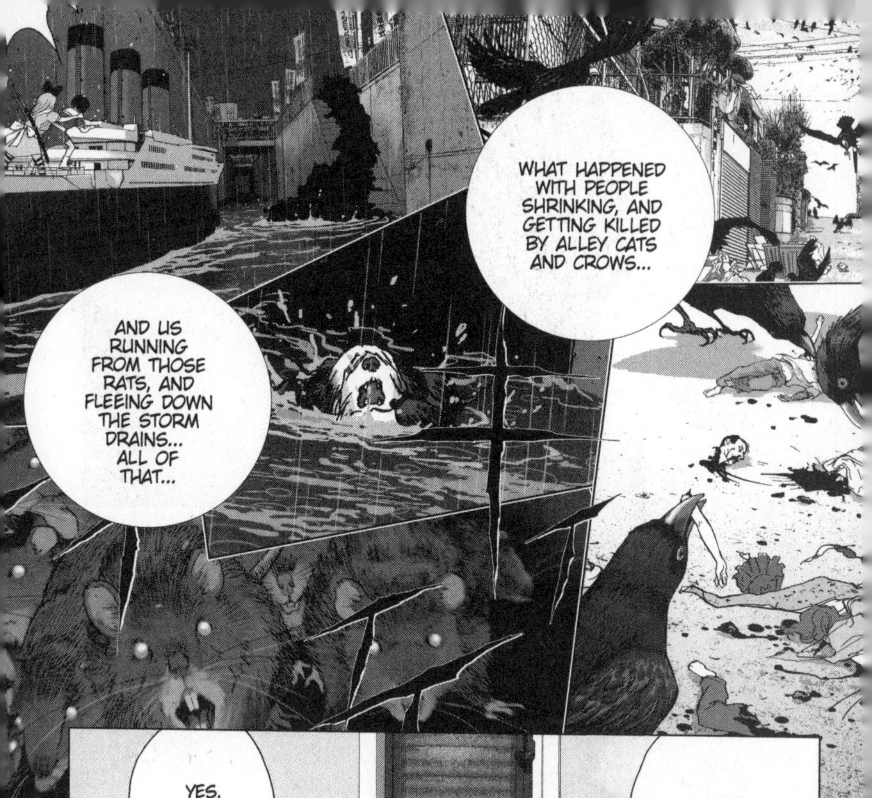
WHAT HAPPENED WITH PEOPLE SHRINKING, AND GETTING KILLED BY ALLEY CATS AND CROWS...
AND US RUNNING FROM THOSE RATS, AND FLEEING DOWN THE STORM DRAINS... ALL OF THAT...

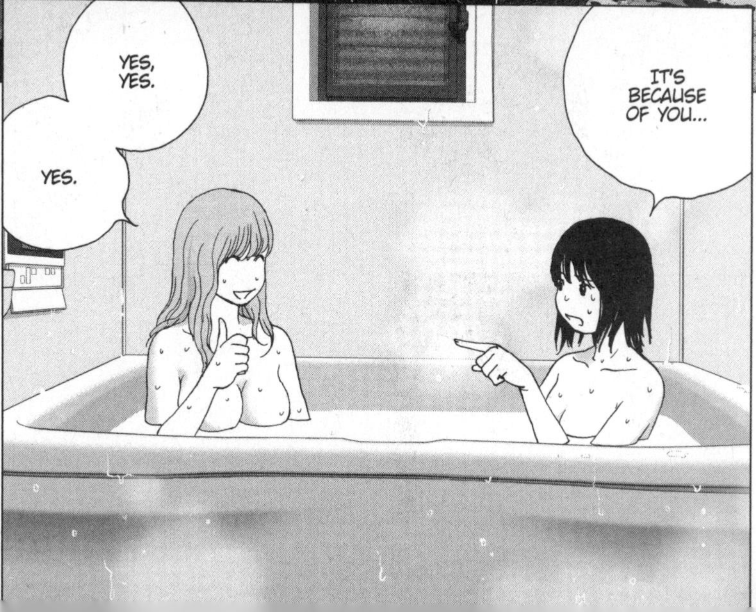
IT'S BECAUSE OF YOU...
YES, YES.
YES.

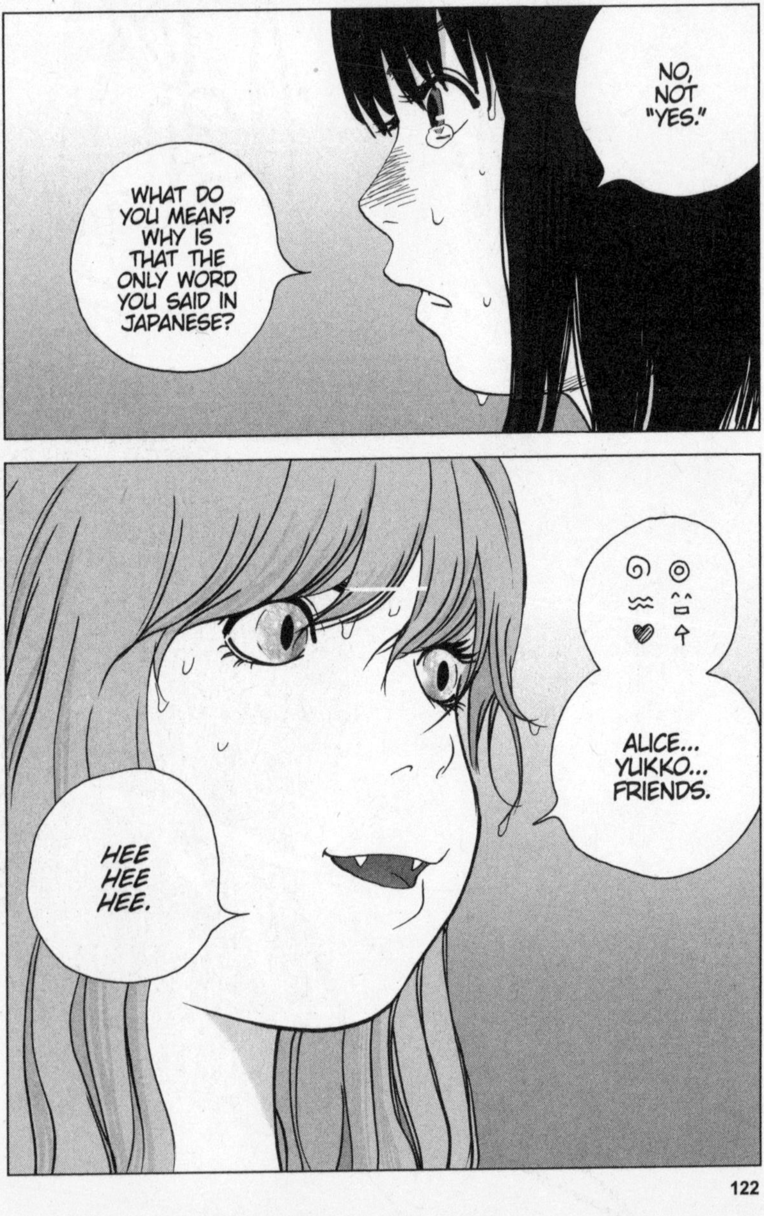
NO, NOT "YES."
WHAT DO YOU MEAN? WHY IS THAT THE ONLY WORD YOU SAID IN JAPANESE?
ALICE... YUKKO... FRIENDS.
HEE HEE HEE.

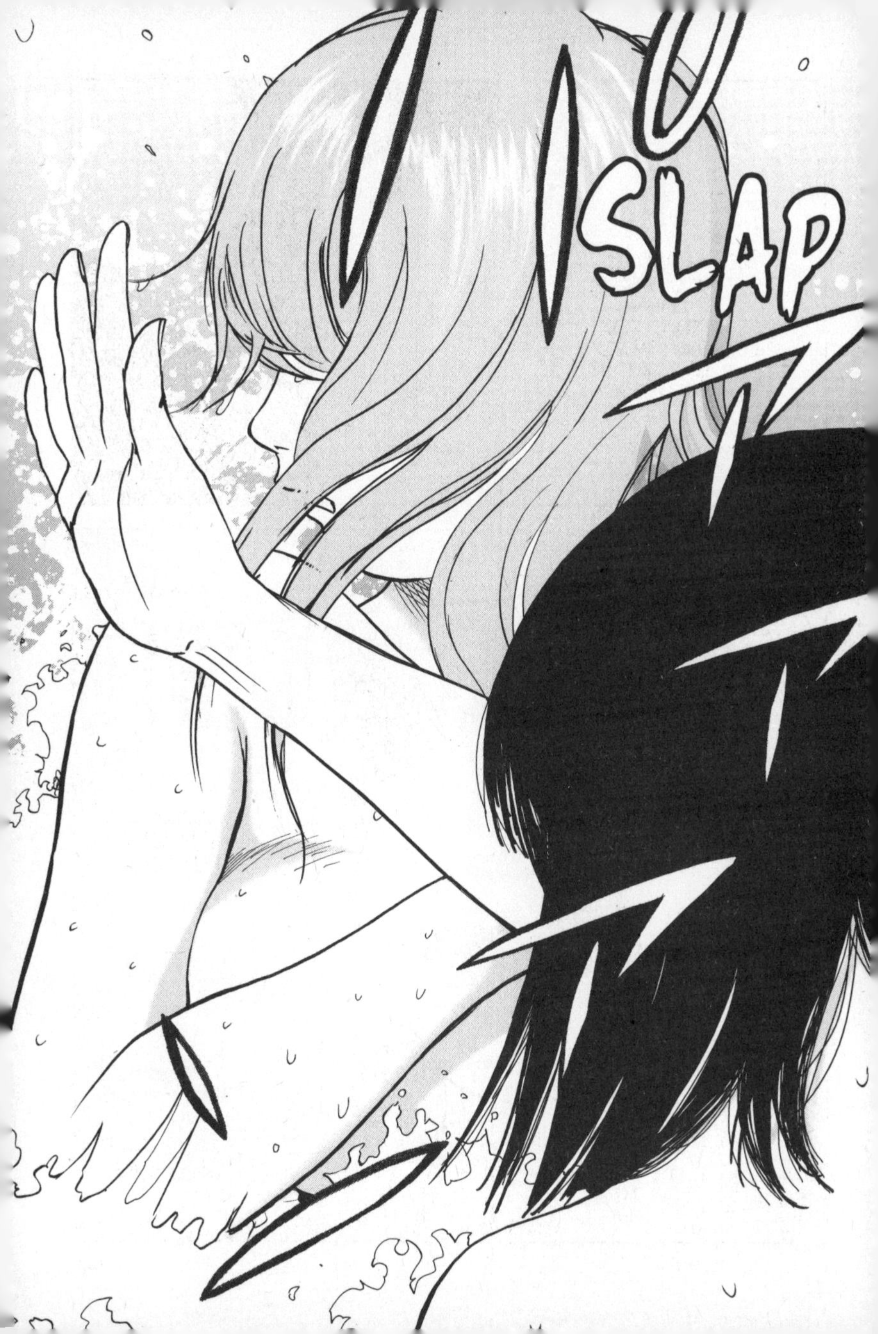
SLAP

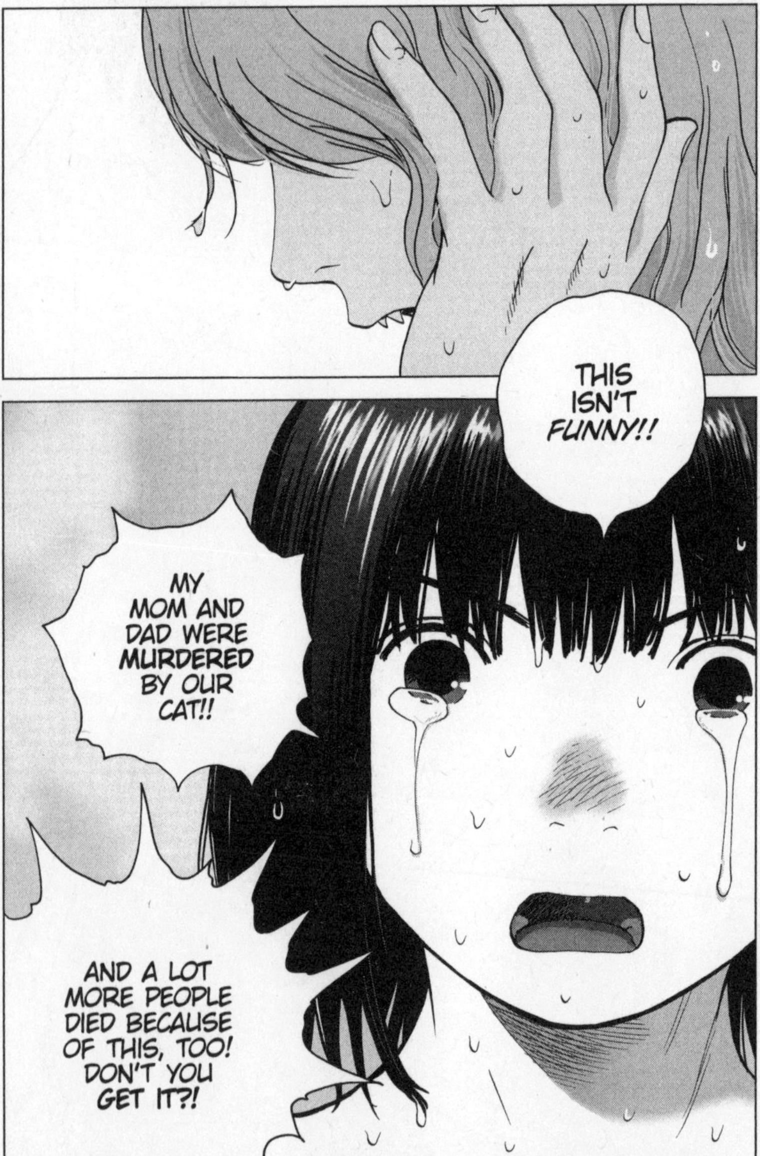
THIS ISN'T FUNNY!!
MY MOM AND DAD WERE MURDERED BY OUR CAT!!
AND A LOT MORE PEOPLE DIED BECAUSE OF THIS, TOO! DON'T YOU GET IT?!

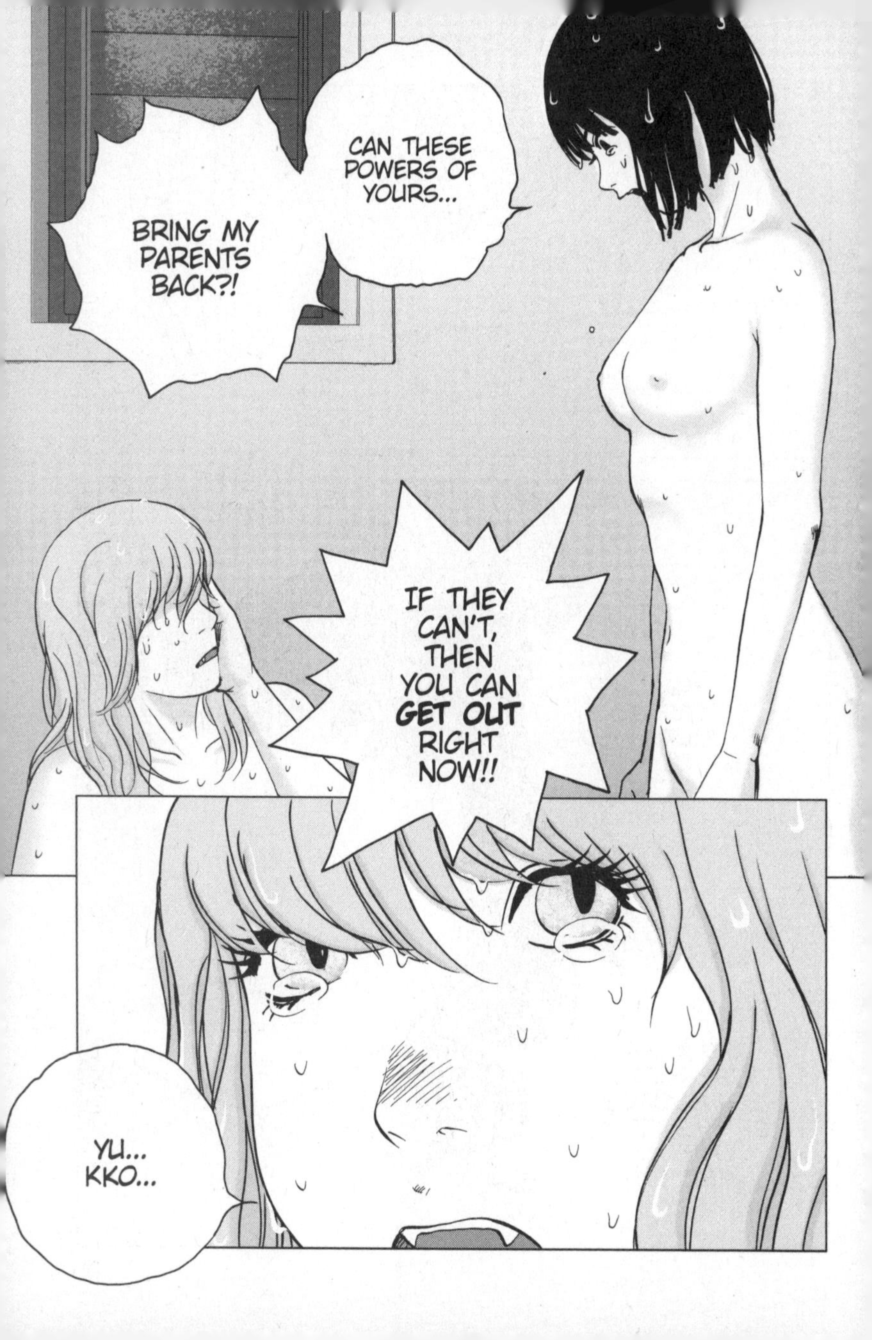
CAN THESE POWERS OF YOURS...
BRING MY PARENTS BACK?!
IF THEY CAN'T, THEN YOU CAN **GET OUT** RIGHT NOW!!
YU... KKO...

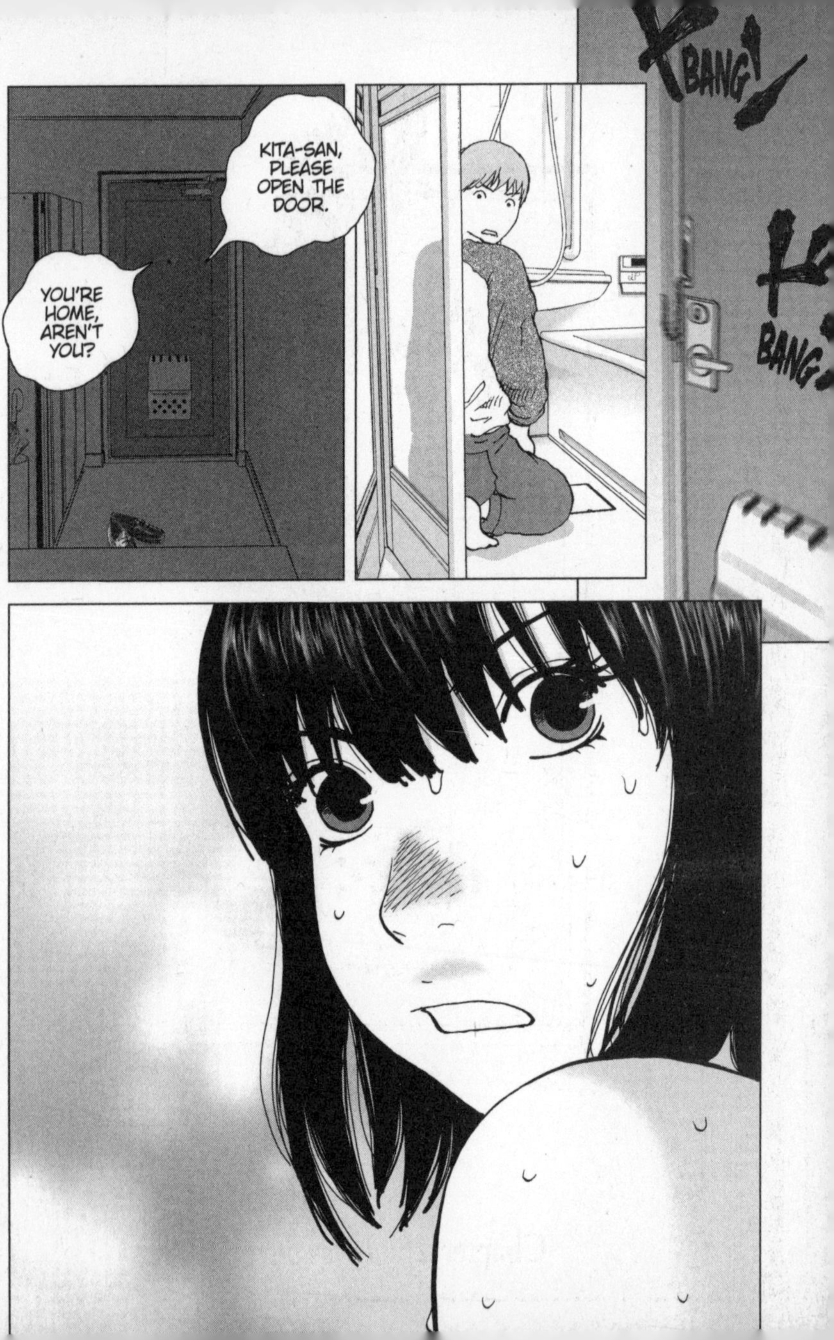
BANG!
BANG
KITA-SAN, PLEASE OPEN THE DOOR.
YOU'RE HOME, AREN'T YOU?

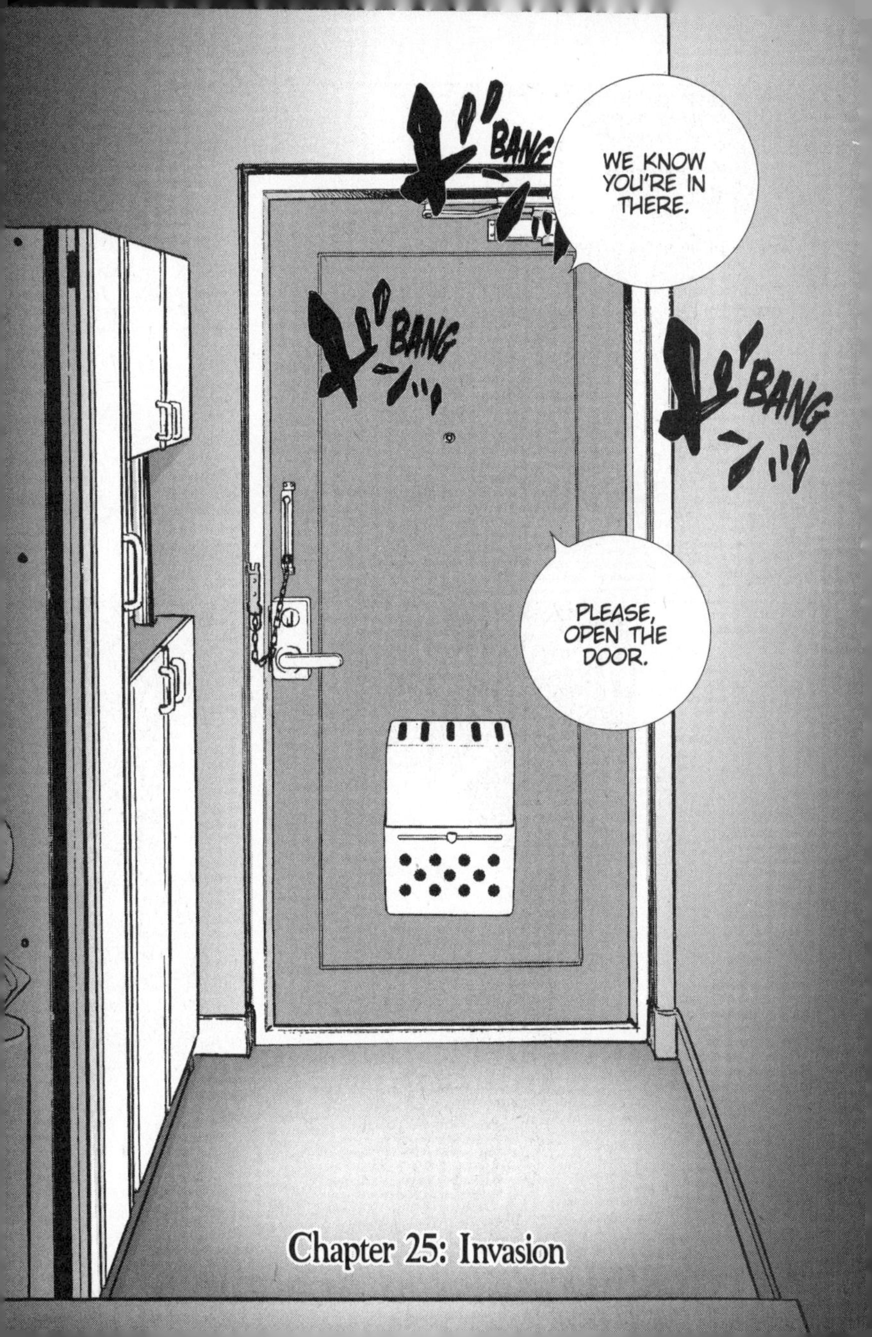
BANG
WE KNOW YOU'RE IN THERE.
BANG
BANG
PLEASE, OPEN THE DOOR.

Chapter 25: Invasion

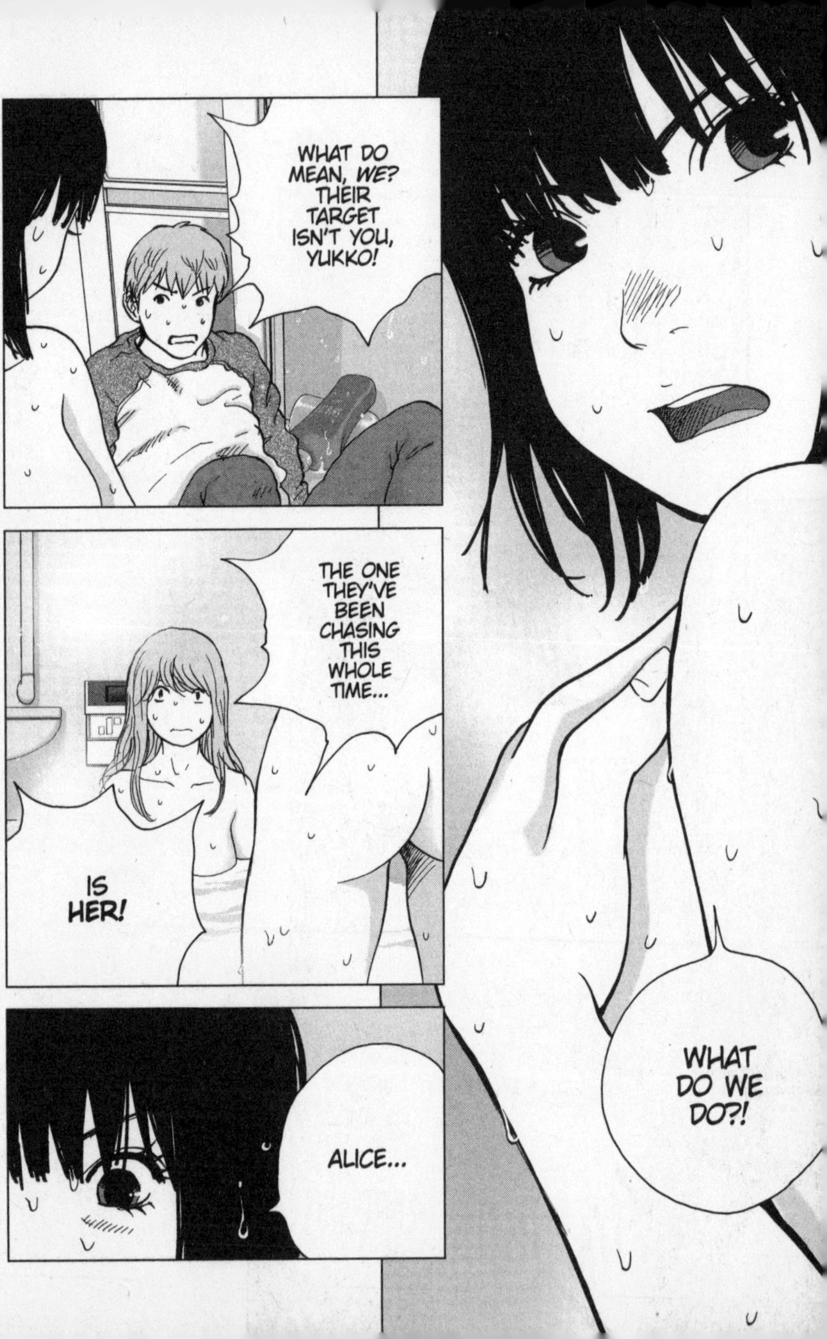
WHAT DO WE DO?!
WHAT DO MEAN, *WE*? THEIR TARGET ISN'T YOU, YUKKO!
THE ONE THEY'VE BEEN CHASING THIS WHOLE TIME...
IS HER!
ALICE...

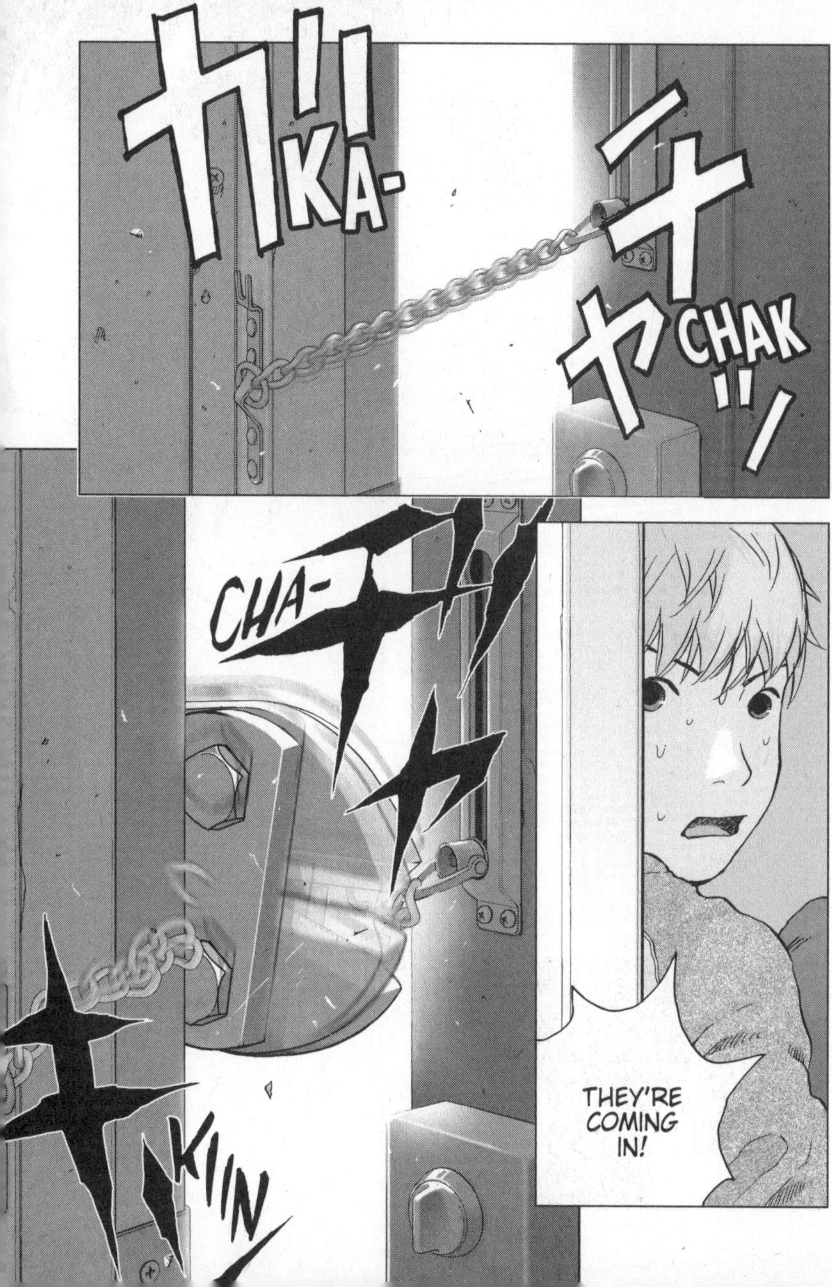
KA-
CHAK
THEY'RE COMING IN!
CHA-
KIIN

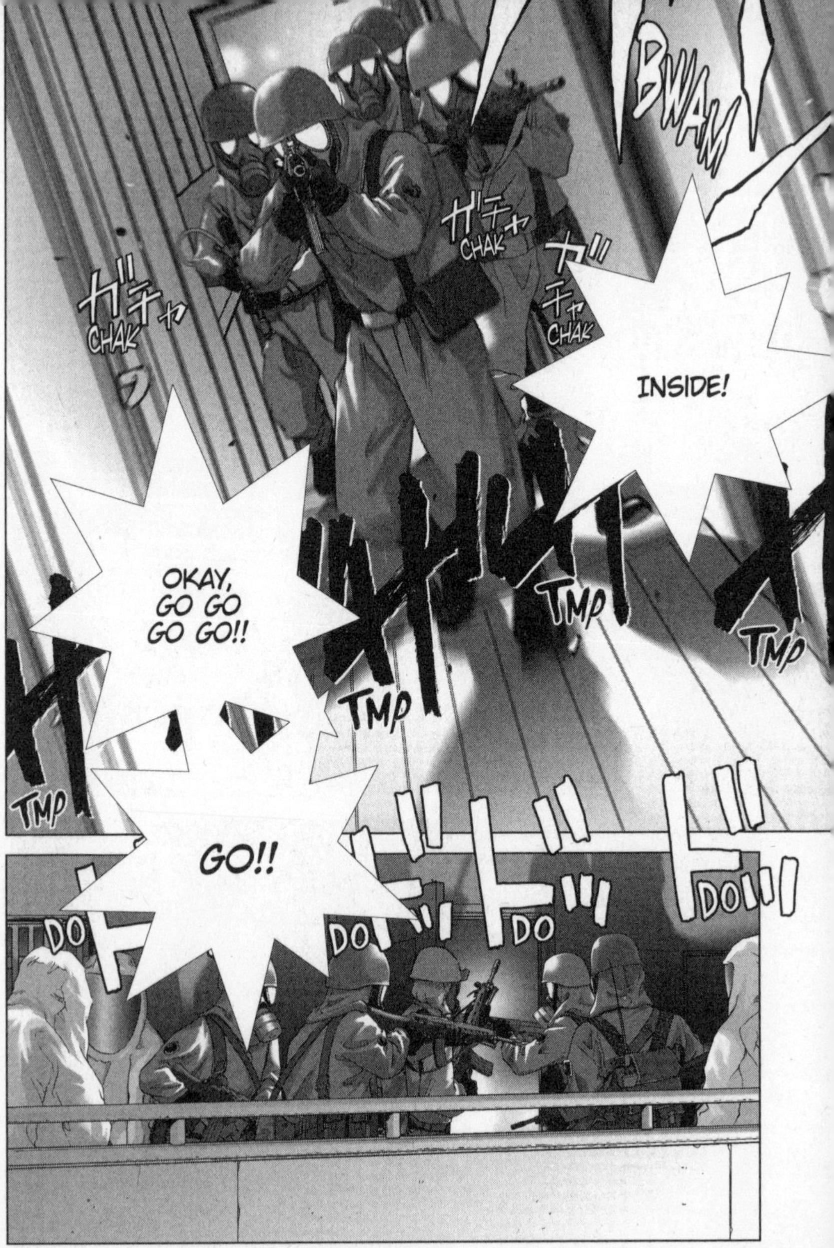

BWAM
ガチャ
CHAK
ガチャ
CHAK
INSIDE!
ガチャ
CHAK
TMP
TMP
OKAY, GO GO GO GO!!
TMP
TMP
GO!!
DO
DO
DO
DO

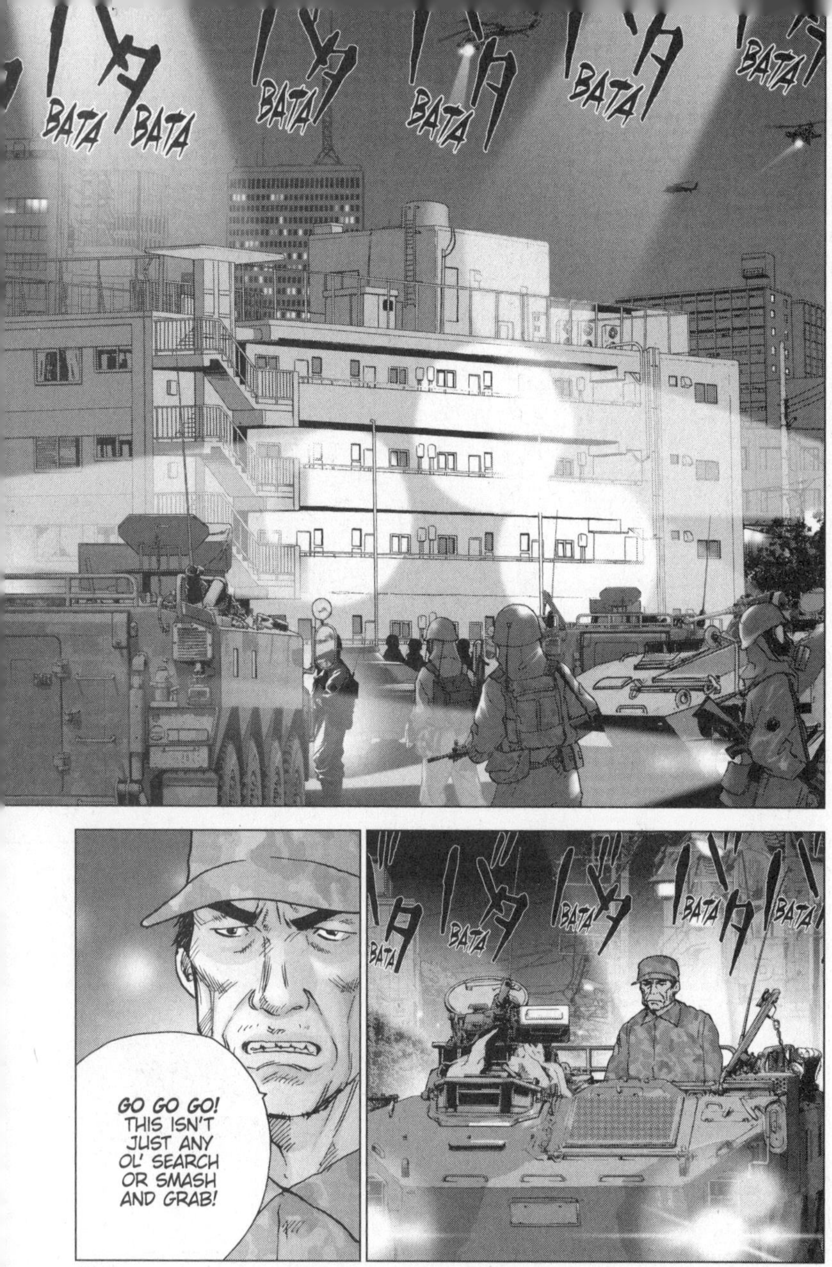
BATA
BATA
BATA
BATA
BATA
BATA
BATA
BATA
BATA
BATA
BATA
GO GO GO! THIS ISN'T JUST ANY OL' SEARCH OR SMASH AND GRAB!

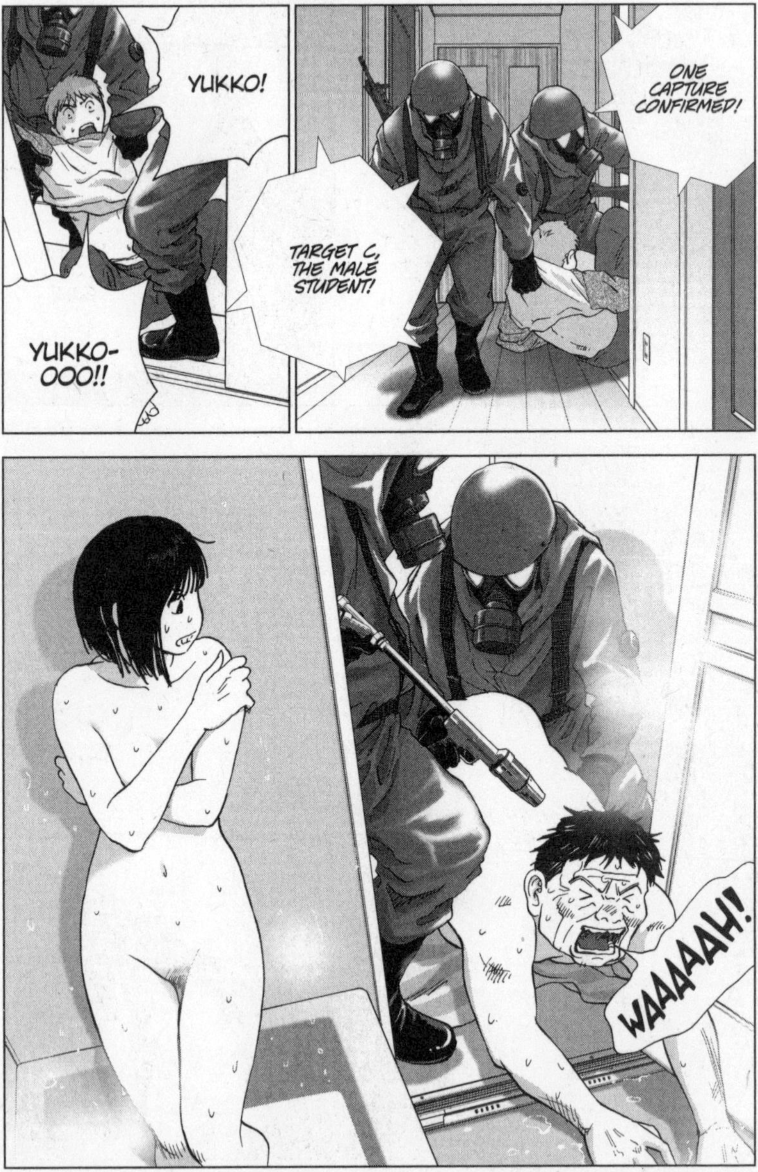
ONE CAPTURE CONFIRMED!
TARGET C, THE MALE STUDENT!
YUKKO!
YUKKO-OOO!!
WAAAAAH!

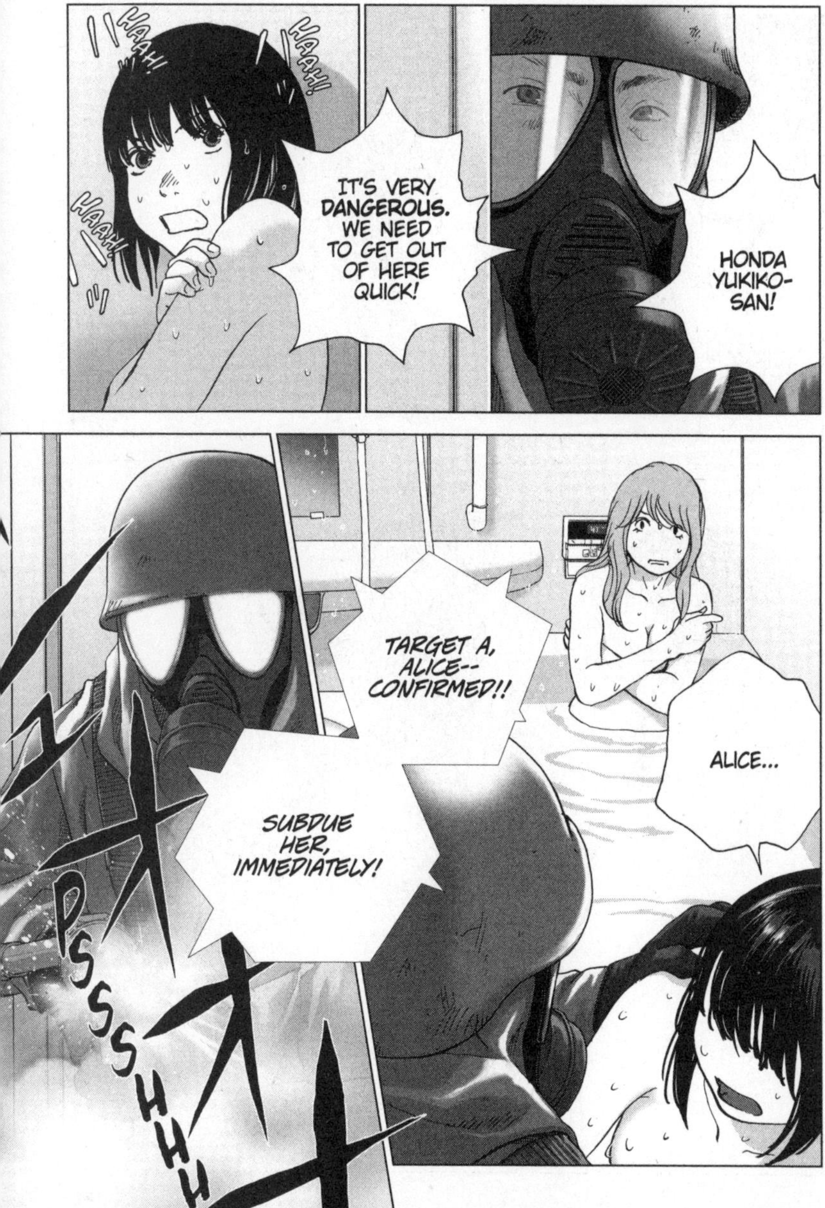
HONDA YUKIKO-SAN!
HAAAH!
HAAAH!
IT'S VERY DANGEROUS. WE NEED TO GET OUT OF HERE QUICK!
HAAAH!
ALICE...
TARGET A, ALICE--CONFIRMED!!
SUBDUE HER, IMMEDIATELY!
PSSSHHHH

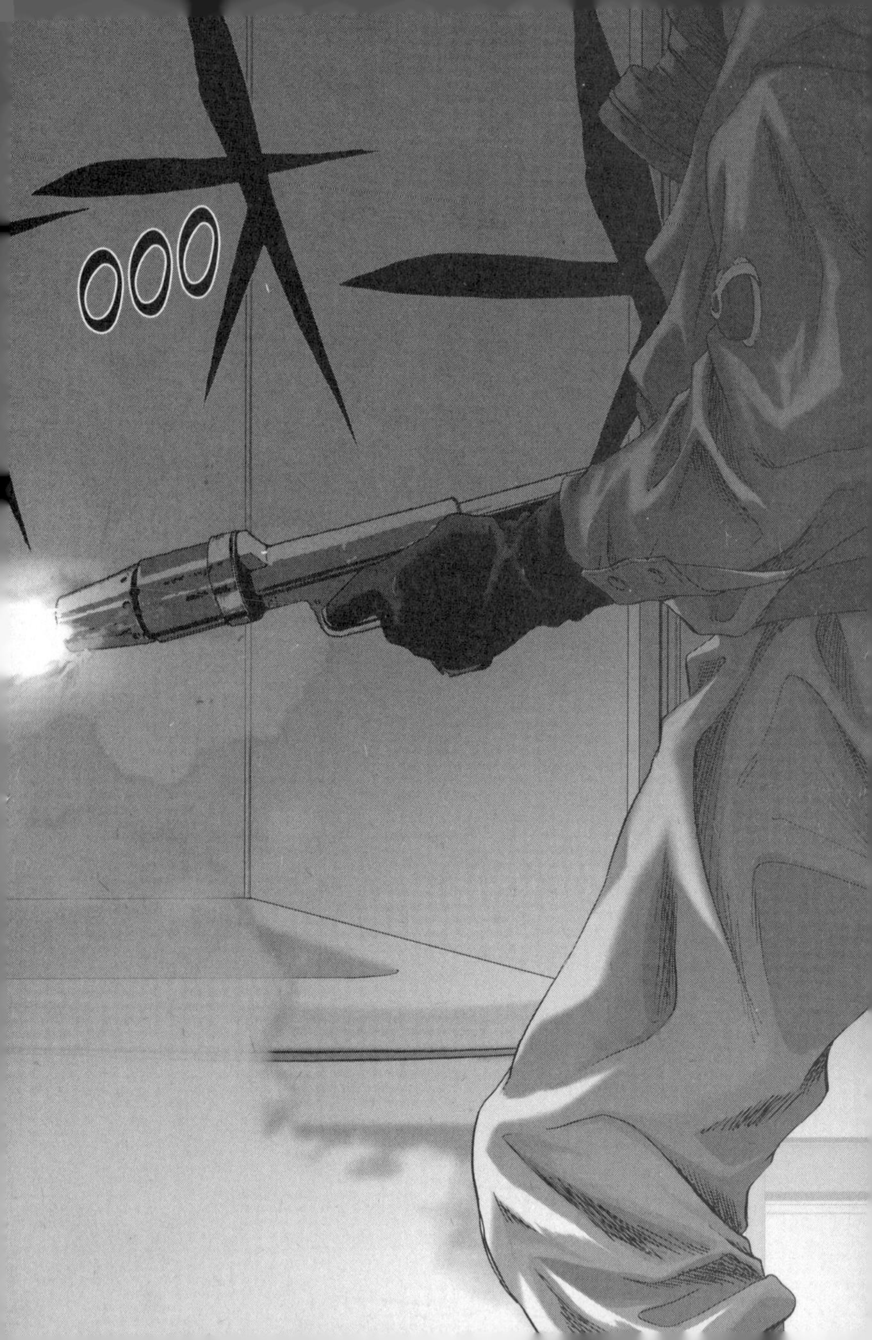

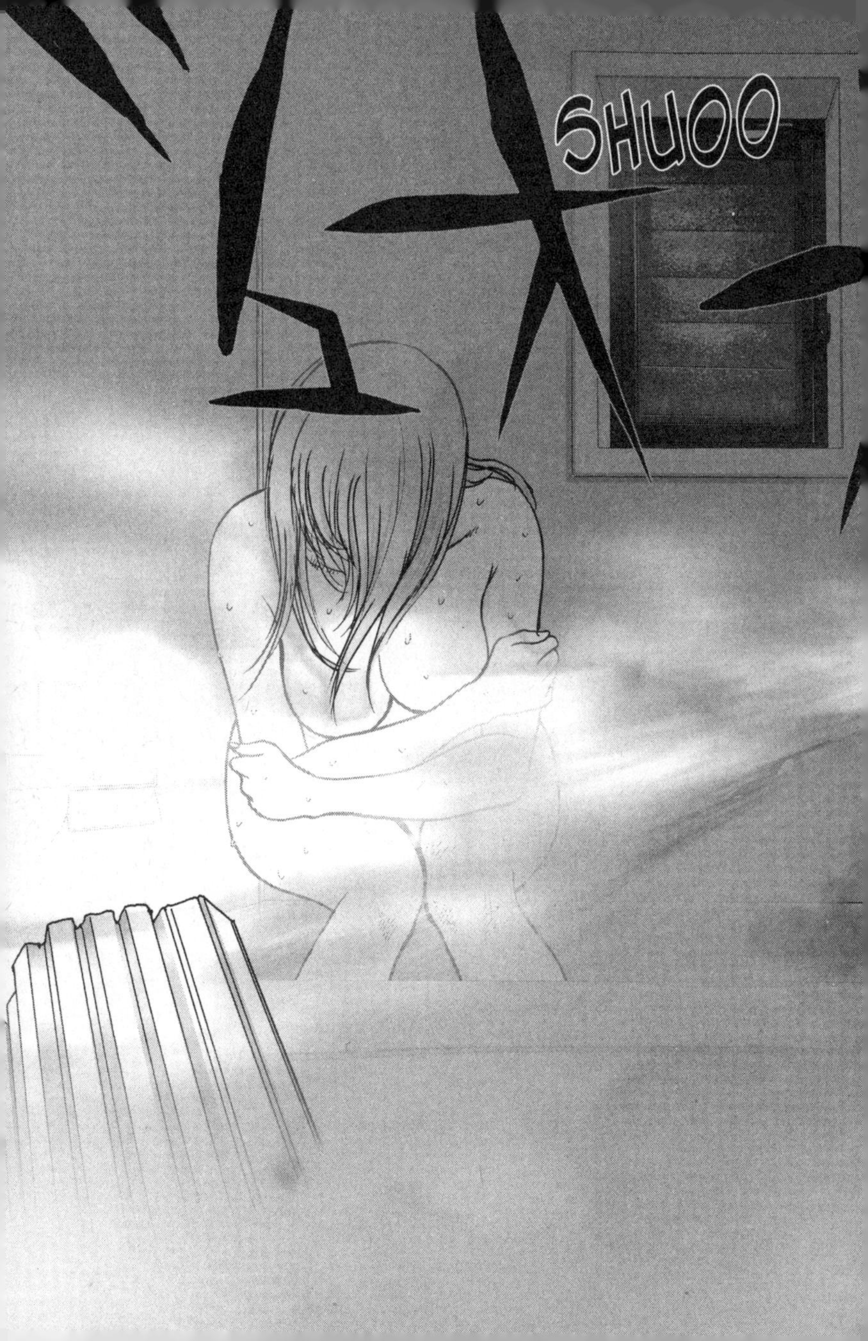
SHUOO

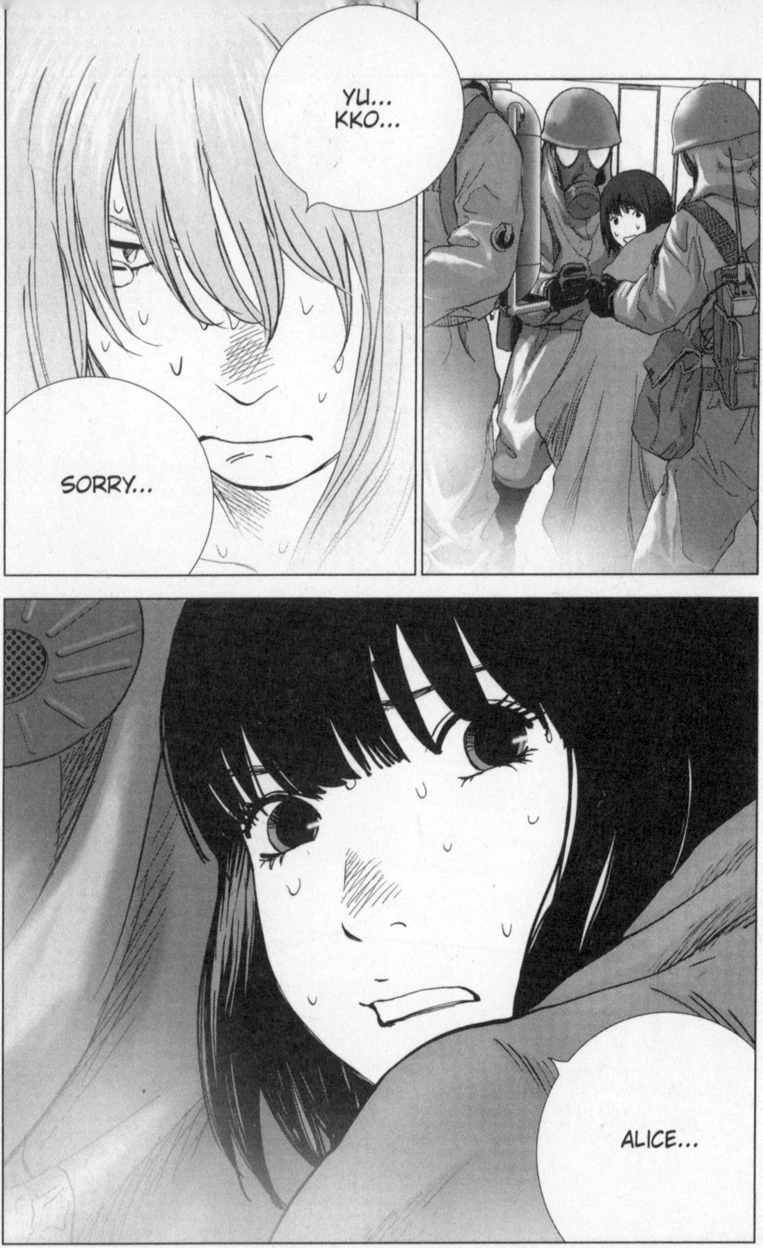
YU... KKO...
SORRY...
ALICE...

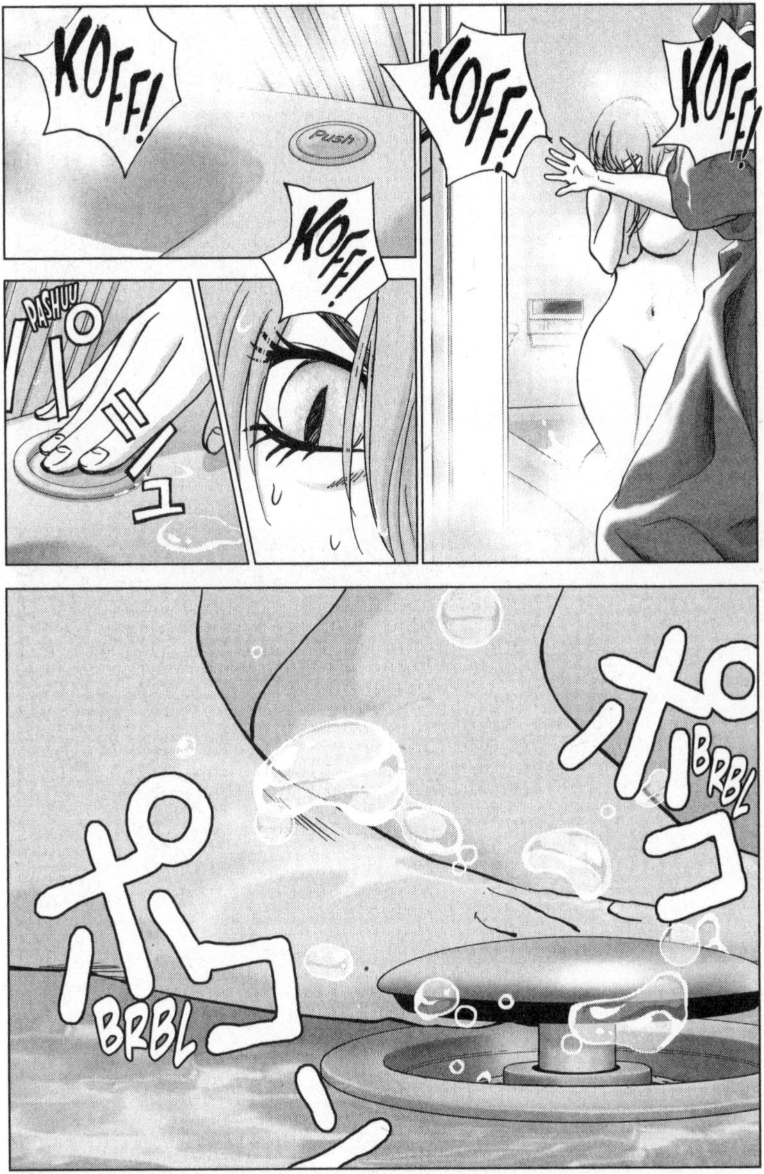
KOFF!
KOFF!
KOFF!
Push
KOFF!
PASHUU
BRBL
BRBL

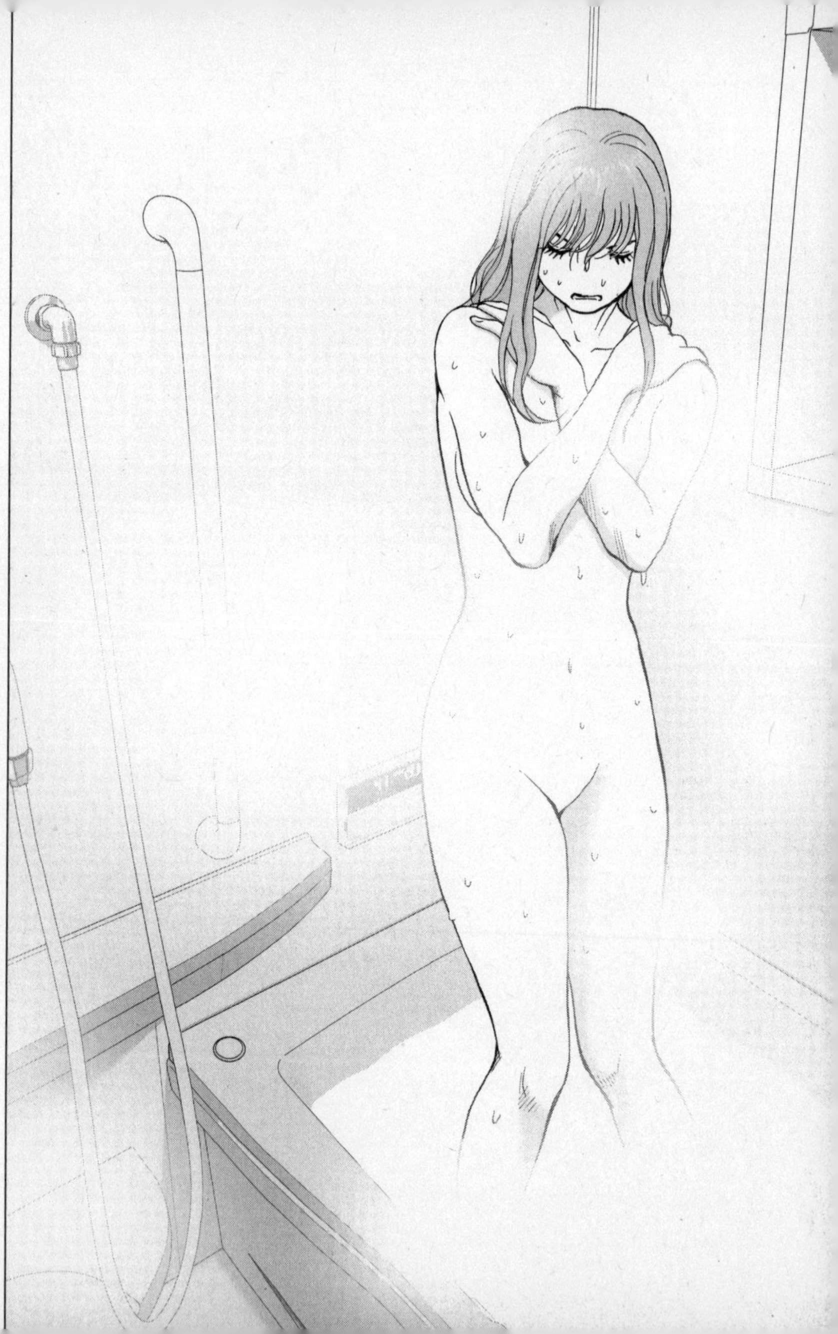

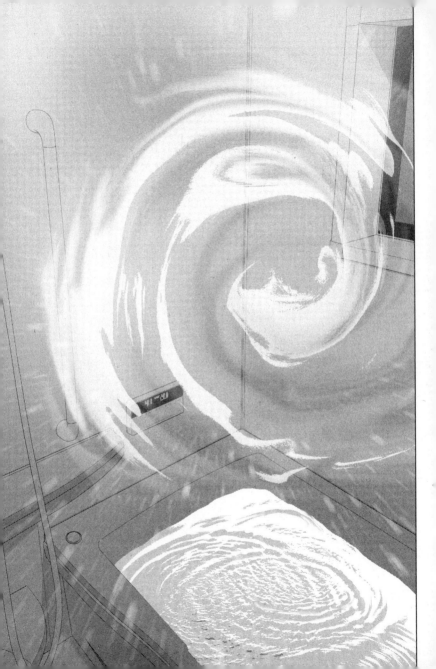

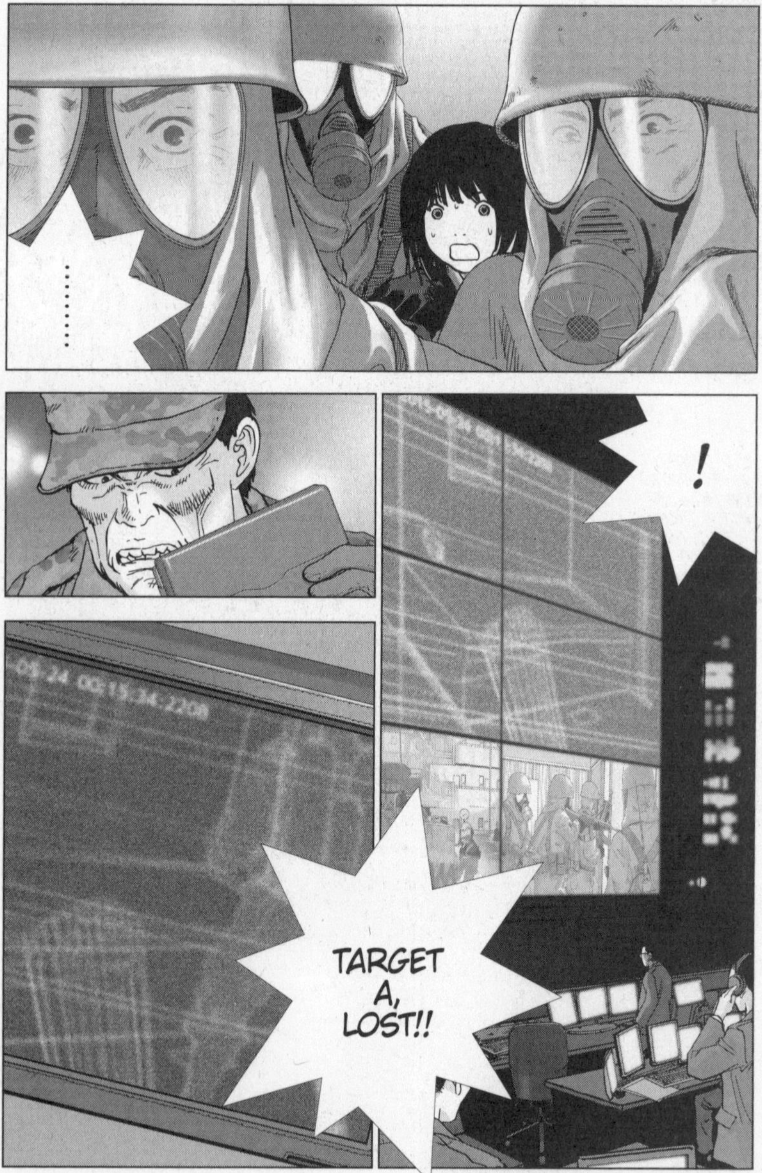

......
!
TARGET A, LOST!!

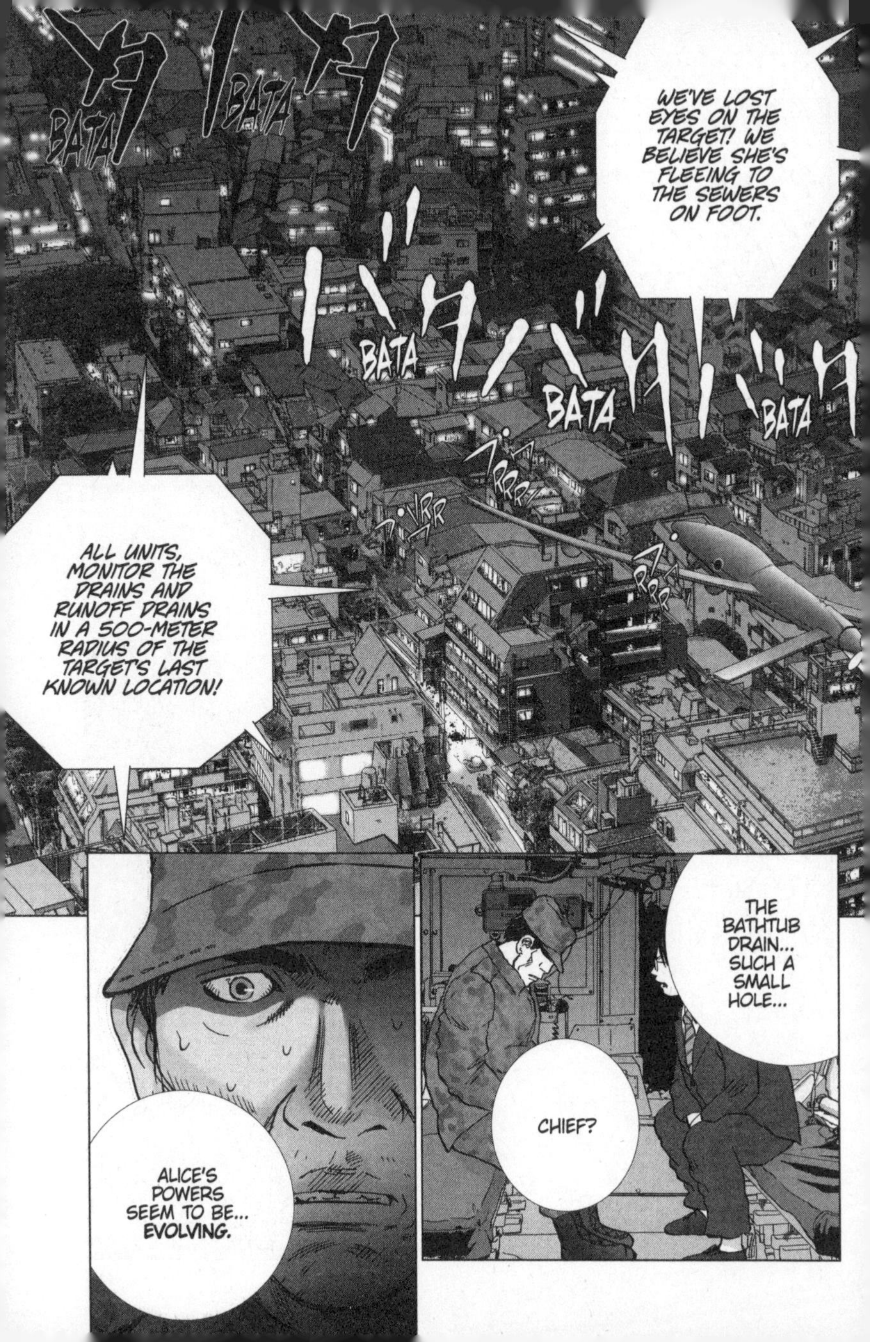
WE'VE LOST EYES ON THE TARGET! WE BELIEVE SHE'S FLEEING TO THE SEWERS ON FOOT.
BATA
BATA
BATA
BATA
BATA
ALL UNITS, MONITOR THE DRAINS AND RUNOFF DRAINS IN A 500-METER RADIUS OF THE TARGET'S LAST KNOWN LOCATION!
THE BATHTUB DRAIN... SUCH A SMALL HOLE...
CHIEF?
ALICE'S POWERS SEEM TO BE... EVOLVING.

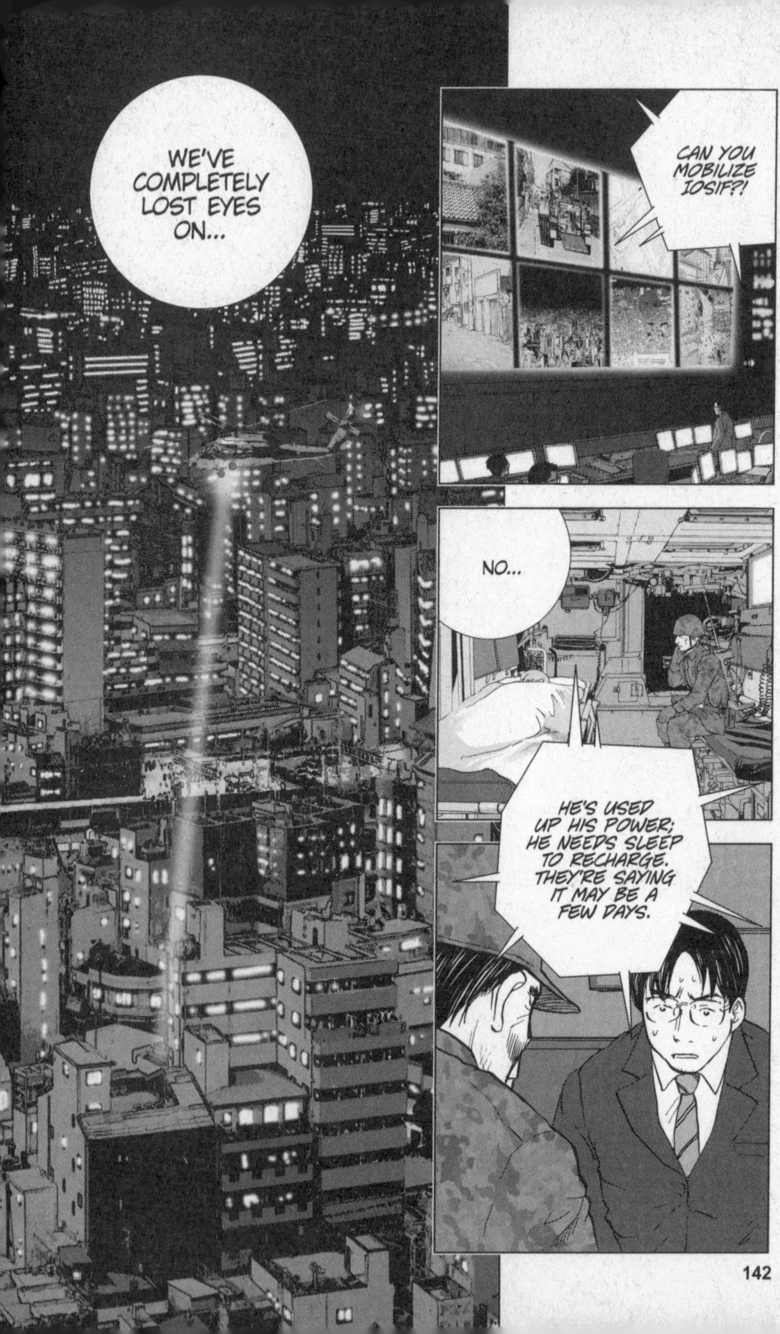
CAN YOU MOBILIZE IOSIF?!
NO...
HE'S USED UP HIS POWER; HE NEEDS SLEEP TO RECHARGE. THEY'RE SAYING IT MAY BE A FEW DAYS.
WE'VE COMPLETELY LOST EYES ON...

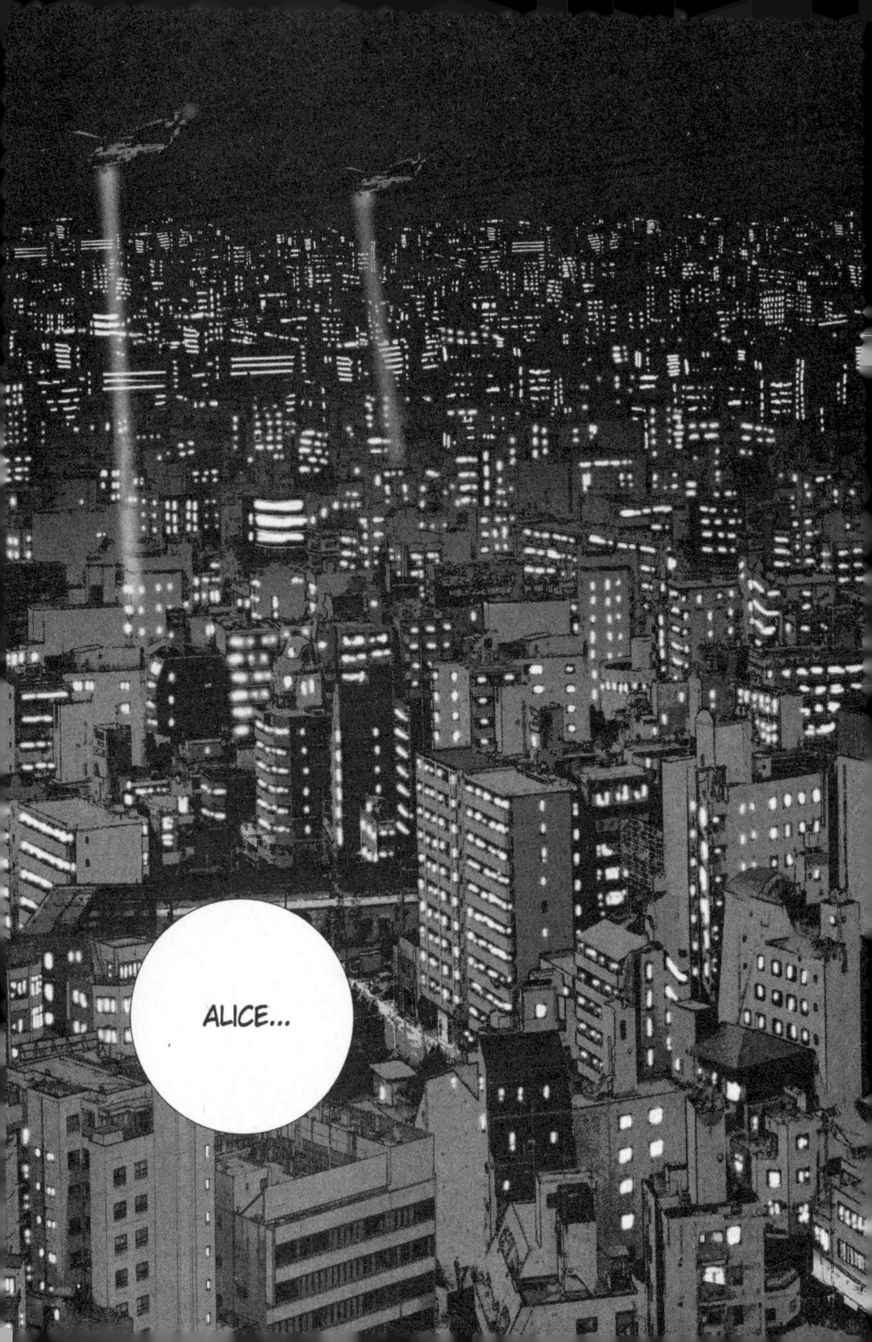
ALICE...

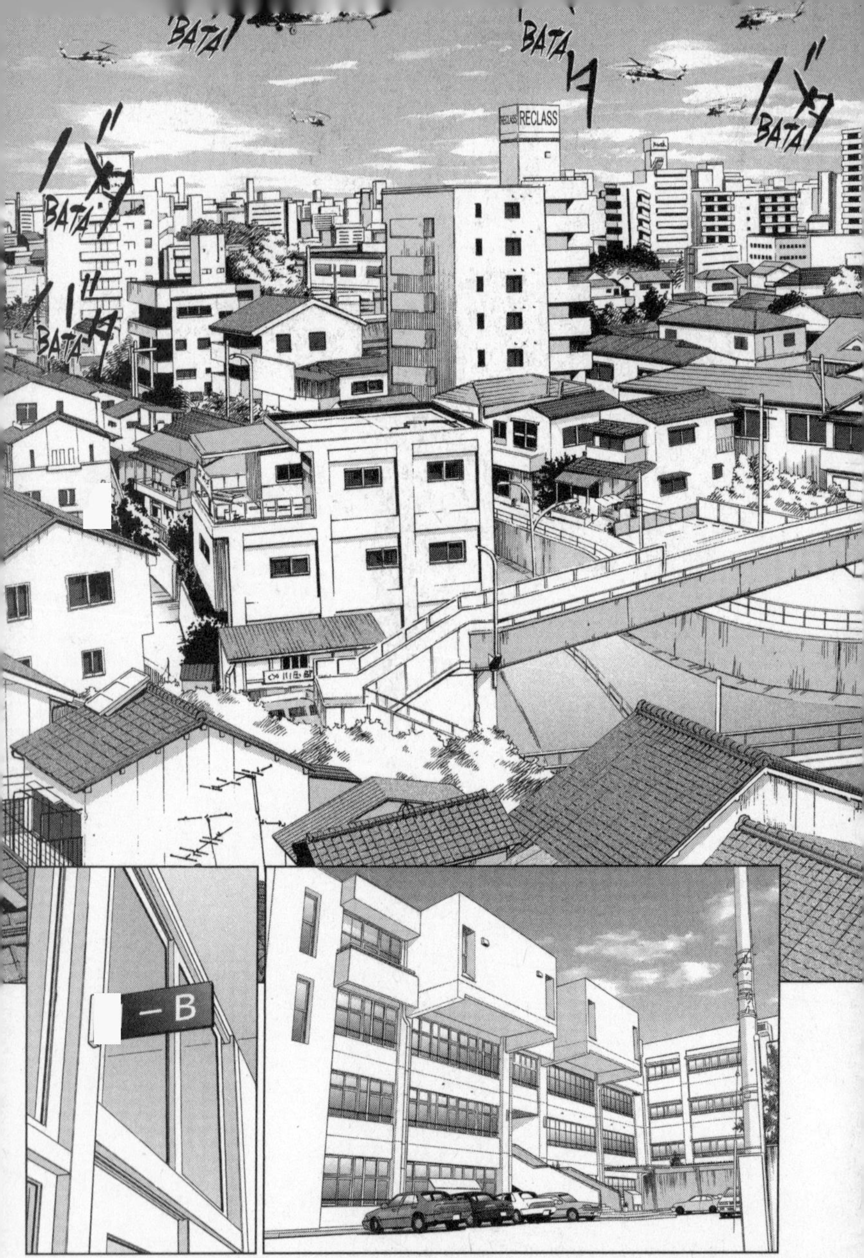
バタ
BATA
バタ
BATA
RECLASS
BATA
BATA
バタ
BATA
バタ
BATA
-B

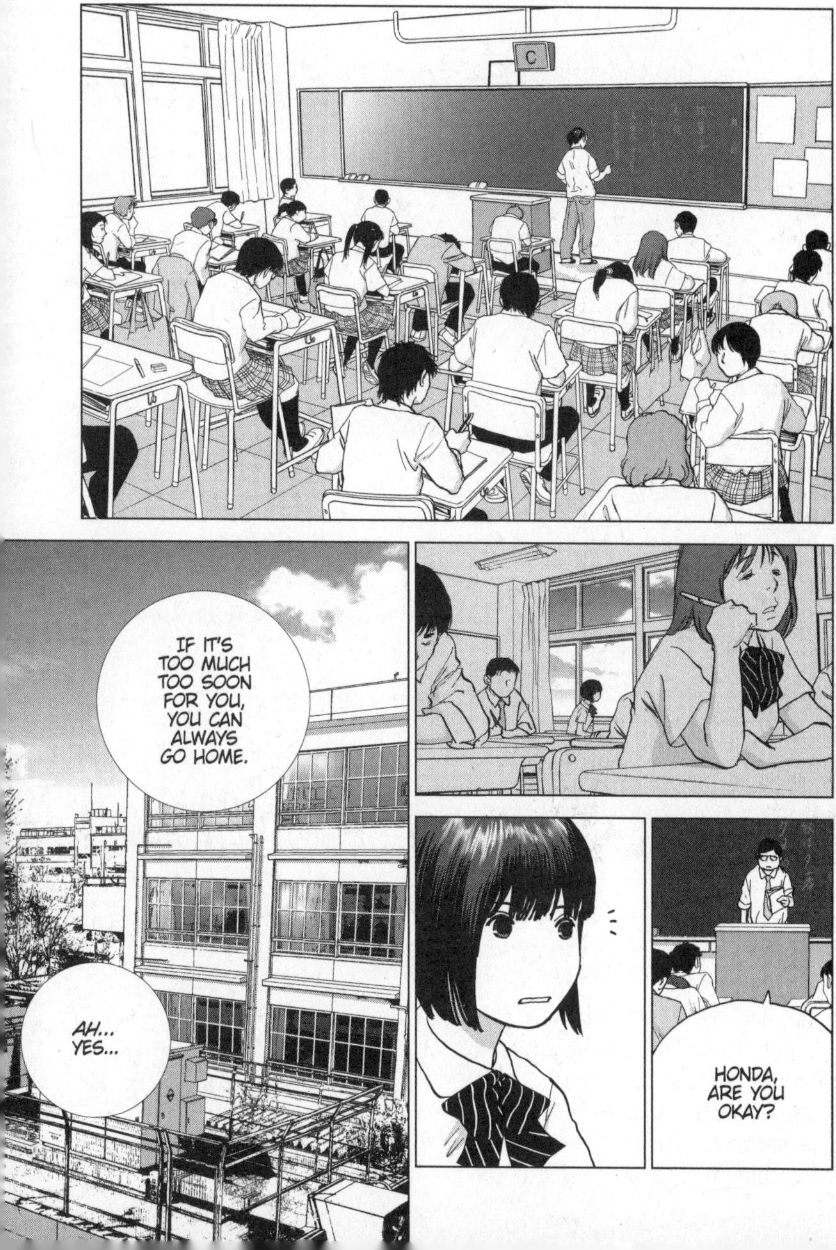
HONDA, ARE YOU OKAY?
IF IT'S TOO MUCH TOO SOON FOR YOU, YOU CAN ALWAYS GO HOME.
AH... YES...

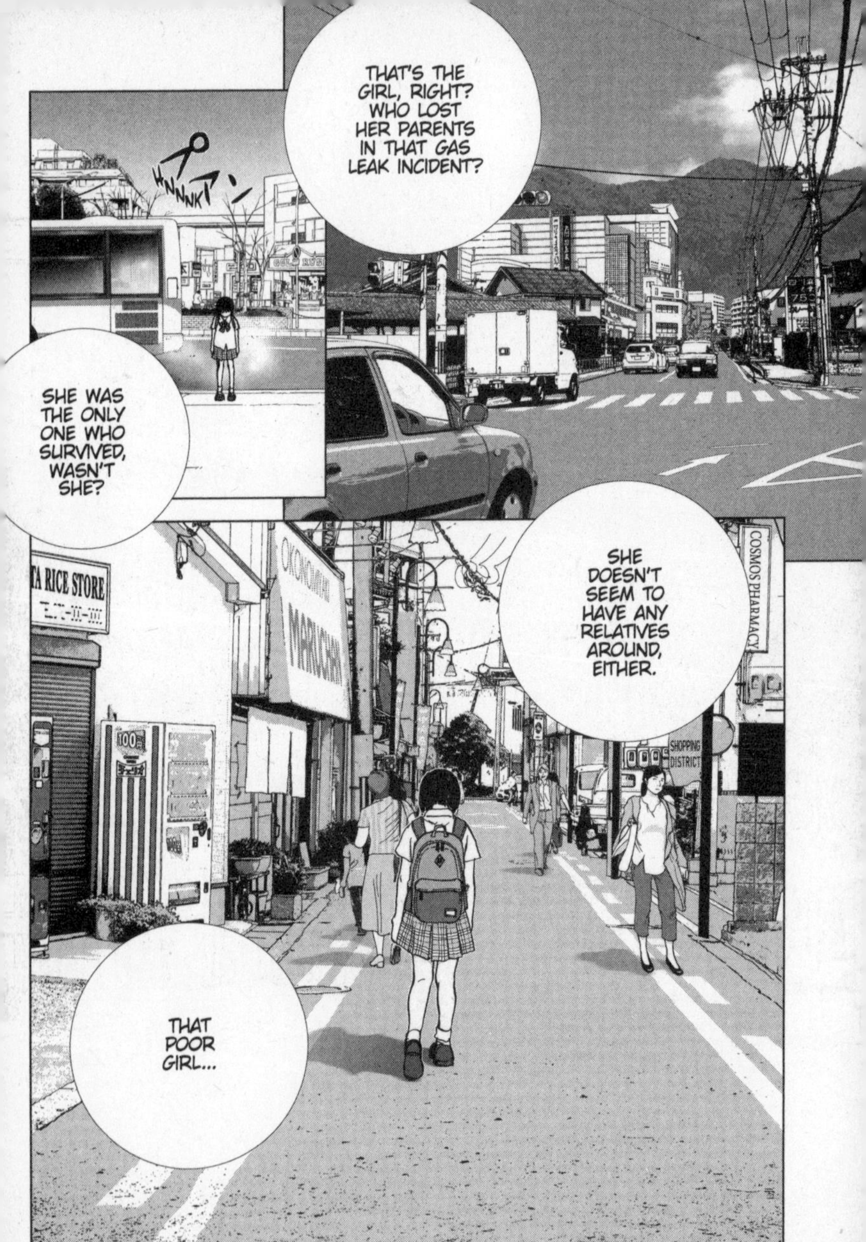
THAT'S THE GIRL, RIGHT? WHO LOST HER PARENTS IN THAT GAS LEAK INCIDENT?
HNNNK
SHE WAS THE ONLY ONE WHO SURVIVED, WASN'T SHE?
COSMOS PHARMACY
SHE DOESN'T SEEM TO HAVE ANY RELATIVES AROUND, EITHER.
SHOPPING DISTRICT
TA RICE STORE
OKONOMIYAKI
THAT POOR GIRL...

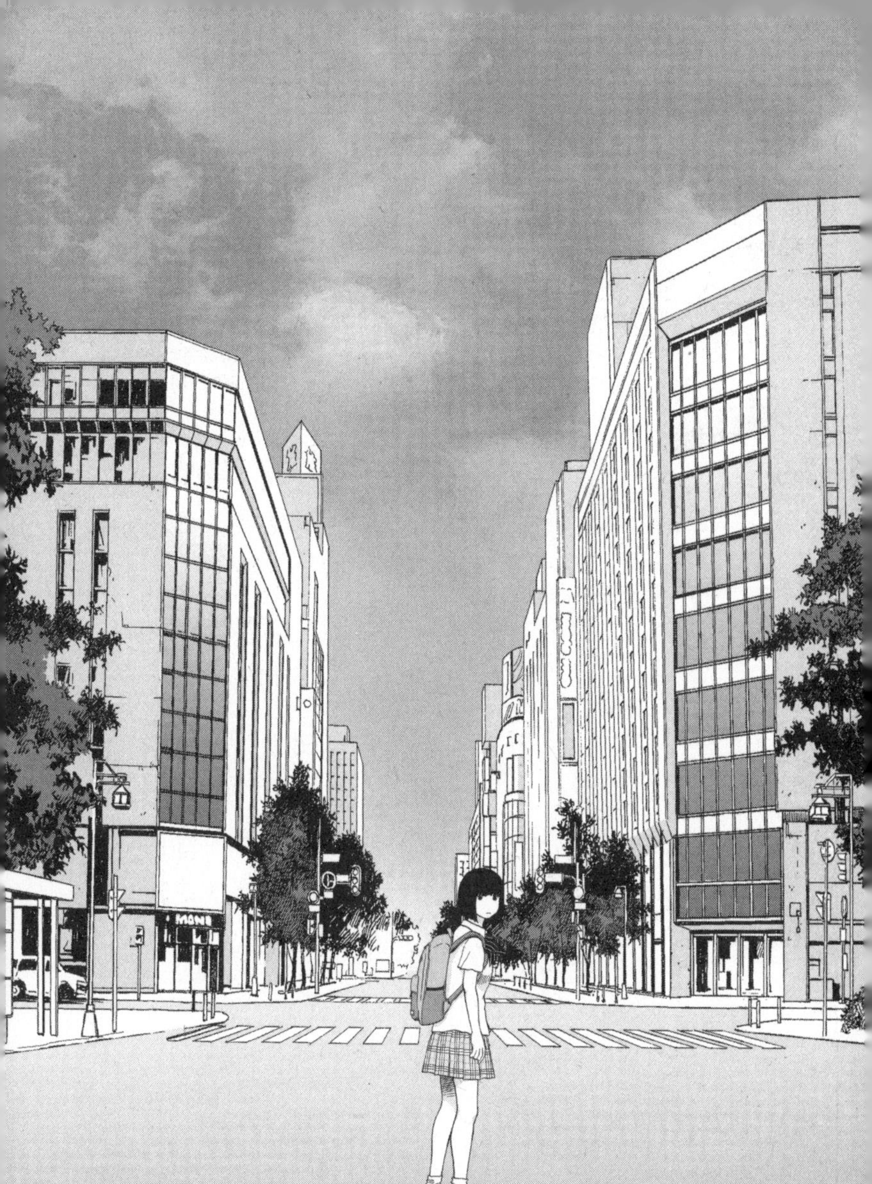

Chapter 26: Asamiya

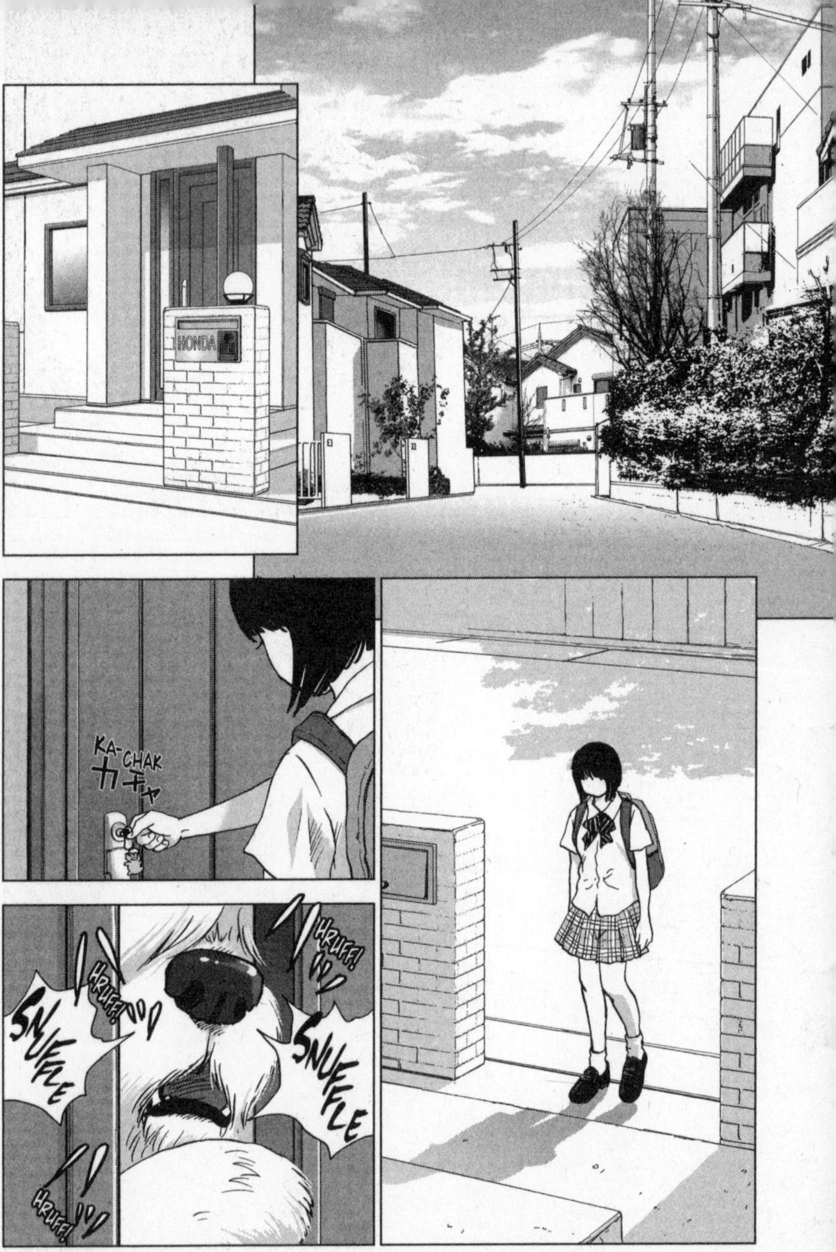
HONDA
KA-CHAK
カチャ
HRUFF!
SNUFFLE
HRUFF!
SNUFFLE
HRUFF!

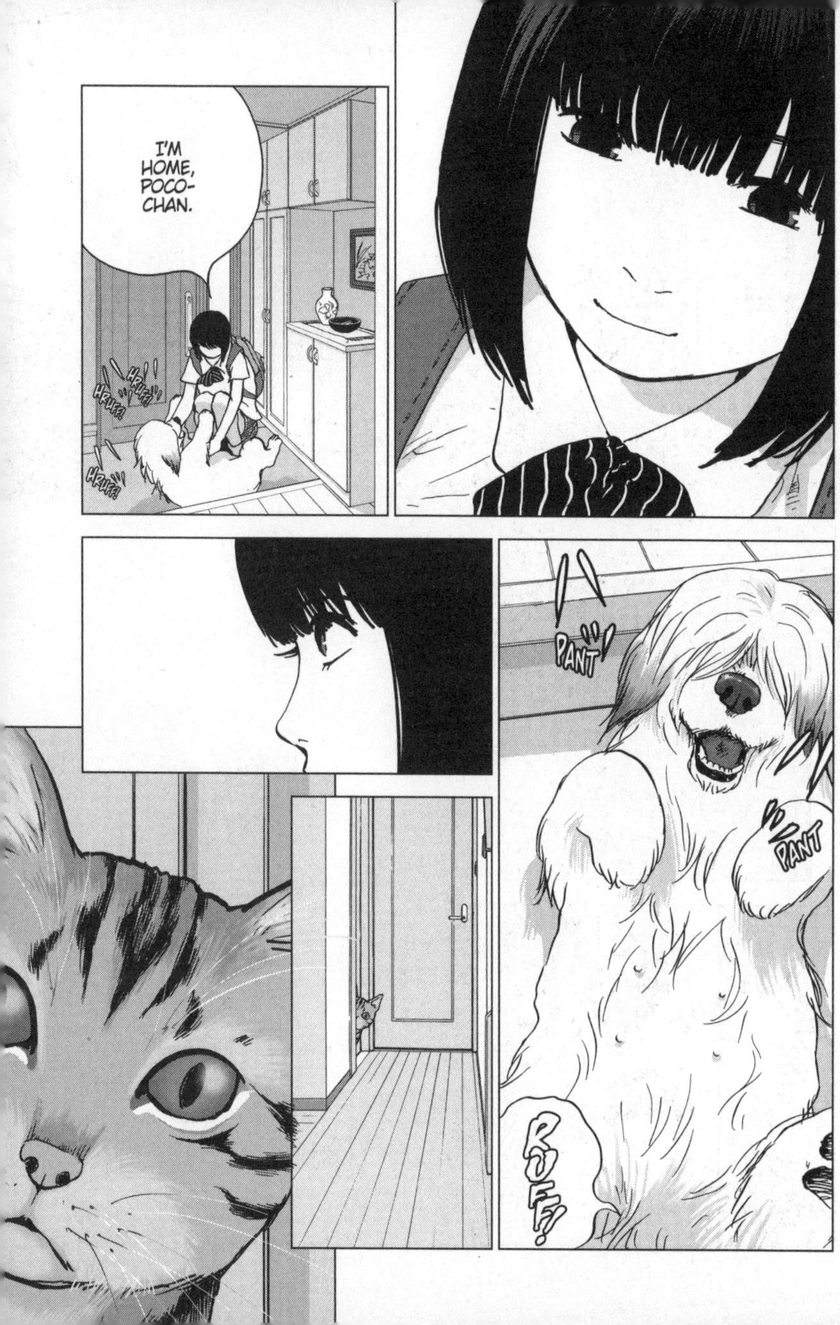
I'M HOME, POCO-CHAN.
HRUFF!
HRUFF!
HRUFF!
PANT
PANT
RUFF!

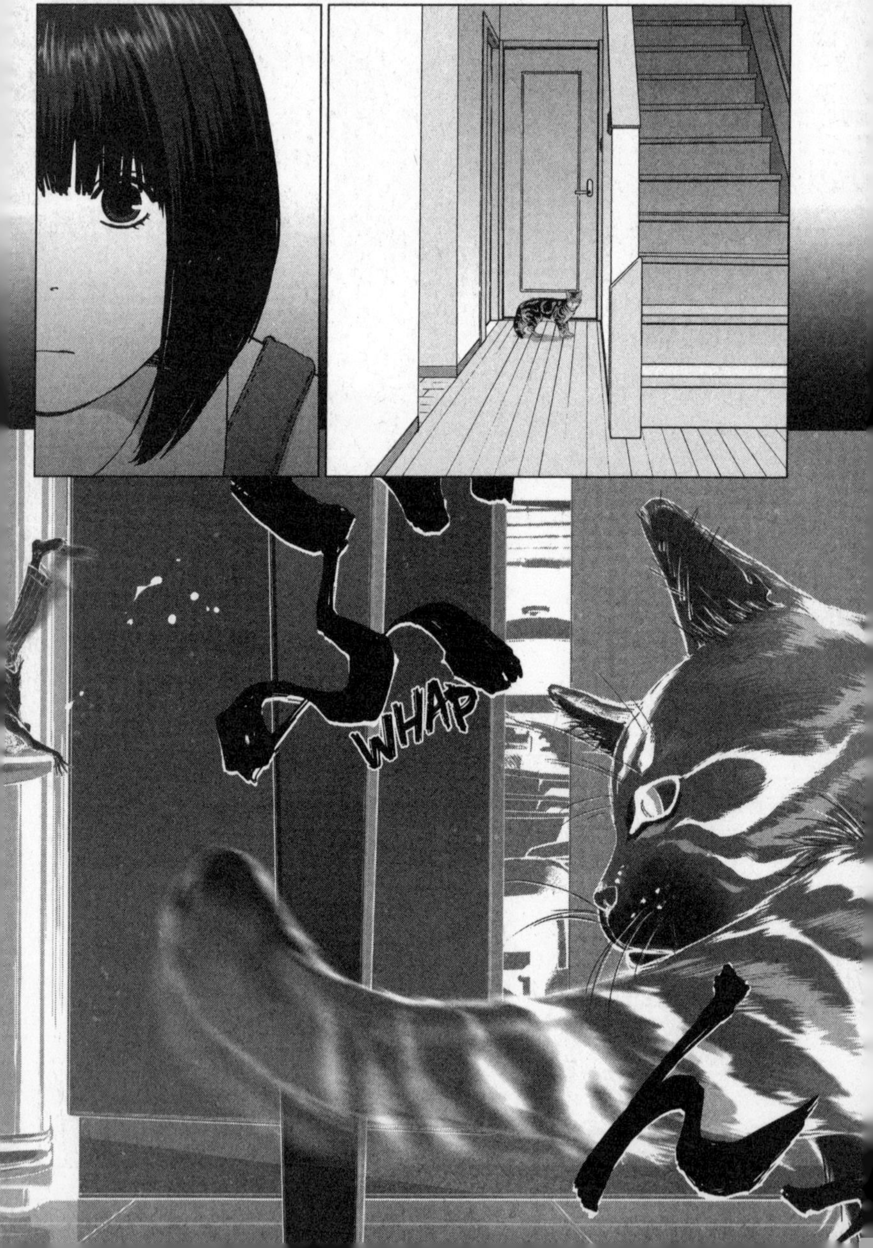
WHAP

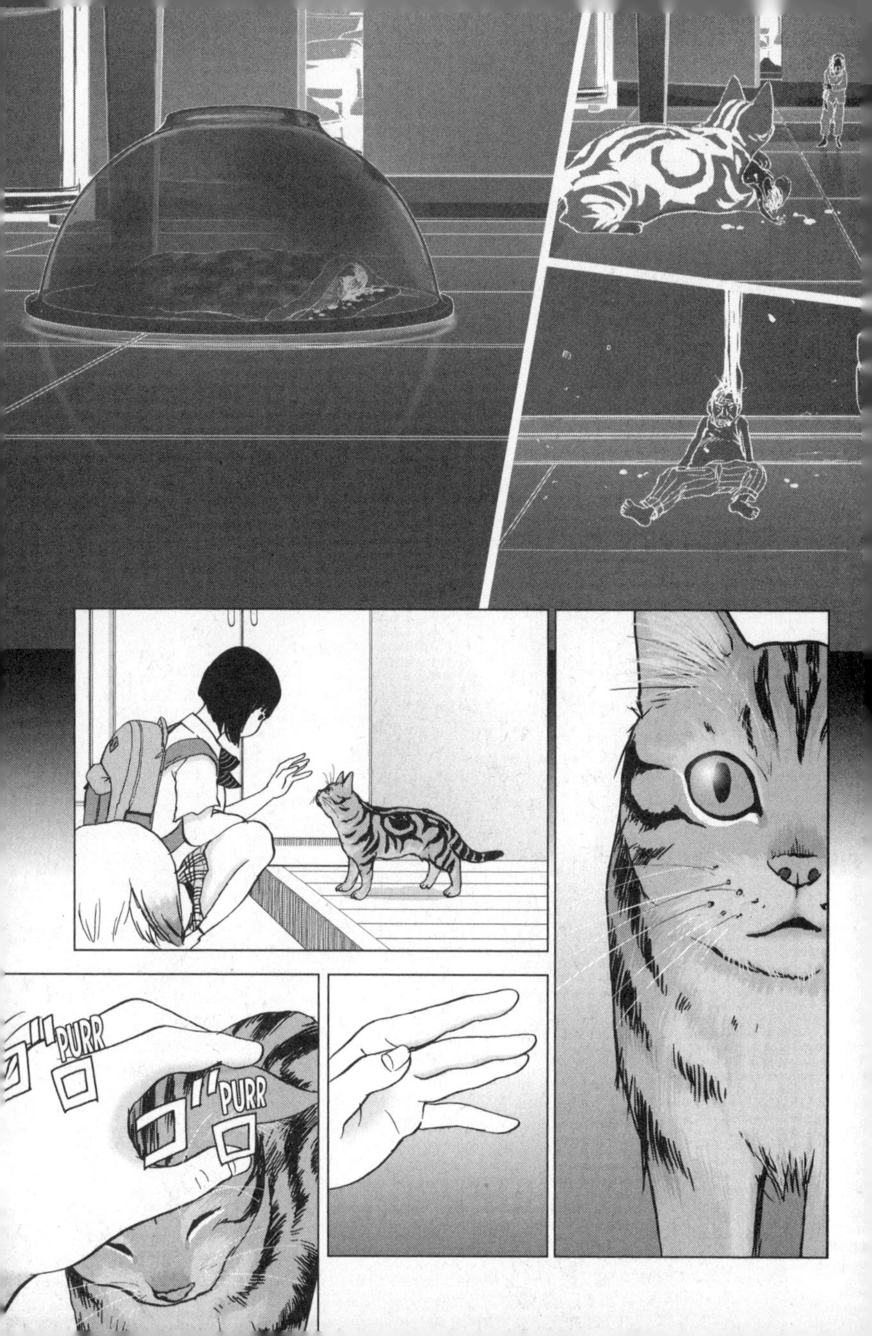
PURR
PURR

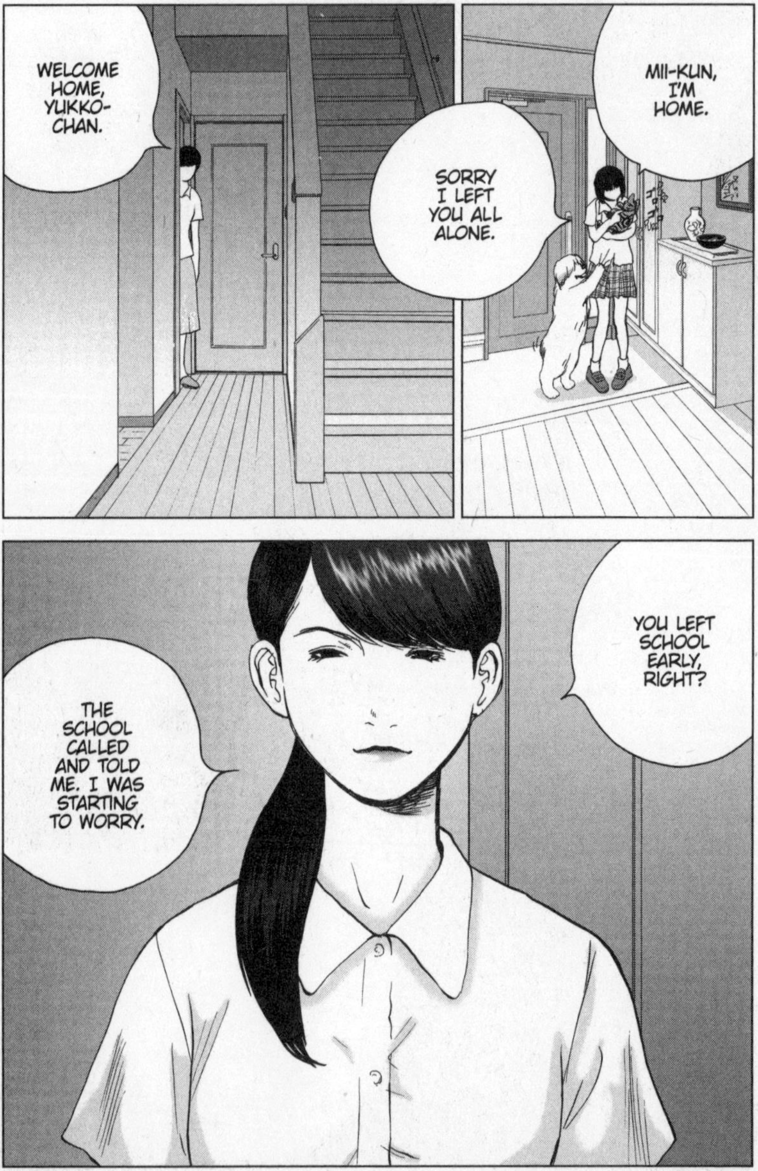
MII-KUN, I'M HOME.
SORRY I LEFT YOU ALL ALONE.
WELCOME HOME, YUKKO-CHAN.
YOU LEFT SCHOOL EARLY, RIGHT?
THE SCHOOL CALLED AND TOLD ME. I WAS STARTING TO WORRY.

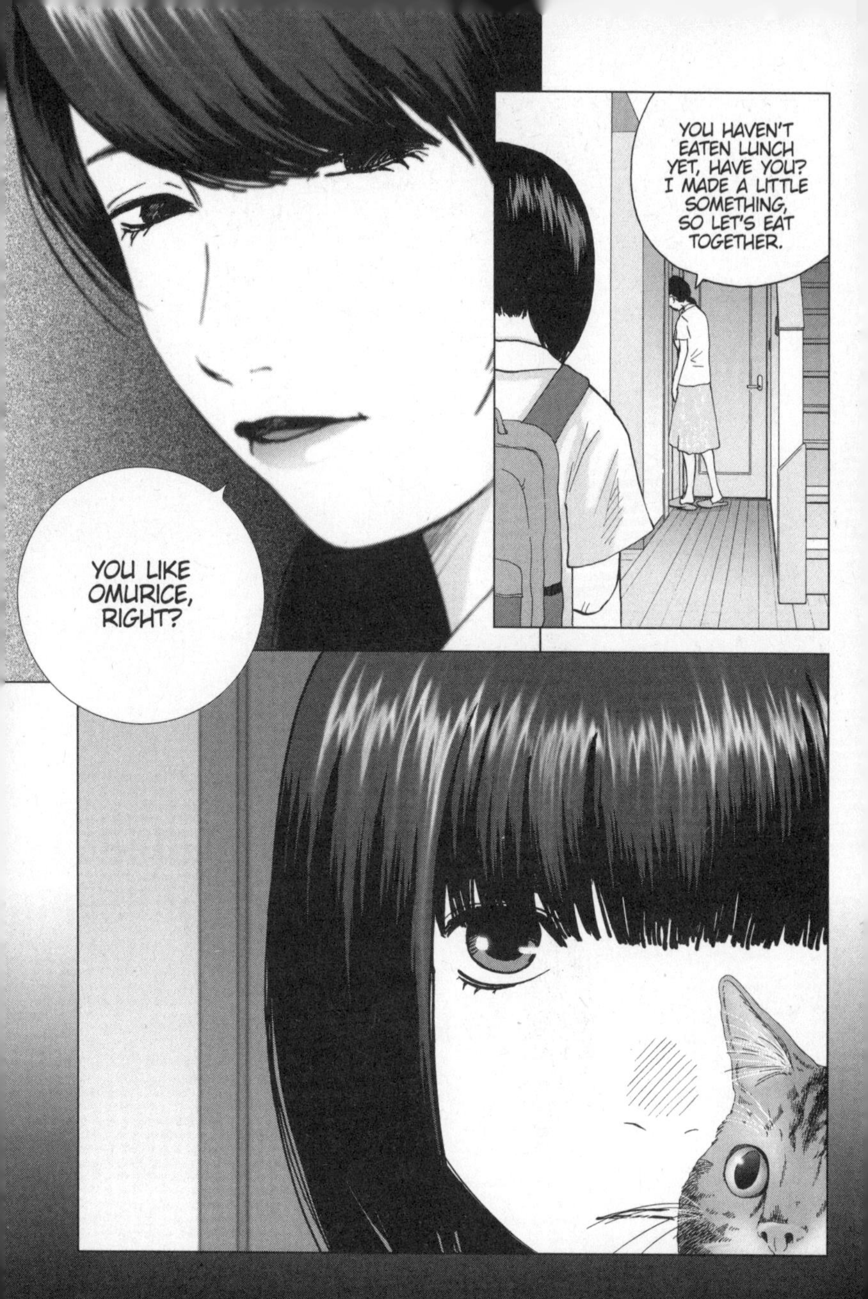
YOU HAVEN'T EATEN LUNCH YET, HAVE YOU? I MADE A LITTLE SOMETHING, SO LET'S EAT TOGETHER.
YOU LIKE OMURICE, RIGHT?

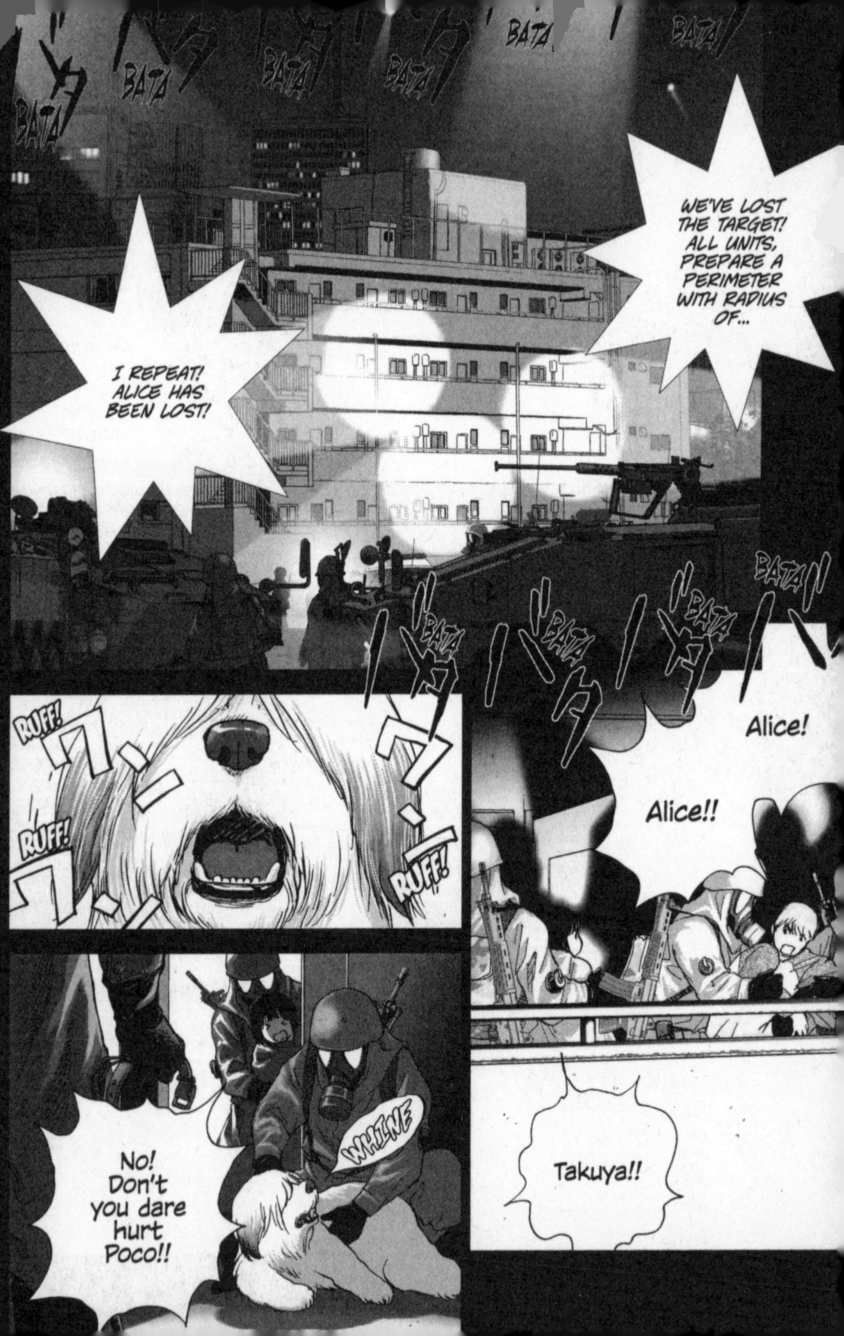
BATA BATA BATA BATA BATA BATA
WE'VE LOST THE TARGET! ALL UNITS, PREPARE A PERIMETER WITH RADIUS OF...
I REPEAT! ALICE HAS BEEN LOST!
BATA BATA BATA BATA
Alice!
Alice!!
RUFF!
RUFF!
RUFF!
Takuya!!
WHINE
No! Don't you dare hurt Poco!!

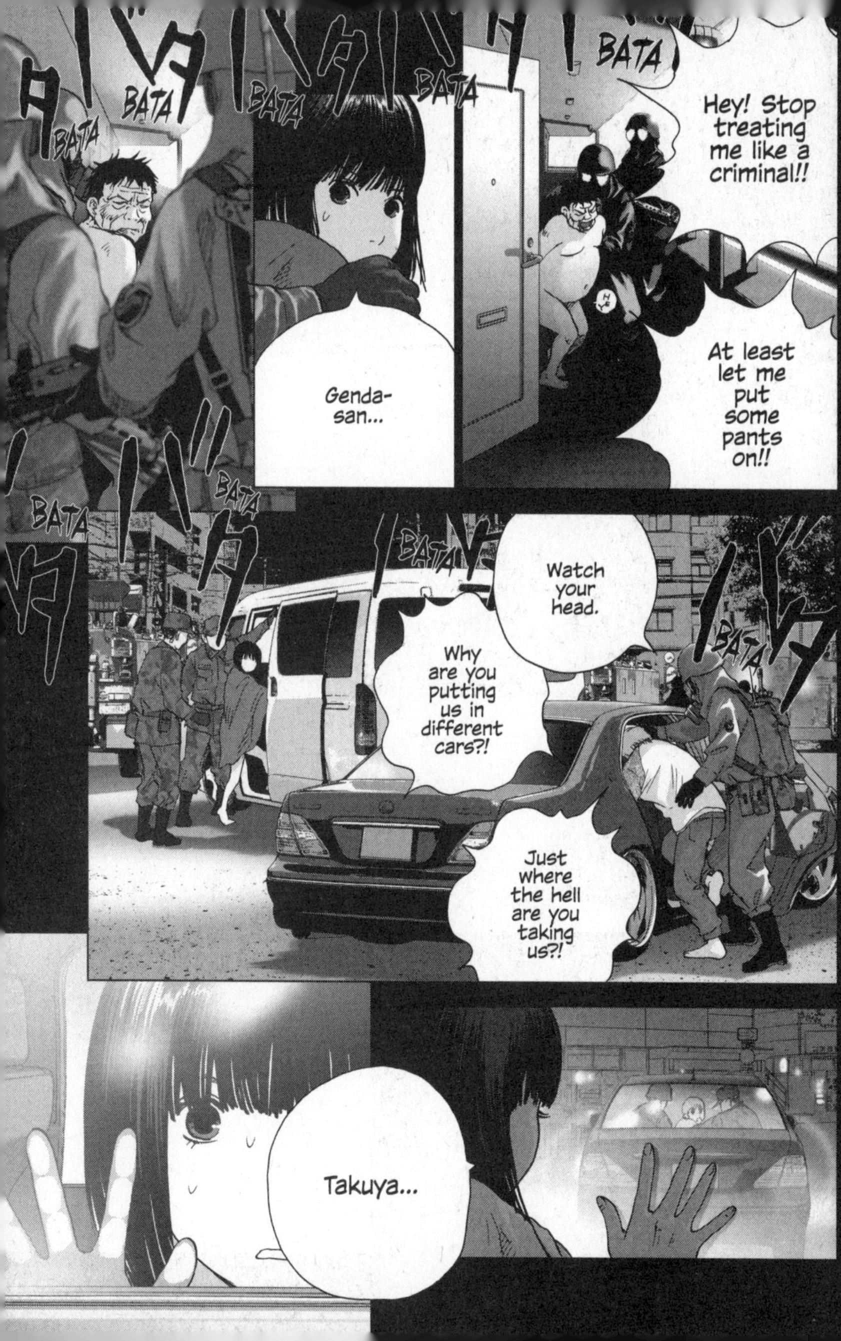
BATA
Hey! Stop treating me like a criminal!!
At least let me put some pants on!!
BATA
Genda-san...
BATA
BATA
BATA
BATA
BATA
Watch your head.
Why are you putting us in different cars?!
Just where the hell are you taking us?!
BATA
BATA
Takuya...

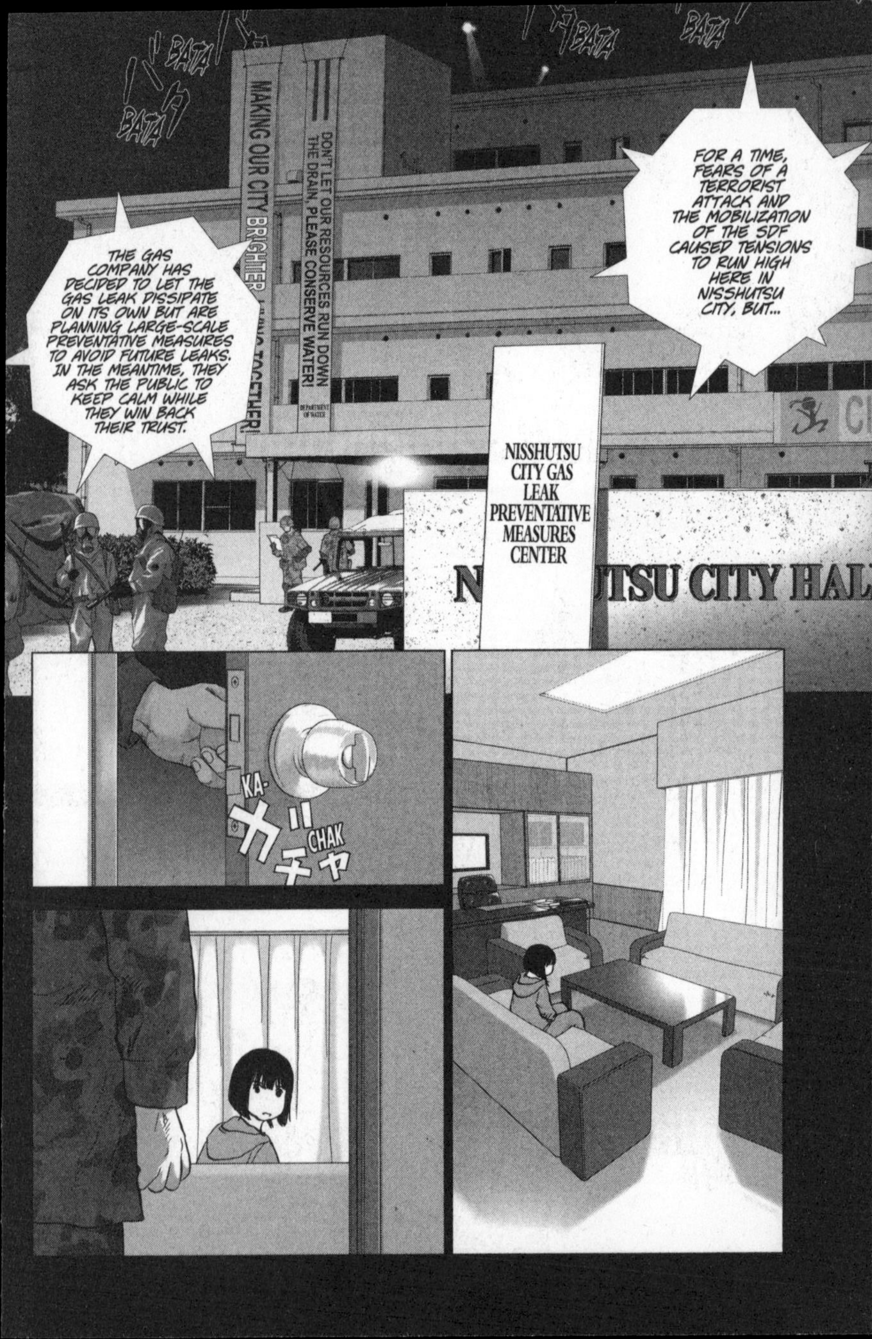
BATA
BATA
BATA
BATA
FOR A TIME, FEARS OF A TERRORIST ATTACK AND THE MOBILIZATION OF THE SDF CAUSED TENSIONS TO RUN HIGH HERE IN NISSHUTSU CITY, BUT...
DON'T LET OUR RESOURCES RUN DOWN THE DRAIN, PLEASE CONSERVE WATER!
DEPARTMENT OF WATER
MAKING OUR CITY BRIGHTER
THE GAS COMPANY HAS DECIDED TO LET THE GAS LEAK DISSIPATE ON ITS OWN BUT ARE PLANNING LARGE-SCALE PREVENTATIVE MEASURES TO AVOID FUTURE LEAKS. IN THE MEANTIME, THEY ASK THE PUBLIC TO KEEP CALM WHILE THEY WIN BACK THEIR TRUST.
NISSHUTSU CITY GAS LEAK PREVENTATIVE MEASURES CENTER
KA-CHAK

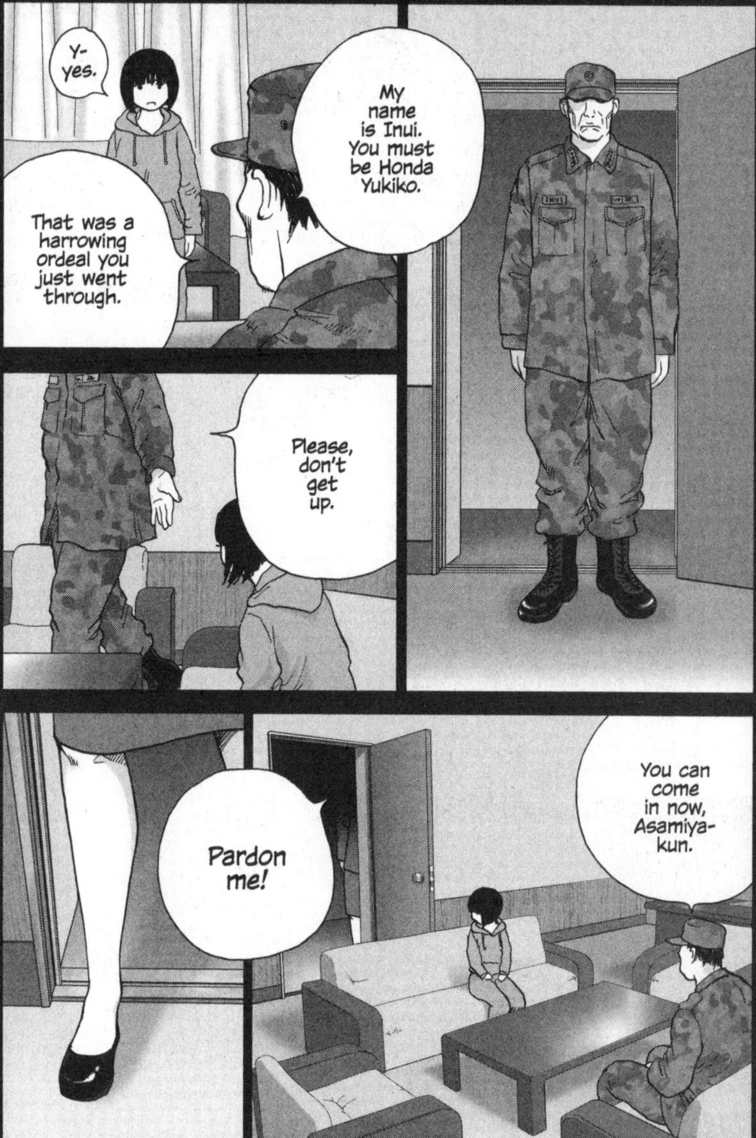
My name is Inui. You must be Honda Yukiko.
Y-yes.
That was a harrowing ordeal you just went through.
Please, don't get up.
You can come in now, Asamiya-kun.
Pardon me!

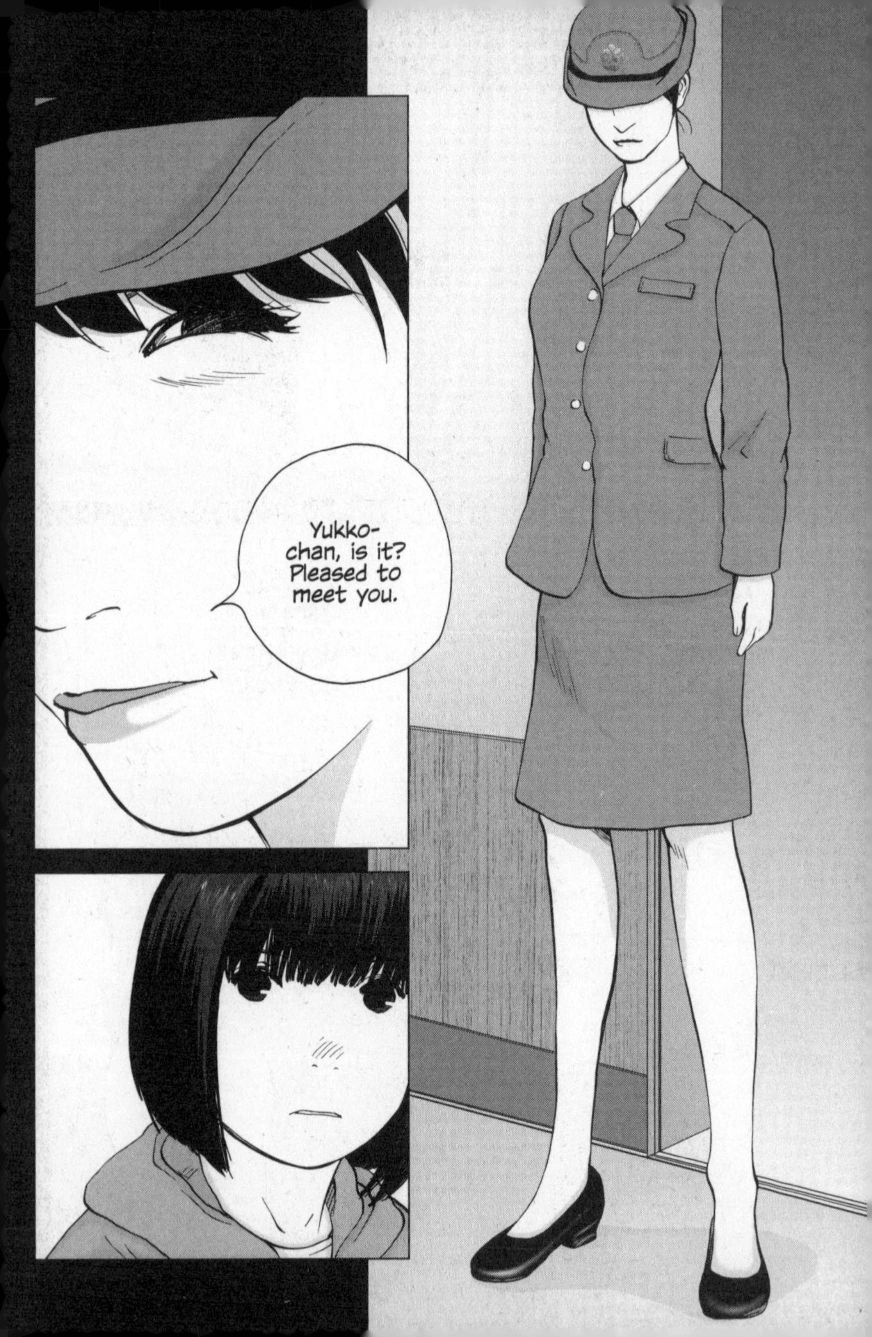
Yukko-chan, is it? Pleased to meet you.

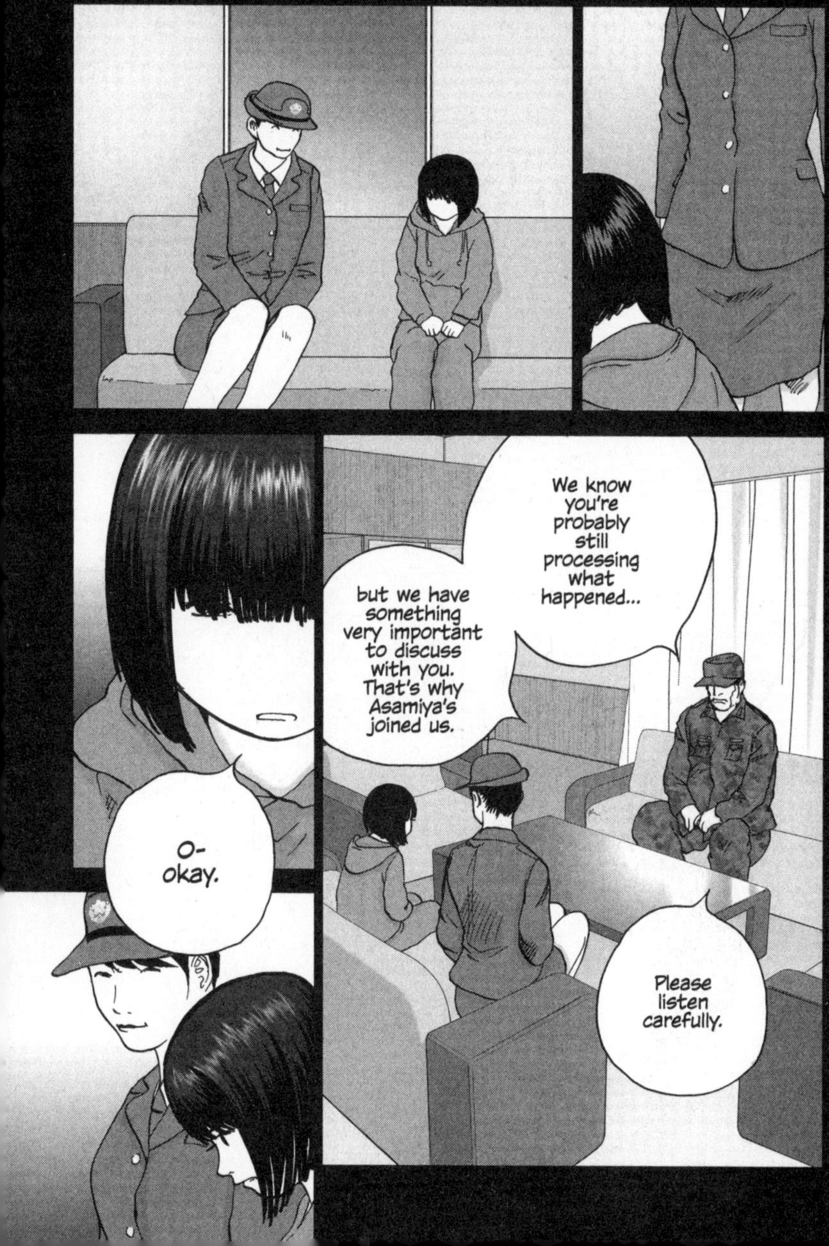

We know you're probably still processing what happened...
but we have something very important to discuss with you. That's why Asamiya's joined us.
Please listen carefully.
O-okay.

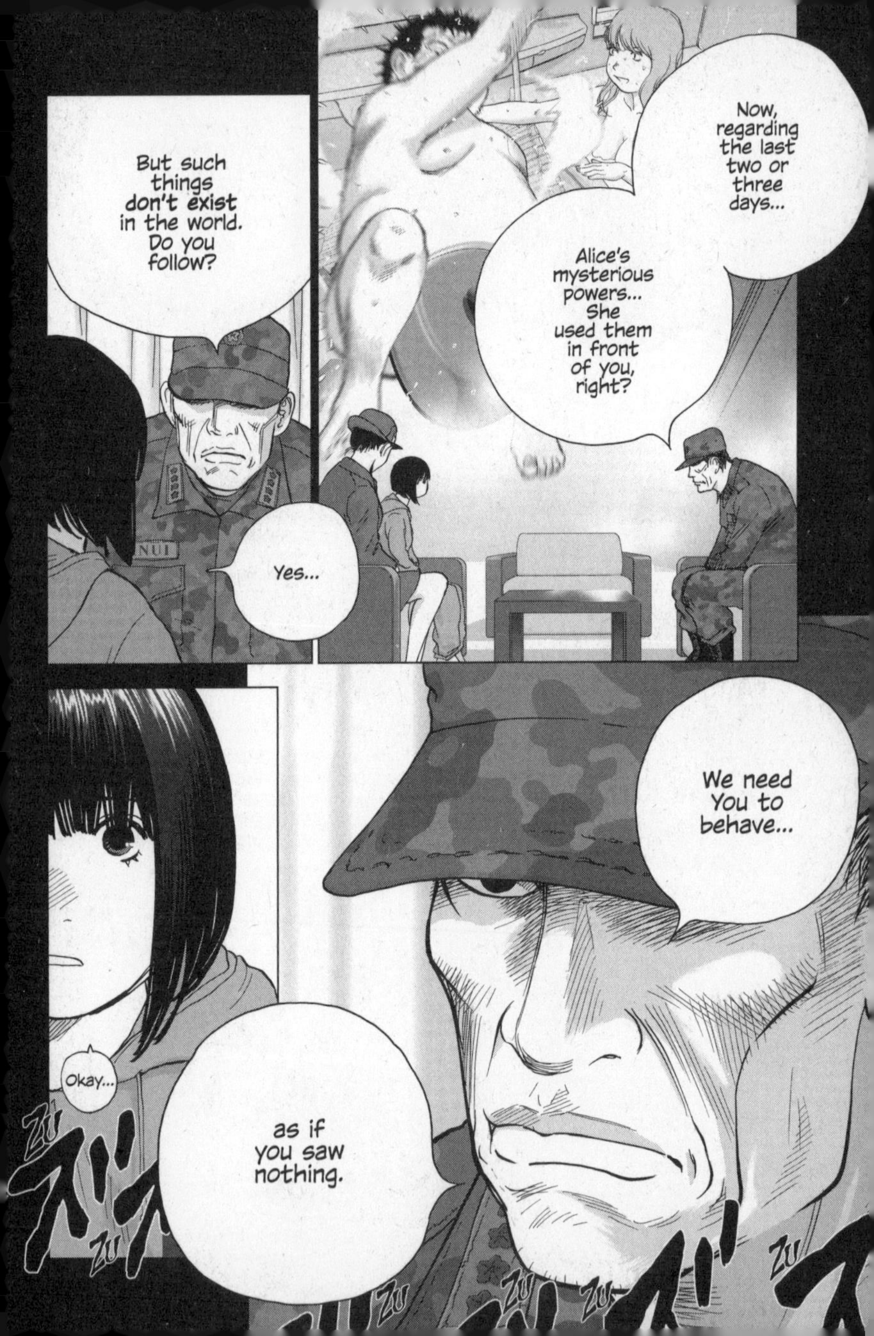
Now, regarding the last two or three days...
Alice's mysterious powers... She used them in front of you, right?
But such things don't exist in the world. Do you follow?
Yes...
We need You to behave...
as if you saw nothing.
Okay...
ZU
ZU
ZU
ZU
ZU
ZU

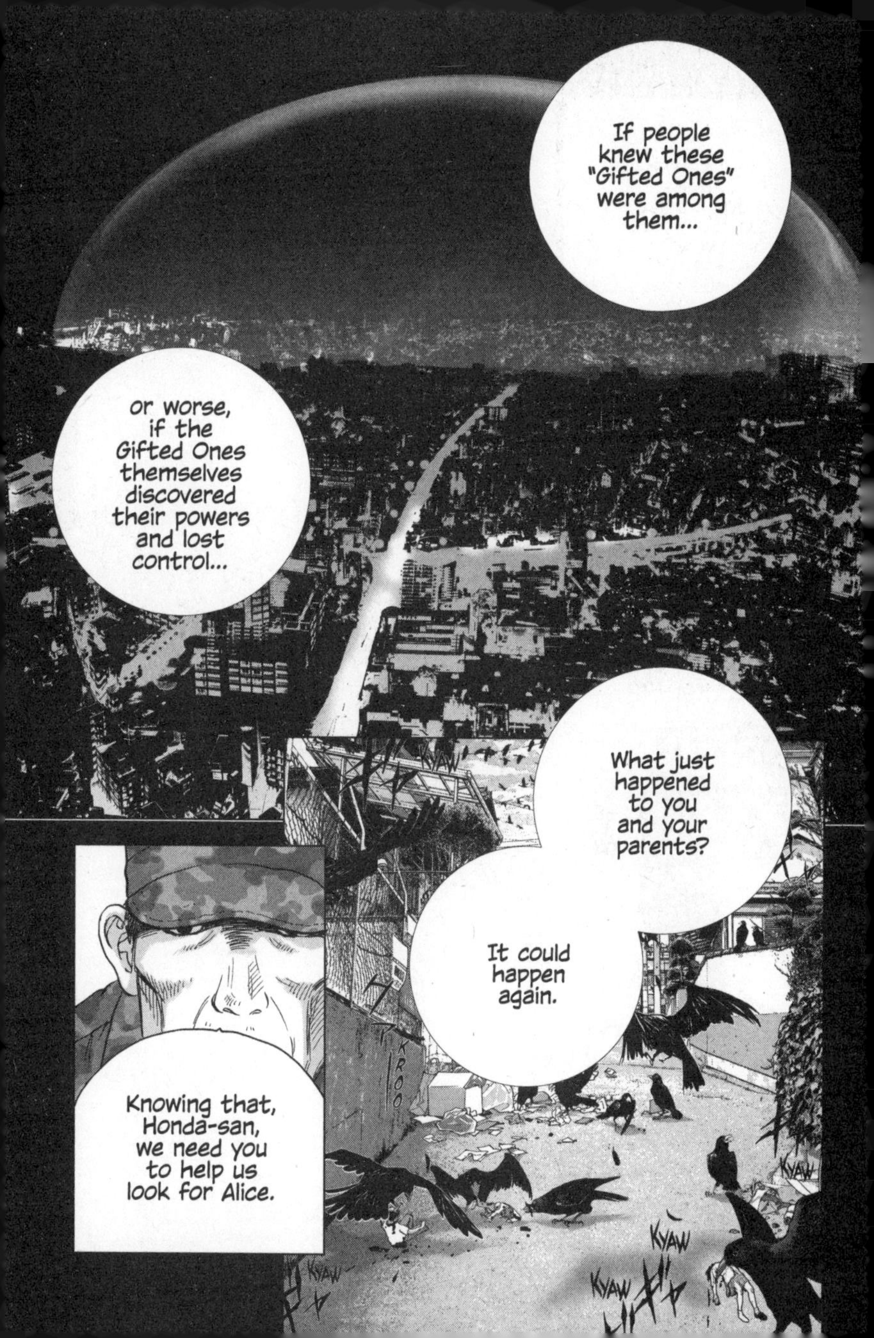
If people knew these "Gifted Ones" were among them...
or worse, if the Gifted Ones themselves discovered their powers and lost control...
KYAW
What just happened to you and your parents?
It could happen again.
KROOO
Knowing that, Honda-san, we need you to help us look for Alice.
KYAW
KYAW
KYAW
KYAW

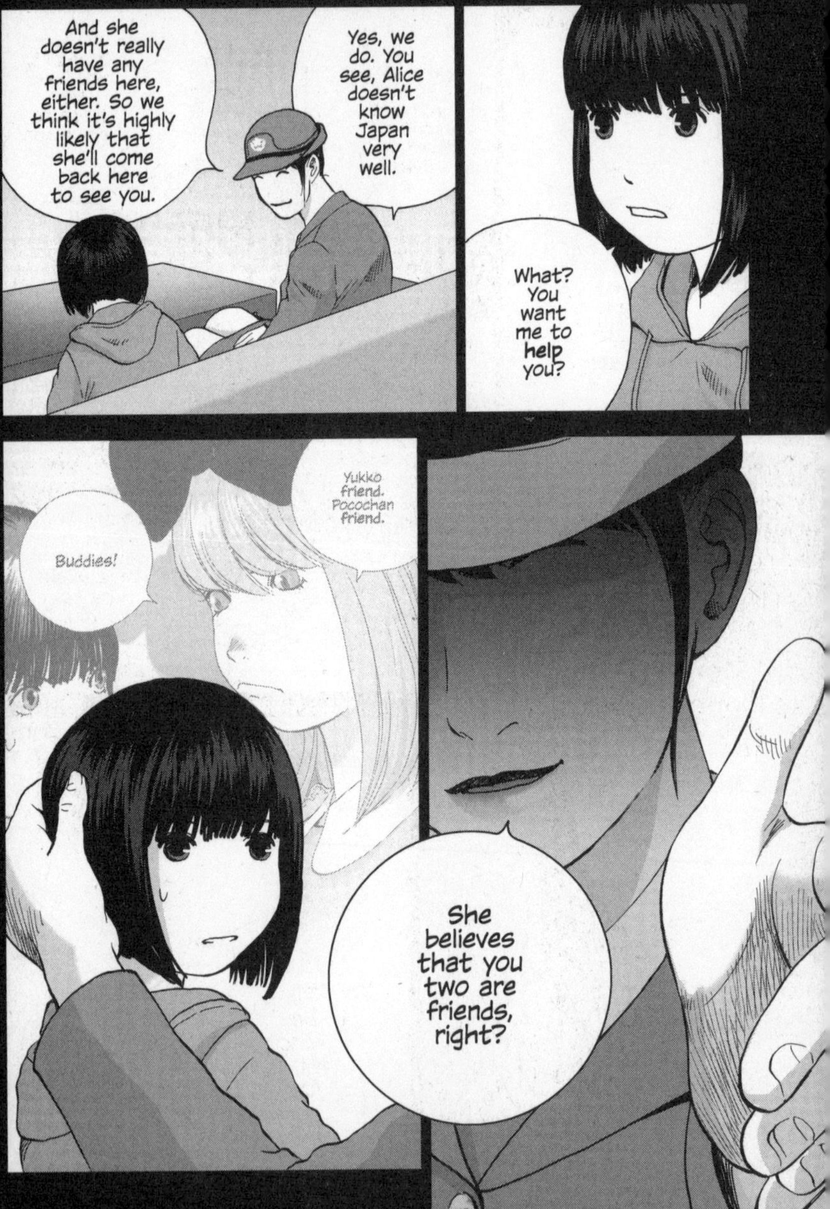
What? You want me to help you?
Yes, we do. You see, Alice doesn't know Japan very well.
And she doesn't really have any friends here, either. So we think it's highly likely that she'll come back here to see you.
She believes that you two are friends, right?
Yukko friend. Pocochan friend.
Buddies!

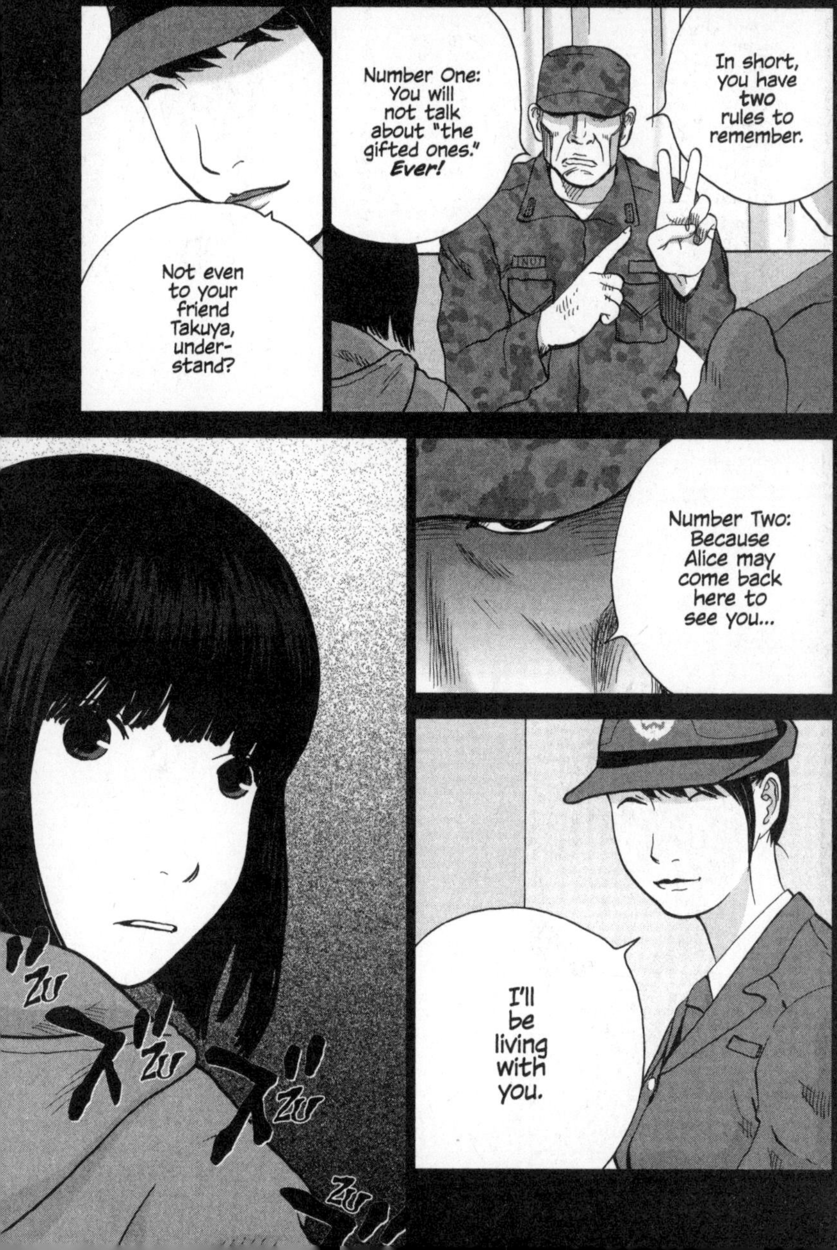
In short, you have two rules to remember.
Number One: You will not talk about "the gifted ones." *Ever!*
Not even to your friend Takuya, under-stand?
Number Two: Because Alice may come back here to see you...
I'll be living with you.
ZU
ZU
ZU
ZU

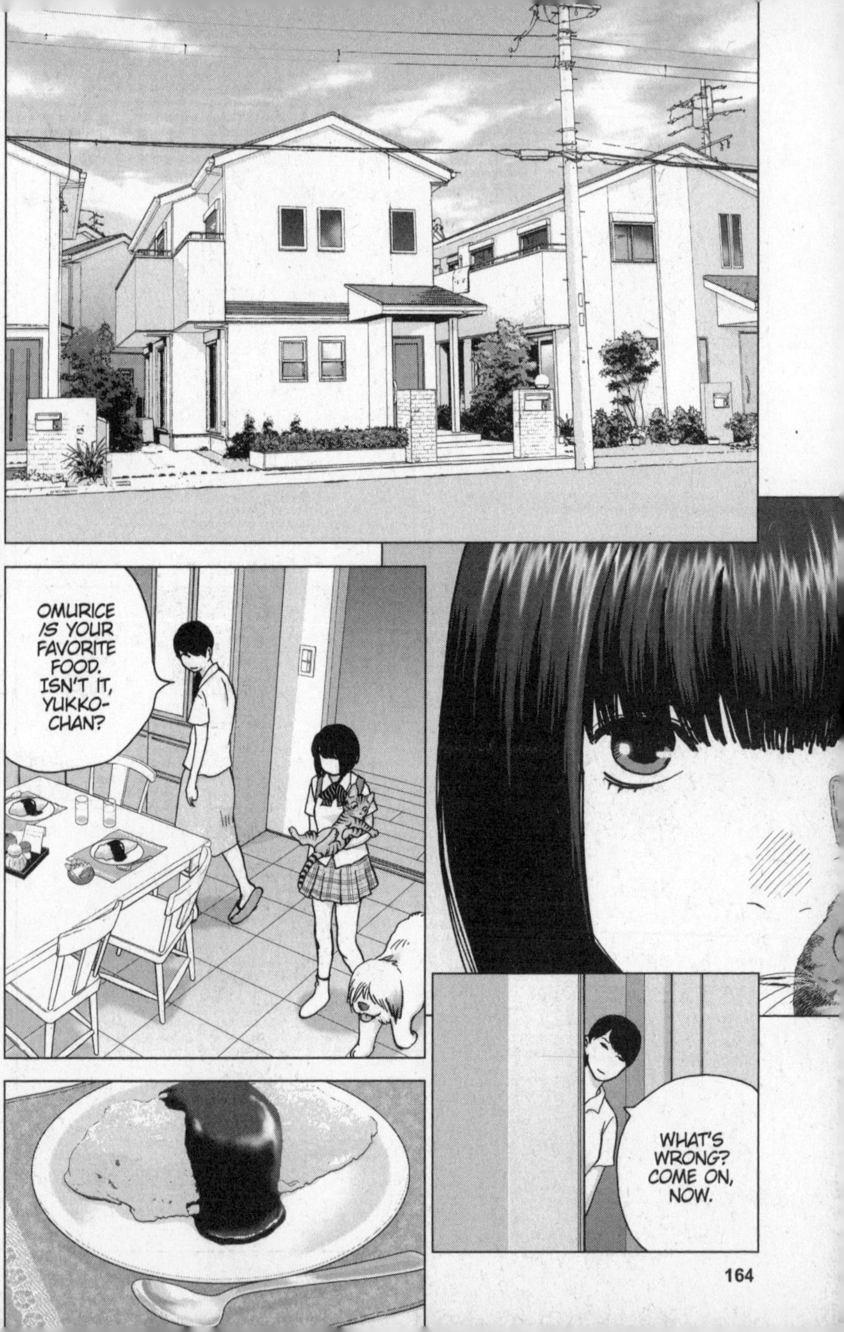
OMURICE IS YOUR FAVORITE FOOD. ISN'T IT, YUKKO-CHAN?
WHAT'S WRONG? COME ON, NOW.

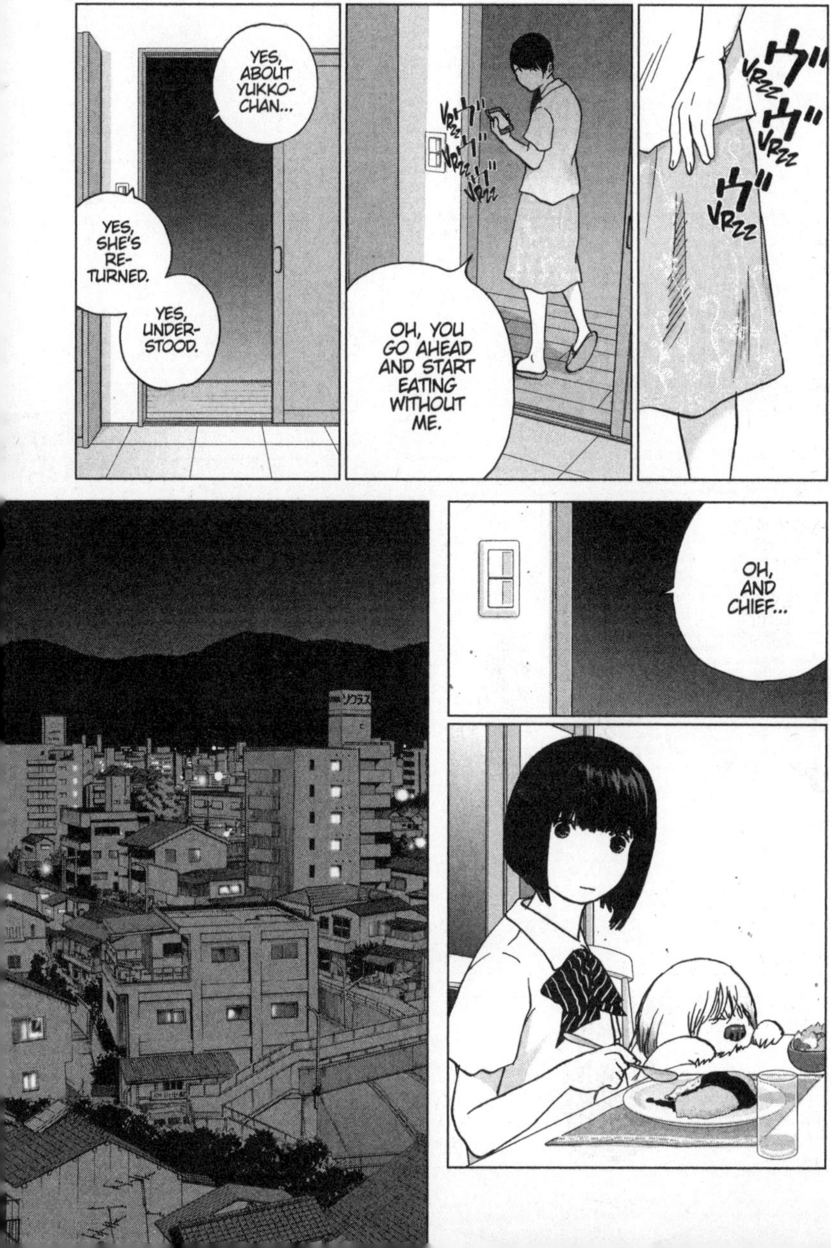
ヴ VRZZ
ヴ VRZZ
ヴ VRZZ
ヴ VRZZ
ヴ VRZZ
ヴ VRZZ
OH, YOU GO AHEAD AND START EATING WITHOUT ME.
YES, ABOUT YUKKO-CHAN...
YES, SHE'S RE-TURNED.
YES, UNDER-STOOD.
OH, AND CHIEF...

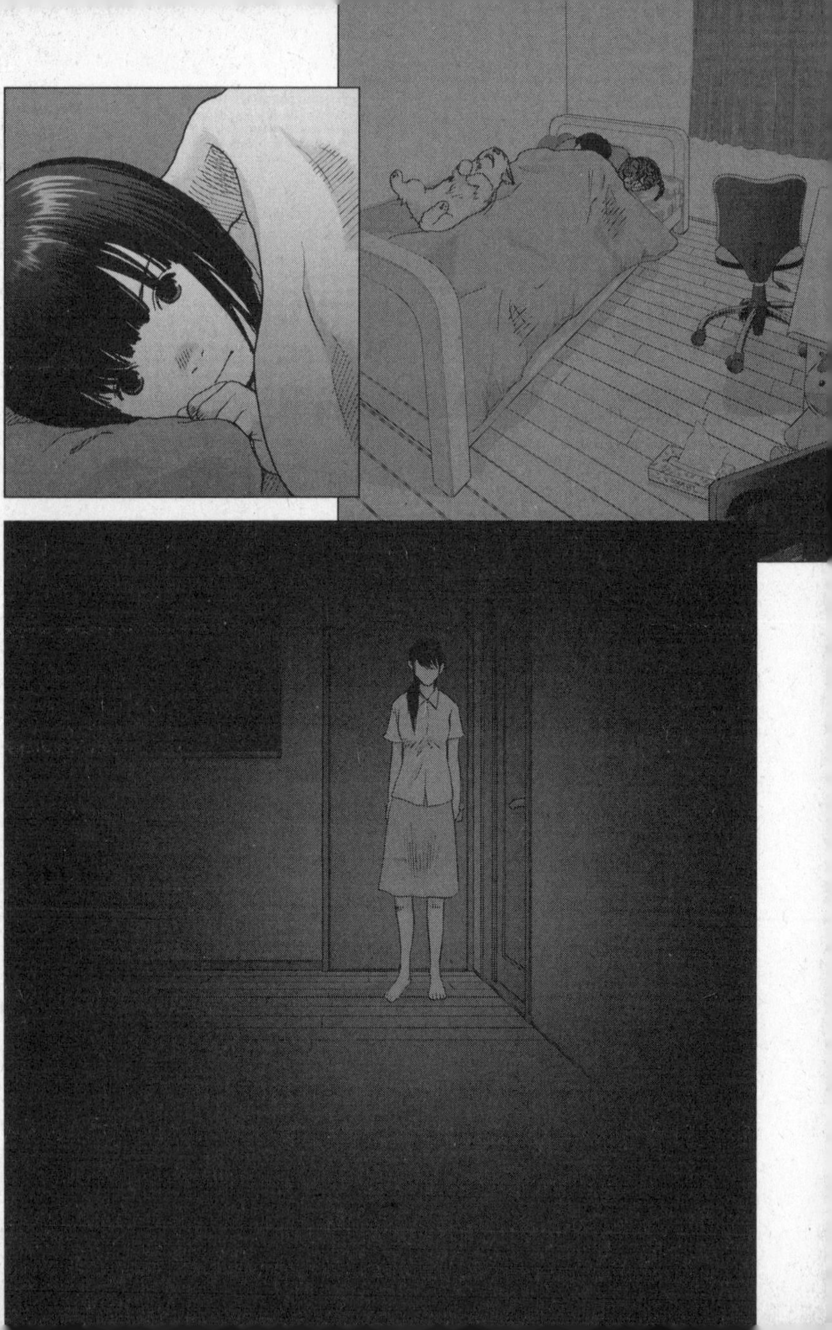

Chapter 27: About That

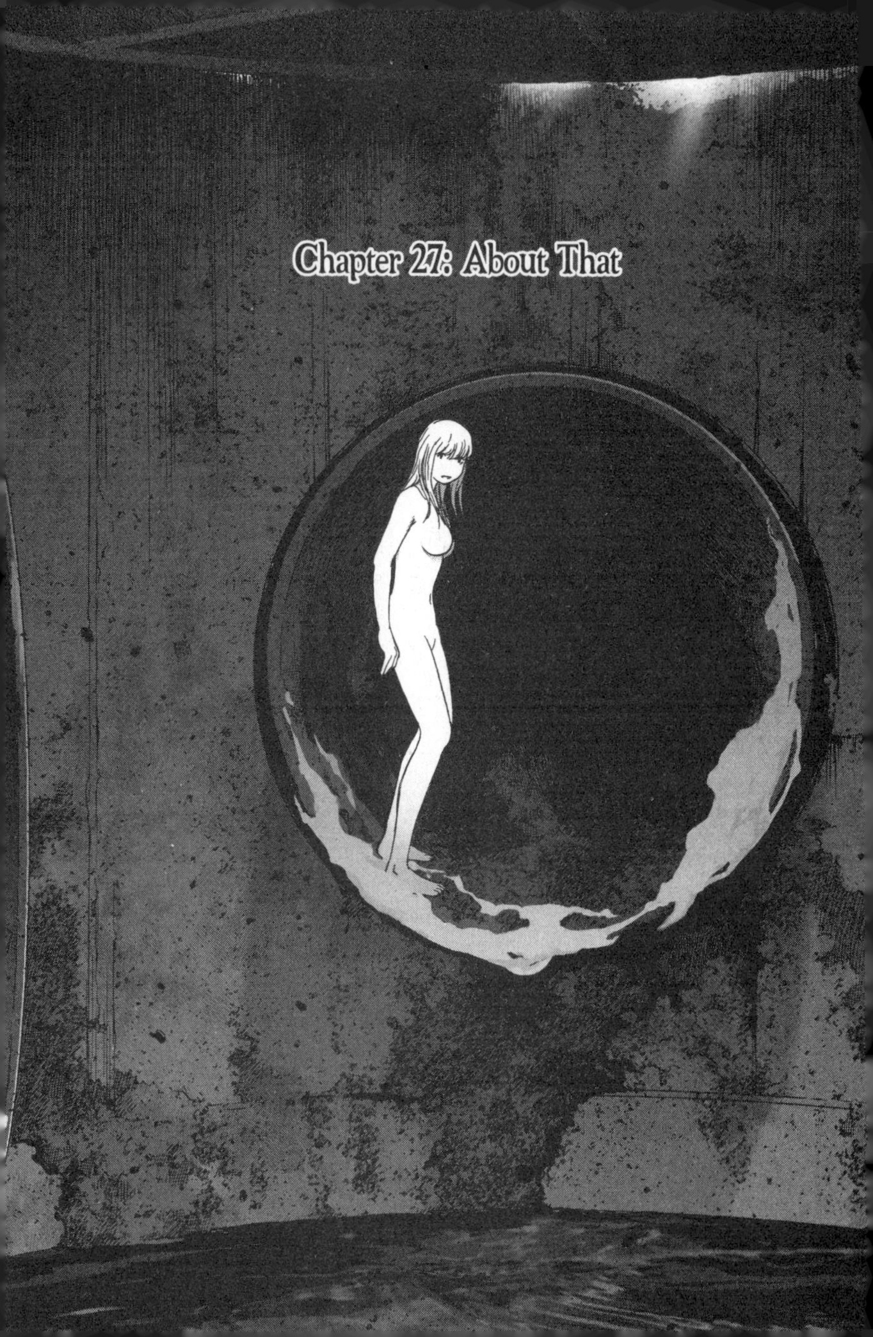

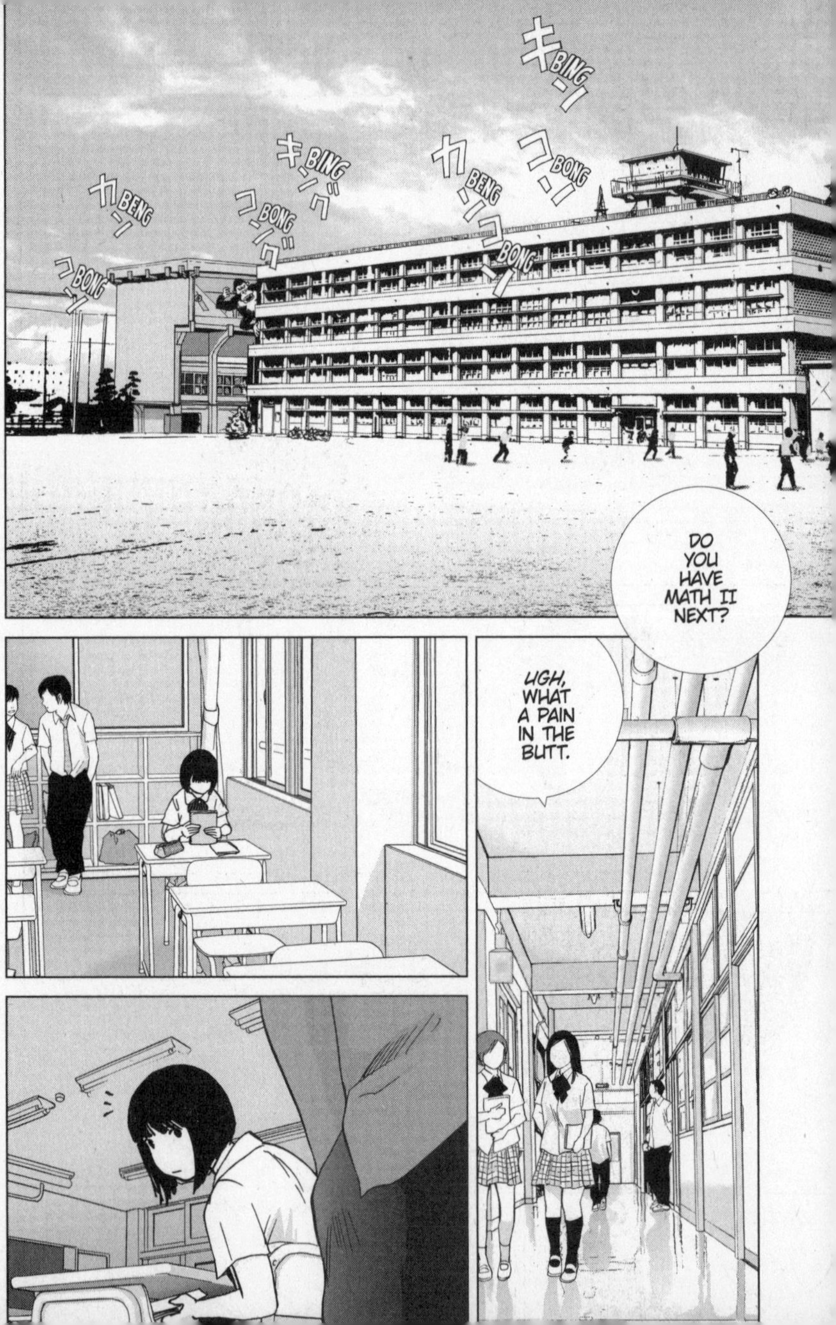
BING
BONG
BENG
BONG
BING
BONG
BENG
BONG
DO YOU HAVE MATH II NEXT?
UGH, WHAT A PAIN IN THE BUTT.

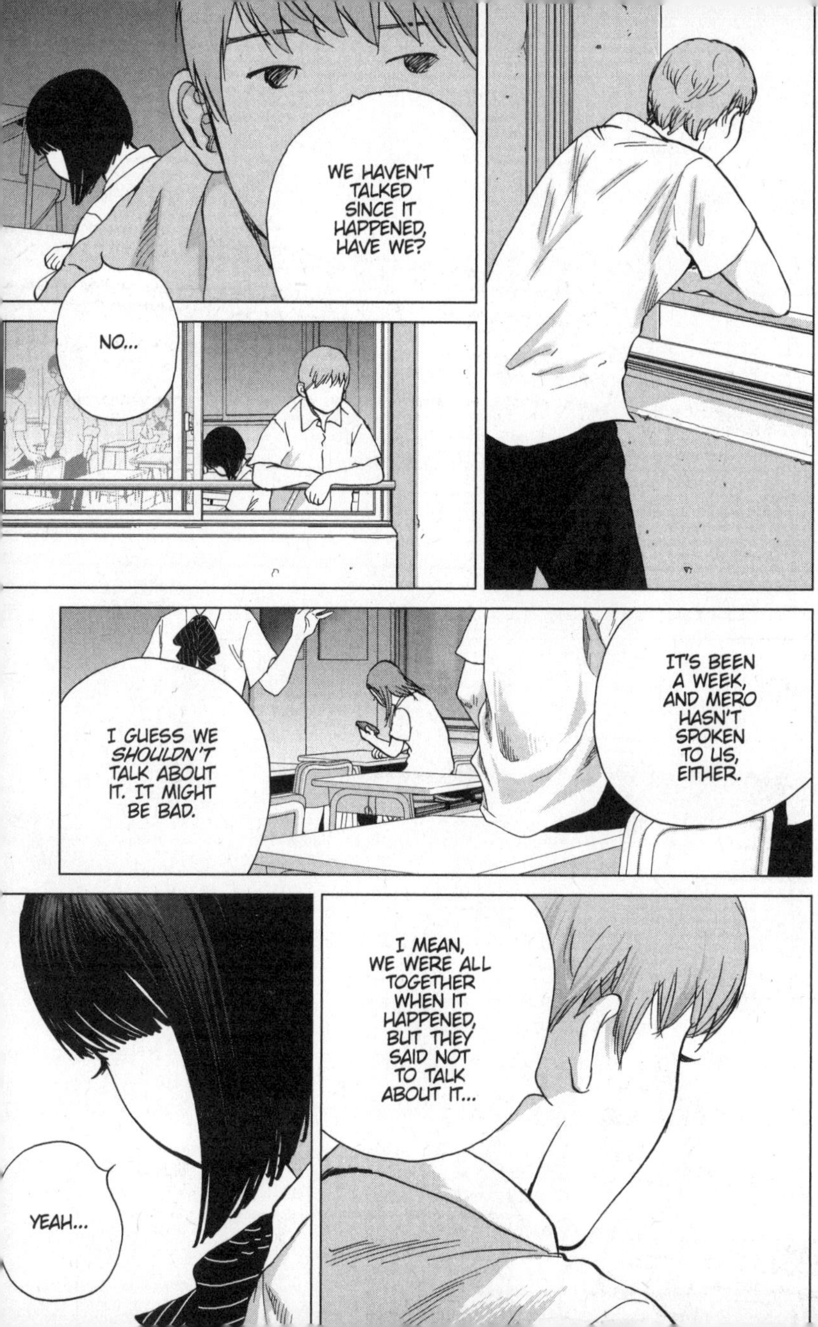
WE HAVEN'T TALKED SINCE IT HAPPENED, HAVE WE?
NO...
IT'S BEEN A WEEK, AND MERO HASN'T SPOKEN TO US, EITHER.
I GUESS WE *SHOULDN'T* TALK ABOUT IT. IT MIGHT BE BAD.
I MEAN, WE WERE ALL TOGETHER WHEN IT HAPPENED, BUT THEY SAID NOT TO TALK ABOUT IT...
YEAH...

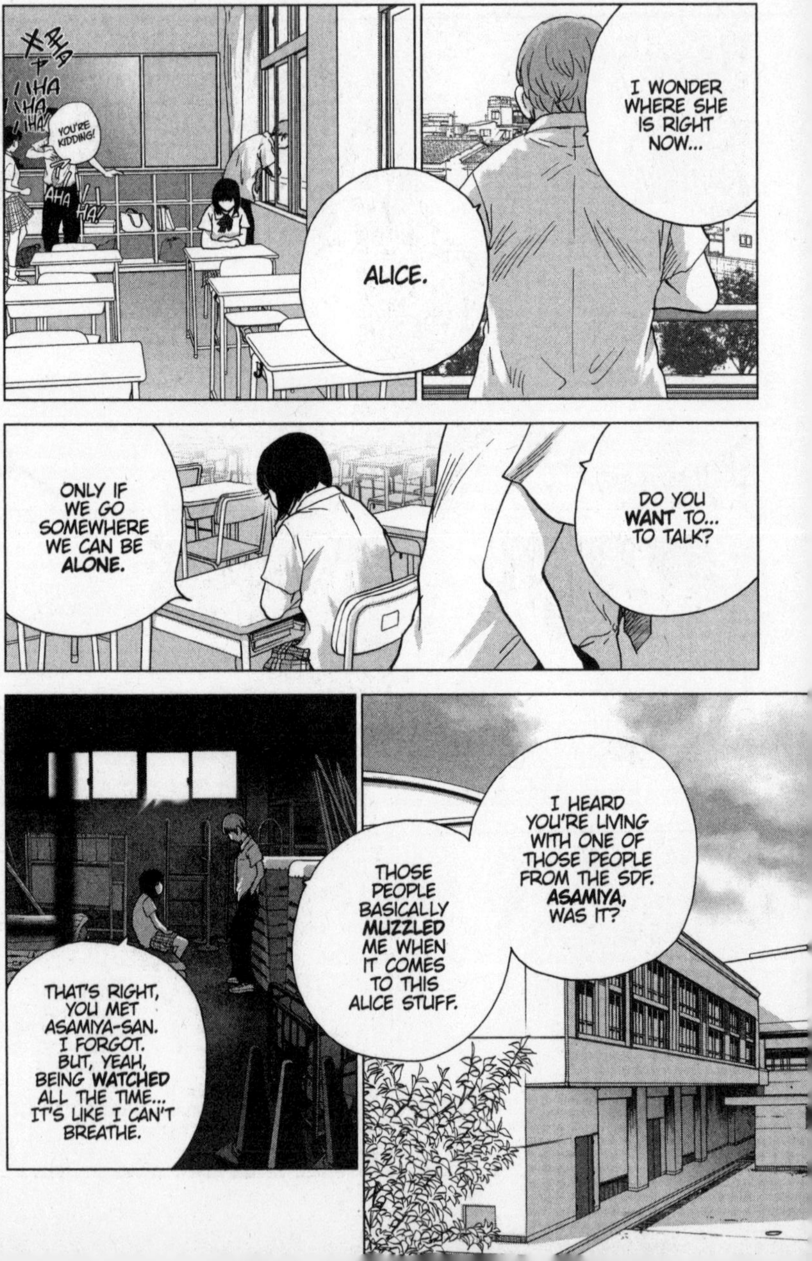
I WONDER WHERE SHE IS RIGHT NOW...
ALICE.
HA HA HA!
YOU'RE KIDDING!
AHA HA!
DO YOU WANT TO... TO TALK?
ONLY IF WE GO SOMEWHERE WE CAN BE ALONE.
I HEARD YOU'RE LIVING WITH ONE OF THOSE PEOPLE FROM THE SDF. ASAMIYA, WAS IT?
THOSE PEOPLE BASICALLY MUZZLED ME WHEN IT COMES TO THIS ALICE STUFF.
THAT'S RIGHT, YOU MET ASAMIYA-SAN. I FORGOT. BUT, YEAH, BEING WATCHED ALL THE TIME... IT'S LIKE I CAN'T BREATHE.

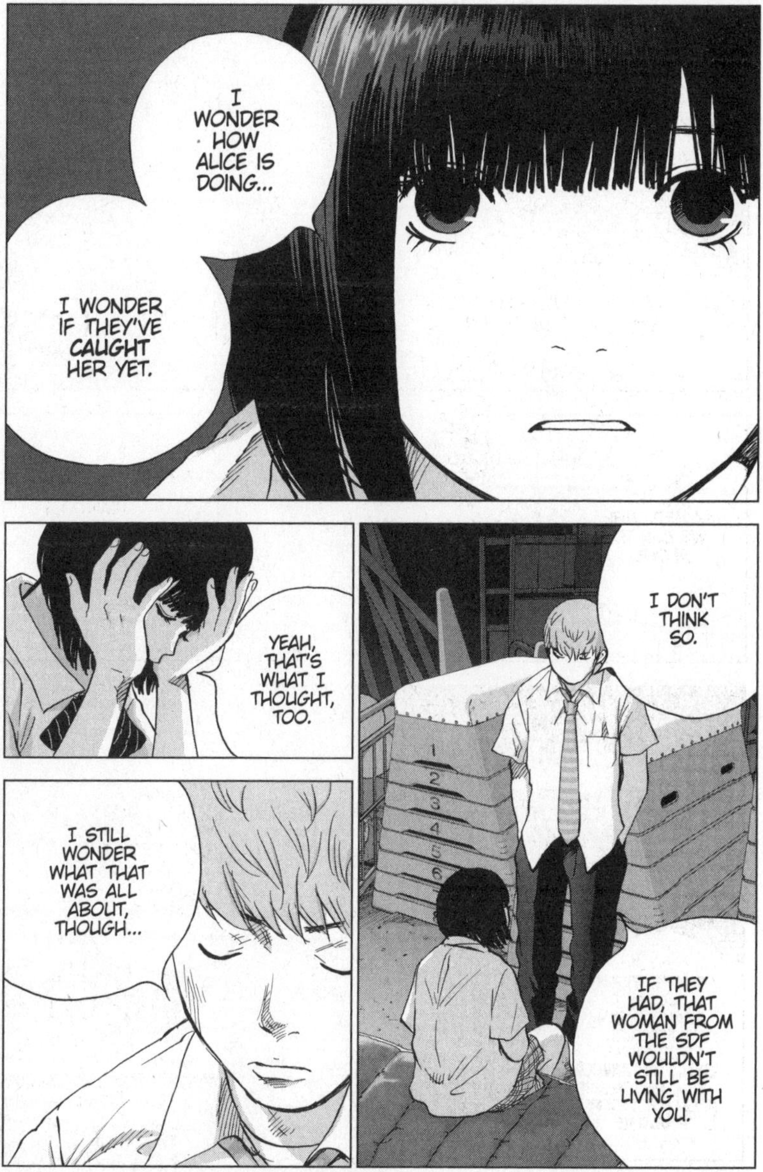
I WONDER HOW ALICE IS DOING...
I WONDER IF THEY'VE CAUGHT HER YET.
I DON'T THINK SO.
IF THEY HAD, THAT WOMAN FROM THE SDF WOULDN'T STILL BE LIVING WITH YOU.
YEAH, THAT'S WHAT I THOUGHT, TOO.
I STILL WONDER WHAT THAT WAS ALL ABOUT, THOUGH...

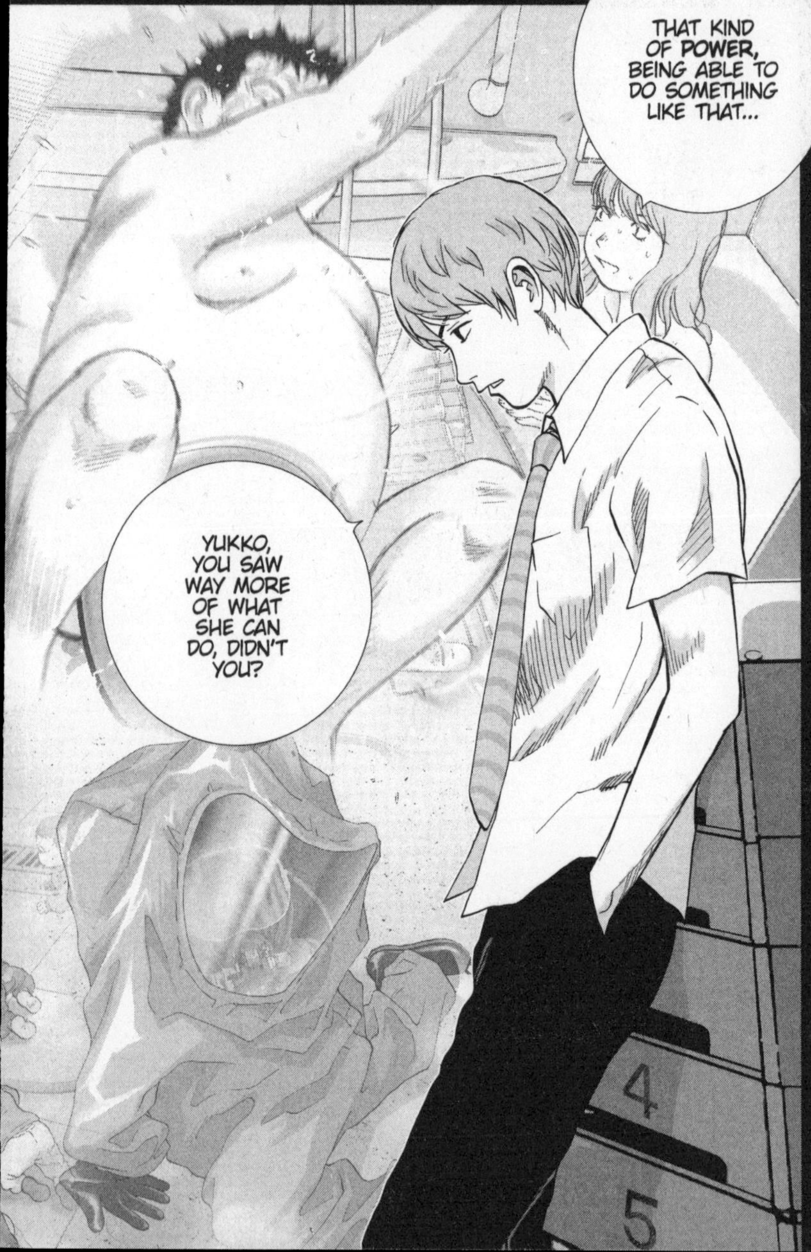
THAT KIND OF POWER, BEING ABLE TO DO SOMETHING LIKE THAT...
YUKKO, YOU SAW WAY MORE OF WHAT SHE CAN DO, DIDN'T YOU?
4
5

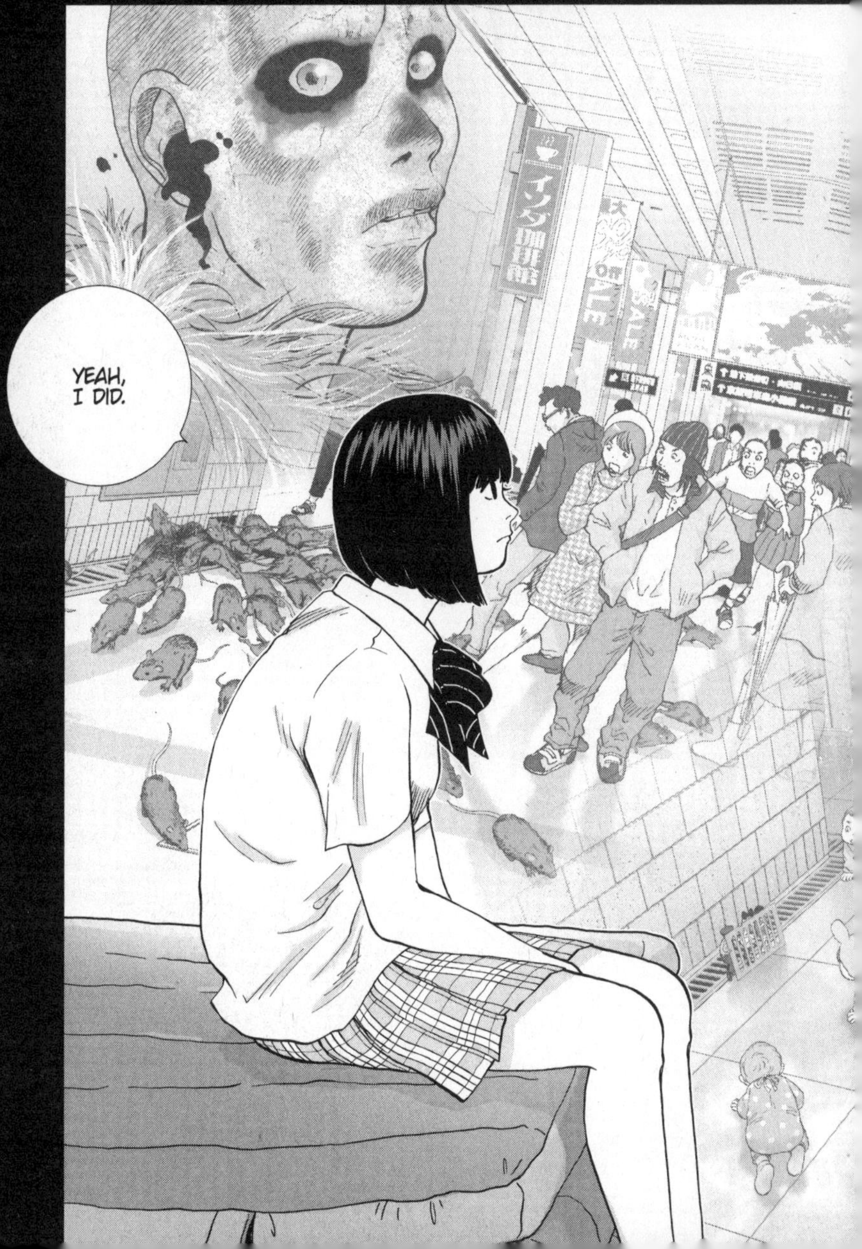
YEAH, I DID.
SALE

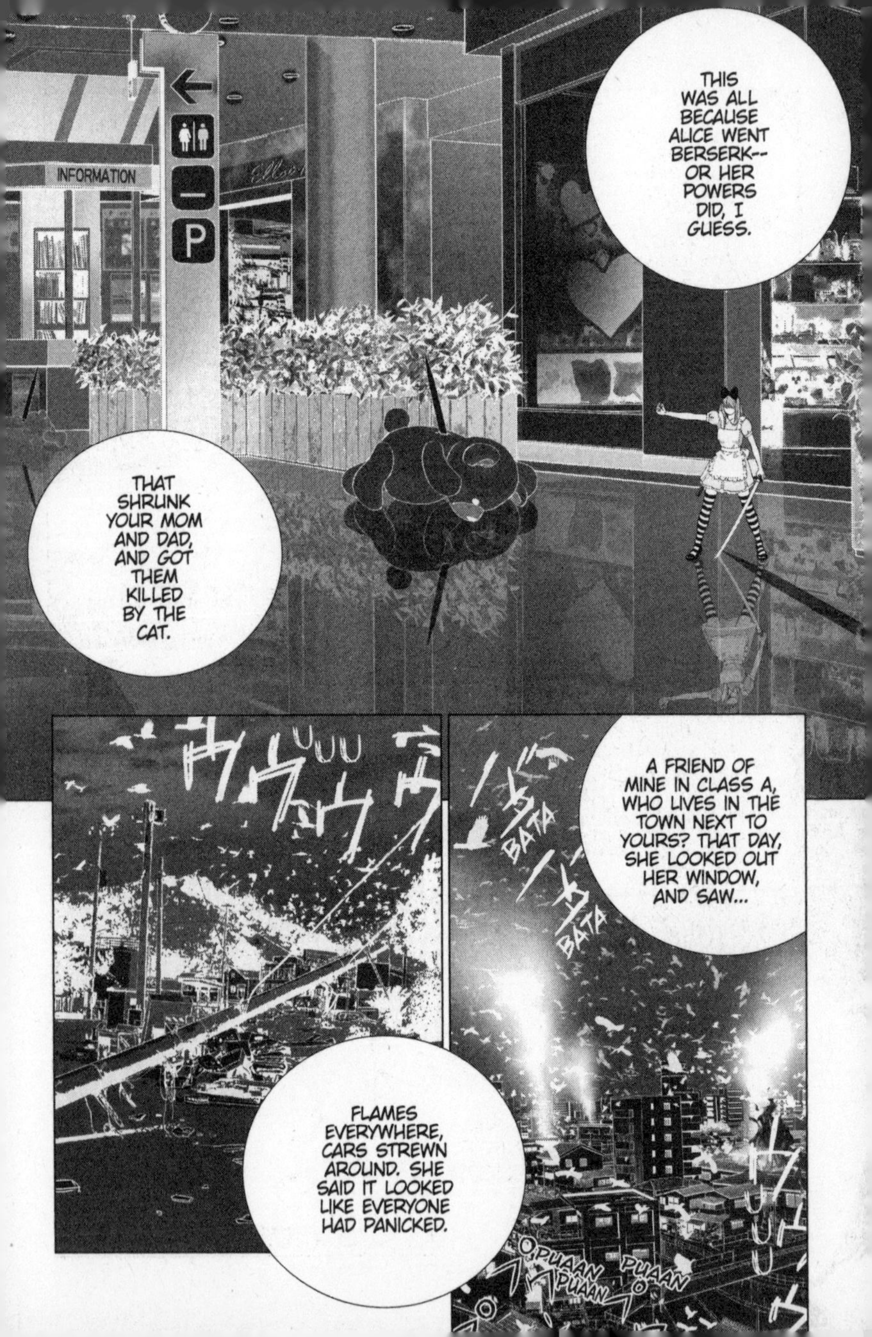
THIS WAS ALL BECAUSE ALICE WENT BERSERK--OR HER POWERS DID, I GUESS.
THAT SHRUNK YOUR MOM AND DAD, AND GOT THEM KILLED BY THE CAT.
A FRIEND OF MINE IN CLASS A, WHO LIVES IN THE TOWN NEXT TO YOURS? THAT DAY, SHE LOOKED OUT HER WINDOW, AND SAW...
BATA
BATA
PUAAN
PUAAN
PUAAN
FLAMES EVERYWHERE, CARS STREWN AROUND. SHE SAID IT LOOKED LIKE EVERYONE HAD PANICKED.

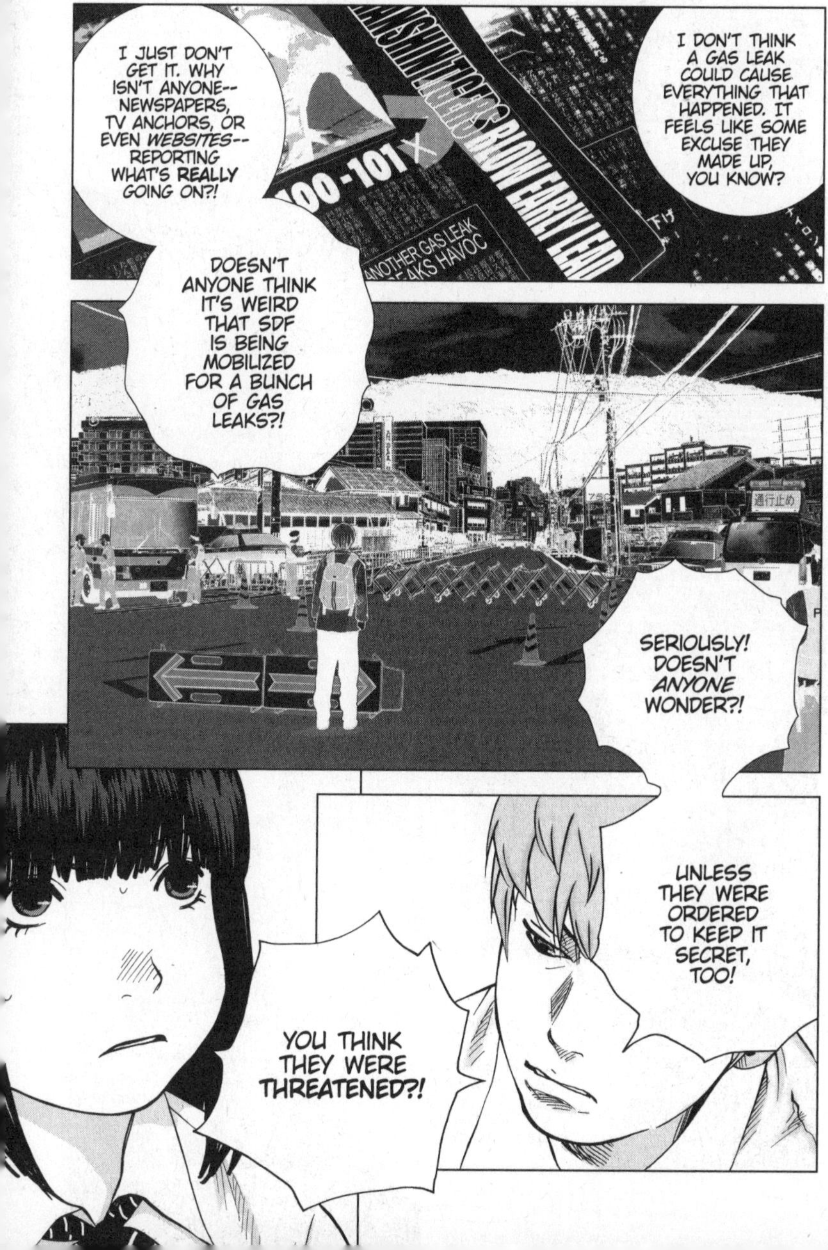
I DON'T THINK A GAS LEAK COULD CAUSE EVERYTHING THAT HAPPENED. IT FEELS LIKE SOME EXCUSE THEY MADE UP, YOU KNOW?
I JUST DON'T GET IT. WHY ISN'T ANYONE-- NEWSPAPERS, TV ANCHORS, OR EVEN *WEBSITES*-- REPORTING WHAT'S **REALLY** GOING ON?!
ANOTHER GAS LEAK
DOESN'T ANYONE THINK IT'S WEIRD THAT SDF IS BEING MOBILIZED FOR A BUNCH OF GAS LEAKS?!
通行止め
SERIOUSLY! DOESN'T *ANYONE* WONDER?!
UNLESS THEY WERE ORDERED TO KEEP IT SECRET, TOO!
YOU THINK THEY WERE **THREATENED**?!

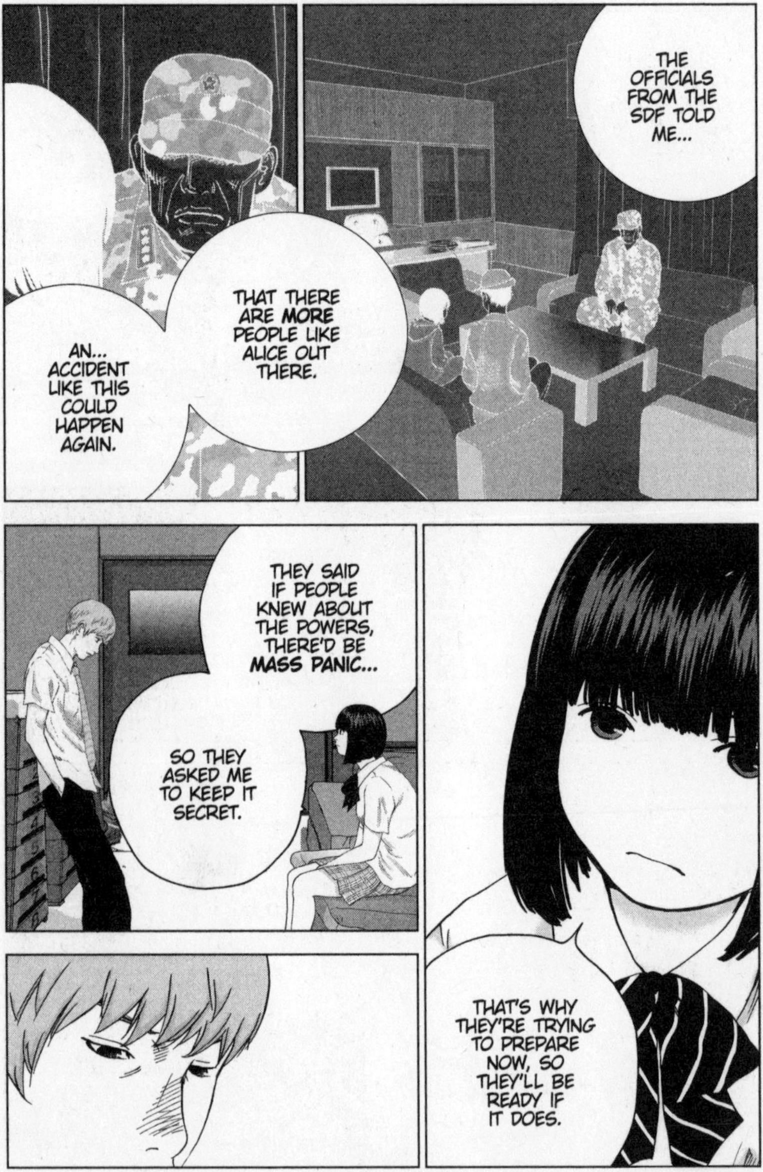
THE OFFICIALS FROM THE SDF TOLD ME...
THAT THERE ARE **MORE** PEOPLE LIKE ALICE OUT THERE.
AN... ACCIDENT LIKE THIS COULD HAPPEN AGAIN.
THAT'S WHY THEY'RE TRYING TO PREPARE NOW, SO THEY'LL BE READY IF IT DOES.
THEY SAID IF PEOPLE KNEW ABOUT THE POWERS, THERE'D BE **MASS PANIC...**
SO THEY ASKED ME TO KEEP IT SECRET.

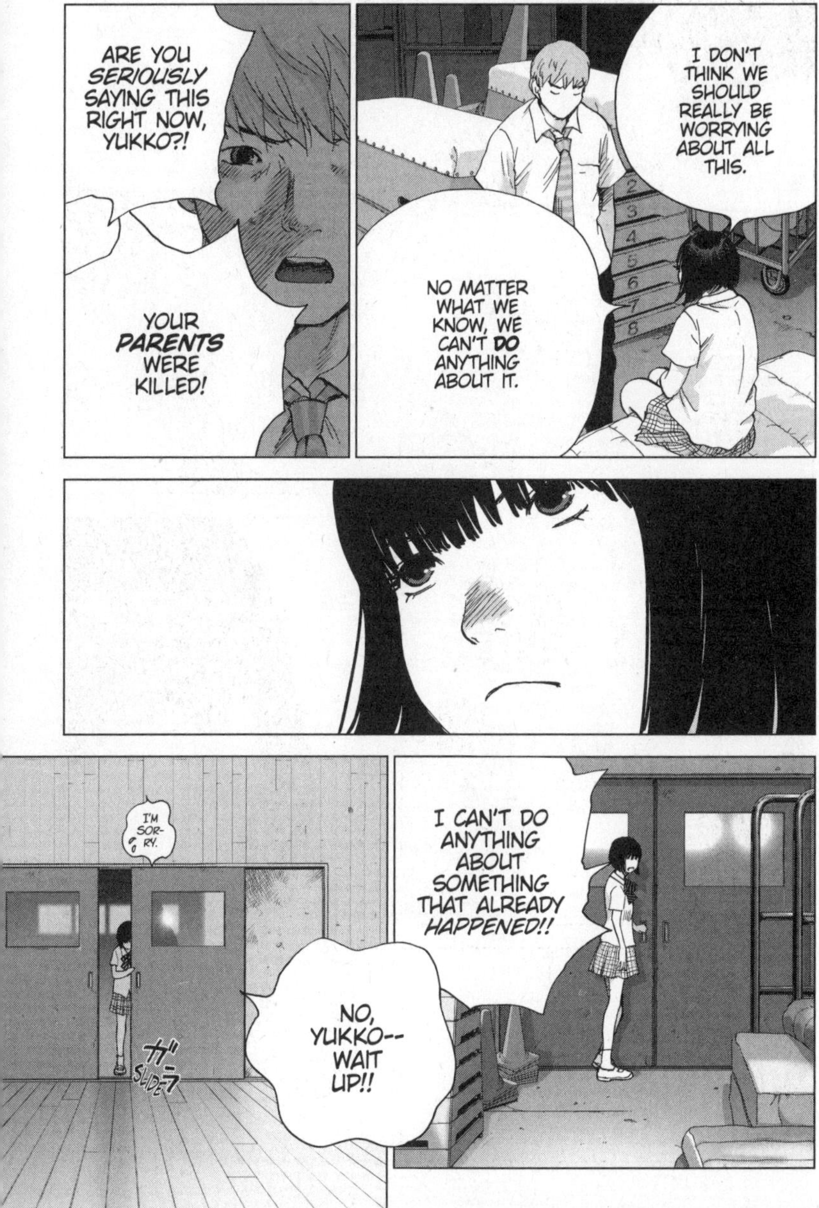
I DON'T THINK WE SHOULD REALLY BE WORRYING ABOUT ALL THIS.
NO MATTER WHAT WE KNOW, WE CAN'T DO ANYTHING ABOUT IT.
ARE YOU SERIOUSLY SAYING THIS RIGHT NOW, YUKKO?!
YOUR PARENTS WERE KILLED!
I CAN'T DO ANYTHING ABOUT SOMETHING THAT ALREADY HAPPENED!!
NO, YUKKO-- WAIT UP!!
I'M SOR-RY.
ガー
SLIDE

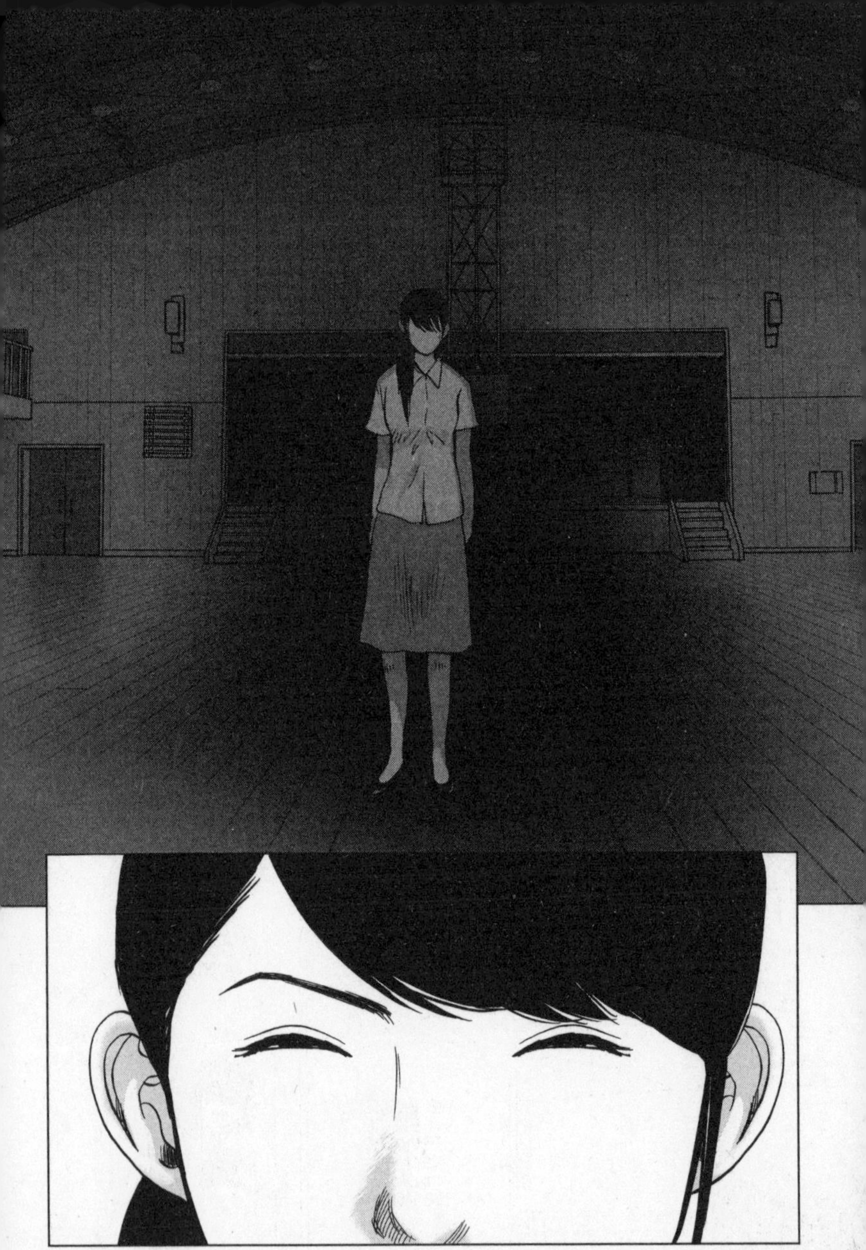

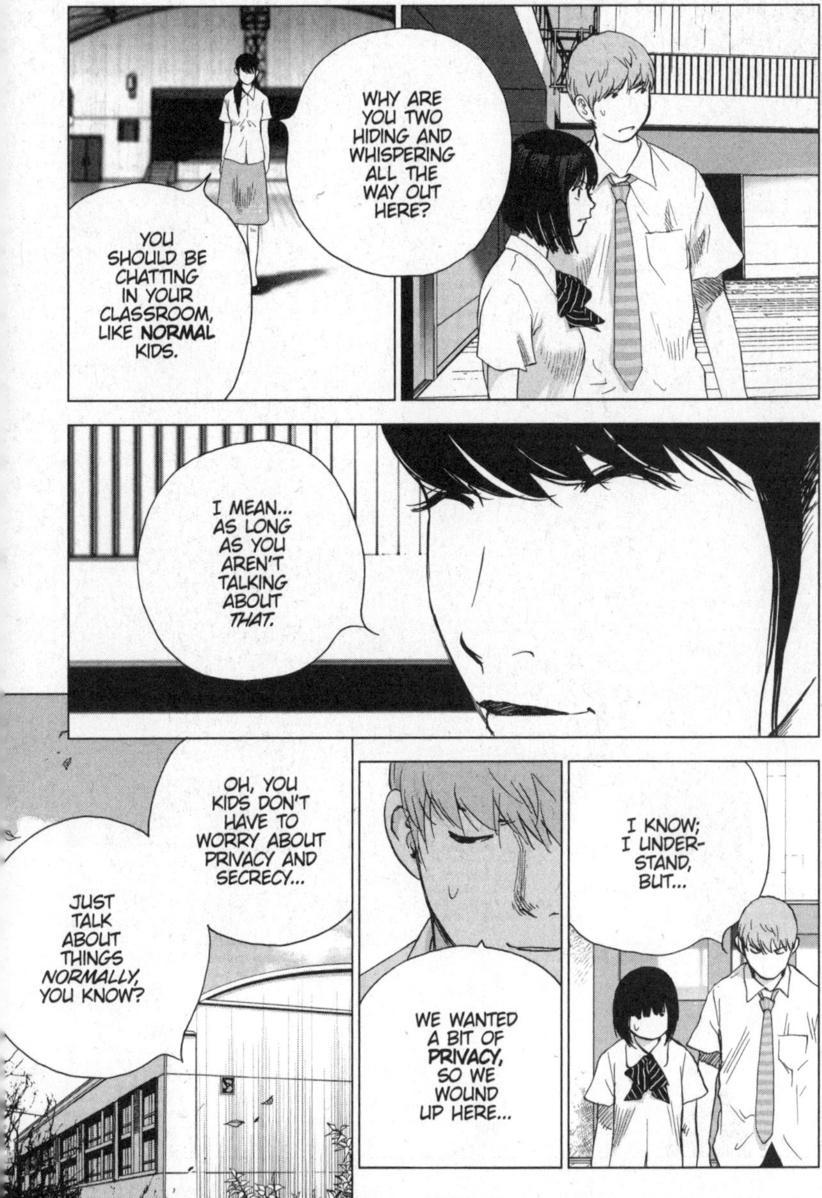
WHY ARE YOU TWO HIDING AND WHISPERING ALL THE WAY OUT HERE?
YOU SHOULD BE CHATTING IN YOUR CLASSROOM, LIKE **NORMAL** KIDS.
I MEAN... AS LONG AS YOU AREN'T TALKING ABOUT *THAT*.
I KNOW; I UNDER-STAND, BUT...
WE WANTED A BIT OF **PRIVACY**, SO WE WOUND UP HERE...
OH, YOU KIDS DON'T HAVE TO WORRY ABOUT PRIVACY AND SECRECY...
JUST TALK ABOUT THINGS *NORMALLY*, YOU KNOW?

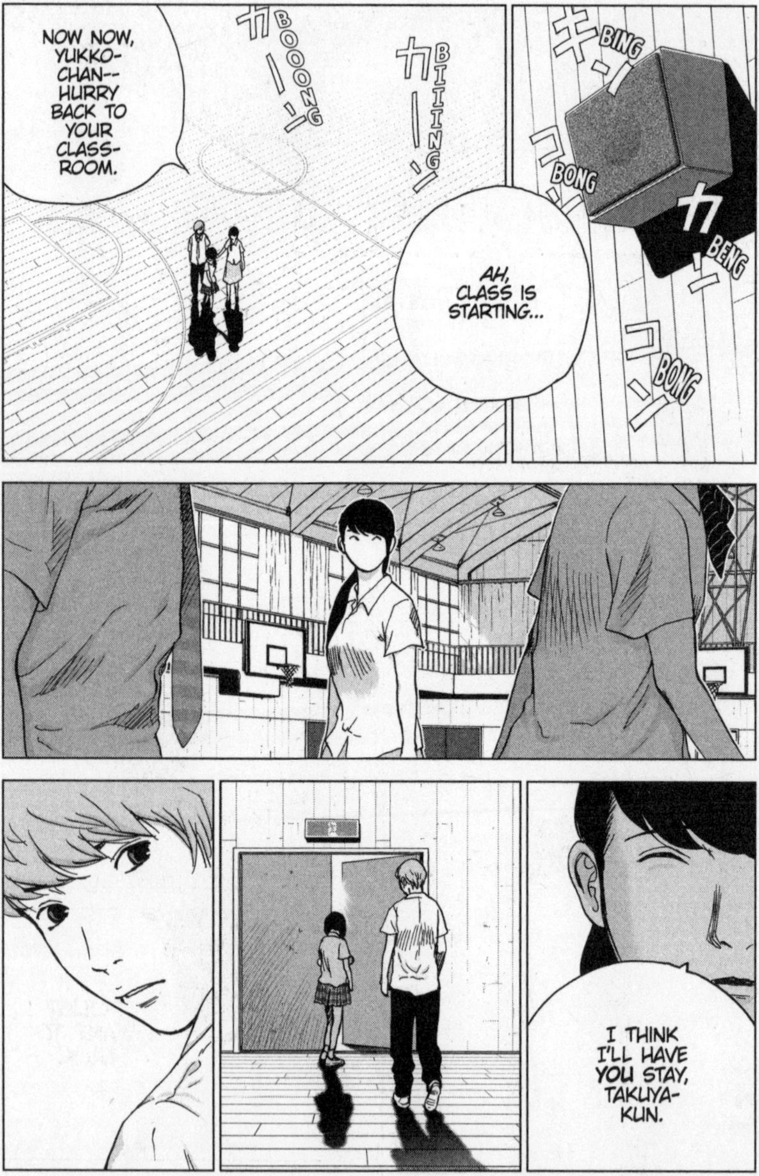
BING
BONG
BENG
BONG
AH, CLASS IS STARTING...
BOOONG
BIIING
NOW NOW, YUKKO-CHAN-- HURRY BACK TO YOUR CLASSROOM.
I THINK I'LL HAVE YOU STAY, TAKUYA-KUN.

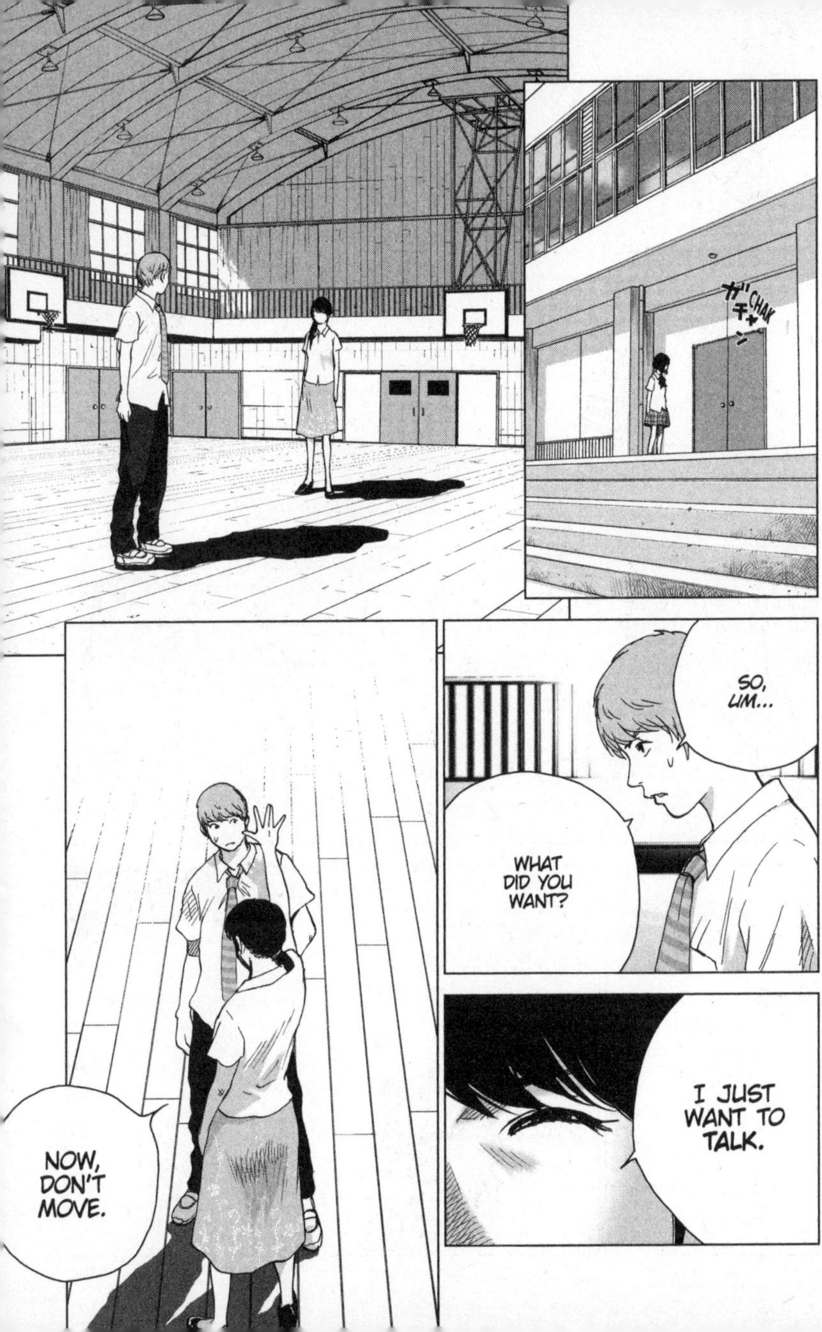
CHAK
SO, UM...
WHAT DID YOU WANT?
I JUST WANT TO TALK.
NOW, DON'T MOVE.

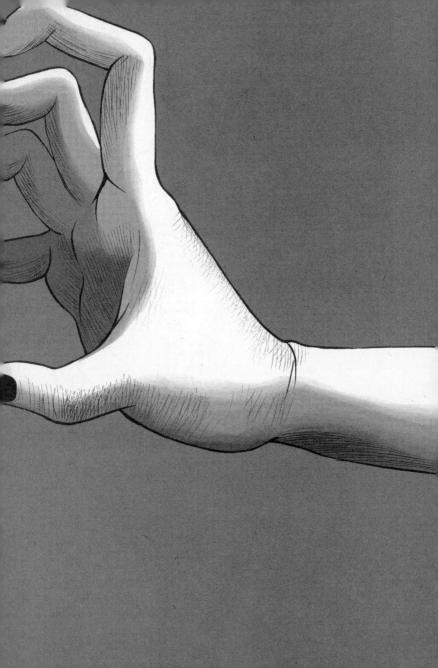

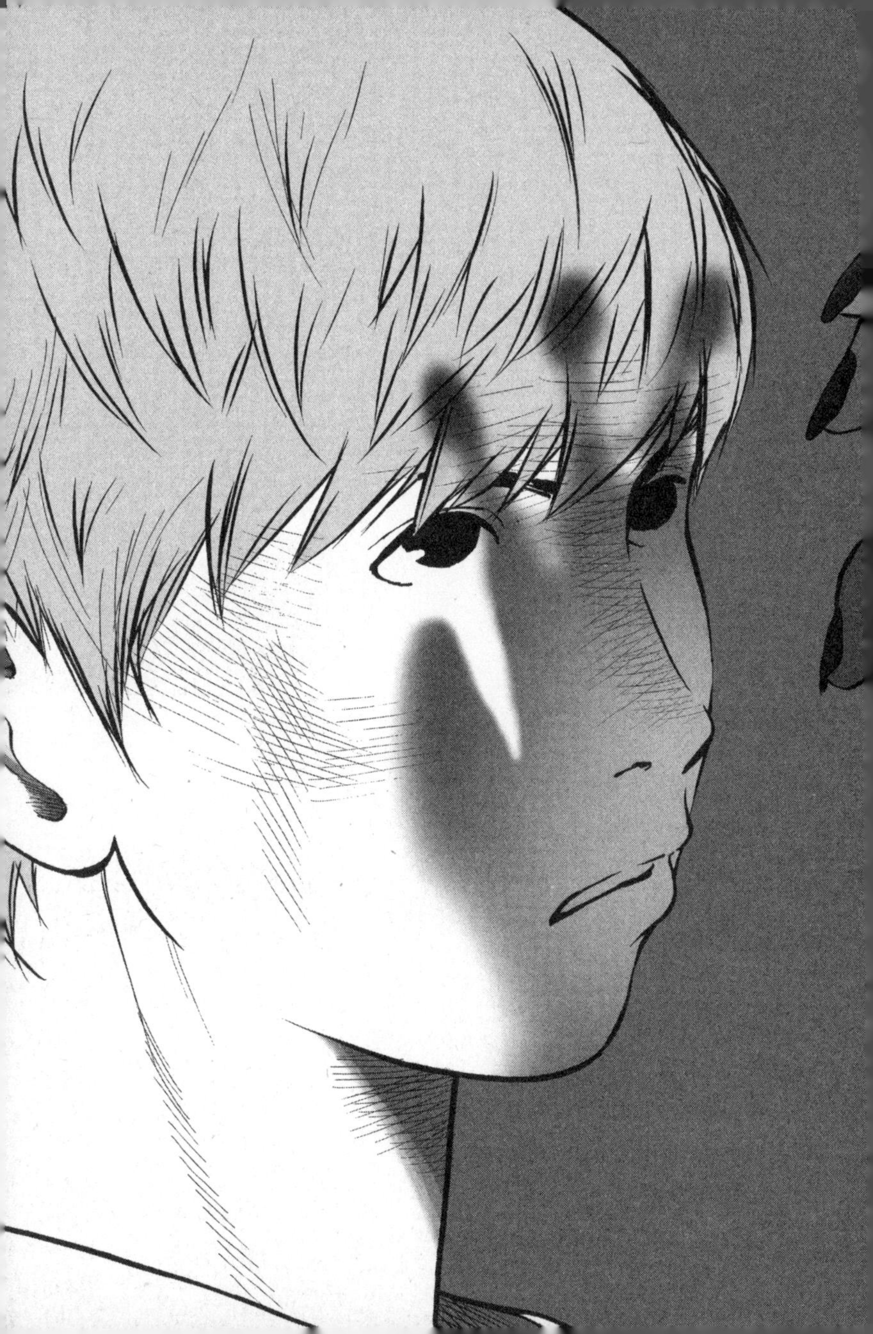

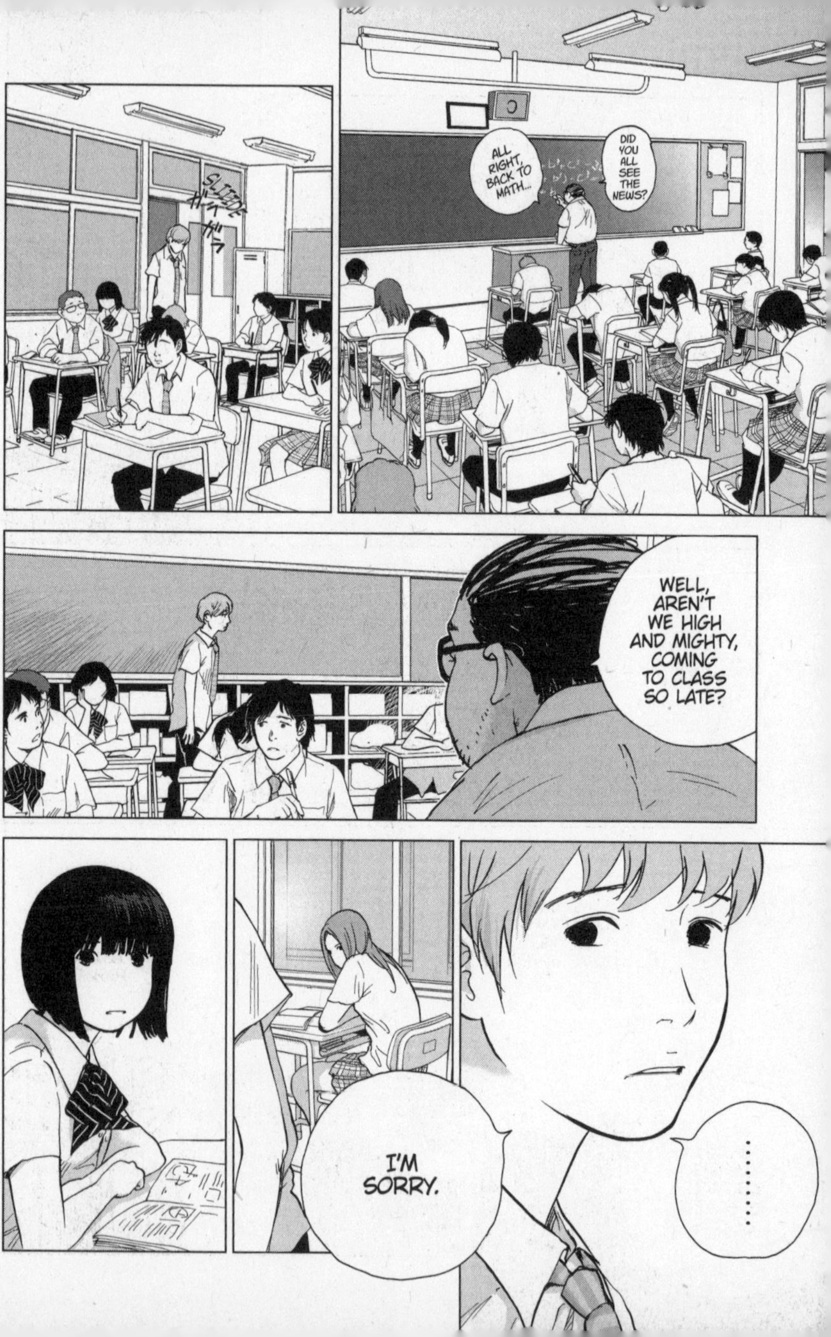
DID YOU ALL SEE THE NEWS?
ALL RIGHT, BACK TO MATH...
SLIIDE
WELL, AREN'T WE HIGH AND MIGHTY, COMING TO CLASS SO LATE?
......
I'M SORRY.

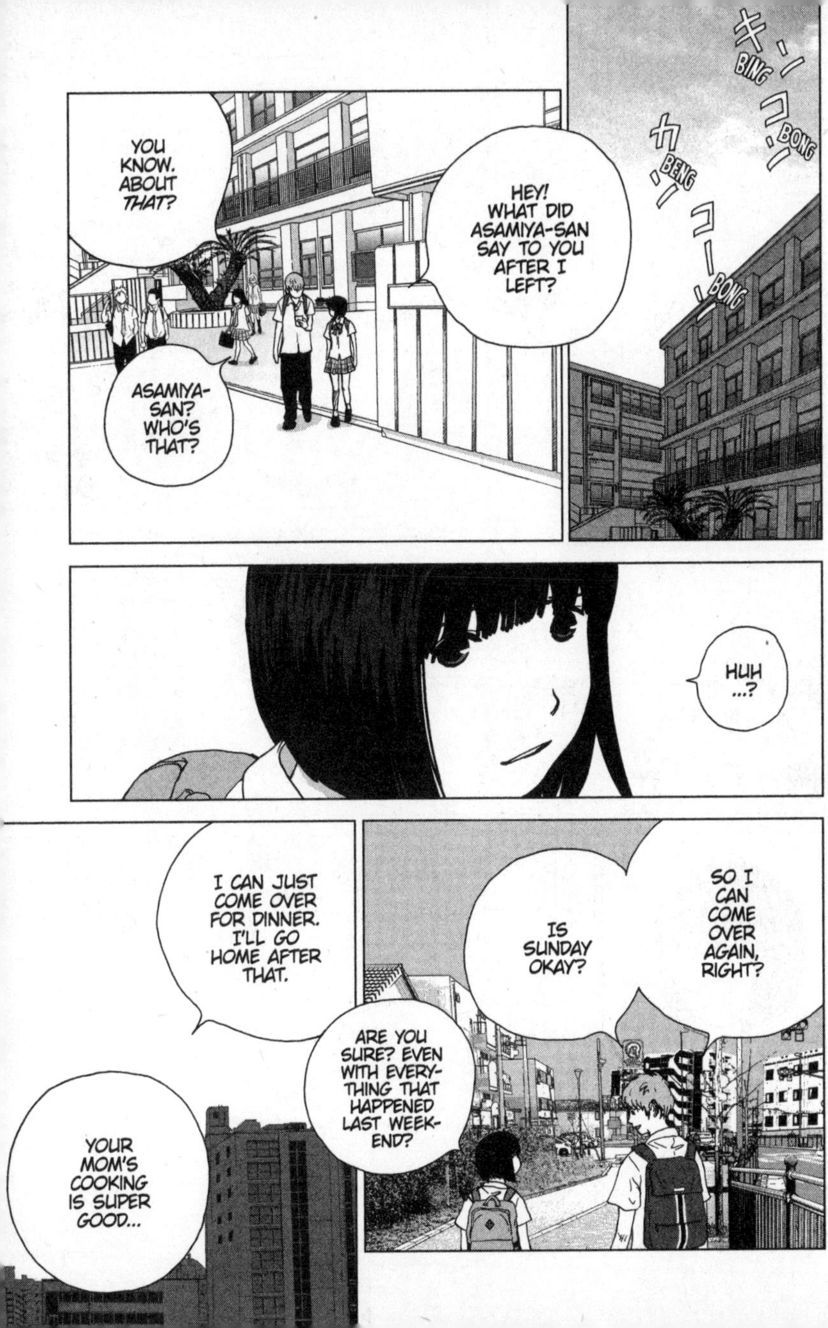
BING
BONG
BENG
BONG
HEY! WHAT DID ASAMIYA-SAN SAY TO YOU AFTER I LEFT?
YOU KNOW. ABOUT *THAT?*
ASAMIYA-SAN? WHO'S THAT?
HUH ...?
SO I CAN COME OVER AGAIN, RIGHT?
IS SUNDAY OKAY?
ARE YOU SURE? EVEN WITH EVERYTHING THAT HAPPENED LAST WEEKEND?
I CAN JUST COME OVER FOR DINNER. I'LL GO HOME AFTER THAT.
YOUR MOM'S COOKING IS SUPER GOOD...

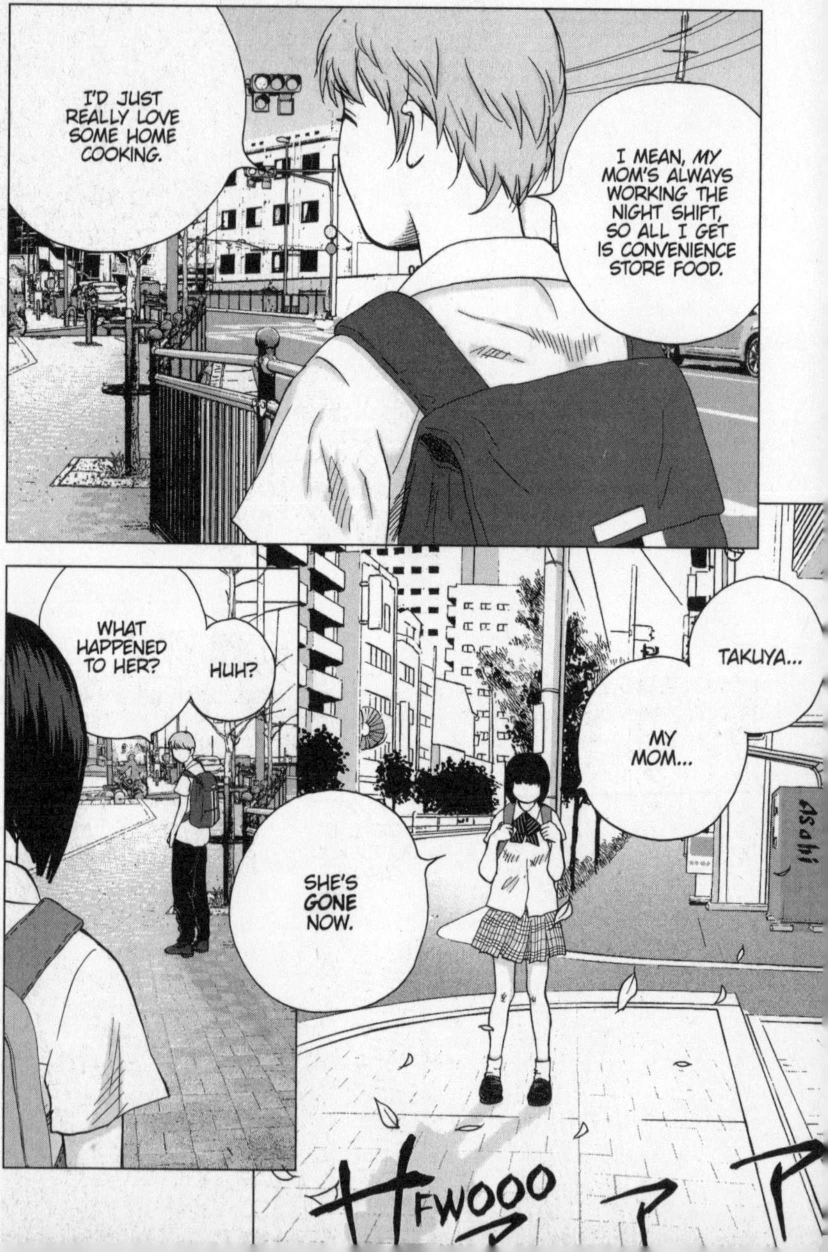
I MEAN, MY MOM'S ALWAYS WORKING THE NIGHT SHIFT, SO ALL I GET IS CONVENIENCE STORE FOOD.
I'D JUST REALLY LOVE SOME HOME COOKING.
TAKUYA...
MY MOM...
SHE'S GONE NOW.
Asahi
HFWOOO
HUH?
WHAT HAPPENED TO HER?

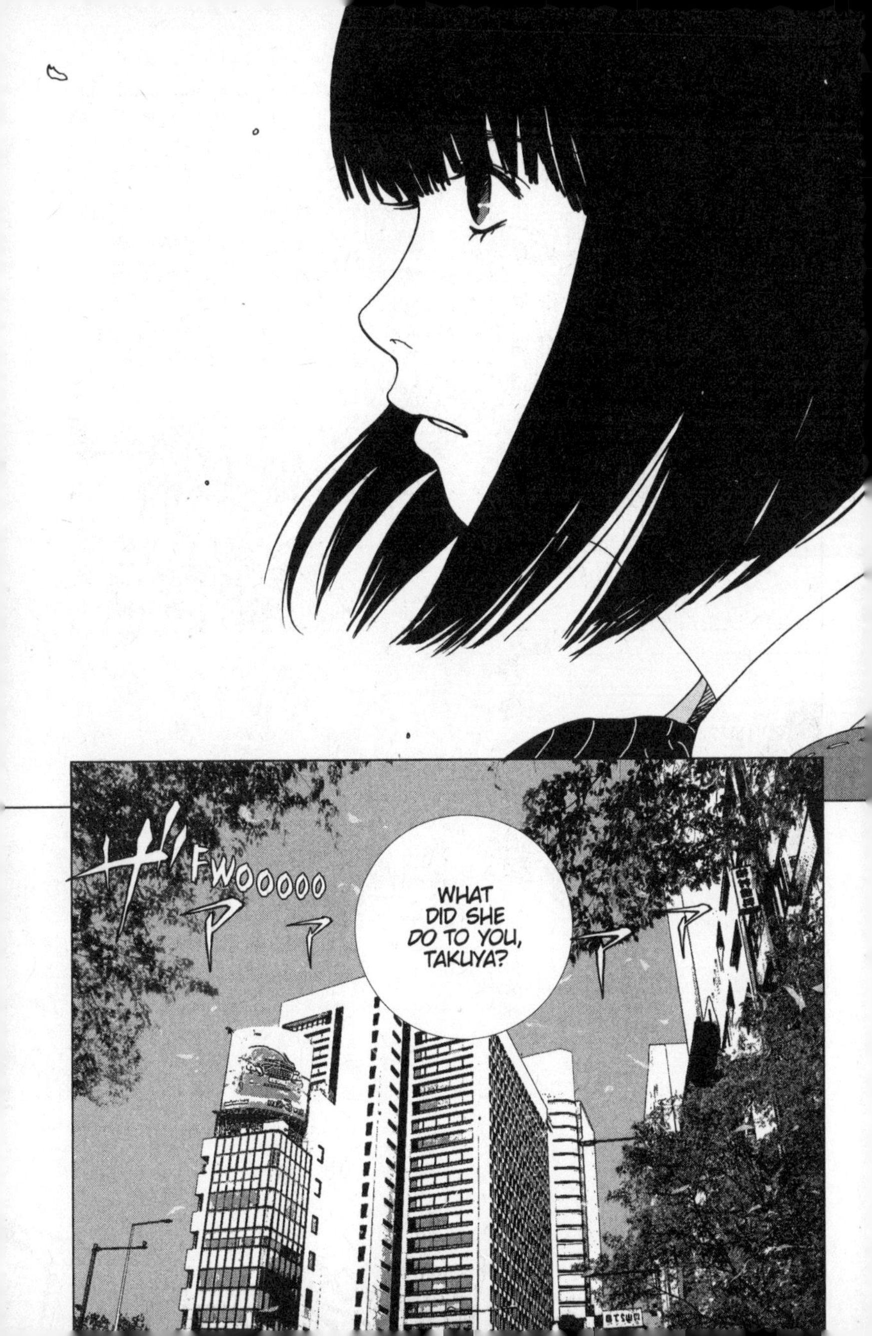
FWOOOOO
WHAT DID SHE DO TO YOU, TAKUYA?

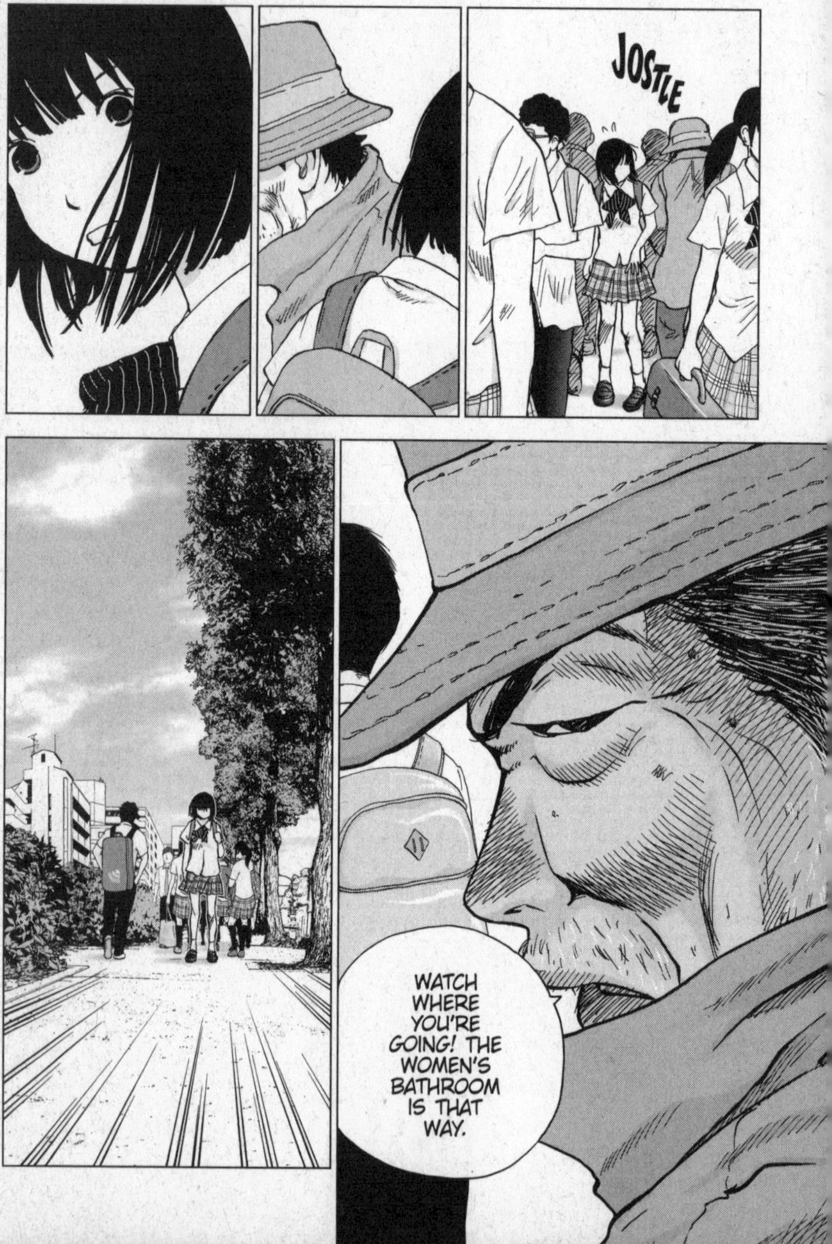
JOSTLE
WATCH WHERE YOU'RE GOING! THE WOMEN'S BATHROOM IS THAT WAY.

Wonderland

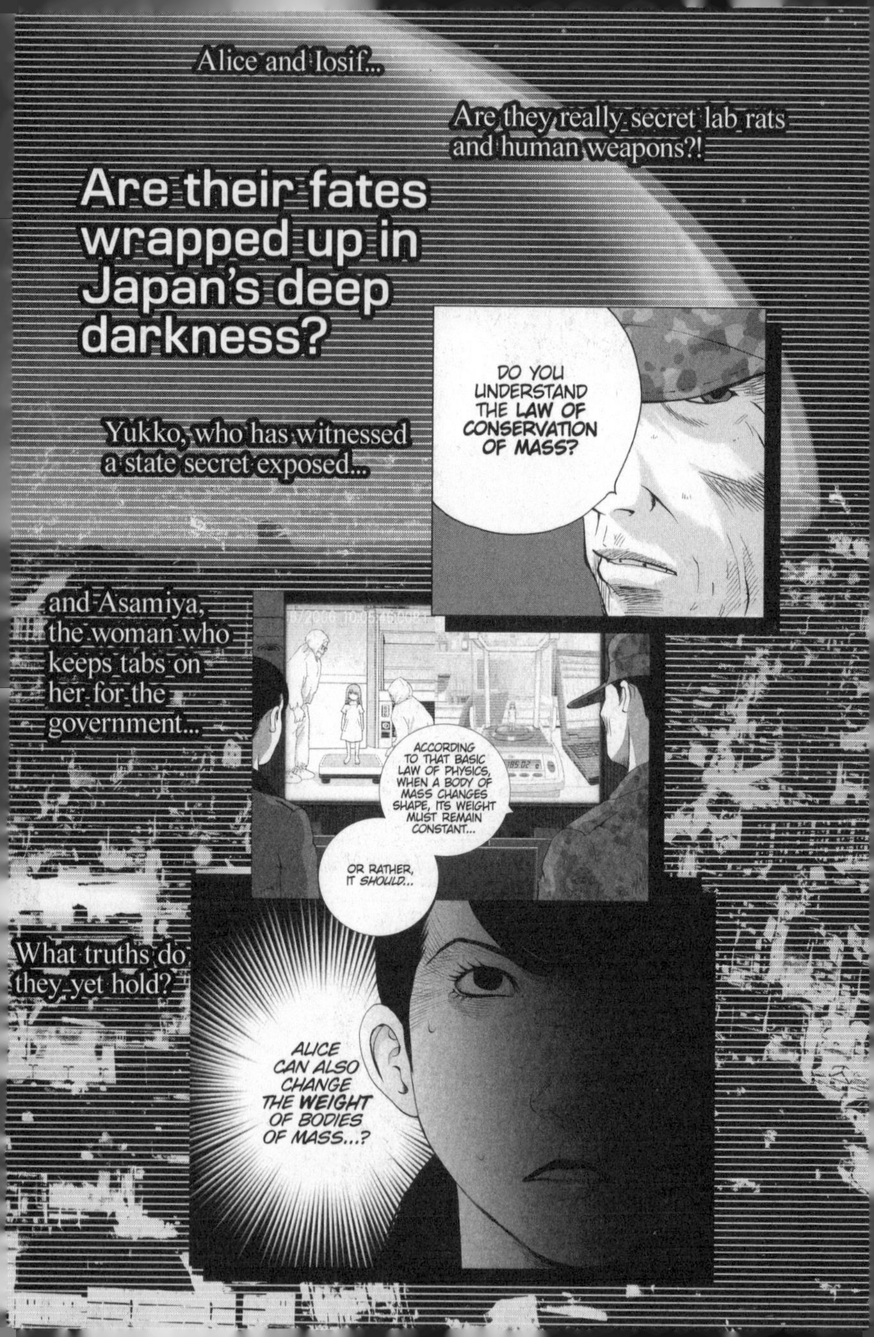
Alice and Iosif...
Are they really secret lab rats and human weapons?!
Are their fates wrapped up in Japan's deep darkness?
DO YOU UNDERSTAND THE LAW OF CONSERVATION OF MASS?
Yukko, who has witnessed a state secret exposed...
and Asamiya, the woman who keeps tabs on her for the government...
ACCORDING TO THAT BASIC LAW OF PHYSICS, WHEN A BODY OF MASS CHANGES SHAPE, ITS WEIGHT MUST REMAIN CONSTANT...
OR RATHER, IT SHOULD...
What truths do they yet hold?
ALICE CAN ALSO CHANGE THE WEIGHT OF BODIES OF MASS...?